❦ THE ❦

MAGICAL STATE

❧ THE ❧ MAGICAL STATE

NATURE, MONEY, AND

MODERNITY IN VENEZUELA

Fernando Coronil

THE UNIVERSITY OF CHICAGO PRESS
CHICAGO & LONDON

The University of Chicago Press, Chicago 60637
The University of Chicago Press, Ltd., London
© 1997 by The University of Chicago

06 05 04 03 02 01 00 99   2 3 4 5

ISBN: 0-226-11601-8 (cloth)
ISBN: 0-226-11602-6 (paper)

Library of Congress Cataloging-in-Publication Data

Coronil, Fernando
    The magical state : nature, money, and modernity in Venezuela /
Fernando Coronil.
        p.   cm.
    Includes bibliographical references and index.
    ISBN 0-226-11601-8 (alk. paper).—ISBN 0-226-11602-6 (alk.
paper)
        1. Venezuela—Politics and government—20th century.   2. Petroleum
industry and trade—Venezuela—History.   I. Title.
JL3831.C67   1997
306.2'0987—dc21   97-8000
                                                          CIP

⊗ The paper used in this publication meets the minimum requirements
of the American National Standard for Information Sciences—Permanence
of Paper for Printed Library Materials, ANSI Z39.48-1984.

Para Andrea y Mariana,

con Julie,

en la memoria de Lya Imber de Coronil

Front cover illustration on the paperback edition of this book: Jacobo Borges, *Meeting with a Red Circle, or Circle of Lunatics,* 1973 (Museum of Monterrey, Mexico). This painting mirrors the history of the state it represents. Borges, inspired by photographs of Venezuelan heads of state, depersonalizes their referents, merging person and institution to show their permanent presence as spectral ciphers of power. Venezuelan president Carlos Andrés Pérez presented the painting as an official gift to Mexican president Luis Echeverría. When subsequently it could not be located in Mexico, Borges painted a duplicate for a European retrospective of his work, but he later found the original. The painting inspired Argentine author Julio Cortázar to write a story titled "Encounter Within a Red Circle," dedicated to Jacobo Borges.

Contents

ILLUSTRATIONS

FIGURES

TABLES

PREFACE

For every poet it is always morning in the world, and History a forgotten insomniac night. History and elemental awe are always our early beginning, because the fate of poetry is to fall in love with the world in spite of History.

Derek Walcott

This account of contemporary Venezuelan history is part of my sustained effort to develop a perspective from which to view societies that are central to the formation of what has been called the modern world and yet are cast as marginal to it. This has involved countering what I call Occidentalism—representational practices whose effect is to present non-Western peoples as the Other of a Western self. I have elaborated this perspective over an extended period, going back and forth between Venezuela, my home country, and the United States, where I was trained and where I now work. At stake in an enterprise of this sort are a host of issues concerning the effects of thinking and translating across cultural boundaries. Here I wish only to note that I have taken the risk that this analysis may confirm prejudices about Latin America's inherent deficiencies, setting it against the chance to question the colonial opposition between the civilized and the backward that still organizes prevailing understandings of cultural difference. By showing how Venezuela's labyrinthine history unfolds within a larger labyrinth, I hope to unsettle the illusion that its history can be contained within fixed territorial, temporal, or cultural boundaries. I could move through these interconnected labyrinths only because I was fortunate enough to have the guidance and support of many people. I wish I could express my gratitude to all of them. As I name here only those who directly contributed to the production of this book, I ask forgiveness of those without whose treasured friendship and support this book could not have come to light.

I did research for this book during various periods: two continuous stretches from 1974 to 1979 and from 1988 to 1989, as well as several fieldwork stints during many of the summers between those two periods and after 1989. During the first period (1974–79), I was affiliated with the Center for the Study of Development of the Central University of Venezuela (CENDES), and my research was funded by a grant from the Consejo Nacional de

Investigaciones Científicas y Tecnológicas (CONICIT). I studied class formation and the mythification of national progress through research on the automobile industry sector, which was defined by the state "as the motor of national development." As part of this work, together with Julie Skurski, I studied numerous automobile enterprises, interviewed their managers and owners, and conducted a survey through which we gathered technical information about the enterprises and the opinions of managers and workers on specific topics. We also interviewed government officials who defined the state development plans and were greatly aided by the *técnicos* who formulated and implemented the automobile industrial policy. I would like to thank the many people who contributed to this research by sharing their experiences and insights, particularly Sebastian Alegrett, Rodrigo Arcaya, José Bisogno, Robert Bottome, Pedro Concha, Mariano Crespo, Roberto Madero, Hugo Pisani, Alfredo Salas Rotundo, Roberto Salas Capriles, and Jack Sweeney. CENDES provided a stimulating forum for the discussion of political and historical transformations in Venezuela. I wish to thank in particular Manuel Beroes, Gastón Carvallo, Germán Carrera Damas, Ocarina Castillo, Luis Gómez, Ivan Gorrín, Margarita López Maya, and Terry Karl. Mónica González, José Seijó, and Nelson Freytes assisted in the collection and organization of data.

Research during the 1988–89 academic year was funded by the Spencer Foundation and the Michigan Society of Fellows and supported by the Center of Latin American Studies Rómulo Gallegos (CELARG). At CELARG, Yolanda Salas de Lecuna and Hector Malavé Mata were a constant source of insight. During that year I explored the interplay between elite and popular conceptions of history in political ideologies and popular religiosity through research on the presidential campaign and the popular religion of María Lionza. In response to rising state repression and popular unrest, I expanded my research to examine the study of the connection among political violence, collective memory, and social transformations. My research on political violence relied on the collaboration of more people than I can mention here; I would like to acknowledge Lígia Bolívar, Matías Camuñas, Liliana Ortega, Antonio García, and Walter Márquez. Much of what I know about the religion of María Lionza comes from the insights of Daisy Barreto and Mariano Díaz. I also want to thank Bernardo Mommer, whose pioneering application of the theory of ground rent to the Venezuelan oil industry, stimulating discussions, and critical reading of two of my chapters significantly contributed to this work.

This book initially took form at the University of Chicago, where I was trained as an anthropologist. The work of two extraordinary teachers and scholars who initiated me into this field continues to orient my thought. Victor Turner made me appreciate William Blake's insight that one can see the universe in a grain of sand. Terence Turner constantly inspires me to push thought to the limit and to ask not just about its truth but about its value. His personal and intellectual integrity and his loyal support in the face of adversity encouraged me to carry on. Many other people at the University of Chicago helped form this book as much by the excellence of their work as by their critical support of mine. Bernard Cohn's pioneering work at the intersection of anthropology and history questioned the limiting assumptions of both disciplines and opened a space which made my work possible. Jean and John Comaroff's imaginative integration of ethnography and history within the study of colonialism has established an exemplary model of what can be accomplished by a critical anthropology. John Comaroff, defying temporal constraints, has always found time for the critical insight. John Coatsworth, a historian, and Adam Przeworski, a political scientist, provided an inspiring disciplinary counterpoint that expanded the scope of my work. Paul Friedrich, Keith Hart, and Nancy Munn, through their encouragement and the example of their scholarship, helped me formulate various aspects of this work. I am also grateful to people at the University of Chicago whose friendship and insights sustained this project at various junctures, particularly Lauren Berlant, Robin Derby, Martha Lampland, Moishe Postone, Rafael Sánchez, Kathleen Swartzman, and Richard Turits.

As a Fellow at the Kellogg Institute of the University of Notre Dame I developed the section on dictatorships and coups d'état; I would like to thank in particular Roberto Da Matta and Guillermo O'Donnell for their helpful suggestions. The book took final form at the University of Michigan. My students there pushed my thinking in unexpected directions, making real the ideal of education as an interactive process through which the educator is educated. Were it not for the asymmetries of this interaction, I would be able to acknowledge more fully the extent to which they have educated me. The Michigan Society of Fellows, the Comparative Study of Social Transformations faculty seminar, and the anthropology and history departments have provided extraordinarily stimulating forums for conversations across the disciplines. I wish to express my gratitude to the many people at Michigan who have offered their comments and support, particularly Jane Burbank, Fred Cooper, Valentine Daniel, Nicholas Dirks, Laurent Dubois, Geoff Eley, Paul Eiss, Michael Fotiadis, Lessie Jo Frazier, Raymond Grew, Daniel Levine, Bruce Mannheim, Brink Messick, Walter Mignolo, Sherry Ortner, David Pederson, John Pemberton, José Rabasa, Bill Rosenberg, Rebecca Scott, Bill Sewell, Ann Stoler, and Ron Suny. My deep gratitude to the members of my writing group, Roger Rouse, Kim Schepelle, David Scobey, and Julie Skurski, who read the manuscript in its early phase, and to a group of graduate students at the University of Michigan, who read the final version and offered valuable suggestions. In its final stage, this work benefited from spirited discussions with the group of Latinamericanists developing a subaltern perspective on the study of the Americas.[1] I would like to acknowledge as well the Undergraduate Research Opportunity Program of the University of Michigan, which made it possible for me to have the assistance of several undergraduate students, in particular Danielle Hayot, who composed the bibliography, and Tomás Grigera, who produced the charts. David Brent, as editor of the University of Chicago Press, trusted and supported this project from the outset; two anonymous readers offered invaluable suggestions. I was fortunate to work with Jim Schaefer, who polished my wording as well as my thoughts and offered a critical and supportive vision of the whole book which helped me bring it to a conclusion. I received invaluable financial support for various phases of this research from the University of Michigan through the Rackham Graduate School, the Office of the Vice Provost for Academic and Multicultural Affairs, the Office of the Vice-President for Research, and the International Institute.

My friends from Liceo Andrés Bello will recognize that the commitment that orients this work was formed long ago by our passion for the possible. For their support and friendship I also wish to thank Jorge Blanco, Maria Elena Coronil, Marisa and Perán Erminy, Mirna Guerra, James Huey, Pablo Livinalli, Stuart McDowell, Elsa Morales, Ana Rodríguez, Zeva Schub, and Gloria Skurski. My gratitude to my parents, Lya Imber de Coronil and Fernando Rubén Coronil, and to my parents-in-law, Irene and Frank Skurski, whose exemplary lives and unconditional support made this work possible. My daughters, Mariana and Andrea, accepted having an often distracted and unavailable father but also found innumerable ways of reminding me that there was life outside this book, and filled me with their joy; perhaps one day they will understand that this book was written for them. Finally, as I review these always insufficient acknowledgments, I am reminded of the Cuban proverb "un solo palo no hace monte" (a single tree does not make a forest). If any book is a collective product, this one is particularly so. From the outset, this work has been a joint project. Julie Skurski participated in its creation

---

1. For a collection of articles that represent some of these views, see *Subaltern Studies in the Americas,* a special issue of *Dispositio/n,* vol. 19, no. 46 (1994), edited by José Rabasa, Javier Sanjines, and Robert Carr.

from beginning to end as companion, friend, and intellectual partner. Her voice is present in every word, making the notion of individual authorship a generous but unfair illusion. My gratitude to all, and to her especially, for creating this necessary illusion.

While these people helped me through the labyrinth, others trapped me within it, obliging me to experience the state's elusive power. Since this book's labyrinthine history mirrors the story it tells about the state, showing how it creates conditions which defy grasping its operations, there is the temptation to recount it. But lest I write a book within the book, I will only offer here a glimpse of its history in order to acknowledge its effect upon the production of this book.

Before undertaking this research, I had carried out fieldwork in Cuba for a year on a project which was truncated by Cuban policy shifts. For a number of reasons I decided not to write about Cuba but to turn to the analysis of nationalist ideology and state power in Venezuela. However, on my return to the United States I was detained, excluded from entry on the ground that I was a subversive agent, denied information about the charges, and after several months ordered to leave the country "within forty-eight hours." As a result of a chance encounter in which family ties and political connections crossed, a well-connected lawyer obtained the suspension of my deportation (after it was mailed!) and undertook my defense.

My defense involved a Kafkaesque "trial." Accused of being a subversive agent but refused information about the charges on the grounds that revealing it would endanger the security of the U.S. government, I had to prepare my defense by imagining what could be construed as my guilt and countering it with a narrative supported by as much evidence as I could provide. An essential part of this defense involved producing an account of my life from my childhood up to that moment. This account had to be backed by letters from official and public figures, as well as by police and intelligence reports from the United States and Venezuela. As part of this process, I obtained the support as well of the then-President of Venezuela, Rafael Caldera (my father was his family's physician), who asked his ambassador in Washington to represent my case vis-à-vis U.S. authorities.

Nevertheless, my situation remained unchanged. After more than a year in the United States trying to resolve my case by legal or political means but without succeeding in securing even a hearing, Julie Skurski and I decided to return to Venezuela in order to carry out our new projects. When I began my work on the structures of political and economic power, however, I learned that my case was an object of rumor and gossip within these circles and that I had been under close surveillance since before my detention in Miami. My inability to prove my innocence, despite the considerable support I had received, proved my guilt. The mistrust, rumors, and surveillance which constrained my research also helped me understand how power creates reality by its effects.

The evidence I have since obtained (including documents through the Freedom of Information Act) suggests that I had unknowingly become entangled in a complex web of power that linked President Nixon's attempt to curtail U.S. dissidence and Latin America dissent to rivalries in Venezuela among different political leaders. At the end of 1978, during Carter's presidency, the case against me was unexpectedly dropped just as it had started with a letter that offered no explanation. In light of these events as well as of the continuing sensitivity of some of the issues I address here, I have had to weigh the impact that publishing my account of state formation in Venezuela might have on my ability to continue working on its transformation. Ironically, the crisis of the state and the challenge to its unbridled power which I examine in this book have opened a political space which this book can now join.

Table 1

Heads of state, 1908–96

1908–35	General Juan Vicente Gómez
1936–41	General Eleazar López Contreras
1941–45	General Isaías Medina Angarita
1945–48	Junta Revolucionaria de Gobierno (presided over by Rómulo Betancourt)
1948	Rómulo Gallegos
1948–50	Military junta (presided over by Carlos Delgado Chalbaud)
1950–58	General Marcos Pérez Jiménez
1958–59	Military-civilian junta (presided over by Rear Admiral Wolfgang Larrazábal)
1959–64	Rómulo Betancourt
1964–69	Raul Leoni
1969–74	Rafael Caldera
1974–79	Carlos Andrés Pérez
1979–84	Luis Herrera Campíns
1984–89	Jaime Lusinchi
1989–93	Carlos Andrés Pérez
1993–94	Ramón Velásquez
1994–	Rafael Caldera

Carlos Andrés Pérez during the 1988 presidential campaign. (Archivo El Universal. Photo: Ivonne Barreto.)

INTRODUCTION:
THE MAGICAL STATE
AND OCCIDENTALISM

We never had to build many theaters in this country. Why should we? The normative structure of power was always our best stage . . . Where did we get our public institutions and our notion of "state" from? From a hat, from a routine trick of prestidigitation . . . With the development of the oil industry a cosmogony was created in Venezuela. The state acquired a providential hue. From a slow evolution, as slow as everything that is related to agriculture, the state underwent a "miraculous" and spectacular development. It would be suicidal for a presidential candidate in Venezuela not to promise us paradise because the state has nothing to do with reality. The state is a magnanimous sorcerer . . . Oil is fantastic and induces fantasies. The announcement that Venezuela was an oil country created the illusion of a miracle; it created, in practice, a culture of miracles . . . Oil wealth had the power of a myth. Betancourt, Leoni, and Caldera did not go very far in this "Venezuelan dream" because our fiscal income did not allow it; we were rich, but not that rich. But then came the other Pérez, Carlos Andrés Pérez, and we found the phrase that defined us. We were building the Great Venezuela. Carlos Andrés Pérez was not a president. He was a magician, a magician who was capable of propelling us toward a hallucination that made the exhibitionism of Pérez Jiménez seem pale in comparison. Pérez Jiménez decreed the dream of Progress. The country did not progress; it got fat. [The rule] of Pérez Jiménez was a début, that of Carlos Andrés Pérez was a flamboyant revival.

José Ignacio Cabrujas

I t is fitting that José Ignacio Cabrujas, an acclaimed writer of plays and serialized television dramas who was intimately familiar with local forms of make-believe in Venezuela, became one of the country's most perceptive political commentators. Invited by the Presidential Commission for State Reform (COPRE) to express his views on Venezuelan politics,[1] he calls attention to what was there for everyone to see yet had eluded

---

1. President Jaime Lusinchi decreed the creation of the Presidential Commission for State Reform (COPRE) on 17 December 1984 in order to promote the democratization of the state. For a discussion of the COPRE that places it in the context of various attempts to reform the Venezuelan state, see Gómez Calcaño and López Maya 1990: 57–116.

social analysis: the deification of the state in contemporary political life in Venezuela.[2]

Reflecting on collectively lived illusions, Cabrujas relates the state's providential appearance to its worldly materiality and highlights the cultural and political effects of its extraordinary financial wealth. As if wishing to acknowledge and yet also to disavow the state's exalted self-representation, he notes that in Venezuela the state is a "magnanimous sorcerer" endowed with the power to replace reality with fabulous fictions propped up by oil wealth. "Oil is fantastic and induces fantasies," Cabrujas says. Its power to awaken fantasies enables state leaders to fashion political life into a dazzling spectacle of national progress through "tricks of prestidigitation." State representatives, the visible embodiments of the invisible powers of oil money, appear on the state's stage as powerful magicians who pull social reality, from public institutions to cosmogonies, out of a hat.

An official version of Venezuelan political cosmogony has come to define the public vision of the nation's past. According to this vision, the birth of the nation's modernity began when General Juan Vicente Gómez died in 1935, thus ending his twenty-seven years of dictatorship. Gómez's death freed Venezuela from the grip of his personalistic rule and allowed the nation to begin a democratizing process that was interrupted only by General Pérez Jiménez's dictatorship from 1948 to 1958. After 1958, this process led to the consolidation of a democratic system that has proven to be the longest-lasting in South America. In terms of this account, while General Gómez kept the country locked in the backward past, General Pérez Jiménez created a dark interregnum that briefly interrupted the democratizing process set in motion by Gómez's death.

Going against the grain, Cabrujas echoes only partially this official story. Instead of focusing exclusively on democratic regimes, he singles out two moments in the state's self-fashioning as the agent of modern progress: the dictatorial rule of Pérez Jiménez, which he describes as the "debut" of the "myth

---

2. Philip Abrams argues that social analysis tends to reproduce the godlike appearance of the state as a unified and self-willed force (1988). In the Venezuelan case, this appearance is heightened by the state's fiscal abundance, which derives from oil revenues rather than from taxation of its citizens, enabling the state to embody powers that seem to come from itself. (For a comment on Abrams's views, see chapter 1.) By examining the intersubjective effects of power relations, Weber's conception of charisma, particularly in its more sociological and anthropological versions (Shils 1965; Tambiah 1984) illuminates the deification of the state. The Marxist conception of state fetishism encompasses both the phenomenology of political power and its underlying social dynamics. For an insightful discussion of Marx's notion of fetishism, see Pietz (1993); for an attempt to apply the concept of fetishism to the state, see Wells (1981).

of progress," and the first presidency of Carlos Andrés Pérez (1974–79), which for him represents this myth's hallucinatory "revival." While Pérez Jiménez was a military dictator and Pérez a democratic leader, Cabrujas suggests that they both promoted the myth of progress more powerfully than other presidents and ruled during periods of extraordinary fiscal wealth and political stability.

Despite their differences, these visions of the nation's past focus on the same post-1935 "modern" period. One of the most effective prestidigitation tricks performed in Venezuela has been the relegation of Gómez's rule to the "backward" age of Venezuela's past. By defining Gómez as the incarnation of primitiveness, later regimes have fashioned themselves, by contrast, as the deputies of modernity. In so doing, they have obscured their foundations in the Gómez regime, their shared dependence on the oil economy, and their extraordinary personalization of state power. Yet it was during Gómez's "traditional" regime, as we shall see, that it became possible to imagine Venezuela as a modern oil nation, to identify the ruler with the state, and to construe the state as the agent of its modernization. That even Cabrujas forgot Gómez is symptomatic, in my view, of a collective amnesia that envelops the dominant memorialization of Venezuela's history.[3]

What is forgotten screens what is remembered. The persuasiveness of a historical account, like that of a magical performance, depends on rendering invisible the artifice of its production. Just as history refers ambiguously to the past in its completeness and to the selective remembering of stories about the past, magic alludes to an extraordinary reality as well as to the selective presentation of the elements that create the illusion of its existence through invisible tricks that exploit distraction and diversion. Like history, magic hangs suspended between fiction and fact, trick and truth. Gabriela, the adopted child secretly taken from *desaparecido* parents in *The Official Story,* the Argentinean film about state terror and historical memory, asks the magician at her birthday party (a party celebrating, in fact, the date when she was adopted): *¿Usted es un mago de trucos, o de verdad?* (Are you a magician of tricks, or a real one; literally, of truth). As the film suggests, asking this question already opens a space for exploring the play of illusion and truth in magic

---

3. Cabrujas recognizes, however, that Gómez marks the beginning of the rapid economic transformation that led to the identification of the state with the government. "In Venezuela the state is the government," Cabrujas says. This identification took place as naturally as the "growth" of the economy. According to Cabrujas, ever since the rule of Gómez up to the rule of Luis Herrera Campíns, Venezuela "grew economically as if following a natural cycle," without being responsible for its own growth (1987:19).

as much as in history, for remembering that they are produced, like memory itself, by performances.

In this book I explore the appearance of the Venezuelan state as a transcendent and unifying agent of the nation. I argue that the deification of the state took place as part of the transformation of Venezuela into an oil nation. As an oil nation, Venezuela was seen as having two bodies, a political body made up of its citizens and a natural body made up of its rich subsoil. By condensing within itself the multiple powers dispersed throughout the nation's two bodies, the state appeared as a single agent endowed with the magical power to remake the nation. I argue that the arduous establishment of state authority was achieved in intimate relation with the exploitation of petroleum. Throughout the nineteenth century the fragile Venezuelan state, chronically assaulted by regional caudillos, was unable to impose its control over the fragmented national territory. It was only when it was transformed into a mediator between the nation and the foreign oil companies in the early twentieth century that the state acquired the political capacity and financial resources that enabled it to appear as an independent agent capable of imposing its dominion over society. Thus, the state itself was produced as an ensemble of practices, institutions, and ideologies of rule in the course of contests over its regulation of oil production and its control over oil-derived money. Its control over oil money enabled it to transform itself as it expanded the range of its rule—controlling production in the mineral sector (oil, gas, petrochemicals, bauxite, iron, steel, alumina, aluminum, and related industrial inputs), regulating and promoting private economic activity (fixing interest rates, establishing tariffs, granting licenses, authorizing subsidies, determining prices and wages, and so forth), and establishing central control in a number of other sectors, from education (for example, defining the content of school curricula and the structure of final examinations) to transport and communications (distributing newsprint and leasing wavelength frequencies to radio and television stations).

Thus transformed into a petrostate, the Venezuelan state came to hold the monopoly not only of political violence but of the nation's natural wealth. The state has exercised this monopoly dramaturgically, securing compliance through the spectacular display of its imperious presence—it seeks to conquer rather than persuade. In this respect, like the Spanish imperial state analyzed by José Antonio Maravall (1986), the Venezuelan state has been constituted as a unifying force by producing fantasies of collective integration into centralized political institutions. As the heir of the culture of the baroque, the state in Venezuela "captivates minds" through highly rhetorical cultural forms which seek the public's compliance by leaving it, in Godzich's words, *boquiabierto* (dumbfounded; literally, open-mouthed) (1994:79). Under the spell of baroque culture, "the audience does not participate, nor does it internalize the arguments: It is conquered, subjugated, carried by the persuasive flow of the rhetoric" (1994:79). Typically, the Venezuelan state astonishes through the marvels of power rather than convinces through the power of reason, as reason itself is made part of the awe-inspiring spectacle of its rule. By manufacturing dazzling development projects that engender collective fantasies of progress, it casts its spell over audience and performers alike. As a "magnanimous sorcerer," the state seizes its subjects by inducing a condition or state of being receptive to its illusions—a magical state.

In the following chapters I examine the state's historical formation during three critical periods: General Juan Vicente Gómez's long dictatorship (1908–35); General Marcos Pérez Jiménez's military rule (1948–58); and the first administration of Carlos Andrés Pérez (1974–79). Borrowing Cabrujas's dramaturgical imagery, I have divided my discussion into four acts: Gómez's "Premiere" in part 1; Pérez Jiménez's "Debut" in part 2; Carlos Andrés Pérez's "Revival" in part 3; and the drama's "Sequel" in part 4. With the exception of the introductory and concluding chapters, each chapter focuses on certain themes and historical junctures when the state defined and intensified the pursuit of "the Venezuelan dream." As Cabrujas notes, other presidents (including the principal architects of Venezuelan democracy Rómulo Betancourt and Rafael Caldera) "did not go very far in this 'Venezuelan dream' because our fiscal income did not allow it; we were rich, but not that rich" (1987:19). By focusing on periods of intense mythification of progress, I offer an interpretation of the dynamics of historical transformation in Venezuela that unsettles dominant accounts not only of its modern history but of modernity itself.

In part 1, I place the forgetting of Gómez within rippling circles of forgetfulness that link national to global amnesias as interconnected dimensions of worldwide processes of nation formation. The first chapter serves as an extended introduction and contains a theoretical discussion of issues which I seek to bring to life through historical and ethnographic narratives in the chapters that follow. The chapter focuses on the erasure of nature in dominant currents of social theory and assesses the significance of this effacing for understanding the division of the world into modern centers and backward peripheries. I argue that this amnesia about nature has entailed forgetting as well the role of the "periphery" in the formation of the modern world, an active "silencing of the past" (Trouillot 1996) that reinscribes the violence of a history made at the expense of the labor and the natural resources of peoples relegated to the margins.

In order to analyze the significance of petroleum for Venezuelan state formation and to account for its monetary value, I develop an approach to the analysis of societies which depend on the export of one or a few primary products. Through a discussion of theories of underdevelopment, neoclassical views of natural resources, the Marxist theory of value, and an analysis of the evolution of oil prices in this century, I orient attention away from the magnitude and direction of value flows (the problematic of unequal exchange which concerns most theories of underdevelopment) and toward the global divisions of labor and of nature implicated in value creation. Treating the creation of value as a process that involves the formation of subjects as much as the production of valuables, I place the domains normally associated with culture, politics, and economics within a unified analytical field. By developing a unifying approach, I seek to examine the historical constitution of subjects as part of the formation of an objectified world of social institutions and understandings and to see the history that forms them as historical creatures as informing their activity as history's protagonists.

Most analysts set apart third-world oil exporters from other third-world countries by virtue of their exceptional financial wealth. Needless to say, these oil exporters share structural features that distinguish them from other peripheral nations. These common features are derived not just from these oil exporters' financial wealth but also from the centrality of the state in their economies.[4] What I find striking, however, is the extent to which oil-exporting countries may help us discern the common predicament of most third-world nations by virtue of their position as primary exporters that depend on ground rents (land-based revenues).[5] The magnitude of these rents may vary widely, depending on such factors as the kind of commodity exported, the patterns of global production and demand, and the competition from alternative products. These rents may arise from different productive structures and from different types of linkages between local and global economies in accordance with the already classic distinction between foreign-controlled enclaves and domestically controlled export sectors (Cardoso and Faletto 1979). Yet these rents help establish similar patterns of in-

4. In a related vein, an analyst argues that "culturally, Venezuela belongs to Latin America; structurally, its economy and patterns of stability and instability are more similar to those of such other relatively populous oil exporters as Algeria, Iran, and Nigeria" (Karl 1995:34).

5. I discuss the category of ground rent in detail in chapter 1.

ternal specialization and external dependence which consolidate the role of third-world nations as what I call nature-exporting societies. Even when these nations seek to break their colonial dependence on primary exports by implementing development plans directed at diversifying their economies, they typically rely on foreign exchange obtained by exporting primary products, intensifying their dependence on these commodities. Paradoxically, in pursuit of their comparative advantage, these nature-exporting nations are frequently recast in their old colonial role as sources of primary products, a role now rewritten in terms of the neoliberal rationality of globalizing capitalism. For them, neocolonialism follows postcolonialism.

The dependence of most third-world nations on a few primary export commodities often subjects them to similar cycles of boom and bust, whether the export commodity is sugar, as in the Cuba and Puerto Rico of the "dance of the millions" after World War I; beef and grains, as in the Argentina of the belle époque; guano (bird droppings), as in the prosperous Peru of the mid-nineteenth century; or oil, as in most oil-exporting nations (examples could easily be extended to other primary producers in Latin America, Asia, and Africa). Export booms tend to overvalue the domestic currency, promote imports of manufactured goods, and undermine productive sectors directed toward the domestic market. Economists who studied the erosion of Dutch manufacturing as a result of the rapid expansion of North Sea gas development named this phenomenon the "Dutch disease," or oil syndrome. The Dutch disease, however, only occasionally afflicts the resilient diversified economies of first-world nations but constitutes an epidemic in the monocrop economies of the third world. As a colonial plague that malformed the third world into narrowly specialized primary product exporters, the Dutch disease should be renamed the third-world or neocolonial disease.[6]

Remembering nature—recognizing theoretically its historical significance—allows us to recast dominant histories of Western historical development and to question the notion that modernity is the offspring of a self-propelled West.[7] A resignified nature allows us to include in our historical accounts not just a more diversified set of historical actors but a more complex historical dynamic. It enables us to replace what Lefebvre refers to

6. For discussions of the Dutch disease, see Corden and Neary (1982); Buiter and Purvis (1983); and Wijnbergen (1984).

7. Following Hegel, thinkers as varied as Habermas (1988), Taylor (1989), and Giddens (1987) view modernity as an European phenomenon. For a critique of this view from a Latin American perspective, see Dussel (1993).

as the "ossified" dialectic of capital and labor by a dialectic of capital, labor, and land (by land, following Marx, he means not only the powers of nature but also the agents associated with it, including the state as sovereign over a national territory). The dialectic of these three elements helps us see the landlord state as an independent economic agent rather than as an exclusively political actor structurally dependent on capital, and to conceptualize capitalism as a global process that mutually forms centers and peripheries rather than as a self-generated system that expands from active modern regions and engulfs passive traditional societies.

By broadening the social and geographical referents of capitalism, this perspective decenters Eurocentric conceptions that identify modernity with metropolitan cultural formations and relegate the periphery to a pre-modern domain. By treating it as the regional product of global center-periphery interactions, it recasts metropolitan modernity as its dominant form rather than as its (self-proclaimed) universal standard. In turn, by recognizing its role in the making of the modern world, this perspective permits us to approach the so-called periphery as the site of subaltern modernities rather than as the region where traditional cultures are embraced by Western progress.

In the second chapter, I explore Venezuela's transformation into an oil nation during the dictatorship of General Juan Vicente Gómez. During Gómez's rule, political power came to be based on the state's control over the exploitation of the nation's subsoil. By making political and economic activities dependent on the independently wealthy state, this centralizing foundation created conditions that simultaneously supported the movement toward political democracy and limited its development. From Gómez onwards the state became the center of political and economic power. Official accounts have buried from view the extent to which the democratic state rests on foundations built during the Gómez regime and must negotiate the underlying tension between the public origin of the state's financial resources and the private character of their appropriation. This chapter shows that if national imaginings are partly sustained, as Anderson argues, by means of communication such as print-capitalism, they also depend on the very materiality of the nation as a life-sustaining habitat—on differing modalities of configuring the metabolism between society and nature.

I argue that during the Gómez regime, as the wealth of the nation came to be equated with its natural body and as social groups identified their particular interests with the nation's interest in the oil industry, the state was construed as the legitimate agent of an "imagined community" (Anderson 1983) formed by its collective ownership of the nation's natural body.

By construing Venezuela's "modern democracy" in opposition to Gómez's "primitive dictatorship," it developed as dictatorship's antithesis: democracy and dictatorship became two sides of the same oil coin. Despite the differences between Gómez's dictatorial rule and the liberal regimes constituted against it, they took form as states of an oil nation. I discuss how this common form took shape during the Gómez regime and its immediate aftermath by examining the self-fashioning of Venezuela into an oil nation through democratic struggles against Gómez's "backward" rule (focusing on debates that took place in 1936) and the formulation of oil policies (up to 1943). The chapter concludes with a critique of the evacuation of materiality in theories about democracy through a critical commentary on the works of Claude Lefort and Slavoj Žižek.

In part 2, I examine how the contest between dictatorial and democratic regimes was played out between 1945 and 1958 through a discussion of several coups d'état (in 1945, 1948, 1952, and 1958). My analysis shows how in the context of the limited diversification of the domestic economy, the state became the focus of intense political competition and the center of economic struggles. Just as under Gómez the independently wealthy state had been the privatized tool of a personalistic ruler, it could subsequently become the partisan tool of a democratic party. The tension between the natural origin of the nation's finite collective wealth and the private destiny of its social appropriation shaped the contest between democracy and dictatorship from 1945 to 1958.

Through the detailed examination of the practical orchestration and public representation of these coups d'état, I explore how the state was constructed as the central site of political power in Venezuela. In chapter 3, I discuss how this role was conceptualized during the process that led to the consolidation of the military dictatorship of General Marcos Pérez Jiménez. I extend this discussion in chapter 4 by examining General Pérez Jiménez's image of progress. I first present a general overview of the contradictory consequences of his economic policies, since they both promoted economic diversification and constrained its further development; and I illustrate this process by means of a detailed analysis of the development of the steel industry. His contradictory policies, I argue, helped turn local capital against the regime and form the alliance with the middle-class parties which led to the coup in 1958. In chapter 5, I discuss the orchestration of the coup d'état of 23 January 1958, widely considered the foundational moment of Venezuela's democracy, South America's most stable and long-lasting democratic regime.

These three chapters place the construction of Venezuelan democracy in the context of recent discussions of worldwide processes of democratization in which it figures as an exemplary case. I argue that the "political" characteristics often invoked to explain the stability and success of Venezuela's democracy—the alleged democratic vocation, negotiating skills, and learning capacity of Venezuelan leaders—must themselves be accounted for. My discussion of the foundational discourses of Venezuelan democracy in part 1 and of the dynamics of class and state formation in part 2 seek to provide an explanation of the conditions that have enabled and limited Venezuela's democracy.

In part 3 I discuss the consolidation of the petrostate during the oil boom period of Carlos Andrés Pérez's first presidency (1974–79). While the quadrupling of oil prices at the end of 1973 led to visions of economic and political decline in the metropolitan centers, in Venezuela, as in other oil-producing nations, it created the illusion that instantaneous modernization lay at hand, that torrents of oil money would change the flow of history and launch the country into the future. Pérez proposed transforming the oil bonanza into a vast project to develop Venezuela at an unparalleled scale and speed, to achieve, in effect, a leap into autonomy. While Simón Bolívar led the nation to political independence by defeating Spain in the battle of Carabobo in 1821, Pérez proposed to win the decisive battle for the nation's economic independence.

I discuss President Pérez's project of national transformation and his plan to "sow the oil" in three chapters. In chapter 6, I examine the attempt by the Pérez administration to develop the automobile industry by producing "fully Venezuelan vehicles" (completing the local manufacture of vehicles) and the political struggle, known as the "motors war," that ensued when the government negotiated with transnational automobile corporations and domestic capitalists the local production of vehicle engines. The bargaining process over apparently technical issues itself became the vehicle for the contestation of existing development goals and the realignment of political forces within the ruling political alliance. The delays in policy decisions, apparently caused by a conflict between the strategy for promoting exports and that for developing local production to replace imports, concealed an underlying reorientation of the global strategy of automotive transnational corporations as well as a chronic local conflict, intensified by the oil boom, between value production and rent appropriation. Domestic debates over policy reflected the tension between the actual social dominance of rent circulation over the production of value and the political need to disguise this dominant business practice and to present the state and the bourgeoisie as champions of production and entrepreneurial autonomy.

While the chapter on the motors wars analyzes the failure to implement the policy of local automobile production, the next chapter examines the short life of FANATRACTO, a state-promoted company jointly owned by the state, a U.S. transnational corporation, and a local conglomerate. Since 1936, the slogan "to sow the oil" had metaphorically expressed the state's policy of using oil resources to finance modern industrial and agricultural production. The establishment of a tractor factory was regarded as a means to promote both industry and agriculture and therefore it stood as one of the highest expressions of this goal. FANATRACTO began with great fanfare and expense, yet it was quietly abandoned as soon as it was built and left to die. In this chapter I discuss FANATRACTO's bizarre history and account for its demise in terms of intrastate rivalries and of its shareholders' contradictory orientations toward productive investments.

In contrast to these two studies in the field of production, chapter 8 explores the murder of Ramón Carmona, a lawyer who was machine-gunned to death one afternoon on a street in Caracas. Public discussion of this murder during the 1978 electoral campaign revealed a vast network of formal, informal, and illegal transactions involving several business deals among a great range of actors extending from poor immigrants to the president and his mistress. While my discussion of the motors wars and of the death of FANATRACTO investigates how productive efforts were undermined by the dominance of rent circulation over the production of value, my analysis of the Carmona case explores the inner logic of the system of rent circulation after the 1973 oil boom, when the flow of rivers of petrodollars throughout the body politic changed its shape, redefining normative standards and projecting the illicit face of state activity onto the public arena as normal and desirable.

These three chapters show how the tension between oil money circulation and value production underlying Venezuelan rentier capitalism was concretely lived through and expressed in the quotidian actions of different social actors. The circulation of torrents of oil money not only undermined productive activity and stimulated the spread of financial speculation and corruption but also facilitated the concentration of power at the highest levels of government. In turn, the extraordinary powers of the president encouraged a vertical style of policy making which often led to arbitrary and contradictory actions and undermined democratic practices.

In part 4 I discuss recent developments in Venezuela and make some

Table 2

State spending, 1900–1979 (in millions of bolivars)

President	Years	Current prices	1979 prices	Annual average
Cipriano Castro	1900–1908	433	2,247	250
Juan V. Gómez	1909–35	3,170	12,885	477
Eleazar López C.	1936–41	805	8,833	1,606
Isaías Medina A.	1941–45	1,798	6,905	1,534
Rómulo Betancourt	1945–48	2,249	7,429	3,715
Rómulo Gallegos	1948	1,644	4,605	4,605
M. Pérez Jiménez	1948–58	24,410	68,926	7,658
Wolfgang Larrazábal	1958	6,260	17,389	17,389
Rómulo Betancourt	1959–64	32,384	84,307	16,861
Raúl Leoni	1964–69	40,133	90,166	18,033
Rafael Caldera	1969–74	59,920	120,210	24,042
Carlos A. Pérez	1974–79	221,840	286,362	57,272

SOURCE: Fundación Polar 1988: 455

general observations concerning the historical arc covered by this book. In chapter 9, I briefly show how the growing hegemony of international capital (including internationalized domestic capital) has led to a shift from the state to the market as the dominant locus of profit-making activities and as the legitimizing source of the categories in terms of which public life is defined. Chapter 10 throws light upon this shift by highlighting the social logic of the historical transformation analyzed in this book, focusing on the twin processes of globalization and abstraction that have accompanied the transubstantiation of petroleum into money. I argue that if the circulation of petrodollars throughout the local economy had subordinated productive structures to the logic of rent capture, now the circulation of petrodollars and debt money in international financial circuits has come to dominate the local economy and to determine the conditions under which it must operate, obliging the local state to act on behalf of an open market. The growing abstraction of the source of state power, from the particular materiality of oil as substance to the general exchangeability of money as the universal equivalent, has entailed not only a shift in the forms of political power and their fetishized representations, but also a weakening of the national state with respect to the expanding hegemony of international money. Circumscribing the need for reform to the domestic, the "internal adjustment" demanded now by neoliberal wisdom promises to make the nation modern by wrenching it from the fantasy world conjured up by the magical petrostate and bringing it to the transparent world of the rational free market.

Jorge Luis Borges once warned against long introductions in an introduction to one of his many books (1978). I have decided to heed Borges's advice, keeping this introduction not much longer than his own, although I perhaps play a Borges trick on the reader by continuing my introductory remarks into the following chapter. I have structured this book as a series of fragments which can be read as separate units or as parts of a larger whole, itself only a fragment of a labyrinthine history. Two related issues, however, require brief comment at this point: first, this book's relation to the critique of Eurocentrism and, second, its focus on the workings of power at the "commanding heights" of the state. The first concerns my effort to view modernity from the bottom; the second, my decision to look at Venezuelan history from the top.

While it may be evident that the view of Venezuelan history presented here draws on contemporary postcolonial critiques, it is perhaps less clear that it does so by linking recent work produced with respect to Northern European colonialism in Asia and Africa to a long Caribbean and Latin American tradition of critical reflection concerning colonialism and modern imperialism.[8] Largely through the influence of Edward Said's pathbreaking critique of Orientalism, the critique of Eurocentrism has focused on Western representations of non-Western societies that were subjected to Northern European colonial domination. This criticism has perhaps been most productively developed by scholars linked to the Subaltern Studies group of India, which has sought to recast Indian historiography through a critique of its dependence on Eurocentric categories shared not only by colonial but also by nationalist and Marxist historiographies. Their extraordinary collective achievement has exerted a significant influence on scholars working in other areas of the world (Cooper 1994; Mallon 1994). From a Latin American perspective informed by a much longer entanglement with European colonialism and imperialism, their reliance on a clear separation between Europe and the colonial world is noticeable, even when they recognize their mutual historical constitution.[9]

8. These references include such central figures as José Martí, Fernando Ortiz, Fernando Henrique Cardoso, C. L. R. James, Frantz Fanon, and Stuart Hall. I would like to acknowledge the influence as well of nonacademic authors in the fields of literature (for instance José Lezama Lima, Pablo Neruda, Alejo Carpentier, Gabriel García Márquez, Augusto Roa Bastos); visual arts (the Mexican muralists, Cuban painter Manuel Mendive, and the Venezuelan painters Apolinar, Emerio Darío Lunar, Miguel Von Dangel, and Jacobo Borges); and last but not least, popular music, particularly Caribbean music, which, through Ortiz, I see as a life-affirming form of transculturation.

9. While Subaltern Studies scholars have productively used this separation between Europe and the colonial world, its use risks reinscribing the imperial assumptions underpinning the three-world scheme (for a critique of this scheme, see Pletsch 1981). For instance, Chakrabarty proposes that European history functions globally as the key to interpret third-world history by invoking Marx's

In my view, the analysis of the West's representation of other societies—the main focus in Edward Said's *Orientalism* (1979)—entails the need to counter these constructs as elements in the West's self-fashioning as the self-made embodiment of modernity. Undoing Orientalism thus requires that we link and problematize further the two entities that lie at the center of Said's analysis: the West's Orientalist representations and the West itself. This move involves reorienting our attention from the problematic of "Orientalism," which focuses on the stereotypical representation of the Orient, toward that of Occidentalism, by which I mean the implicit conception of the West animating its representation of non-Western societies. This perspective does not involve a reversal of focus from Orient to Occident, from Other to Self. Rather, by guiding our understanding toward the relational nature of representations of human collectivities, it brings out into the open their genesis in asymmetrical relations of power, including the power to obscure their genesis in inequality, to sever their historical connections, and thus to present as the internal and separate attributes of bounded entities what are in fact historical outcomes of connected peoples. Occidentalism, as I define it, is thus not the reverse of Orientalism but its condition of possibility. While any society may produce stereotypical representations of cultural difference as part of its own self-production, what is unique about Occidentalism is that it entails the mobilization of stereotypical representations of non-Western societies as part of the West's self-fashioning as an imperial power. Occidentalism is inseparable from Western hegemony not only because as a form of knowledge it expresses Western power but because it establishes a specific bond between knowledge and power in the West.

Occidentalism is thus the expression of a constitutive relationship between Western representations of cultural difference and worldwide Western dominance. Challenging Occidentalism requires that it be unsettled as a

---

famous analogy between evolutionary biology and social development (his notion that just as the human anatomy is the key to the anatomy of the ape, the abstract categories of bourgeois society are the key to understand ancient societies) (1992 : 3 – 4). This key applies to contemporary societies only if we do not resist the imperial denial of coevalness that makes them appear to stand in evolutionary relation to each other rather than side to side (contra Fabian 1983). The argument that "a third-world historian is condemned to knowing Europe as the home of the modern" (Chakrabarty 1992 : 19) reveals but also confirms Europe's ideological role as the indispensable key to the inner reality of the third world. While Chakrabarty analyzes the effectivity of this ideological division between Europe and its Others, one wonders whether the acceptance of this division at the same time risks reinscribing a notion of Europe as civilized ("human anatomy") and of the third world as savage ("the anatomy of the ape"). Elsewhere I have built on Ortiz's concept of transculturation both to problematize the separation between first and third worlds and to question the notion of Europe as the home of theory (1995).

mode of representation that produces polarized and hierarchical conceptions of the West and its Others and makes these conceptions central figures in accounts of global and local histories by a series of operations: separating the world's components into bounded units; disaggregating their relational histories; turning difference into hierarchy; naturalizing these representations; and therefore intervening, however unwittingly, in the reproduction of asymmetrical power relations.[10]

This analysis of state formation in Venezuela hopes to contribute to the subaltern critique of Occidentalism from a Latin American perspective. Since the European conquest of the Americas, the West and its peripheries have been mutually constituted through processes of imperial transculturation and capital accumulation that continue, in different forms, in the present. I analyze the formation of the Venezuelan state by placing regional developments within global transformations, resisting the desire to privilege a bounded singularity or a determining totality. This task, oscillating between a critical localism and a critical globalism, is premised on the possibility of attending to a singular history at the local level without either subsuming it within, or separating it from, the encompassing social totality within which it necessarily unfolds. This unfolding totality, as my analysis shows, is not strictly "social" but is also "natural"—it involves the exchange between society and nature not only at the local but at the global level. Thus, my work also reflects the effort to overcome the separation between what are often regarded as material and cultural factors by developing a cultural materialist perspective capable of apprehending the production of meaning and the reproduction of life as distinct moments of a unitary process.

From what I have already said it should also be evident that this book explores Venezuelan history by looking at its making at the highest centers of political power. A history of this sort shares the problems of top-down histories, even if it seeks to place "the top" within a complex ensemble of relations and to view it from its margins. One obvious limitation is the restricted access that most analysts have to what is often a highly secretive, and powerful, social arena. The most serious risk, however, is that of becoming trapped at the top by the rigors of work and the osmotic complicities of power, with the result that the subordinated sectors are excluded from view or remain shadowy figures in the background. When this happens, analysis

10. I develop this argument about Occidentalism through an elaboration of Said's critique that builds on a critical evaluation of three Occidentalist modalities of representation. For an important contribution to the analysis of the mutual formation of Europe and its colonies, see Cooper and Stoler (1989).

unwittingly tends to reinscribe the arrogant view from above and reproduce its self-proclaimed universality and fundamental disregard for the lives and forms of knowledge of subaltern subjects.

Focusing on the view from the commanding heights of the state, I have tried to offer a perspective of the top from within but also from without. Producing this book while also carrying out work among popular sectors in Venezuela, moving back and forth between Venezuela and the United States, and keeping an international and a Venezuelan audience in mind has encouraged me constantly to shift perspectives, to trace links between local and global forms of power, and to see the state as dominant and as dependent, even as subaltern.

Countering essentialist taxonomies of the subaltern, I view subalternity as a relational and a relative concept that refers to heterogeneous social actors that share a common condition of subordination. In my opinion, there are times and places where subjects appear on history's stage as subaltern actors, just as there are times or places in which they play dominant roles. Moreover, at any given time or place, an actor may be subaltern in relation to another, yet dominant in relation to a third. And, of course, there are contexts in which these categories may simply not be relevant. Subalternity defines not the being of a subject but a subjected state of being.[11] Yet because enduring subjection has the effect of fixing subjects into limiting positions, a relational conception of the subaltern requires a double vision that recognizes at one level a common ground among diverse forms of subjection and, at another, the intractable identity of subjects formed within uniquely constraining social worlds. While the first optic opens up a space for establishing links among subordinated subjects (including the analyst who takes a subaltern perspective), the second acknowledges the differentiating and unshareable effects of specific modalities of subjection.[12]

Taking a subaltern perspective, I examine in this book the formation

11. Building on Guha's classificatory grid of subaltern and dominant subjects, Spivak focuses on Guha's least powerful subaltern subject in order to develop her argument about the subaltern subject's subjection as a political actor, in her words, its inability "to speak." In my discussion of her argument, I concentrate on Guha's midlevel subaltern subjects in order to develop a relational conception of subalternity which I use to analyze state transformations in Venezuela as its populist leaders turned into advocates of an IMF austerity program in 1989 (1994).

12. This elaboration of my previous understanding of subalternity (1994) owes much to discussions with members of the Grupo de la Playa of the Latin American Subaltern Studies Group in Puerto Rico (March 1996), and especially to Josefina Saldaña's insistence on the radical alterity of subaltern subjects and Alberto Moreiras's suggestion that we use a "double register" in our approach to the subaltern.

of the Venezuelan state within the context of the historical production of Venezuela's subaltern modernity. In treating dominance and subalternity as relational characterizations, I find it productive in certain situations to see the neocolonial state as permeated by relations of subalternity, without disregarding its considerable power or its difference from subaltern actors subjected to more absolute forms of subordination. By breaking down homogenizing categories into their relational historical forms, a subaltern perspective provides a basis for a general critique of power in its multiply fetishized forms. Instead of organizing my account in terms of narratives which present the state as a sovereign and central agent in the nation's transformation from tradition to modernity, I take these narratives as my object of analysis.

I have tried to keep in mind that the process of state formation in Venezuela is part of a global project of modernity that claims for itself a singular universality, rationality, and morality that depend on the subordination, exclusion, or destruction of alternative forms of sociality, rationality, and values (Chatterjee 1993). If narratives of modernity are constructed on the basis of exclusions and denials, I have sought to pay attention to the hidden operations that select and naturalize historical memory, to the filter that creates national and global memories and their respective forms of amnesia.

While anthropology has shied away from studying the state, paradoxically, it prepared me to approach some of the tasks that I have faced in this book. Its usual units of study are subaltern or subordinated peoples—the West's Others, and within the West, its marginal communities or subcultures. I began this work at the University of Chicago as an effort to push anthropology beyond its previously established legitimate limits. Conventional wisdom in political anthropology was that the anthropologist "has a 'professional license' to study the interstitial, supplementary, and parallel structures in complex societies—the peripheral gray areas surrounding Lenin's strategic heights of sovereign power" (Vincent 1978:176). I proposed to accept this license while questioning its limits, and to center directly on the study of the strategic heights of sovereign power. In focusing on the opaque zones of state and corporate decisions at the heart of processes that have shaped the modern world, I have sought to preserve the unifying perspective that has distinguished anthropology as well as the decentering impetus that animates this work.

The decentered perspective developed in this book seeks to establish a position from which to transcend the opposition between the universal and the regional that underwrites Western modernity. "Decentering," like Mignolo's "pluritopical" (1995) and Shohat and Stam's "polycentric" (1994), works as a sign that expresses the desire for modes of apprehending, and constructing, difference within equality. By taking this perspective, I hope not simply to broaden the geopolitical referents of modernity, but to transcend its conceptual horizon. As Dussel proposes,

> The "realization" of modernity no longer lies in the passage from its abstract to its "real," European embodiment. It lies today, rather, in a process that will transcend modernity as such, a trans-modernity, in which both modernity and its negated alterity (the victims) co-realize themselves in a process of mutual creative fertilization. (1993:76.)

In his book *Oil: The Juice of the Earth,* Juan Pablo Pérez Alfonzo, the leading architect and a subsequent critic of Venezuela's oil policies, stated that "oil is the most important of the fuels indispensable for modern life" (1961: 83). His life work was informed by an acute sense of oil's centrality in the making of the modern world both as a vanishing source of energy and as a substance that enters into the object world of modernity—from the clothes we wear and the vehicles that transport us to the homes we inhabit. Oil has helped mold a highly stratified and ecologically unsound world shaped in the image of disconnected peoples and things that have in common their separation from each other and from the history that engendered them. If modernity is a process characterized by the incessant, obsessive, and irreversible transformation of a world splintered into distinct entities, then the effects of oil production and consumption reflect the spirit of modernity.[13] Susan Buck-Morss has argued that "a construction of history that looks backward, rather than forward, at the destruction that has taken place, provides a dialectical contrast to the futurist myth of historical progress (which can only be sustained by forgetting what has happened)" (1995:95). If a subaltern vision of the past—what Walter Benjamin called "the traditions of the oppressed" (1969:253–64)—is sustained by the hope of a future without subalternity, this book's construction of Venezuelan history seeks to look forward toward a form of progress shaped by that hope.

13. I owe this conceptualization of modernity to Jim Huey.

❧ I ❧
Premiere

THE NATURE
OF THE NATION:
STATE FETISHISM AND
NATIONALISM

Man holding a bust of Simón Bolívar during looting in Caracas following General Juan Vicente Gomez's death on 17 December 1935. (Instituto Autónomo Biblioteca Nacional.)

Previous page: General Juan Vicente Gómez with family and friends in Maracay. (Instituto Autónomo Biblioteca Nacional. Photo: Felipe Toro.)

1

HISTORY'S
NATURE

Nature is perhaps the most complex word in the language. It is relatively
easy to distinguish three areas of meaning: (i) the essential quality and character of something; (ii) the inherent force which directs either the world
of human beings or both; (iii) the material world itself, taken as including
or not including human beings. Yet it is evident that within (ii) and (iii),
though the area of reference is broadly clear, precise meanings are variable
and at times even opposed. The historical development of the word through
three senses is important, but it is also significant that all three senses, and
the main variations and alternatives within the two most difficult of them,
are still active and widespread in contemporary usage.

Raymond Williams

A construction of history that looks backward, rather than forward, at the
destruction of material nature as it has actually taken place, provides dialectical contrast to the futurist myth of historical progress (which can only be
sustained by forgetting what has happened).

Susan Buck-Morss

Jorge Luis Borges once remarked that the absence of camels in the Koran
reveals the book's authenticity. It has roots in a culture in which camels
are taken for granted. By the same logic, the neglect of nature in contemporary Western social theory perhaps shows the extent to which the massive
appropriation of natural resources upon which the modern world depends
has come to be assumed as a fact of life. Yet if one instance of habituation
expresses a millenarian dynamic between society and nature, the other reflects the abrupt rise of a short-term perspective that threatens the future of
both nature and humanity.

"We can bury our heads in the sand and say we don't want to be well
informed on these issues," states one of the authors of "the first full review
of the health of the American [U.S.] landscape." [1] Yet this study calls for

---

1. An article about this report appeared on the *New York Times* front page on 15 February 1995. For
the view that the protection of endangered species cannot be taken as an absolute goal but must be
balanced with the promotion of human needs, see Mann and Plummer (1994).

a collective awakening: "Vast stretches of formerly vibrant natural habitat, once amounting to at least half the area of the 48 contiguous states, have declined to the point of endangerment." Another of its authors, warning that "we're not losing single species here and there, we're losing entire assemblages of species and their habitats," proposes that "the burden of proof ought to be on developers to demonstrate that their activities will not be harmful." At a time when the free market is exalted as the natural embodiment of rationality, I believe it is more likely that the burden of proof will fall on the state whose regulations concerning conservation (including the Endangered Species Act in the U.S.) are in danger of being eliminated "as unnatural" in response to pressure from advocates of property rights and their conservative allies in the U.S. Congress. Ironically, the conservative move to open new spaces for profit making by removing constraints upon the "natural" play of the market threatens to erode the physical foundation which makes long-term profits, and life itself, possible.

It is noteworthy that this report depicts the destruction of nature as taking place at the very center of the capitalist system. The available information for the rest of the Americas and for other nonmetropolitan regions provides a disturbing image of the devastation of nature that has occurred in neo-colonial nations in which a colonial culture of plundering nature continues to inform present-day practices. Despite postindependence efforts to diversify their economies, these former colonies typically continue to depend on agricultural or mineral products for export, and are ruled by states whose lenient environmental policies are frequently sidestepped by "developers" in collusion with state functionaries.[2]

A typical example illustrates the erosion of the natural foundation of third-world economies. The United Nations considered El Salvador "rich" in hydraulic resources a decade ago but today defines it as being near the "poverty line." The country is now experiencing a severe water shortage due to poor planning, waste through ill-maintained pipelines, and landholder abuse. The flow of the country's largest river, the Lempa, has diminished 62.9 percent between 1985 and 1993. The head of the Salvadoran Center for Appropriate Technology, Ricardo Navarro, states that water "will become a strategic resource, and a large part of future political and military actions will be defined by the supply of water for powerful inhabitants." He adds, "In the future we will talk about ecopolitics rather than geopolitics, because geo-

2. For a classic statement of the destructive impact of the conquest and colonization of the Americas, see Crosby (1972).

graphical limits will be less important than ecological ones in defining areas
of interest and power relationships." In Navarro's words, "What should be a
source of life will become a source of disagreements and violence" (cited in
Dalton 1995). Navarro's distinction between ecological and geographical
concerns forcefully calls attention to the need to include a fuller appreciation
of the importance of nature in contemporary geopolitics. While this example
appears to have only domestic relevance, the destruction of the Amazonian
rain forest, a source of oxygen for the whole planet, makes evident that ecological concerns raise issues about national sovereignty and international
rights which question traditional geopolitical boundaries.

From the dawning of global trade originating with the conquest of the
Americas to the globalization of the market hastened by advanced technologies of production and communication, the worldwide commodification of
natural resources has tended to proceed, despite conservationist constraints,
as if they were inexhaustible. For all practical purposes, in societies in which
business practice has come to define the commonsensical aims of existence,
nature is taken for granted.

WESTERN SOCIAL THEORY AND NATURE

No generalization can do justice to Western social theory's diverse and complex treatments of nature. I think, however, that the dominant paradigms in
Western social science tend to reproduce the assumption permeating modern
culture that nature can be taken for granted. Post-Enlightenment visions of
historical progress typically assert the primacy of time over space and of culture over nature. In terms of these polarities, nature is so deeply associated
with space and geography that these categories often stand as metaphors of
each other. In differentiating them, historians and social scientists usually
present space or geography as the inert stage on which historical events take
place and nature as the passive material with which humans make their
world.[3] The separation of history from geography and the dominance of

---

3. This statement excludes subdisciplines that attribute to nature a decisive influence on social affairs,
such as sociobiology and various types of geographical determinisms whose reductionist logic and
reified categories hinder understanding and discourage transformative action; paradoxically, these
modes of viewing nature may have the effect of inhibiting, by fear of being associated with them,
alternative attempts to integrate nature in social analysis. On the other hand, my characterization
unintentionally does injustice to a substantial body of work that has illuminated the complex unity
of society and nature (by geographers, ecological anthropologists, feminist critics), including many
studies which inform this book but which I can only partially acknowledge in this discussion.

time over space has the effect of producing images of societies cut off from their material environment, as if they were fashioned out of thin air. If nature is included, it typically appears in the likeness of the appearance of the air itself, eternally and readily available. Bathed in this deceptive light, the social appropriation of nature does not seem to require particular analytical attention.

I intend to have this characterization serve only as a rough guide to help locate my argument in relation to dominant theoretical paradigms as I see them from my perspective as a cultural anthropologist and historian. Part of a countercurrent, my work builds on studies which resist the prevailing prioritization of time over space, not by reordering it but by redefining these categories so as to integrate a spatialized conception of time with a temporalized notion of space. A major body of these works has been produced in the interface between radical geography and political economy. In a discussion of this scholarship, entitled "The Postmodernization of Geography: A Review," Edward Soja comments that the growing attention paid by non-geographers to spatial and geographical issues has reached the point where these outsiders "are even daring . . . to proclaim what most geographers still hesitate to make explicit—that space and geography may be displacing the primacy of time and history as the distinctively significant interpretive dimensions of the contemporary period" (1987:289).

If the complex set of cultural transformations associated with post-modernity entails a crisis of metanarratives and a related privileging of simultaneity over sequentiality and of surfaces over depth, it is understandable that the "postmodernization of geography" may be believed to lead, as Soja suggests, to the displacement of time by space. While modernity's *grands récits* pushed geography to the background, postmodernity's bricolage brings it back to center stage. Geography may indeed be occupying a leading role at this juncture; but to the degree that this reversal of roles preserves the meanings commonly attached to spatial and temporal categories, its protagonism is inhibited by a postmodern anxiety concerning any form of agency and the possibility of historical protagonism itself.

For example, Fredric Jameson sees postmodernism as a "cultural dominant" that expresses the homogenization of the world under late capitalism. The expansion of capitalism colonizes domains that had served to establish standards of difference and grounds of historicity. In this respect, Jameson assigns a critical role to the third world. At times he unabashedly includes it with the unconscious as part of nature: "Late capitalism can therefore be described as the moment in which the last vestiges of Nature which survived on into classical capitalism are at length eliminated: namely the third world and the unconscious" (1984:207). In other writings, he locates it as a pre-capitalist formation within a rather conventional evolutionary framework (1986, 1988, 1990). In either case, to the extent that the third world is colonized by postmodernism, it ceases to function as an alter ego in relation to which the first world can recognize its own advancement and historicity.[4] Without an outside (that is, nature or the third world) that can serve as a source of radical difference and with an inside constituted by the generalization of a depthless postmodern space produced by new technologies of production and communication, the world becomes unrepresentable. In response to an opaque and impenetrable world that has dissolved the prospect of radical political action by sovereign subjects, Jameson proposes an "aesthetics of cognitive mapping." To the loss of a sense of historicity associated with the emergence of postmodern space corresponds a weakening of political agency.

In contrast to Jameson, Ernesto Laclau celebrates the political possibilities opened up by postmodernism, which he sees as an epochal shift in the conditions of identity formation. In place of the unitary political protagonists of modernity whose preordained roles were fixed by master metanarratives, it now becomes possible to imagine multiple political strategies around a plethora of fluidly constituted identities and alliances. In a book revealingly entitled *New Reflections on the Revolution of Our Time* (1990), Laclau supports this argument with an extended discussion of space and time as contrasting principles of organization. In this work he views space as a field of repetition, stasis, and determination, in opposition to time as the realm of innovation, change, and freedom. Conceptualizing freedom as the absence of determination (in affinity with liberal definitions of freedom as absence of constraints), Laclau sees history as an expression of freedom and thus as the proper realm of the political. As the domain of repetition or stasis, space is restricted to a nonpolitical sphere of structural determination.

It is significant that despite their differing evaluations of postmodernity, Jameson and Laclau reproduce a commonly held view of space and time as contrasting categories. While they appreciate space's new role in postmodern culture, they preserve its familiar subordination to time as the primary locus of agency in social theory. The new valorization of space, however, reduces

4. For Jameson, however, third-world texts somehow remain outside the reach of postmodernism. Presumably because as expressions of a resistant culture they reflect a pre-postmodern reality, they still have a "tendency to remind us of outmoded stages of our own first-world cultural development" (1986:65). For a critique of Jameson's conception of third-world literature, see Ahmad (1987).

history's effectivity. Freed from modernist metanarratives and unmoored from structural conditions that infused it with momentous power, history is now associated with microprocesses of uncertain effects. By locating the making of history in contingent situations, human agency is freed from structural determination but is also rendered less capable of effecting historical transformations.

A postmodern inclination to divorce cultural formations from social intercourse has often meant that they are viewed as texts whose meaning can be elucidated by textual analysis independently of the conditions under which they are produced and received. Insofar as a postmodern sensibility leads to the theorization of nature and space in these textualized terms, space appears as a disembodied discursive construct. If nature and the spatial phenomena associated with it were once treated as the material stage on which modernist dramas depicted history's fateful progress, they are now brought to a decentered stage as ethereal bodies on which history's representability and advance are cast in doubt. Whether displaced as material background or dematerialized as a discursive protagonist, nature has eluded these dominant modes of social analysis.

If one conceptualizes society and nature from the outset as distinct but unified, it ceases to make sense to treat nature as external to society or to neglect the sensuous and signifying materiality of the human-made world. Nature can be recognized as given and yet as made into a "second nature" by human beings who are part of it and yet participate in its transformation as they transform themselves.[5] This recognition permits historicizing rather than ontologizing the relationship between nature and society. Building on Marx's conception of the fundamental unity between society and nature, Ollman argues that society and nature are linked by "internal relations" rather than external interaction, that is, by the dialectical constitution of related entities rather than the interaction between separate entities (1971: 28).[6] Similarly, Schmidt suggests that for Marx, "while natural processes

---

5. The concept of second nature was used by Hegel to distinguish the natural, external environment or first nature from the meaningful social environment that human beings create. In capitalist societies, according to Marx, this second nature also appears as external to human beings, since they do not control the conditions of its production. Marx's concept of the metabolism between society and nature expresses both their fundamental unity and their variable historical differentiation and separation. For a discussion of Marx's concept of nature, see Schmidt (1971), Smith (1984) and Lippi (1983).

6. According to Bertell Ollman, a philosophy of "internal relations" posits not only that relations are internal to things but that things are inherently relational. "No one would deny that things appear and function as they do because of their spatial-temporal ties with other things, including man as a creature with physical and social needs," says Ollman. He adds: "To conceive of things as Relations is simply to interiorize this interdependence . . . in the thing itself" (1971: 28).

independent of men are essentially transformations of material and energy, human production itself does not fall outside the sphere of nature," for human beings are a part of nature whose human nature is transformed by acting upon external nature. As a result of this "metabolic interaction," as Marx referred to the exchange between society and nature, "nature is humanized while men are naturalized" (1971:78–79).

This unifying perspective can also be brought to the study of space and time. What Soja calls the "reassertion of space and geography in critical social theory" (in effect, the subtitle of his 1989 book) could then be taken as the opportunity not to install space and geography in place of time and history as "the distinctively significant interpretive dimensions of the contemporary period," but to reassess the meaning of these polarized categories. Just as time occupies space, space unfolds in time; as "mediums" for each other, they share a fundamental unity-in-difference.[7] Doreen Massey notes that the issue is "not to argue for an upgrading of the status of space within the terms of the old dualism (a project which is arguably inherently difficult anyway, given the terms of that dualism) but to argue that what must be overcome is the very formulation of space/time in terms of this kind of dichotomy" (1992:75).

This dualist opposition is being challenged by different academic and intellectual fields. Massey's own reconceptualization creatively integrates findings from radical geography, feminist theory, and physics. It involves three considerations. First, the need to develop an alternative view of society as a four-dimensional entity, rather than "as a kind of 3-D (and indeed more usually 2-D) slice that moves through time" (1992:79). Second, the need to conceptualize space "as constructed out of interrelations, as the simultaneous coexistence of social interrelations and interactions at all spatial scales, from the most local level to the most global" (1992:80). Space is to be viewed not as an absolute dimension but as a form of relationality, as simultaneity, a "moment in the intersection of configured social relations" (1992:81). Third, the need to think of space as both ordered and chaotic and thus to transcend dichotomies that have served, as in Laclau's work, to treat spatiality as "a structure that establishes the positive nature of all of its terms" (1990:69). No longer restricted to the structured domain of order, space can be brought back from its unwarranted exile from politics. Freedom can be seen substantively, instead of identifying it formally with unconstrained, immaculate action.

7. Gregory and Ury use this notion of "medium" in relation to space: "Spatial structure is now seen not merely as an arena in which social life unfolds, but rather as a medium through which social relations are produced and reproduced" (Gregory and Ury 1985:3).

Henry Lefebvre's pathbreaking *The Social Construction of Space* ([1974] 1991) has provided a foundation for thinking about space in terms which integrate its socially constructed significance with its formal and material properties. Unlike theorists who take the argument that space is socially constructed as a license to detach society from nature, Lefebvre sees it as involved in the challenge to examine how nature enters into the social construction of space. His triad of "spatial practice, representations of space, and representational spaces" offers a useful framework for investigating how the multiple forms of perceiving, conceiving of, and living in space have been produced historically and given cultural significance. For him, human beings, located in nature and making use of nature's materials, construct space but do not produce it as a thing, as a "kilogram of sugar or a yard of cloth is produced." Spaces are produced from social relations and from nature, which form their "raw material" (1974:84). They are both the product of and the condition of possibility of social relations. As a social relation, space also involves a natural relation, a relation between society and nature through which society produces itself as it appropriates and transforms nature. "Is space a social relation?" asks Lefebvre. His answer highlights the role of power in the social production of space: "Certainly—but one which is inherent to property relationships (especially the ownership of the earth, of land) and also closely bound up with the forces of production (which impose a form on that earth or land)" (1974:85). While nature's effects necessarily depend on its physical properties, these properties are always constructed culturally through social interactions occurring in fields of power. As we will see, this critical perspective—as refined by feminist scholars and radical geographers—informs my examination of the relationship between the state and the oil economy in Venezuela.

THE THIRD WORLD'S NATURE

It is evident that all nations are located in space and that they are constituted through specific relations to the natural world. Yet the relationship of nations to nature assumes particular significance in countries dependent on the production of primary products—commodities whose comparative advantage in the international market typically rests on a combination of natural factors and cheap labor rather than on higher social productivity. In most neocolonial nations, these products are either agricultural or mineral commodities; except for capital-intensive mining, their production generally involves the abundant use of labor. For this reason, it is likely that cheap labor will remain an important comparative advantage of third-world economies. Yet, given the power of capital to substitute machines for labor, and the development of an informal economy in metropolitan societies based on cheap domestic and migrant labor, the special qualities of the third world's natural resources, rather than its cheap labor, ultimately secures a role in the international division of labor for this region as a whole.[8]

Even this natural foundation, however, is not stable. According to Alexander Kouznetsov, economic affairs officer of the United Nations Conference of Trade and Development, there is evidence that supports "a generally neglected dimension of long-term structural change which can be characterized as a 'dematerialization' of production—that is, a reduction in the demand for the products of the more raw-material-intensive industries in industrialized countries and a decline in the intensity of raw materials use in existing industrial sectors" (1988:70). This "dematerialization of production" will affect in particular, according to Kouznetsov, "the majority of the developing countries [which] depend on the ability to exploit and market their natural resources, which represent the principal part of their export potential and often the only reliable source of foreign exchange earnings" (1988:67).[9]

The international division of labor is not solely a social division of labor but also a global division of nature. "The earth, underground resources, the air and light above the ground," as Lefebvre argues, "all are part of the forces of production and part of the products of those forces." The division of labor, therefore, "affects the whole of space—not just the 'space of work,' not just the factory floor" (1991:347). What may be called the international division of nature provides the material foundation for the international division of labor: they form two dimensions of a unitary process. An exclusive focus on labor obscures from view the inescapable fact that labor is always located in space, that it transforms nature in specific locations, and thus that its worldwide structure involves as well a global division of nature.

Once nature is brought into social analysis, the organization of labor can

8. The industry of tourism confirms the third world's reliance on "nature." While tourism in the first world involves the consumption of human-made environments and cultural products, in the third world it is heavily dependent on the consumption of natural environments that have been minimally modified to provide adequate comforts for the experience of "nature" away from "civilization."

9. For a fuller discussion of the role of raw materials in evolving productive structures, see *Materials Technology and Development,* the fifth issue of the *Bulletin for the Advanced Technology Alert System,* published by the United Nations.

no longer be abstracted from its material foundation. The worldwide expansion of capitalism and the creation of a global market of commodities has been driven by the profit-seeking effort to control not only cheap labor, technology, or markets, but also nature. The abstract notion of "the commodity world," as Lefebvre notes, "cannot be conceived apart from the world market, which is defined territorially (in terms of flows and networks) and politically (in terms of centres and peripheries)" (1991 : 350). The construction of the "first" and "third" worlds as regional categories is premised on a distinction between areas where capitalism develops, promoting new technologies and products, and regions where it expands, controlling labor, markets, and nature. While this schematic taxonomy masks the complex interactions through which first and third worlds have been formed historically, it does reflect the role assigned to the periphery as a source of cheap labor and raw materials.

If, as radical geographers propose, geography matters, it is in no small measure because matter itself is made to matter. Since the significance of nature is always constituted historically, the point of recognizing the importance of geography, in my view, is not to displace history but to integrate historical and geographical perspectives. As I have argued, this synthetic perspective is particularly important for examining societies in the third world, a region constituted by changing forms of colonial and imperial control over their populations and natural resources. It is by developing this perspective that I seek to recognize how oil was made to matter in the transformation of Venezuela into an oil nation. Far from being a local process, this transfiguration was effected through links that related, and transformed, the nation and the world in the process of producing wealth.

THE WEALTH OF NATIONS:
NATURAL PRODUCTS, SOCIAL PRODUCTS

The produce of the earth—all that is derived from its surface by the united application of labour, machinery, and capital, is divided among three classes of the community; namely, the proprietor of the land, the owner of the stock or capital necessary for its cultivation, and the labourers by whose industry it is cultivated. But in the different stages of society, the proportions of the whole produce of the earth which will be allotted to each of these classes, under the names of rent, profit, and wages, will be essentially different; depending mainly on the actual fertility of the soil, on the accumulation of capital and population, and on the skill, ingenuity, and instruments employed in agriculture. To determine the laws which regulate this distribution, is the principal problem in Political Economy.

David Ricardo

In the Western world, the complex social transformation associated with the rise of modernity has entailed a radical redefinition of the relationship between society and nature. The reorganization of work spurred by what Weber ambivalently called the "rational pursuit of profit" has raised a number of questions, central among which has been, in Smith's words, the "cause and nature of the wealth of nations." The great accomplishment of classical political economy was to have made labor central to the discussion of this issue. While mercantilism had seen the source of value in trade and physiocracy in agricultural land, classical political economists located it in productive labor. They came to distinguish between natural riches as invariable givens and labor as a value-creating force. For them, while the wealth of nations results from the combination of nature and labor, only productive labor could expand its existing magnitude.

This argument was first formulated in this form by Adam Smith and was developed by David Ricardo and Karl Marx. Yet the focus on labor became immediately so widespread that Marx in his own time had to remind his followers that wealth results not only from socially created value but also from naturally available "material wealth"; or, as he also said, following William Petty, labor is the "father" and the earth the "mother" of value (1967: 43). Still, followers of the labor theory of value have tended to focus on the extraction of surplus value either domestically or internationally and to neglect the role of nature in the creation of wealth. This neglect of nature also characterizes the work of neoclassical economists, for whom natural resources deserve no special treatment because they become simply commodities in a market of goods whose value is determined by the subjective orientations of economic actors.

Using the labor theory of value, a number of scholars have produced critical accounts to explain the lack of development of the periphery in terms of the exploitation of labor. Theories of unequal exchange posit that the goods produced in the periphery have a larger component of labor incorporated in them than the goods it obtains in exchange for them. Given this focus, as well as the fact that nature plays no role in the creation of value, it is understandable that the theorists who are most concerned with analyzing international inequality have neglected the role of natural resources in the organization and reproduction of peripheral societies.

Since commodity production in the periphery is generally organized around the exploitation not only of labor but of natural resources, I believe the study of neocolonialism requires a shift of focus from the unequal flow of value to the unequal structure of international production. This approach brings to the center of analysis the relationship between the production of social value and natural wealth. In bringing attention to production as a holistic process the aim is to examine the ensemble of social relations and understandings formed through the mutual commodification of labor power and of natural resources rather than to study natural resources as discrete commodities (as in neoclassical economics) or to focus exclusively on the transfer of value (as in unequal exchange theory).

In societies in which revenues derive predominantly from the commodification of labor, value creation is both the primary aim of production and the underlying principle of economic organization. In societies in which revenues depend on the commodification of nature, rent capture conditions the organization of economic activities. In one case, productive structures must be constantly transformed in order to increase productivity and profits; in the other, rents must be maximized and access to their distribution ensured by a variety of political means. Needless to say, the commodification of nature and that of labor depend upon each other. The point of this schematic distinction is to help us distinguish dominant tendencies in different social orders. While in any particular society the elements that are contrasted here are blurred, my argument is that the first and third worlds tend to be polarized in terms of these modes of producing and distributing wealth. This difference has profound political and cultural consequences, which need to be explored further.

BEYOND APPEARANCES

"The Wealth of societies in which the capitalist mode of production prevails appears as an 'immense collection of commodities'" (Marx 1977: 125). With this simple observation Marx opened his classic analysis of capitalist society. Critics and followers have argued about Marx's findings and method but have tended to share the two assumptions expressed in his starting position: the conception of the nation as the fundamental unit of analysis and of national wealth as being represented by commodities. While this perspective has been useful for the analysis of nations at the center of the international capitalist system, it has profoundly obscured the understanding of societies at its periphery.

Capitalism has developed not just within nations but among them. Yet the treatment of the nation as a self-contained unit often leads to the interpretation of international economic phenomena as the outward projections of the endogenous dynamics of the more advanced nations. As one critic has noted:

> The tendency is to take the national economy—the developed, monopoly capitalist system in which the capitalist mode of production is universal, the development and the socialization of the means of production has gone furthest, the dominance of capital and its movement is most clear—and then to analyze the forces projecting out from this system into the outside world. (Radice 1975:18.)

As this statement suggests, advanced capitalist nations are typically studied as autonomous units, while peripheral societies are seen in terms of the impact that center nations have on them. An alternative position argues that the dynamics of the "world system" explains the development of nations (Wallerstein 1976). This latter position shifts the focus from the dominant nations to the international system but risks preserving the view that peripheral nations are to be understood as being shaped by external forces. Even when an explicit effort is made to account for the histories of non-European peoples and to observe the interaction between expanding metropolitan nations and peripheral societies, the tendency is to cover these societies under the mantle of capitalism and to see capitalism as an external force.[10]

In fairness to Marx, the focus on a closed economy in *Capital* is a simplifying assumption aimed at clarifying the logic of capitalist accumulation. But since in this work the links between the national economy and the international system—links forged through primitive accumulation, colonialism, world trade, foreign investment, and overseas banking—are suggested, but not developed, this working assumption has reinforced a tendency to treat the national economy as if it actually were an independent system. By abstracting from external conditions, Marx's model directs attention to the inner dynamic of capitalist society conceived of as a national unit. It is a society driven by the constant expansion of value that results from the transformation of labor into increasingly productive labor power under conditions of capitalist competition. Competition for profits leads to the formation of a productive system of increasing specialization and differentiation and to

---

10. Through the discussion of works by Wolf (1982), Mintz (1985), Taussig (1980), and Mitchell, among others (1988), I have noted how the development of capitalism in the periphery tends to be seen as an "external" force that originates in metropolitan centers (1996).

the expanding production of a growing variety of commodities. Commodities for Marx are both the product of a society's total productive power and factors in the organization of a society's productive system. As symbolic tokens of a society's productive power, they form a system of signification through which domestic value is represented; in this sense, they are "national" commodities. It is from this perspective that the wealth of capitalist society appears as an "immense collection of commodities."

But Marx's concern was to ascertain not only the means of representing wealth but the ends of representation—not just how, but why, the representation of value assumes the form it does in capitalist society. He shared with Smith and Ricardo the view that the wealth of nations depends on the productive organization of labor. He called Adam Smith "the Luther of political economy" for having demolished the fetishes of vulgar economy—the notions that land, money, or trade are in themselves the origin of wealth. But Marx took another step. He showed how fetishism arises from the functioning of capitalist society and revealed a connection between the mode of producing and the form of representing value.

In his view, capitalist society generates a set of illusory beliefs about itself that are essential constituents of capitalist relations. These beliefs are real in the sense that they participate in the social construction of reality, and provide a rationale for economic behavior that accurately represents subjective experience as it is shaped within a given system of social relations. But they are deceitful in that they misrepresent the fundamental processes of value creation and distribution in capitalist society: they do not show their origin in the reproductive dynamic of social life. Fetishism is the representational complex through which objects appear as the source of the powers which human labor inscribes in them.

What is concealed, Marx's work suggests, determines not only what is represented but the nature of representation itself. Exchange in the sphere of circulation, which is ruled by notions of equivalence, hides the creation of value in the sphere of production, which is structured in terms of relations of inequality. In the arena of the market, the appearance of equivalent exchange of wages for labor power conceals the creation of surplus value by unpaid labor power in the abode of production. Thus, exchange in capitalist society creates the illusion that wages, profits, and rents are created by labor, capital, and land, respectively, and that each of these forms of revenue is the fair compensation to its corresponding factor of production. The apparent equivalence of exchange thus conceals the inequality in production. On this illusion capitalist legitimacy rests.

THE WEALTH OF POOR NATIONS

When this classic model is transposed from the center to the periphery of the capitalist system, Marx's simplifying assumption—that the nation constitutes a unit—mystifies more than it illuminates. For what typifies the economies of peripheral societies, if one may generalize, is that they in fact do not form integrated domestic systems and are connected to the world market through the export of primary products. Of course, no nation's economy constitutes a self-sufficient system in an absolute sense. But advanced capitalist nations have diversified productive structures which grant them a degree of internal coherence and enable their states and dominant classes to exert relative control over domestic economic decisions. Peripheral societies, in contrast, tend to be linked to the world market through the export of one or a few primary products and the massive import not only of capital and intermediate goods but also of a wide range of consumer goods. The prices of these primary products, which depend on shifting natural factors, tend to vary widely and are subjected to competition from other third-world regions and from increasing productivity at the center, as well as from substitution by human-made products. Domestic productive structures in the periphery—which often combine and rearticulate precapitalist and capitalist relations—depend on imports to achieve internal coherence. Primary export products are less important as concrete goods—as use values—than as means to obtain foreign currency in the international market—as exchange values. A significant proportion of the foreign exchange that these products bring to the country is used to import the foreign goods that have become increasingly vital for the reproduction of third-world societies. This dependence on manufactured imports maintains the fragmentation of the local economy and the need for integrating the domestic and international spheres.

For these nations, primary exports are principally a source of foreign exchange. The worth of domestic products and of the national currency that represents local productive capacity is measured in terms of the international system of production and exchange; their monetary value expresses, in crystallized form, the intersection of the national and the global. Is the wealth of these societies represented as "an immense collection of commodities"? In the case of societies organized around the capture of rent or in which rent plays an important role, a mechanical transposition of Marx's observation will not do.

In these societies there is no single "collection of commodities." The world of commodities is fragmented, reflecting and reinforcing the disarticulation of economies in which rents play a key role. The commodities that circulate domestically are the product not just of different nations but of different cultural orders and bear upon them the mark of this difference. Imported commodities that come from metropolitan centers represent the cultural orders of these nations. The differentiated collection of imported commodities, in contrast to the limited range of domestically produced ones, becomes a privileged vehicle for the representation of wealth. But these imported commodities are no simple representations of wealth, for they embody another society's productive organization and, by implication, its place in a hierarchy of cultural development. Through trade an apparent equivalence is established between the value of the commodities of different societies. But this formal equivalence does not conceal but, rather, heightens the inequality between the productive and cultural orders of metropolitan and peripheral societies.

The increasing globalization of metropolitan production renders this difference less evident. While a large range of products, as their labels indicate, are now produced in third-world locations, their production is controlled in fact by metropolitan transnational corporations. Beneath the surface impression that production is being dispersed throughout the world lies the reality of a growing concentration of capital and polarization of global productive structures (Palloix 1978; Mandel 1978; Sassen 1991). A number of processes which include the internationalization of third-world capital and the emergence of corporations not limited by borders—truly transnational corporations that do not have a national home (Miyoshi 1993)—blur the continent-based boundaries that define the center/periphery model. Just as the first world has generated a third world within, the third world has produced its own first-world enclaves.

In third-world societies, commodities have thus become profoundly charged symbols, social things that carry their worldly life inscribed in them.[11] Imported goods are at once the tangible evidence of the domestic capacity to import and, therefore, of local wealth and inescapable reminders of the local incapacity to produce them. Primary export products, when they are reduced to mere intermediaries, appear strictly as the material counterpart of alluring metropolitan commodities, representing at once the

---

11. For an insightful discussion of some of the theoretical issues involved in the examination of the "social life of things," see Appadurai (1988), as well as a critique by Ferguson (1988). For a treatment of commodities and exchange in a colonial context, see Thomas (1991). Haug offers a pioneering analysis of commodity culture under capitalism (1986). Fernando Ortiz's *Cuban Counterpoint: Tobacco and Sugar* remains a classic analysis of the "social life" of the two main agricultural commodities of Cuban society (1995).

level of local productive development and the narrowness of its specialization. Commodities express hierarchies among cultures, not just magnitudes of value. In the quest for foreign exchange, domestic productive powers are channeled into the production of one or a few commodities, such as sugar, bananas, coffee, rubber, gold, copper, and oil. These commodities mark the place of primary exporters in the international division of labor and to a significant extent define their national identity, specifically labeling them as oil nations, banana republics, or plantation societies, for example, or broadly as underdeveloped or backward nations.

International trade appears to establish a relation of equivalence between the commodities and the productive capacity of different societies. For theorists working within the premises of unequal exchange, prices (as the expression of market forces) would have to correspond to values (as the objectification of abstract labor power) for this equivalence to reflect actual social relations in the sphere of production. But international market prices are particularly affected by the interplay of political and natural factors, causing prices to deviate sharply from values.

What, then, makes primary export products competitive in the world market, and how is it that they become a source of foreign exchange? Despite their considerable differences, primary goods exporters share a common fortune: the international competitiveness of their export products is determined by (in addition to locational factors) the degree to which the export sector possesses either cheap labor or a natural advantage. The latter may consist of land especially suitable for a product, the presence of scarce or unique natural goods, or rich mineral resources. Historically, when it has been the source of comparative advantage in trade, cheap labor has tended to reflect, rather than the local generalization of capitalist relations of productions, the persistence of noncommoditized relations, which cheapens the cost of reproduction of the labor force. Cheap labor also indicates the existence of political control on workers, which reduces the expansion, mobility, and autonomy of free labor.

Nevertheless, as capitalist competition has standardized labor processes worldwide, cheap labor has become a crucial factor in manufacturing. This is most evident in the case of such export platforms as Hong Kong, Singapore, South Korea, and Taiwan.[12] According to Mandel, labor-intensive

---

12. Some of these nations have managed to develop backward linkages and integrated industrial structures. According to Gereffi and Hempel, the key to the success of East Asian newly industrialized countries lies in having used state protection to transform export-oriented industrialization into

manufacturing in late capitalism is not declining in importance relative to capital-intensive industries, but the latter tends not to be transferred to the periphery (1978:364–76). An unexpected development has been the emergence of a vast "informal economy" at the core of the highly developed nations which reflects not only the presence of immigrant labor but also of structural conditions which lead to the formation and expansion of labor-intensive processes that generate a large proportion of inputs used in the "formal economy" (Sassen 1993). Thus, the third world, as many commentators have noted, has grown within the very confines of the first world; and one author has even baptized Los Angeles as the capital of the third world—the title of his book (Rieff 1991).

In the case of many primary export goods, the same worldwide processes that standardize international production highlight the importance of natural factors for creating comparative advantage in trade. This suggests that the competitiveness of these goods arises from a mixture of social and natural factors. By 1965 only $4 billion of third-world exports out of a total of $40 billion were industrial products. Despite a significant expansion of third-world industrial production, slightly transformed raw materials and agricultural products remain the major exports for most peripheral nations (*Pearson Report,* cited by Mandel 1978:370). Trends in aggregate production by nation or region do not convey the transformations in productive structures taking place worldwide in response to the globalization of production under the control of a relatively small number of transnational corporations. While there is evidence of significant growth of manufacturing in certain enclaves within the third world, it is also clear that the industrialized nations—mainly through transnational corporations still "located" in their respective home countries—maintain global dominance in both productive technologies and production itself. With 80 percent of the world population, the third world accounts for only 20 percent of world output. Primary commodities account for almost one half of third-world exports, but for only about a quarter of the U.S.'s world trade (ECLA 1993:219–34).

Cheap labor has always been a focal point for the analysis of third-world nations. Heated debates have centered on the role of cheap labor in unequal exchange and in the reproduction of an international division of labor that

---

a means to upgrade and develop internal productive enterprises. The major mechanism used to ensure this has been a type of contract manufacturing (original equipment manufacturing, or OEM) in which there is a sharp separation between the actual producer and the supplier of product specifications and marketing (1996).

blocks the balanced development of the periphery. In contrast, natural resources remain a highly neglected and untheorized dimension of center-periphery relations. The focus on cheap labor has resulted in part from an understandable reaction against reductionist interpretations which attribute economic underdevelopment to cultural or psychological factors. The emphasis on the costs of labor has directed attention to the manner of structuring worldwide productive processes.

This focus on productive relations has also provided the basis for a critique of the prevailing theory of international trade. The fundamental principle of neoclassical exchange theory, the Ricardian law of comparative costs, posits that in time all nations gain from trade. Just as in Adam Smith's seamless world the pursuit of individual interest leads to collective welfare, in the uniform universe of neoclassical economics free trade among nations benefits them all. In this world of "universal harmonies," as a critic has remarked ironically, "no nation need be afraid of free trade, for it humbles the mighty and raises the weak. Something like God, only quite a bit more reliable" (Shaik 1979b:205).

Empirical evidence of the growing inequality among nations has encouraged the study of the interaction between international trade and production. Raul Prebisch in the 1950s focused on the "deteriorating terms of trade" for primary exporters (1959); Paul Baran offered a pioneering analysis of the international mechanisms of surplus investment and extraction (1957). During a decade when political economy occupied a central place in social analysis, Arghiri Emmanuel (1972), Samir Amin (1974), and Ernest Mandel (1978) examined the mechanisms of unequal exchange through trade. Despite significant differences among them, these authors share a view that underdevelopment results from a constant drain of surplus value from periphery to center. This common assumption leads them to focus on the mechanism of this transfer. Although they disagree about the particular mechanism, their basic argument is that underdevelopment is rooted in unequal exchange, which consists of a significant lack of correspondence between prices and values; the appearance of equal exchange at the level of prices thus conceals an asymmetry at the level of values. As Mandel puts it, "Equal international values are exchanged for equal international values. Where, then, does 'unequal exchange' lie hidden behind this equivalence? It is to be found in the fact that these equal international values represent unequal quantities of labor" (1978:359). That is, "through exchange, advanced countries appropriate more labor time in exchange than they generate in production" (Weeks 1983:500).

It must be recognized that these authors also analyze the specific features of the social structures of third-world societies, not just the flow of value out of them. Amin distinguishes between the integrated "autocentric" economies of the center and the "extroverted" ones of the periphery. Mandel criticizes Emmanuel for emphasizing the cost of wage labor to the exclusion of an analysis of its productivity. For him, "The problem of unequal exchange ultimately goes back to the problem of the different social structures of the underdeveloped countries" (1978:365). But, as often occurs in social analysis, ultimate factors often become explanatory principles, not problems that themselves should be explained. Underdeveloped social structures turn into tautological explanations for underdevelopment.

Despite their differences, these critics focus on the transfer of value because they share a common assumption. They criticize the findings of orthodox trade theory, not its foundation in the law of comparative cost (which posits that trade that flows from the comparative advantage of each nation benefits them all). Using Marx's theory of value, Shaik has demonstrated how free trade leads instead to the absolute advantage of the stronger economy (1979a; 1979b; 1980). From this perspective, unequal development becomes the consequence of free trade itself. "Instead of negating uneven development, free trade is shown to enhance it. Instead of closing the gap between rich and poor countries, direct investment is seen to tighten the grip of the strong over the weak" (Shaik 1979b:57).

I find Shaik's insight into the nature of underdevelopment particularly suggestive. The crucial issue, according to him, is not the drain of value from the periphery to the center but the uneven development of world productive structures brought about by international competition. Shaik is thus critical of authors who derive underdevelopment from the transfer of value from the underdeveloped to the developed regions of the capitalist world. "On the contrary," he argues, "since uneven development on a world scale is a direct consequence of free trade itself, these transfers of value and the theories of unequal exchange which rely on them emerge as secondary phenomena, not primary causes of underdevelopment." He concludes by asserting that "in fact, a critical examination of the theories of unequal exchange shows that even the net direction of value transfers cannot be simply established" (1980a:57). By restricting the analysis of value to the problem of its magnitude, unequal exchange theory stays within the orthodox theory's fetishized conception of wealth and runs the risk of fetishizing labor itself.

Shaik's perspective entails a shift in focus: it directs analysis from the unequal flow of value among nations to the unequal structures of production through which they are linked, from the concrete products of labor to the international division of labor itself. This focus encourages a closer examination of the structures within which value is created and distributed. It can also help place the international division of labor and that of nature within a unitary analytical field.

By focusing on labor, unequal exchange theory has paid insufficient attention to the role of natural resources in forming the social relations that give rise to unequal exchange. Since what is socially significant in the case of natural resources is how the material properties of these resources are made to matter by the network of social relations woven around them, this focus should lead to an examination of the spatial structures and political units produced in the process of producing and distributing wealth. Paradoxically, a focus on the exploitation of natural resources may encourage a more comprehensive view of the labor process itself.

The process of value creation involves at once the production of objects and the transformation of social relations. As Marx never tired of saying, value is not a thing but a social relation mediated and represented by means of things. The task is to study how the production of value entails the reproduction or transformation of social and cultural formations. In terms of this emphasis on the constitution of labor through the process of production, the labor theory of value can be properly seen as a "value theory of labor," that is, a theory about "the determination of the structure of production as well as the distribution of labor in that structure" (Elson 1979:128). Similarly, the labor theory of value should also be seen as a value theory of nature; it can illuminate the organization and division of nature just as it does that of labor.

A holistic approach to production encompasses the production of commodities as well as the formation of the social agents involved in this process and therefore unifies within a single analytical field the material and cultural orders within which human beings form themselves as they make their world (Turner 1984:11). This unifying vision seeks to comprehend the historical constitution of subjects in a world of human-made social relations and understandings. Since these subjects are historically constituted as well as the protagonists of history, this perspective views the activity which makes history as part of the history that forms them and informs their activity.

I seek to develop this perspective in this study of the historical transformation of state and nation in Venezuela during a period when that country became a major oil exporter. Oil's "mixed blessings"—to use Amuzegar's expression (1982)—have puzzled most analysts, for they express the paradox of "wealthy" peripheral nations which nevertheless are subjected to the typical problems that afflict third-world countries. While during the oil boom of the midseventies Venezuela obtained more dollars from its oil exports than those given to all European nations by the Marshall Plan, Venezuela in 1995 had the highest inflation and the lowest growth rate in Latin America. When they remark on the inability of oil-exporting nations to use their resources productively, analysts speak of the "inexorable dynamic of an oil-reliant economy" (Amuzegar 1982; see also Attiga 1981). In this study of Venezuela, I examine the social dynamic of what appears to be the "inexorable dynamic" of petroleum-led economies. In order to understand this social process, we must first have a sense of how mineral wealth is valorized.

NATURAL RESOURCES: MAINSTREAM VIEWS

Neoclassical economics represents a break from classical economics' concern with the relation between production and exchange. While classical economics seeks to establish the foundation of value in production, neoclassical economics determines value through the subjective preferences of economic agents. By positing a market-centered, subjective theory of value, neoclassical economics defines the value of natural resources in the same way that it defines the value of any commodity: by its utility, that is, by its usefulness for consumers as measured in the market. The price of goods expresses their relative utilities as established through their exchange among economic agents in the market. Revenues paid to the owners of capital, land, and labor are regarded as compensation for their contribution to the production of value through a calculus of utilities or similar mechanism of defining subjective preferences.

In addition, as Mommer has suggested, natural resources are analyzed in neoclassical economic theory from two major perspectives: either from a microeconomic vantage point that reflects the position of an individual or from a macroeconomic standpoint that takes the outlook of society as a whole (1983:45). From a microeconomic perspective, natural resources are seen as "natural capital." As Alfred Marshall says, "Land is but a form of capital for the individual producer" (Mommer 1983:3). From this perspective, natural resources are bought and sold like any other commodity; they thus figure either as a cost of production or as a source of gain. Their price is determined by supply and demand; scarcity is therefore a crucial factor in price determination. Their cost of production is based on the evaluation of the investor's opportunity costs, alternative costs, or disutility. As Marshall stated, "While demand is based on the desire to obtain commodities, supply depends mainly on the unwillingness to undergo 'discommodities'" (1961:140).

From this perspective, earnings derived from natural resources appear as profits, in the case of renewable resources such as crops and as payment for preexisting capital in the case of nonrenewable resources such as oil. Mining royalties to landowners are thus considered a payment for "natural capital." The products of human labor and of nature are treated as if they were essentially the same; they are defined as commodities. Thus, Marshall argues that mining royalties are the price paid for a commodity which was "stored by nature but is now treated as private property." For this reason, Marshall argues, the marginal price of minerals includes a royalty besides the marginal costs involved in exploitation of the mine (1961:430). In an article considered to be "the classic work explicating the economics of exhaustible resources" (Moran 1982:95), Hotelling argues the same point. Nonrenewable resources such as minerals are assets like any other asset: they yield a return to the owner either as capital appreciation—if they are left in the ground as capital—or as current dividends, if they are sold (1931).

A macroeconomic perspective recognizes that natural resources in fact do not have a cost of production; this viewpoint is therefore more sensitive to the actual mechanism through which owners of natural resources receive an income. Their income depends on the relative differences among natural resources of the same type but which are of different origins. Since the market price tends to be set by the cost of production of the least efficient producers, landowners receive a rent the magnitude of which depends on the difference between the average market price of the commodity produced in the sector and its lower cost of production on lands or from mines which are of above-average productivity. Therefore, the revenues received by landowners represent a transference of income from capitalists.

From a microeconomic perspective, the price paid to landowners for the use of their land or for their resources reflects the value assigned to the resources as natural capital. From a macroeconomic standpoint, the rent that landowners receive is determined by the price of the commodity produced in the sector; thus, the royalty paid to the landowner is a transference of income, not a payment for natural capital. As Morris Adelman argues in relation to oil, "rents or royalties are not costs." Therefore, "the whole problem of rents and royalties is superfluous in the determination of prices" (Adelman 1964:109).

As Mommer has shown, both perspectives are reflected, respectively, in the tax and accounting systems of most capitalist societies. Tax systems generally represent the viewpoint of the individual taxpayer, while national accounting systems adopt the perspective of society as a collectivity. Thus, most domestic tax codes grant a depletion allowance for mineral producers, treating minerals as "natural capital." Yet no such depletion of capital is recognized in the national accounting system; from the perspective of society, the products of nature are not treated as capital (1983 : 4) but as a transference of income from capitalists to landowners.

Scholars working on societies in which agricultural or mineral production plays a central role often use a neo-Ricardian conception of rent to explain the price of agricultural and mineral products.[13] While treating land and minerals as a form of capital, they determine the magnitude of the rent on the basis of natural comparative advantages and the relationship between domestic production and international levels of supply and demand at specific temporal conjunctures. Mamalakis's attempt to formulate a "mineral theory of growth" in relation to Latin America is particularly interesting because of the richness of its comparative scope (1978). Yet, to the extent that they treat natural resources as capital, they conflate wealth and value and make it difficult to understand the relationship between different forms of income-generating activity. A fundamental feature of societies analyzed under the rubric of the "mineral theory of growth" is that the income generated by mineral commodities is largely unrelated to the domestic productivity of labor, and its high level, particularly during boom periods, often has the "perverse" effect of inhibiting its development.[14] The experiences of the guano boom in Peru, of nitrates in Chile, and of oil in Venezuela demonstrate this tendency.

In fact Mamalakis concludes his article by mentioning the cases of Peru

13. From this perspective, rent is generally seen as an extraordinary, fiscally unearned income to low-cost producers of a commodity in short supply; since capitalist competition tends to equalize costs of production, rent tends to be temporary. Rent also refers to rewards obtained by producers due to their monopoly of technology, production, or political control in certain economic areas.

14. Many authors have analyzed the "perverse" effects of petroleum rents and other forms of windfall profits on society, often referred to as the "Dutch disease." For a classic discussion of the "Dutch disease" theory of resource booms I have already mentioned the work of Corden and Neary (1982). In Venezuela, the expansion of oil production in the 1920s was accompanied by a critique of its effects. One of the most vocal critics has been Arturo Uslar Pietri, who as early as 1936 expressed concern that the nation might become a parasite of petroleum. The most authoritative critic was Juan Pablo Pérez Alfonzo, who was the architect of AD's oil policies and a founder of OPEC and became increasingly concerned with the effects of petroleum on Venezuela after the 1973 boom. For a discussion of ideas concerning petroleum held by prominent Venezuelan economists, including Uslar Pietri's and Pérez Alfonzo's positions, see Baptista and Mommer (1987). For an attempt to locate the economic discourse about the oil industry in Venezuela within a larger symbolic universe, see Pérez Schael (1993). For a study of the "perverse" effects of oil rents in a local region of Venezuela, see Briceño León (1990).

and Chile as examples of the rather typical "inefficient" use of mineral income and notes that "the most promising use of surplus mineral rents has occurred in Venezuela since 1974, where the government is putting into effect a massive conversion of its mineral surplus into physical, human, and technological capital" (1978:875). Yet Venezuela, like most oil exporters, faces today more serious economic distortions than before the boom periods of 1973 and 1979; it is such results that make it necessary to examine the "social dynamic" of an oil-reliant economy.[15]

NATURAL RESOURCES: THE MYSTERY OF MADAME LA TERRE

As for most third-world primary producers, for oil producers the determination of the international price of oil is a matter of extraordinary importance. If we wish to ascertain how oil prices have been determined, we must leave the neoclassical world of market exchange and turn to the thinkers who first analyzed capitalist production as a social process that engages people and nature in mutual transformation. Among classical political economists, Adam Smith and David Ricardo provided some of the most interesting discussions of the origins of value in production and of the determination of the exchange value of natural resources in the market. Building on their work, Marx developed their theory of value by unveiling the mystified appearance in which factors of production such as land or capital appear as sources of value under capitalism.

Classical economists were centrally concerned with analyzing the origin of wealth and the mechanisms of its distribution. They thought that the value of a commodity depended on the conditions of its production, that economies were capable of producing a surplus, and that the wealth of a nation depended on the expansion of its productive capacity. For them there were two kinds of prices: prices of production, which reflect the actual costs of production and which they explained by means of a theory of value; and market prices, which describe the actual exchange price of commodities in response to fluctuations of supply and demand. The interesting issue for them was the interplay between production and exchange and, therefore, the relation between values (as natural prices or prices of production) and market

15. Although oil-exporting nations share many common features, they also have distinct histories, which makes comparisons both more difficult and more interesting. Even authors who work with different theoretical perspectives tend to agree that oil production in third-world nations tends to have wide-ranging effects, and most would agreed that oil has been, at best, a "mixed blessing" (Amuzegar 1982).

prices. As I indicated above, neoclassical thought does not continue this concern with the origins of wealth in production, for it treats the determination of value as the result of the subjective preferences of economic agents through the market; it explains production in terms of exchange. Agents invest or consume in accordance with their subjective preferences and prices result from the play of supply and demand. Therefore, there is only one kind of price: market price.

In the market the conditions of the original production of value fall completely out of sight; under its blinding light, value is invisible. All that can be seen are different forms of revenue: wages paid to labor, profits to capitalists, rents to landowners. Even Adam Smith, who saw labor as the source of value, was bewitched by the same fetishes that he had shattered. Contradicting his own labor theory of value, Smith asserted in *The Wealth of Nations* that "wages, profits and rents are the three original sources of all revenues, as well as of all exchangeable value" (quoted in Marx 1968:347). As Marx pointed out, "In accordance with his own explanation he should have said: original sources of all revenue, although none of the these so-called sources enters into the formation of the value" (1968:347−48).

For Marx, the "trinity form," by which he meant the relationship among capital-profit, land−ground rent, and labor-wages, "holds in itself all the mysteries of the social production process" (1981:953). The fact that this magic formula appears as natural shows the extent to which capitalism has succeeded in establishing as normal its fantastic conception of reality:

> As the connection between the components of value and wealth in general and its sources (this trinity) completes the mystification of the capitalist mode of production, the reification of social relations, and the immediate coalescence of the material relations of production with their historical and social specificity: the bewitched, distorted and upside-down world haunted by Monsieur le Capital and Madame la Terre, who are at the same time social characters and mere things. (1981:969.)

In this bewitched world these forms appear together as sources of value but, according to Marx, actually have nothing in common. Labor, divested of any specific social form, is an abstraction without historical reality. As the source of value, it is absurd that it should have a price—"The price of labor is just as irrational as a yellow logarithm" (1981:957). Capital, in turn, is not a thing but a social relation specific to a specific mode of production. It is not the means of production but the means of production transformed into capital, that is, monopolized by a particular sector of society and used to make profits: capital seeks to expand itself. When capital seeks self-expansion through its form as money rather than as the means of production, it then generates interest rather than profits. Here the fetishism of capital appears in its most "estranged and peculiar form," for "interest seems independent both of the wage-labor of the worker and of the capitalist's own labor; it seems to derive from capital as its own independent source" (Marx 1981:968): money begets money. Finally, land, by definition a nonproduced condition of production that partakes as a material element of any process of production, can have price but no value, for "value is labor" (Marx 1981:954).

By land, Marx meant "every power of nature," not just agricultural land but also mines, rivers, and waterfalls (Marx 1968:342). While for Ricardo rent was an attribute of nature itself and landed property determined simply its distribution, for Marx it was an attribute of landed property, and its extent was determined by the level of excess profits possible under a given set of productive conditions. From Marx's perspective, the mystery of Madame la Terre is solved when it is recognized that rents do not add value because they are unambiguously a deduction from surplus value. Since value derives not from nature but from society, rents pertain to the distribution of surplus value, not to its creation. But insofar as production involves the use of natural resources, the intrinsic differences among them affect differentially the productivity of human labor and therefore the profitability of capital. Thus, rents represent a deduction from the capitalists' profits that accrue to landowners by virtue of their ownership of a natural factor of production. Rents depend, therefore, on the existence of both surplus profits and the institution of landed property.

The source of surplus profits gives rise to two kinds of rent: differential and absolute. Differential rent depends on surplus originating from the competition between sources of capital within the same economic sector, for instance, the oil sector, which may expand to a wider energy sector if the price of oil approximates the price of coal. Absolute rent results from surplus arising from capitalist competition between different sectors; it is the rent that must paid to the landowner independently of the fertility of its land. Both forms of rent derive from the monopoly of land.

Competition within a sector, given differences in the natural conditions of production (such as soil fertility and richness of mines) or in the intensity of capital (varying amounts and type of capital invested, such as the use of fertilizers and mechanized agriculture) brings about uneven rates of profits. The landowner can obtain a rent the size of which depends on the excess of the rate of profit over the average. If excess profits derive from advantageous natural conditions, this rent is called differential rent I; it is named differential rent II if surplus profits result from the more intensive use of capital. In either case, the level of the rent is set by the size of the existing surplus profits within the sector. Let us assume that prices in the oil sector are determined by the cost of production in the United States. If Standard Oil makes higher profits in Venezuela's oil fields than in its mines in the United States, the Venezuelan state, as landowner, is in the position to claim a higher rent.

In other words, the amount of the rent received by the landowner depends on the market price of the commodity produced by the capitalist. Differential rent, as Marx explained, "does not enter as a determining factor into the general production price of commodities, but rather is based on it" (1974:646). Differential rent "invariably arises from the difference between the individual production price of a particular capital having command over the monopolized natural force, on the one hand, and the general production price of the total capital invested in the sphere of production concerned, on the other" (1974:646).

Within a productive economic sector (the oil sector or the wider energy sector), landed property promotes competition by offering capital different natural conditions of production and therefore of profitability. In contrast, between productive sectors, landed property acts as an obstacle to capitalist competition by demanding a rent as a condition for capital investment to use land. For instance, capitalists must decide whether to invest in manufacture, with minimal rent obligations, or in mining, which includes a substantial rent payment. Because a rent is demanded, market prices in the sector rise above the average prices of production. Absolute rent, as the expression of the social power of landed property, creates the conditions that generate a sectoral increase in the rate of profit over the average rate of profit in the economy as a whole; landed property (such as that of private landowners and oil-exporting states) captures this increase in profit in the form of absolute rent. Thus, absolute rent reflects the power of landed property over capital in the struggle over the distribution of the mass of surplus value. While the level of differential rent is limited by the existing market price, the level of absolute rent depends on the power of landed property to increase the market price through extramarket means; in one case, rent is determined by price; in the other, price is determined by rent.[16]

---

16. There is a vast and inconclusive literature on the labor theory of value; the theory has been criticized as vigorously as it has been defended. Marx developed this theory in the *Grundrisse* (1973), *Capital* (1967) and *Theories of Surplus Value* (1968). For interpretations and discussions of the theory

BLACK GOLD

Oil, more than any other commodity, illustrates both the importance and the mystification of natural resources in the modern world. An essential commodity for the capitalist system, oil has fueled not only its industrial, transportation, and heating systems but also the popular and academic imagination worldwide. Not surprisingly, as Mommer's analysis shows (1983), the price of oil has generally been interpreted in terms of the same two commonsense outlooks informed by the neoclassical view of natural resources.[17]

From a microeconomic perspective, oil is natural capital. This definition emerged from the conflict between private landowners and capitalists in the United States during the late nineteenth century at the outset of the oil industry's development. In the confrontation between landlords and capitalists which took place in that period, an implicit understanding was reached that profits should be shared equally between the owners of the resource and the capitalists who extracted it. The payment to the landlord of a royalty of one oil barrel out of eight reflected this understanding. By the last quarter of the nineteenth century, profits in the oil industry in Pennsylvania were considered to be around 25 percent of the commercial price; half of 25 percent was 12.5 percent, or 1:8, the size of the royalty for the landowner.

This microeconomic view was recognized by U.S. tax legislation. A series of legislative acts, culminating in the 1932 depletion allowance law, validated a conception of oil as natural capital. Just as income derived from capital gains is taxed by half (in principle, to protect the capital structure of society), taxes on the sale of oil were reduced by 27.5 percent, to compensate for the depletion of this natural capital. (The depletion allowance for oil is granted both to the capitalist and to the landowner: 7:8 and 1:8, respectively.) The significance of this depletion allowance cannot be overstated; by

---

of value and related issues, see Bohm-Bawerk (1946), Hilferding (1949), Rubin (1973), Rosdolsky (1977), Meek (1956), Brunhoff (1973), Elson (979), Fine (1986), Morishima and Catephores (1978), Mandel and Freeman (1984), Steedman et al. (1981), Shaik (1977, 1980). For discussions of the theory in relation to ground rent, see Ball (1977,1980), Edel (1976), Fine (1979, 1980), Murray (1977). For analysis of ground rent in relation to urban spaces, see Harvey (1989), Lojkine (1977), Edel (1976). See also the polemic among Samuelson, Sweezy, and Baumol in the *Journal of Economic Literature* (1974). These debates range from the hypertechnical to the almost theological. I find the labor theory of value useful as a way of comprehending the formation of subjects in a world of objectified values, rather than as a technical tool to determine prices.

17. This discussion of the conceptualization of pricing mechanisms in the mineral sector and of the evolution of oil prices is drawn from Mommer's pathbreaking work (1983, 1986).

1970, income tax on manufacturing activities was 43 percent, while for the oil industry it was only 21 percent (Mommer 1986 : 31).

The same microeconomic perspective has been adopted by oil-producing nations. While in the United States oil belongs to the private owner of the soil, in most other nations oil is considered to be public or national property. Oil-producing nations in the third world took the standpoint of the individual landowner in their confrontation with international oil companies, and their governments chose to act at the international level as represen tatives of the nation as an individual property-owning unit. They came to justify their demand for a share of the profits derived from the sale of this natural resource by invoking the idea that oil has an inherent value and should thus be treated as "natural capital." The mining legislation of most oil countries reflects this viewpoint.

This view was explicitly recognized by the Organization of Petroleum Exporting Countries (OPEC) in 1962. In its struggle to increase its participation in oil revenues, OPEC redefined the commonly accepted goal of dividing profits equally between states and oil companies. Before this historic OPEC meeting, these oil-producing states tended to include the royalty as part of the percentage of profits distributed to the state. Following OPEC's new initiative, the royalty was defined as compensation for the intrinsic value of oil as nonrenewable resource, that is, as a form of depletion allowance. Profits were to be shared after discounting the company's operating costs and distributing the royalty. By separating royalty payments from their share in oil profits, oil states increased their total oil revenues.

The macroeconomic perspective, on the other hand, does not regard the rent paid to landowners as entering into price formation. As Adelman argues throughout his examination of the petroleum market, the price of oil is determined by supply and demand, with increases based on scarcity. Rents (royalty payments) do not constitute a cost and therefore do not affect prices. They do represent a residue, a difference due to natural advantages. The conditions of production on the least productive oil fields determine the price of oil in the world market. Since prices of comparable types of oil become uniform whether extracted from poor or rich fields, the more productive oil fields yield a rent (Adelman 1972).

Following closely Ricardo's theory of rent, Adelman takes into account the importance of differing conditions of production, in contrast to neoclassical analysts who adopt a microeconomic perspective. But since his theory recognizes only natural features as determinants of rents, it is unable to take into account the social forces that actually determine the price of oil. In the introduction to his 1972 study of the oil industry, Adelman predicted that oil prices would decline: "The conclusions of this study are that crude oil prices will decline because supply will far exceed demand even at lower prices, and because—a separate issue—there will continue to be enough competition to make price gravitate toward cost, however slowly" (quoted in Hausmann 1981:230).

This theoretical framework could not account for the 1973–74 four-fold increase in oil prices. For Adelman, the movement of oil prices is determined by supply and demand. For him, the payment of rent to states in oil-exporting nations depends on the level of the market price for oil. This theory assumes that capital has access to the oil fields; it does not understand the economic significance of landed property as a barrier to capital.

When they attempt to find an underlying logic behind the apparently chaotic events—wars, revolutions, coups—that have led to rapid shifts in prices, neoclassical interpretations remain at the level of supply and demand, where supply itself is established by an exchange-determined view of production. At best, they introduce "political factors" into their models (Moran 1982); but since these models are premised on the postulate that value is determined in exchange, they are ultimately unable to account for the origin of value in production. "Politics," in this context, does not include the deployment of power by landowners as such, in which their ability to claim an absolute rent is exercised.

Thus, despite the considerable degree of sophistication of these attempts, the movement of prices is seen as constrained by a ceiling set by supply and demand within the oil or energy sectors. Thus, Adelman, using a Ricardian conception of differential rents, sees oil rents as a residual category. For him the ceiling on energy prices was determined, at the supply side, by the potential competition of more expensive sources of crude oil before the boom (1973:1256) or, after the oil booms of the seventies, "by opportunities to invest in greater thermal efficiency more than by new sources of crude oil" (1982:32).

As the price of oil moved upward, Adelman broadened the ceiling on oil prices to extend from the oil industry itself to the entire energy sector. In this respect he was right, for as oil prices jumped, the use of alternative sources of energy set limits on further oil price increases. The oil booms of the seventies made it evident that differential rents are best seen as arising not from within the confines of a narrowly defined industrial sector (oil) but from within the limits set by alternative resources such as coal within a broader sector (energy). Massarrat's analysis of the oil industry in the context of the energy sector illustrates this point (1980). Adelman's view of the larger field within which differential rents are established does not consider, however, the role of landed property itself as a barrier to capital investment in natural resources. It simply extends the boundaries within which landed property plays this role.

The sharp increase of 1973 and 1974 in oil prices did not result from a world shortage of oil. It was, rather, the outcome of a long historical process by which OPEC nations, acting as landowners, developed the means to extract a rent on the basis of their ownership of the oil fields—an absolute rent—in addition to the differential rents they had collected in the past. In 1973 a set of converging political and economic conditions helped establish their collective ability to restrict the world supply of oil. With this power, OPEC felt entitled to set the market price of oil, thus freeing the level of rent from the previous constraint of the market price. Now rent itself (absolute and differential) would determine the market price of oil.

This shift, from a rent the level of which was determined by the market price to a market price determined by the level of rent, expressed a historical change in power relations between capital and landed property throughout the capitalist world. The original 1 : 8 Pennsylvania oil royalty, while ideologically construed as being a payment to the landlords for the use of their natural capital, represented in fact the power of landowners to claim an absolute rent; that is, a payment due them as landowners, regardless of the productivity of their oil fields. As profits in the oil sector expanded, this royalty came to represent an increasingly smaller percentage of oil profits, not an equal sharing of profits. Thus, it became what it really was all along: a minimum payment to landlords, an absolute rent. Landlords in the United States devised various contractual arrangements to increase their participation in the growing oil industry profits but lacked the collective organization and knowledge to preserve the original goal of equal profit sharing.

Initially, oil-exporting nations behaved very much like individual domestic landlords in the United States, acting as passive and atomized independent agents with limited knowledge of the oil industry. In their struggle to increase their participation in oil profits, however, they were better placed than individual landlords to learn about the industry, to share information, and to act together. As sovereign states, they could obtain crucial information about this secretive industry; as the major suppliers of oil for the capitalist world, they could affect the level of world production. The key to understanding the evolution of oil prices is the analysis of how these states consolidated their power as landowners, both separately, as sovereign states confronting oil company subsidiaries, and collectively, through OPEC's actions at the international level.

These states were able to define the level of absolute rent by setting market prices. Given this redefinition of power relations, absolute rent has functioned as a new barrier that redefines the field within which it functions. By promoting the expansion of the field, it redraws the boundaries of the expanded field. Thus, the underlying logic of oil price formation cannot be found in the market as defined by neoclassical economics but in the complex political arena in which states and oil companies, landed property, and capital struggle for the production and appropriation of value. In these struggles, labor figures as a force through the mediation of the state in nations in which it has contributed to defining nationalist demands.[18]

ONE HUNDRED YEARS OF OIL PRICES

I can now draw, on the basis of Mommer's work, the broad outlines of the evolution of oil prices. From the origins of the oil industry in Pennsylvania in the nineteenth century until 1959, the world market price of oil was set by U.S. oil companies, which were the world's major oil producers during most of this century. From 1917 until 1958, U.S. oil accounted, on average, for 55 percent of total world production. Since 1928, the International Oil Cartel (a U.S.-dominated alliance of British, Dutch, and U.S. oil companies) controlled world oil production and set the world market price on the basis of the elevated cost levels prevailing in the United States. Oil production was significantly cheaper in all other oil-producing nations. This was in part because in some cases they had richer oil fields but also because oil extraction was more rationally organized than in the United States. Since the subsoil in these countries is public property, oil fields are not anarchically subdivided into scattered small plots, as in the United States, which are costlier to mine. Given uniform market prices determined by high-cost U.S. oil, this cost difference was the source of surplus profits for the oil companies that operated overseas.

---

18. The significance of labor in global struggles over price formation in the oil sector remains to be determined, but it is evident that labor's role is mediated through its influence on the states of oil producing nations. In the case of Venezuela, several scholars have emphasized the significance of labor in defining a nationalist oil policy, particularly in the early stages of the oil industry, before the trade union movement became controlled by Acción Democrática (Tennassee 1979; Bergquist 1986). The collection of articles brought together by Nore and Turner in *Oil and Class Struggle* (1980) seeks to underline the relevance of labor in the domestic and international politics of oil in various countries.

As they sought to increase their oil revenues, the oil-exporting states claimed for themselves a portion of these surplus profits. To the extent that they were successful, they in effect transformed these surplus profits into rents—differential rents. Given a certain level of consumption, the ceiling of these rents seemed to be set by the world market price of oil as fixed by the U.S. oil industry (which, it must be remembered, included the royalty—an absolute rent). Insofar as this perception determined the action of economic agents, it was an accurate reflection of reality. Until 1960, the struggle of oil-producing nations to increase their oil revenues was constrained by the magnitude of surplus profits within the international oil industry. In other words, rent was determined by price.

The conditions that enabled oil-producing states to increase their participation in oil profits by turning the industry's surplus profits into differential rents could not last indefinitely. Oil prices had been remarkably stable. In fact, since 1934 they had slowly increased for a quarter century. As oil production overseas expanded, U.S. participation in world oil production declined; between 1959 and 1972 it accounted for only 25 percent of the total. Already by 1947 the U.S. had become an importer of oil. The United States began to exert influence on world oil prices not only as a major producer but also as an increasingly large consumer. In 1959 oil prices declined for the first time in twenty-five years. As could be expected, this reduction deeply concerned oil-exporting nations. In 1960 OPEC was founded, in large part at the initiative of Venezuela, which had more experience as an oil exporter and as a sovereign state than Middle Eastern oil exporters. A cartel of landowners, not of producers, OPEC originally attempted to make oil prices stable. But its pursuit of larger revenues, within existing market conditions, necessarily entailed an increase in oil prices, that is, the establishment of an absolute rent.

This shift from a rent determined by price to a price determined by rent began in the 1960s and culminated in the 1970s. The crucial moment came in 1968. OPEC nations, limited in their earnings by the existing market price of oil, decided that, for tax purposes, the price of oil would be fixed by the oil-exporting states. The stated purpose of these state-set fiscal prices was to capture the companies' surplus profits. Ostensibly, their limit was set by the level of surplus profits obtained by the oil companies, which were defined as profits above the customary level that would have been necessary to induce capitalists to invest. As Mommer has argued, "OPEC was on the road to transforming any existing or possible surplus profits into ground rent" (1986:183).

Mommer's analysis shows how the mechanism of this transformation created the conditions for the generation of surplus profits in the oil industry. Surplus profits were to be transformed into rents not by increasing the taxes of oil companies but by raising the fiscal price of oil and defining taxes as a proportion of the increased price of oil itself. Given an existing magnitude of surplus profits in the oil sector, a tax increase transforms surplus profits into ground rent. In contrast, an increase in the fiscal price of oil establishes a priori the level of rent, regardless of the existing magnitude of profits in the sector. It may, therefore, push market prices upwards in the effort to maintain the present rate of profit in the sector. Thus, OPEC nations, by potentially pushing prices upwards and demanding an absolute rent, were in fact not only capturing existing surplus profits but creating the conditions for the continued existence of surplus profits in the oil sector (1986:182–83).

At the 1968 meeting, OPEC nations formulated the goal of achieving national control over their domestic oil industries. This goal was to be achieved by increasing state participation in all phases of the oil industry. According to this plan, the role of foreign companies would eventually be reduced to that of minor partners or licensees. Once government-owned oil companies had developed their capacity to operate the industry, foreign companies would derive income only from payments for their limited services. Thus, the OPEC states' pursuit of an absolute rent was intimately related to their political consolidation as sovereign states in the domestic and international arenas and to the development of specific state capacities.

The quadrupling of oil prices in 1973–74, and then again in 1979, was the culmination of this process. Surplus profits were transformed into rents by transferring value at the international level between different economic sectors, rather than within the oil sector. This movement of value toward the oil sector shook the entire world economy. It was perceived as a shift of the world's wealth toward the oil-exporting nations. It entailed a redistribution of profits underwritten by oil consumers in all sectors, from basic industry to the general public. For this reason, OPEC nations became the target of attack of oil-consuming nations on an unprecedented scale.

In this context, transnational oil companies lost interest in remaining as oil capitalists in the third world: they wanted to avoid public attack at a moment when they were making large profits in their own operations. Moreover, the capacity of OPEC states to extract an absolute rent not only reflected, but also heightened, their power. These states could now assume control over their respective oil industries. By 1976, the oil industry in every oil-exporting nation had been nationalized. Transnational oil companies now were contracted for their services to the nationalized industries. The stated goals of the 1968 OPEC meeting had been achieved.

Two events highlighted in this brief sketch point to the significance of political relations in the determination of oil prices. The 1968 OPEC meeting was preceded in 1967 by the third Arab-Israeli war. The 1973–74 oil price increase was preceded in 1973 by the fourth Arab-Israeli war. On each occasion, oil was used as a political weapon. It would be simplistic to argue that political conflicts caused the increase in oil price by affecting the supply of oil. Rather, through these confrontations, oil-producing states tested and extended their power. If oil became a political weapon, it is because oil states turned into an economic force.

The history of oil prices, then, reflects political struggles over the distribution of value within and among sectors of the world economy. Underlying the diverse events that conditioned the evolution of oil prices was the growing power of OPEC states, acting individually and collectively, as owners of a natural resource. In turn, the most evident consequence of their power as landlords, the increase in oil revenues and the nationalization of oil industries, affected not only the extent of their power, but its basis, the social relations through which state power was constituted both domestically and internationally.

HISTORY'S NATURE: FROM A BINARY
TO AN OPEN DIALECTIC

I have used some Marxist categories to illuminate aspects of the international political economy of oil and to introduce my discussion of state formation in Venezuela. From the perspective informing my work on Venezuela, I wish to conclude this chapter by offering a view of both capitalism and the state that seeks to overcome Eurocentric and androcentric biases present in the vision of capitalism that Marx handed down to us.

Marx's relationship to capitalism was marked by a deep ambivalence. He recognized at once its achievements and liberating potential, as well as its alienating consequences and limited historical horizon. Only by inhabiting capitalist culture, immersing himself in its categories and examining its implicit assumptions could he subject it to a critique that remains exemplary in its comprehensiveness and imagination. Yet nineteenth-century European capitalist culture also inhabited Marx, limiting his critical reach. His deconstruction of political economy's categorical system did not free him from its heterosexist identification of activity with masculinity, passivity with femininity, and productivity with fertility (Arendt 1958:106; Parker 1993·35)

His conception of history's progress assumes a trajectory defined by the dialectical union of capital and labor which increasingly displaces nature—as well as the social classes and regions of the world identified with it—from history's center stage. Not only the bourgeoisie and the working class but city and country, landowners and peasants, metropolitan centers and capitalist periphery are defined by their assigned role in his narrative of history's advance. His account of the productive engagement of Monsieur le Capital with Madame la Terre unwittingly serves to confirm dominant representations of a world polarized into a masculine and creative order which is the home of capital in the metropolitan centers and a feminized and subjected domain where nature passively awaits capital's fertile embrace in the periphery.

The neglect of nature in Marxist thought is related to the identification of capital and labor with activity and of nature with passivity. In the spirit of Hegel's master/slave dialectic, Marx's capital/labor dialectic posits the antagonism between these two agents as the source of history's emancipatory movement. While this binary focus informs most of his work, through his discussion of the role of ground rent under capitalism Marx brings out a third actor: nature (together with the cluster of factors associated with it). Although nature forcefully enters analysis only at the end of volume 3 of *Capital,* Marx makes rather large claims for the role it plays in union with capital and labor. They are the leading protagonists of capitalist societies: "Capital-profit (profit of enterprise plus interest), land–ground rent, labor-wages, this trinity form holds in itself all the mysteries of the social production process" (1981:953).

Since most Marxists, following Marx, have devoted themselves to solving the mystery of the capital/labor relation, it is no surprise that the mystery of Madame la Terre still remains to be deciphered. Few thinkers have noted that Marx's binary system clashes with his "trinity formula." Henry Lefebvre is exceptional in noting this tension and brilliantly exploring its consequences. He suggests that a fuller inclusion of nature would bring to center stage the role of additional social agents and of politics itself, understood as a specific social relation. Recognizing that by "land" Marx meant a social relation, not a thing (agricultural or mineral resources not as inert objects but as elements of social formations constituted through the socialization of nature), Lefebvre argues that land includes "landlords, country, aristocracy" and, most significant for my argument, the "nation-state, confined within a specific territory" and therefore, "in the most absolute sense, politics and political strategy" (1991:325). Thus for him, Marx's "binary opposition of a conflictual (dialectical) character implies the subordination of the historical to the economic, both in reality and in the conceptual realm" and also "the dissolving or absorption, by the economic sphere proper, of a multiplicity of formations (the town, among others) inherited from history, and themselves of a precapitalist nature" (1991 : 324).

Lefebvre suggests that with Marx's treatment of nature at the end of *Capital* his analysis of capitalism "comes to a halt" (1991 : 325) because it presented him with difficulties which he could not resolve. The main difficulty was to acknowledge the implication of the growing importance of nature for capitalist production, given that he had a binary model of capitalist development. Contrary to the historical progression envisaged in Marx's model, mobilized as it was by the capital/labor relation, Lefebvre argues that the growing importance of land has entailed a more complex development: "On a world scale, landed property showed no signs of disappearing, nor did the political importance of landowners, nor did the characteristics peculiar to agricultural production. Nor, consequently, did ground rent suddenly abandon the field to profits and wages." He underlines the expanding significance of natural resources and spatial considerations: "What was more, questions of underground and above-ground resources—of the space of the entire planet—were continually growing in importance" (1991 : 324).

Marx's inability to account for the importance of nature, according to Lefebvre, is reproduced in contemporary social theory's remarkable insensitivity to the significance of ground rent: "Any attempt to restore to its proper place the concept of ground rent has for decades been utterly squelched, whether in France, in Europe or in the world at large, in the name of a Marxism that has become mere ideology—nothing but a political tool in the hands of apparatchiks" (1991 : 324). He does not explain why the recognition of ground rent's centrality has been so threatening, but I believe that it would entail integrating temporal and spatial dimensions and replacing Eurocentric and formulaic conceptions of capitalism with a more historical, political, and global understanding of its historical development.[19]

However, since Marx wrote volume 3 of *Capital* before volumes 1 and 2

19. The concept of ground rent, however, has been used to study societies in which mining or agricultural products play a key role. While these studies have made valuable contributions to the analysis of specific nations, they have not modified dominant conceptions of capitalism. My work in this area builds on the contributions of scholars who have used the category of rent to analyze primary producers, and in particular, oil-producing nations. One of the earliest attempts to bring together a number of essays that use the theory of ground rent to study of oil-exporting states is Nore and Turner (1980). The journal *Peuples Mediterraneans/Mediterranean Peoples* dedicates a special issue (no. 26, 1984) entitled *Pétrole et société*, to the analysis of petroleum-based societies. Among the authors who are sensitive to the cultural or political implications of oil rents, see the work by Watts (1983; 1987; 1994) and Graf (1988) on Nigeria.

(Rosdolsky 1977), the acknowledgment of the importance of land in volume 3 (at that "late" point) thus does not account for its subordination to the capital/labor dynamic in the rest of this work . Moreover, Marx's neglect of nature cannot be explained strictly by what Lefebvre calls the "subordination of the historical to the economic." Although a fuller recognition of land's role in capitalist production would have certainly challenged Marx to present a more political and global conception of capitalism, I think that one of Marx's accomplishments is to have begun to show that the apparent separation of the "economy" from "politics" under capitalism is itself an effect of politics. Through his work he demonstrated that what came to be called the economy in bourgeois society was constituted through class struggle and state regulation, as can be clearly seen in his historical writings as well as in *Capital*.[20]

I believe that Marx's oversight had to do with his aims. From his location in England in the midst of the industrial revolution, he sought to advance the cause of socialism by presenting workers as an exploited class that has an interest in the universal emancipation of humankind. He saw the roots of exploitation in the extraction of surplus value in the production process. Thus, he focused on the dialectic between capital and labor and on the relation between profits and wages in order to make visible, at a relatively high level of abstraction, the hidden operations that secure the extraction of surplus labor and obscure this process from view. In contrast to labor, land does not produce value. Like capital, it only appropriates it but does so not by engaging labor in the production process like capital but by blocking capital's mobility and its ability to exploit labor. In this sense, land is parasitical on both labor and capital.

Marx thus saw land as a conservative force that inhibits capital's advance. His work suggests that in time, land would be subsumed under capital, that is, capital would control land's power as a social relation opposed to it. Given this view, and his concern to lay bare the logic of capitalist accumulation from a perspective that privileged the problem of the exploitation of labor, it is understandable that he did not focus on nature as a source of wealth or as the basis of landed property and ground rent. Marx's strictly social conception of exploitation avoids fetishizing capital, money, or land as sources of value. But in the end it excludes the exploitation of nature from the analysis of capitalist production and erases its role in the formation of wealth.

---

20. I have in mind in particular several chapters of *Capital*'s volume 1 (1967): on money (chapter 3), the working day (chapter 10), and primitive accumulation (chapters 26–33).

This erasure of nature also takes place in Marx's discussion of the main form of wealth under capitalism: the commodity. He takes such pains to show that the value of commodities depends only on the social relations that stamp upon them a definite quantity of abstract labor power that he neglects the role of nature in their constitution as commodities: "The existence of things *qua* commodities, and the value-relation between the products of labor which stamps them as commodities, have absolutely no connection with their physical properties and with the material relations arising therefrom" (1967:72). While it is true that the value-relation between commodities has nothing to do with their physical properties, their existence qua commodities cannot be separated from their physical properties.

As things that embody exchange values and use values, commodities are, as Marx emphasizes elsewhere, intrinsically sensual objects, dependent on a physical medium for their constitution as such; they have a material or "natural form" and a social or "value form" (1977:138). This is true not only for unquestionably material commodities such as cars or mangos but also for those that are less tangible, such as musical performances or poems. What makes a particular song or mango into a commodity, of course, is not its real or imagined usefulness alone but its marketability; its participation in market exchange transforms it into a commodity. The mango I buy in the market is a commodity, the one I pick freely from a tree is not; in one case I eat a commodity, in the other a thing. The same is true of a song, which can circulate freely, as when I receive it from a friend "who sings like a bird" (Marx 1977:1044), or dressed as a commodity weighed down by a price tag, as when I buy a ticket to a concert to listen to her. Commodities circulate through the medium of their physical properties, not independently of them. The particular form of their sensuous materiality is an intrinsic element of the form they take as commodities.[21]

My argument about the importance of the physical properties of commodities is not restricted to recognizing the role of matter in defining their usefulness as things. Many scholars have noted that *Capital* focuses on exchange value and pays little attention to use value (Baudrillard 1981; Sahlins 1976). Given Marx's aims, I find this focus understandable. In my view, the materiality of commodities also participates in their constitution qua com-

---

21. As Marx noted, commodities are no simple things, and it is not always easy to identify what is in fact a commodity. Marxists often attribute great significance to goods produced by wage labor for exchange, but then goods could be produced for exchange under a variety of labor conditions and still be commodities. For an interesting discussion of the commodification of music as a program to which labor is later applied, see Attali (1977).

modities and therefore in defining their role as the form of appearance of wealth under capitalism. If it is true, as Marx argues from *Capital*'s opening sentence, that "the wealth of societies in which the capitalist mode of production prevails appears as an 'immense collection of commodities'" (1967: 125), I think it is so because commodities embody not only abstract labor power but also material wealth. The commodity, qua commodity, embodies social value and natural wealth; as "sensuous things which are at the same time suprasensible or social" (Marx 1967: 165), they cannot be understood independently either of their physical or their social properties.

In his discussion of the commodity form, Marx's major concern is to dissipate the mist of familiarity "through which the social character of labor appears to us to be an objective character of the products themselves" (1967: 74). For Marx, the fetishism of commodities involves the inscription of abstract labor power into objects and the simultaneous erasure of the mechanism of this inscription from collective awareness. Ironically, in his zeal to demonstrate that a commodity's value resides in the inscription, not the object, Marx erases William Petty's insight (which he makes his own) that labor inscribes value through a material medium and that wealth is generated from the union of labor, "the father," and nature, "the mother" (Marx 1967: 43). As far as I know, this is an unremarked aspect of Marx's discussion of the commodity form.

An appreciation of the role of nature in the formation of wealth offers a different view of capitalism. The inclusion of nature (and of the agents associated with it) should displace the capital/labor relation from the ossified centrality it has been made to occupy by Marxist theory. Together with land, the capital/labor relation may be viewed within a wider process of commodification, the specific form and effects of which must be demonstrated concretely in each instance. In light of this more comprehensive view of capitalism, it would be difficult to reduce its development to a dialectic of capital and labor originating in advanced centers and expanding to the backward periphery. Instead, the international division of labor could be more properly recognized as being simultaneously an international division of nations and of nature (and of other geopolitical units, such as the first and third worlds, that reflect changing international realignments). By including the worldwide agents involved in the making of capitalism, this perspective makes it possible to envisage a global, non-Eurocentric conception of its development.

The aim of shifting from a binary to a triadic dialectic is to open our view of the historical development of capitalism rather than to limit it by defining a priori the identity of its agents and the logic of its transformation. A focus on the commodification of land, labor, and capital—Marx's trinity formula—embraces within social analysis, as Lefebvre proposes, a wider range of social actors and social formations, unifies temporal and spatial dimensions, and brings out more forcefully the play of structure and contingency in history. The critical purpose is to apprehend the relational character of the units included in the making of the modern world, not to multiply their number as independent entities.

In Marx's account of capitalism, land appears ambivalently both as necessary natural powers that participate in the production of commodities and as a social class that acts as an obstacle to the expansion of capital. When Marx speaks of landowners as a class, his ambiguity resolves itself into sheer negativity: "a class that neither works itself nor directly exploits workers, and cannot even, like interest-bearing capital, launch forth in edifying homilies about the risk and sacrifice in lending capital" (1981 : 968). Given his negative evaluation of land's social role, it is understandable that he paid little attention to its role in the evolution of capitalism. From the perspective of the periphery of the capitalist system, however, it is necessary to recognize the centrality of land as an active social force of ongoing economic significance and remarkable political eloquence.

If land is brought to the center of analysis in the multiple forms which it assumes in the contemporary world—not just as a class that represents a declining mode of production, but as an active social force in the reproduction of modern relations—it would be difficult to continue to view capital accumulation as an economic drama enacted by capital and labor *in* society. Instead, one would have to include as well, as Lefebvre suggests, the "nation-state confined within a specific territory" and, therefore, "in the most absolute sense, politics and political strategy."

From this perspective, the Marxist critique of the reified appearance of politics and economics as independent spheres in both capitalist culture and mainstream social theory can be made to include a criticism of their persistent separation within Marxist theory itself. The vast literature on the state in advanced and peripheral capitalist societies focuses on the relationship between politics and economics. Within mainstream analysis, inspired by Weber's programmatic rather than historical writings, most works seek to establish the independence of the state from its socioeconomic context and to privilege the intentional role of political agents in both the domestic and international domains. Within Marxism, debate has centered on competing modes of apprehending the links between the state and capitalism, on the assumption that states are constituted and organized in response to their role in reproducing capitalist social relations. Thus, while neo-Weberians tend to posit an essential separation between state and economy and are concerned with the assessment of relative degrees of "state capacities" (Skocpol 1985), Marxists generally assume the existence of a structural connection between state and society and are thus interested in exploring its significance for the form and relative autonomy of the state (Miliband 1969; Poulantzas 1976).

Studies of states on the periphery—such as "modernizing states" (Almond and Verba 1963), "colonial states" (Chandra 1980; Alavi 1972), and "dependent states" (Cardoso and Faletto 1979; Frank 1978; Amin 1980)—tend to reproduce the terms of these debates. Given the prevailing forms of theoretical discourse, it is understandable that attempts by neo-Weberians and Marxists to "bring the state back in" (Evans, Rueschemeyer, and Skocpol 1985) and to see "state making" as a continuous historical process (Bright and Harding 1984) have been framed in terms of the dual problematic of the relative autonomy of the state and of the capacity of state agents to generate and pursue specific courses of action. These approaches tend to assume capitalism and to problematize the state's relation to it.

The conception of capitalism advanced here provides a different perspective on state theories. A curious feature of these theories is the ease with which they present state and society as separate spheres. While the state is treated as the "public" order of real or imagined general interests, "society" is viewed as the domain of private interests. Given this opposition, society, capital, and the economy often come to function as synonyms of each other. The separation of the political and the social is so deeply embedded in liberal theories of the state that defining the "boundaries" dividing society and state (or the "political system," the term embraced by David Easton and Gabriel Almond in the 1950s) has been a central problem in liberal political theory.[22] While Marxist state theories typically historicize the relation between these separate spheres or domains, their mode of historicizing them reproduces Marx's tendency to identify the expansion of the wealth of nations with the production of value. This conflation of value and wealth reduces the generation of wealth to the capital/labor relation and excludes the role of land, viewed as a social relation, in its formation.

The exclusion of nature has important consequences for Marxist theories of the state. Whether theorists focus on the relationship between the ruling class and state rule (as in instrumentalist and structuralist positions) or

22. For a useful review of liberal conceptualizations of the state that underlines the difficulty of defining the state and of identifying the boundaries that separate it from society, see Mitchell (1991). Mitchell's solution to the problem rests on a Foucauldian conception of the state as the structural effect of dispersed disciplinary formations.

on the form and function of the capitalist state (as in the German derivation-ist school), they generally assume that the state depends on society or capital for its economic resources. Analysts may conceptualize the state in sharply differing ways, viewing it as a cohesive apparatus which fulfills specific "func-tions" for capital, or as a conflict-ridden social complex with contradictory "interests," but they agree that, whatever its form or function, it must rely for its revenues on society.

It is thus not surprising that this prevailing assumption is reproduced without comment in one of the most lucid recent attempts to "retrieve" the Marxist theory of the state. In *Alien Politics: Marxist State Theory Retrieved,* Paul Thomas takes as a given the state's dependence on capital: "One of the reasons why it does make sense to employ the category of the capitalist state is that the state has long been dependent upon the activities of capitalism, and on the accumulation of capital, which is after all the source of its own revenues" (1994:21). On the basis of Giddens's distinction between two forms of authority, command over persons and command over allocable re-sources, Thomas treats the decisive separation of the political and economic spheres as the distinctive feature of capitalist societies. "Command over per-sons and command over resources are separate processes or spheres, falling into different hands, under capitalism." Thomas's argument is complex, but its thrust is unambiguous: in capitalist societies, command over persons rests in the hands of the state, while command over resources lies in the hands of capital. Capitalists need the state to control its citizens, but the state, "after all," needs capital to finance its activities, for capital accumulation is "the source of its revenues" (1993 : 19).

In capitalist societies, an economic surplus is produced by labor under the domination of capital; in a fundamental sense, the revenues of all social actors ultimately depend on capital as the agent that controls the production process. This justifies, at a general level, the notion of the structural depen-dence of the state on capital. Yet the surplus produced by labor under the rule of capital accrues to capitalists as profits but also to landlords as rents and to workers as wages. Moreover, the state often participates directly in the exploitation of labor through its involvement in productive activities and may act as landlord as representative of the nation.

Thus, while it is indeed true that they depend on capital and its profits, states also depend on land and its rents; and both profits and rents derive not just from domestic, but from international activities. If, as Marx suggested, the state, as a general representative of a capitalist society, is an abstract capi-talist, as the sovereign authority over a national territory it plays the role of an abstract landlord. Moreover, these abstract roles assume concrete expression through the state's direct involvement in the economy. Thus, the state can become an active capitalist when it participates directly in financial and productive sectors—often in so-called basic industries such as steel and petrochemicals. It can also effectively become a landlord when it controls natural resources,[23] which in third-world countries are often major means of foreign exchange. In this case, domestic capitalists may come to depend on the resource-rich state for their revenues through multiple forms of state protection and promotion of private industry, from direct export subsidies to high tariffs against imports. Given the varied forms of the state's involvement in the economy of capitalist nations, the boundaries separating the political and the economic spheres in these nations are variously drawn and seldom clear-cut.

Theories of the state, like theories of capitalism, need to be decentered in order to encompass the totality of capitalist states and the global process of their formation. To the extent that state theories have construed the states of advanced capitalist nations as the general model of the capitalist state, the states of peripheral capitalist societies, when they are considered at all, are represented as truncated versions of this model; they are identified by a regime of deficits, not by historical differences.[24] But a unifying view of the global formation of states and of capitalism shows that all national states are constituted as mediators of an order that is simultaneously national and international, political and territorial. This conception does not deny the inequality in power and development among national states or the significance of modular influences among them. Rather, by placing states within a unified temporal and spatial matrix, it views their inequality as the expression of mutually constitutive transcultural exchanges among the allegedly bounded societies they represent.

These considerations inform my analysis of state formation in Venezuela as the Venezuelan state, by virtue of its ownership of the oil-rich subsoil, was turned into a major landlord and capitalist during a period when oil became

---

23. For a discussion of the state's involvement in the oil sector in both metropolitan and third world nations, see Klapp's *The Sovereign Entrepreneur: Oil Policies in Advanced and Less Developed Countries* (1987). Focusing her comparative study on four countries, she approaches the question of why "the governments of seventy-four governments become entrepreneurs in the oil industry rather leave this business to the private sector" (1987:9).

24. It is sufficient to read the excellent synthetic studies of Marxist theory by Carnoy (1984) and Jessop (1982; 1990) to see that "dependent" states, as Carnoy calls them, appear only as imperialized and inferior models of the "normal" capitalist state.

one of the world's most valuable and essential commodities. While my discussion seeks to throw light upon the specific example of Venezuela, my presumption is that the revelation of a unique national formation offers a general illumination, since it reflects upon the circumstances from which other singular national histories spring. I believe this perspective can throw new light on societies also dependent on primary exports for foreign exchange and recast the analysis of struggles over land, which have emphasized the relations between landlords and peasants but have neglected to include the significance of agricultural rents in these relations. Although the identities of most third-world nations have come to be so intimately bound up with specific primary export products that in some cases they have been identified with them—banana (Central America), oil (OPEC nations), coffee (Colombia and Brazil), nitrates and copper (Chile), wheat and cattle (Argentina), and sugar (Cuba)—it has proven difficult to think through the economic, political, and cultural significance of this bond. While the Venezuelan case is exceptional in certain respects, it makes more visible processes that also shape other third-world societies.

As I have suggested, struggles over oil have helped draw the contemporary map of the world. In recognition of oil's crucial role in making our "hydrocarbon societies," a noted analyst of the oil industry proposes that the "twentieth century rightly deserves the title of 'the century of oil'" (Yergin 1991 : 14). At the beginning of this century, the world's most advanced transnational corporations established themselves in Venezuela, a precariously organized agricultural society, and began pumping oil from its subsoil. In a few years this society became the world's major oil exporter and came to see itself as an "oil nation." In the following chapters I examine this transfiguration, focusing on the state's capture of oil wealth and on the transformative effects of its circulation within the body politic.

2

THE NATION'S
TWO BODIES

The future of the nation will be written with oil. This liquid will penetrate
into all our cells and will take possession of our destiny.[1]

Domingo Alberto Rangel

The essence of a nation is that all individuals have many things in common, and also that they are obliged to have already forgotten many things.

Ernest Renan

Lest we forget Renan's insight that "forgetting is a crucial factor in the
creation of a nation" (1990:11), Benedict Anderson has reminded us
that national imaginings conjure up a timeless image of the nation by inducing specific historical amnesias (1991). Through selective rememberings
that mythologize a nation's past and displace from consciousness conflictual
aspects of its historical origins, these national imaginings evoke a sacralized
conception of the nation as an eternal community.

At the close of the twentieth century, Venezuela is commonly identified
as an oil nation.[2] Strange as this may seem, a mere material commodity serves
to represent its identity as a national community. The remarkable fact that
this rather common manner of identifying a neocolonial nation by its major
export product seems unremarkably natural only highlights the need to understand why some nations have become so bonded to some commodities
that they have come to be identified by them.

Although in Venezuela the coupling of nation and oil occurred as recently as the 1930s, it has achieved the force of a timeless reality. As if it
were an imperceptible cloud, oil wealth enveloped Venezuelan society, leaving its fresh mark everywhere and yet making its presence seem part of an

---

1. "El futuro del país se escribirá con petróleo. Este líquido penetrará en todos nuestros poros y
llegará a adueñarse de nuestro destino" (Rangel 1970:9).

2. I am tempted to say, "Venezuela is *still* imagined as an oil nation." Growing poverty, political
instability, inflation and deepening uncertainty concerning the future have transformed, if not
eroded, the meanings attached to Venezuela as an oil nation. Yet opinion polls taken in 1995 and
1996 indicate that Venezuelans still believe that their country is wealthy and that they are entitled to
its wealth. Each return of rising oil prices, as in 1996, fuels that belief.

immemorial landscape. In this chapter I wish to unsettle amnesiac nationalist rememberings in order to call back the time when Venezuela was first
imagined as an oil nation. In these forgotten memories I hope to find clues
that may help explain the significance of this manner of imagining the nation
for the transformation of the state both as an ideal complex and as an institutional construct.

FORGETTING JUAN VICENTE GÓMEZ

The abrupt transformation of Venezuela from an indebted agricultural nation into a wealthy oil exporter took place during General Juan Vicente
Gómez's rule. While Gómez provided the oil companies with what was
widely regarded as an exceptionally advantageous investment climate, the
oil companies established political and economic conditions that helped
consolidate his dictatorial rule and turned him into one of America's wealthiest men. During this formative period, the Gómez regime and the domiciliated foreign oil industry conditioned each other. Together, they defined
the social landscape in which Venezuelans began to recognize the elusive
presence of oil and to fashion their political identity as citizens of an oil
nation.

Yet in the public national imagination as well as in official historiography, Venezuela emerged as a modern nation essentially unpolluted by its
links to the Gómez period. This purification was largely the effect of the
ideological work of emerging political actors who drew a sharp demarcation
between Gómez's privatization of the state and their project for democratizing it. This demarcation was presented as a historical turning point, as
in Mariano Picón Salas's frequently repeated dictum that Gómez's death
marked Venezuela's entrance into the twentieth century. Up to this day, this
phrase has circulated as a mythical charter of Venezuela's birth as a modern
nation.[3]

If a trick of prestidigitation could turn Gómez's death into Venezuela's
magical entrance into modernity, the same type of trick converted his life
into a model of the nation's primitive past. Yet both tricks depended on con-
juring away the links that joined the oil industry to the Venezuelan state
during the Gómez regime. As we have seen, for playwright José Ignacio
Cabrujas oil wealth made possible such magical tricks. In the hands of politicians oil wealth created the illusion that modernity could be brought to

---

3. Mariano Picón Salas (1969; 1976) was a noted essayist closely identified with Acción Democrática.

Venezuela as if pulled out of a hat. Cabrujas singles out two statesmen as Venezuela's foremost magicians: General Marcos Pérez Jiménez (1948–58), who "decreed the myth of progress," and Carlos Andrés Pérez (1974–79), who transformed progress into a "hallucination."

I take Cabrujas's forgetting of Juan Vicente Gómez as symptomatic of a collective amnesia. Dominant accounts, intent on signaling a disjuncture between the regimes established after Gómez's death and his dictatorial rule, have buried from view the extent to which the contemporary state rests on a structure built during the Gómez regime. Yet Venezuela's "modern democracy," feverishly constructed in opposition to Gómez's "primitive dictatorship," is in effect its antithesis, the other side of the same oil coin. Despite the significant differences between Gómez's dictatorial rule and the liberal regimes erected against it, both took form as the state of an oil nation. I will explore here how this common form took shape during the Gómez regime and its immediate aftermath by examining oil policies (up to 1943) and struggles for democracy against Gómez's "backward" rule (focusing on formulations produced in 1936).

The purpose of initiating this drama about the Venezuelan state with Gómez, however, is not so much to restore repressed memories as to recast hegemonic rememberings in light of what they forget: the moral of the drama is revelatory, not restitutive. By bringing to light the state's earthly foundation as it was laid down during the Gómez regime, we will be better placed to understand the conditions that have both enabled and circumscribed Venezuela's long-lasting democracy, as well as the unprecedented moral and economic crisis that, since the 1980s, has eroded its basis.

THE FIRST MAGICIAN: JUAN VICENTE GÓMEZ

In 1902, Venezuela's ports were blocked by the combined navies of England, Italy, and Germany, which threatened to invade if the government's foreign debts were not paid, and the port of Puerto Cabello was bombarded at the end of that year.[4] Yet in 1930, in honor of the hundredth anniversary of Simón Bolívar's death, the Venezuelan government paid its entire foreign debt.[5] In the context of a history of state financial shortages which reflected

4. Venezuela's foreign debt reached Bs. 189 million in 1900. In 1901 the government, suffering a steady decline of fiscal income, was forced to suspend payment of interests on the foreign debt, which steadily increased, reaching Bs. 224.7 million in 1905 (Pardo 1973:162).

5. By that time the debt amounted only to Bs. 23.76 millions at a yearly 3 percent interest rate. This gesture, "used to intensify praise of Gómez, lacked an economic rationale" (Pardo 1973:180).

the government's limited control over a weak and fragmented national economy, this was a rather exceptional happening. However, it was the kind of achievement that came to be expected from the spectacular rule of Juan Vicente Gómez, who seized leadership of the government in 1908 and managed to centralize and control state power until he died in bed in 1935 at the age of 76.[6]

According to Ramón Díaz Sánchez, a perceptive Venezuelan writer, Gómez's death was his "last miracle": after twenty-seven years of rule people had come to believe that his death "would never happen" (Díaz Sánchez 1973:24; López 1985:659–60). During his lifetime, through a succession of extraordinary performances that wove his private and public lives into a singular model of state power (Skurski 1995), Gómez produced his own rule as the most astounding miracle of all in the republican history of Venezuela, a nation torn by civil war and warring caudillos since it became independent in 1821.

How to explain this miracle, or more significant, how to account for Gómez's rule being imagined as one? Until recently, a sharp polarization of the Venezuelan ideological climate has rendered these questions difficult to answer. As I indicated, the establishment of democratic rule entailed a reconstruction of history that posits a sharp opposition between Venezuela's primitive past, represented by Gómez, and the liberal regimes that followed it; within this scheme, the Pérez Jiménez dictatorship from 1948 to 1958 is presented as a dark parenthesis, a sort of temporary resurgence of the turbid past within the enlightened present.

Yet it is no mere coincidence that by 1930, the year when Gómez paid the national foreign debt, Venezuela had consolidated its position as the world's leading oil exporter. Venezuela's first major oil deposit was discovered in 1914; oil exports began in 1918; and by 1928 the country had become the world's second largest oil producer and the top oil exporter (Pardo 1973: 172). Although the state's oil income in 1924 scarcely reached Bs. 6 million, by 1930 it increased more than fiftyfold to over Bs. 300 million. Supported politically and financially by the oil industry, Gómez surrounded himself during his twenty-seven-year rule with some of the most distinguished

---

According to Pardo, it made more economic sense to invest this money productively than to pay a debt that was being paid regularly at very low interest.

6. Gómez came to power in 1908 through a bloodless coup d'état. As a result of his importance as a military leader during the civil war that led to Cipriano Castro's ascent to power in 1902, Gómez became Castro's vice president. When Castro left for Europe in 1908 for medical reasons, Gómez seized power.

professionals of his time and implemented a number of economic and social reforms which modified significantly the economic and political foundations of Venezuela and helped consolidate his ruthless and idiosyncratic dictatorship. Paradoxically, the most modern industry of the world contributed to consolidating Gómez's autocratic rule as a model of the traditional Latin American caudillo.

As the Gómez regime was redefined as a backward dictatorship that stood in opposition to Venezuela's civilizing democracy, its analysis was shaped by the ideological need to construe it as the embodiment of primitivity. Mariano Picón Salas, as I said, defined what came to be the official view of history with his oft-repeated assertion that Gómez's death marked Venezuela's entrance into the twentieth century. Set in opposition to modern Venezuela, Gómez has stood as an internal other against which contemporary Venezuela is evaluated (Skurski 1994). Gómez became the embodiment of democracy's antithesis. As a result, the study of Gómez's rule has been covered by the same obscurity that has been attributed to Gómez himself. Yet the intangible ideological barrier that has hidden Gómez from view, as Skurski has shown, has also surrounded him with an aura of mystery that heightens the fascination that his charged political figure has never ceased to exert. Always a submerged presence, the specific form of Gómez's enduring appeal has fluctuated with changing circumstances. Until the recent crisis, it has been hard to break through the wall separating Gómez from the more liberal regimes that followed his rule. This wall has cracked as a result of the general deterioration of the economy and the loss of faith in Venezuela's democratic institutions. Through these cracks Gómez is being viewed in a different light. The Gómez period is no longer a taboo subject, or it is at least a less forbidding one; new studies are exploring the period and removing the dark mantle that had covered Gómez's rule.

In a special issue of a history journal dedicated to the regime on the fiftieth anniversary of Gómez's death, Venezuelan historian Elías Pino Iturrieta argues, in an article provocatively entitled "To Kill Gómez," that the aim of current historiography is to unsettle both the (dominant) image of Gómez's regime as Venezuela's Dark Ages and the (repressed) view that he was a model of peaceful and productive rule (1985a:535). Gómez was never buried, Pino Iturrieta explains, because his rule ended not by means of a collective upheaval but with his natural death. His unburied presence has therefore permeated Venezuela's collective life in unacknowledged ways. According to Pino Iturrieta, "Every five years, with each new government, our life is determined by the rule of Gómez-like figures who have no links to civil society" (1985a:534). Not restricted to the figure of the president, these Gómez-like characters are "state functionaries at every level" who "model themselves after him, holding power and distributing favors as in the past" (1985a:534). Gómez "must be killed," he claims, and released into the open so that his figure could be finally recognized for what it was. He proposes to see the Gómez period as the origin of modern Venezuela: "the first chapter of contemporary Venezuela" (1985a:535).

In another account, the origin of Venezuela's modernity is pushed even further back. Criticizing both Picón Salas's dictum that Venezuela entered the twentieth century in 1936 and AD's notion that it did so on 18 October 1945 (the date of its coup d'état against General Medina), Dávila suggests that the origins of Venezuela's modernity must be traced to the rule of General Guzmán Blanco in the last quarter of the nineteenth century (1992:57). During the times that he ruled (1870–77, 1879–84, and 1886–88), Guzmán Blanco unified the national currency, established a national printing press, promoted the construction of roads and waterworks, expanded the railway system, and built a large number of monumental buildings.

Although the new revisionist history is succeeding in illuminating anew an old territory, it is also casting its own shadow over it.[7] If earlier the emphasis was placed on differentiating Gómez as a primitive tyrant from the liberal regimes that succeeded him, now the revisionist tendency is to focus on their continuities. Debates center on issues of periodization and typically include efforts to specify the precise timing of Gómez's historical death. If until recently his biological death marked Venezuela's entrance into modernity, now that Gómez is no longer the unquestionable embodiment of primitivity, discerning the origin of Venezuela's modernity has invited new answers.

My contribution to this collective effort involves not an alternative trac-

---

7. Countering the notion that Gómez was a primitive dictator, in *El tirano liberal,* Manuel Caballero, a noted Marxist historian, portrays him as a liberal tyrant, a contradictory embodiment which expresses the unresolved tensions between autocracy and liberalism permeating Gómez's rule (1992). Tomás Polanco Alcántara's more traditional biographical work presents a nuanced image of Gómez that shows the complexity of his persona, including evidence that unsettles such myths as Gómez's illiteracy (1980). Yolanda Segnini has highlighted how Gómez surrounded himself by some of the most outstanding intellectuals and professionals of the period, whose projects of health, educational, and economic reform he supported (1982). Ramón Velázquez has reconstructed through fictional dialogues Gómez's intimate subjectivity (1988). While in this chapter I restrict my focus to certain aspects of Gómez's rule, I have been influenced by these works, and particularly by Skurski's pioneering analysis of Gómez's model of rule (1994; forthcoming).

ing of Venezuela's modern origins but rather an interrogation of the categories used to draw these landmarks. The "historicism that projected the West as History" (Prakash 1995:1475) has constructed Europe as the home of modernity and the rest of the world as only its belated recipient with no alternative than to catch up or remain in a backward state. Prevailing geopolitical taxonomies reflect and reinforce worldwide processes of polarization that essentialize rather than historicize difference; nations are placed in the slots of imperial taxonomies by virtue of their allegedly sociocultural characteristics without taking into account the fact that these national characters are the transcultural products of interrelated histories. While the modern West has been made to include economically successful non-European nations (Chomsky refers to Japan as an "honorary European" [1991:13]), the third world is condemned to remain in an eternal state of "transition," if not of regression. Many third-world countries, now abandoned by the imperial powers that once exploited them, are seen as intrinsically unable to chart new paths for themselves or to tread along the historical tracks set by History's protagonists. Trapped in a historical limbo, they are presented as the quintessential embodiment of primitivity or of the banality of politics in the postcolony (Mbembe 1992).[8]

The self-fashioning of Europe as the home of modernity has been premised on the colonization of vast regions of the world that are seen as backward and in need of civilization. The ambivalent Latin American discourse of modernity, in its rejection of European domination but its internalization of its civilizing mission, has taken the form of a process of self-colonization which assumes distinct forms in different political contexts and historical periods. In this respect, it is, like nationalism, a "derivative discourse" (Chatterjee 1986) that simultaneously rejects Europe's imperial hegemony but reinscribes its changing values and rationality, except, as we need to remember, that the periphery is not just the passive recipient but frequently the coauthor of this

---

8. For Mbembe's views, see his "The Banality of Power and the Aesthetics of Vulgarity in the Postcolony" (1992) and the discussion of this article in the following issue of *Public Culture*. In my contribution to this exchange, I suggest that there is a connection between modern modes of essentializing cultural difference and certain forms of postmodern analysis that refuse to locate power in historically constituted structural relations. I argue that this approach, "directed against metanarratives of history, produces disjointed mininarratives which reinforce dominant worldviews; reacting against determinisms, it presents free-floating events; refusing to fix identity in structural categories, it essentializes identity through difference; resisting the location of power in structures or institutions, it diffuses it throughout society and ultimately dissolves it" (1992:99–100). From either modern or postmodern perspectives, the periphery is typically viewed as modernity's Other.

allegedly derivative discourse, as Anderson reminds us in relation to nationalism itself.[9]

If we see the formation of the modern world as a unitary global process that has entailed the mutual constitution of core and peripheries, the project of provincializing Western modernity (Chakrabarty 1991; Rafael 1993) involves as well recognizing the periphery as the site of subaltern modernities. The aim is neither to homogenize nor to catalogue modernity's multiple forms, least of all to uplift the periphery by semantic fiat, but to undo imperial taxonomies that fetishize Europe as the sole bearer of modernity and erases the transcultural constitution of imperial centers and colonized peripheries. The criticism of the locus of modernity from its margins creates conditions for an inherently unsettling critique of modernity itself. Undoing the periphery's depiction as the incarnation of barbarous backwardness demystifies as well Europe's self-representation as the embodiment of universal reason and historical progress.[10]

Far from the blinding light of Europe's Enlightenment, among peoples who wear the scars of modern violence as a second skin, it becomes difficult to clear from sight or to displace onto foreign Others the barbarous underside of modern civilization. In Latin America, from Argentina to Mexico, the incessant insistence upon the need to protect imported civilization from local primitivity reveals both the limits of Europe's civilizing mission and the extent to which its rationality has become part of Latin America's self-fashioning. In societies formed by the violence of a culture of conquest, the state's appearance as civilization's agent can hardly conceal the violence that sustains its power.

Writing in the midst of a Europe engulfed by its own savagery, Walter Benjamin grasped the horror before him with the assertion that "there is no document of civilization which is not at the same time a document of barbarism" (1969:256). Reading Latin American history as a double-sided

---

9. In the second edition of *Imagined Communities,* Benedict Anderson explains that his intent had been to stress the New World origins of nationalism but that his critics, "accustomed to the conceit that everything important in the modern world originated in Europe, too easily took 'second generation' nationalisms (Hungarian, Czech, Greek, Polish, etc.) as the starting point in their modelling" (1991:xiii). He adds, "I was startled to discover in many of the notices of Imagined Communities that this Eurocentric provincialism remained quite undisturbed, and that the crucial chapter on the originating Americas was largely ignored. Unfortunately, I have found no better 'instant' solution to this problem than to retitle Chapter 4 as 'Creole Pioneers'" (1991:xiii).

10. As some observers have noted, the critique of modernity cannot be separated from decolonizing struggles after World War II (Young 1990). I have sought to relate the critiques of modernity and Orientalism in a discussion of Occidentalist modalities of representation (1996).

document reveals the unity of reason and violence that lies at the root of its formation as Europe's periphery. By historicizing the specific forms in which metropolitan civilization has been the mother of colonial barbarism,[11] we can recast our understanding of centers and peripheries alike. From this perspective we may begin to see the rule of Gómez not just as an obstacle to modern progress in Venezuela, or as its effect and condition, but as a form of modernity that recasts its (one-sided) metropolitan rendition.

OIL IN VENEZUELA

The existence of what we know today as oil in the territory that now is Venezuela was known before the arrival of Columbus by the natives of the land, who used it for medicinal purposes. The first written reference to oil appeared in the chronicles of Gonzalo Fernández de Oviedo y Valdez in 1535, and already by 1839 Venezuelans were carrying out scientific studies of oil in order to promote its development (Martínez 1973 : 31−53). The first oil-producing well in the world was drilled in Pennsylvania in 1859; six years later the first oil concession was granted in Venezuela (Martínez 1973 : 65). While oil production expanded rapidly in the United States after 1859, reflecting not only the abundance of oil but also the power of U.S. capital, in Venezuela it did not begin on a large commercial scale until the second decade of the twentieth century. Until then foreign interest in Venezuela had focused on asphalt; local capitalists, who had been the first to exploit oil, did not have sufficient resources to carry out the necessary investments in exploration and drilling to compete internationally.

The expansion of the world economy at the beginning of this century created worldwide demand for oil. Oil became the central commodity of the capitalist system when World War I proved the superiority of motorized vehicles and the mass production of the automobile began to redefine forms of production and consumption, reconfiguring the very structure of social space in the modern world. At this time, increasing European demand for oil turned Venezuela into an attractive investment site. While in the United States, John D. Rockefeller's Standard Oil of New Jersey (now Exxon), facing an anarchic mass of private landowners, achieved supremacy by monopolizing oil's distribution (the "downstream") in Europe, Henri

11. Markoff and Baretta, in a pioneering discussion of the colonization of space in the cattle frontiers of the Americas, advanced this project by showing how in the Americas "civilization" was indeed the "mother" of "barbarism" (1978).

Deterding's Royal Dutch Shell led the control of oil fields overseas (the "upstream").

In Venezuela, General Juan Vicente Gómez, facing a "chaotic economy" (Sullivan 1976:249) after overthrowing General Cipriano Castro in 1908, sought to restore order by inviting foreign capital to invest with the guarantee of labor peace and flexible business conditions. Gómez only managed to attract investments from oil companies, but he reciprocated by maintaining "the most liberal oil policy in all of Latin America" (Sullivan 1976: 258). Deterding's Shell, and later Rockefeller's Standard Oil, as well as other firms, invested heavily in Venezuela. Gómez, propped up by their support, kept his promise: he preserved unrestrictive conditions and guaranteed "social peace" during the twenty-seven years of his ruthless rule. By the late 1930s, Standard Oil and Shell had come to control 85 percent of oil extraction in Venezuela (50 and 35 percent, respectively).

As foreign oil companies immersed themselves in the business of extracting oil in Venezuela, the state acquired a new role as a national landlord. This role entailed its expansion into an increasingly complex system of institutions and rules—mining codes, tax legislation, bureaucratic institutions, government agencies, and ideologies of rule—designed to regulate oil's exploitation and to retain within Venezuela a share of the profits obtained by the oil companies. In this novel capacity, the state also assumed a new relationship with society as manager of income derived from the nation's major source of wealth. As it began to affect society in unprecedented ways, the petroleum state became the central referent for heightened public discussions about the role of the state in an oil nation.

THE STATE SYSTEM

At the beginning of this century the state was so weak and precarious as a national institution that its stability and legitimacy were constantly at risk. Without a national army or an effective bureaucracy, in an indebted country that lacked a national road network or an effective system of communication, the state appeared as an unfulfilled project whose institutional form remained limited to localized sites of power with but partial dominion over the nation's territory and sway over its citizens.

Under Gómez the state underwent a metamorphosis. As the representative of the nation in negotiations with the foreign oil industry, the state became intimately tied to its presence in the national territory and benefited in multiple ways from its association with it. In addition to political support and legitimacy, the oil industry provided a growing proportion of the state's income, first through import duties and the sale of concessions, and in the 1920s through the taxation of oil exports. Continuing what Veliz has examined as a Latin American "centralist" tradition (1980), but propped up by the oil industry, the state implemented a series of administrative reforms, some of which had been initiated by presidents Guzmán Blanco at the end the nineteenth century and Cipriano Castro at the beginning of this century, which enabled it to increase its fiscal income (Quintero 1985; Vallenilla 1986), develop a national army (Ziems 1979), promote the integration of the territory through a national road system (Arcila Farías 1974; Martín Frechilla 1994), and make and enforce decisions that affected the national community. Like many nineteenth-century caudillos in Venezuela, Gómez became the head of state as a result of his military and political skills; but by becoming the ruler of an oil nation, he stabilized his rule and consolidated his power.[12]

The influence of the oil industry cannot be reduced to the financial contribution of oil exports to the state. There is consensus among historians that Gómez offered favorable conditions to oil companies after 1908 and that they reciprocated by providing him with critical political and economic support. Needless to say, during the second decade of the twentieth century agricultural exports continued to be Venezuela's main source of foreign exchange. Cárdenas's reorganization of the Treasury Ministry expanded and organized the state's tax base and increased its income (Quintero 1985). While this reform, together with the expansion of the army (Ziems 1979), continued a long-standing tradition of state centralization, it cannot be seen in isolation from the powerful presence of the oil industry in Venezuela and from the growing political and economic support it provided to the state. Salazar Carrillo notes that statistics covering oil's impact during this period must also include payment for concessions, indirect taxes, and import duties, which are difficult to determine given the available data. According to him, one additional difficulty is that at that time the state could not be readily separated from Gómez: "The Venezuelan state was not, during those years, easily distinguishable from the clan of Juan Vicente Gómez, which dominated the

---

12. The effects of the oil industry on society are multiple but not readily discernible. For an attempt to quantify the economic "contribution" and "effects" of the oil industry in Venezuela which includes this period, see Salazar Carrillo (1994: 33–103). Pacheco correctly notes that oil exports provided significant state income only in the 1920s but then argues that the oil industry could not be seen as the source of Gómez's power, at least in the early phase of his regime. Instead, he underlines the importance of Gómez's consolidation of the army and the reorganization of public finances under minister Román Cárdenas in the 1910s, which he sees as part of a process of national unification which started with Cipriano Castro (1984).

country . . . the compensation for the use of the concessions went to Gómez's favorites, and possibly to him as well through them" (1992:39–40). Baptista has also noted the limitations of statistical information for this period, including the lack of data on the companies' benefits before 1936 (1991:105). It is even more difficult to measure the extent to which the oil companies' support protected Gómez from his enemies and made him even more indispensable among his supporters.

During this period, the state's income shifted from resources derived from import duties and the taxation of agricultural products cultivated by private producers to rents produced by the sale of a natural resource that belonged to the nation. Coffee remained, until 1925, Venezuela's main export and a basic sector of the national economy. Yet while during this period coffee production expanded in Colombia and Brazil, reaffirming its significance in their economies and strengthening the social classes associated with it, it remained stationary in Venezuela, in part because circulating oil rents began to shift the focus of profit-making activities from agricultural production in the countryside to commerce and real estate development in urban centers (de la Plaza 1970; see also Rodríguez 1983; Roseberry 1983; Ascanio 1985). In less than a decade, oil displaced coffee as Venezuela's major export product. Mining regulations reflected the changing domestic perception of the significance of the oil industry. In turn, these regulations, as they increased domestic control over the industry and participation in its profits, consolidated its centrality.

"OUR NATIONAL WEALTH" AND GÓMEZ'S OIL POLICIES

The complex history of oil industry regulation has been told in detail from different perspectives.[13] My concern here is not to trace this history once again but to explore changing representations of the nation which these regulations expressed and helped bring about. While Gómez always offered flexible conditions to the oil industry, as time passed he sought to increase the state's oil income. At first Gómez placed practically no demands on foreign capital. The 1910 Mining Law only required that companies pay a small tax, no different from taxes paid on other economic activities. It was a minimal tax—Bs. 2 per ton of oil and Bs. 1 per hectare of land—to be paid contractually during the duration of the concession.

13. Betancourt (1979), Liewen (1961), MacBeth (1983), Malavé Mata (1974), Martínez (1966; 1973; 1980), Mejía Alarcón (1972), Mommer (1983; 1986), Pérez Alfonzo (1971), Tugwell (1975), Salazar Carrillo (1994), Vallenilla (1973).

Plaque commemorating the initiation of oil production in Venezuela: "Zumaque I, the well that started the era of commercial production in the country. The oil industry began to participate in the progress of Venezuela with the start of production on 31 July 1914." Only the logo indicates that this plaque was installed by Shell Oil Co.

In part these extremely liberal conditions reflected the initial uncertainty about the possibility of developing the oil industry in Venezuela. At the outset there developed a system by which the local elite mediated between the government and the oil companies. The government granted land concessions to the local elite land, and the elite, in turn, sold these concessions to the oil companies at a high profit. In effect, "the early history of the Venezuelan oil industry shows the difficulty encountered by the oil concessionaires in attracting foreign capital. Only after considerable time and effort were they able to transfer their oil concessions to foreign companies"

(MacBeth 1983 : 13). This situation began to change in 1913 when Shell made its entry into Venezuela, buying two large concessions that had been given to two members of Gómez's clique (the Valladares and the Vigas concessions) in a transaction that Shell's Deterding called "our most colossal deal" (MacBeth 1983 : 12). The presence of Shell in Venezuela "with its ample resources was not only welcomed by the oil concessionaires, but by the Gómez administration too, which had tried since the December 1908 coup to encourage the development of the mining and oil industries" (MacBeth 1983 : 13).

As awareness of the magnitude of Venezuela's oil reserves increased, so did local efforts to participate in the industry's profits. These efforts resulted in the closer regulation of the oil industry, as well as in the centralization in the executive branch of decision making power regarding it. In 1923 Gómez created the Compañia Venezolana de Petróleo, S.A. (CVP), which monopolized all oil concessions and negotiated the sale of these concessions and national reserves to the oil companies. The major source of oil profits for Venezuelans throughout this period had been the sale of concessions to foreign oil companies. Since 1908, oil regulations had therefore focused on this aspect. The creation of the CVP consolidated a shift of power from private landowners, who as recipients of concessions had been mediators between the state and the oil companies, to the state, which, personified by Gómez, practically monopolized this business for his own benefit and that of his entourage of relatives and allies.

The most significant change, however, occurred between 1917 and 1922, when Development Minister Gumersindo Torres issued regulations intended to increase the state's participation in the industry's profits. In 1920 he drafted the first oil law, which legally distinguished oil extraction from other mining activities. Torres was not an expert in this field but a medical doctor with strong nationalist convictions. His regulatory work focused on the extractive character of the oil industry. After studying the oil legislation of Mexico and the United States, he concluded that Venezuela was entitled to receive a significant share of the oil industry's profits. He claimed that this was not an industry like any other because nationally owned natural resources were removed forever and sold overseas. Thus, oil industry taxes should not be seen as ordinary taxes but as the means by which the state asserts its right to participate in the industry's profits.[14] In effect, Torres, in-

---

14. Despite Betancourt's opposition to the Gómez regime, he praised Torres as a fierce nationalist who confronted those who sold out Venezuela (1975 : 17).

spired by the rights conferred to private landowners by the U.S. legislation of the oil industry, was claiming for the nation, as landlord, the right to charge a rent for the use of its subsoil. Through Torres, ironically, "ground rent, as it was developed under conditions of private property in the U.S., became the criteria to define Venezuelan national property" (Mommer 1983:27, 1986:65–73).

The new oil legislation both reflected and was instrumental in effecting a transformation in the conception of the nation. Economic discourse began to shift its focus from private agricultural production to public mining rent capture. For Torres, oil, seen as an "article" that played an important role in "universal industry," was part of "national wealth." The state, as representative of the nation, was responsible to this and future generations of Venezuelans for safeguarding this "sure source of wealth" (1917:xviii). In 1917 he justified a policy of halting further oil concessions in terms of the state's responsibility to protect the nation's wealth for the welfare of future generations. The new regulations would be drafted after the ministry had "obtained all the knowledge required to evaluate the situation reasonably, so that future generations will not be entitled to criticize us for not knowing how to safeguard our national wealth" (1917:xviii). The notion that oil constituted "our national wealth" and that the role of the state was to "safeguard it" eternally for the nation, were the foundations of an emergent political discourse of national identity.

The Gómez government was torn by conflicting demands as it began to rely on oil income. On the one hand, it sought to increase its revenues, for which it required the development of its regulatory capacity and of a legitimizing nationalist discourse. Yet this was a personalistic government with an extremely narrow social base. It neither sought, nor could it afford, to antagonize the oil companies, and it remained highly responsive to their pressures.

In part as a result of this tension, Torres was ousted from the ministry in 1922 but was returned to his post in 1929. Gómez could not do either without the backing of the oil companies or the support of the small urban professional and commercial elite which sought to promote the nation's economic modernization. The laws and regulations enacted during the Gómez regime reflect this conflict between the particularistic interests and limited mobilizing capacity of the personalistic state and the new demands for political and economic development made by urban sectors whose growth depended on maximizing oil rent distribution.

The 1920 law which regulated oil concessions until 1943 established an average royalty of only 9 percent. Gómez, in addition, granted the oil companies tax exemptions on their imports. Thus, during the period from 1923 to 1930, the oil companies paid the government less in royalties than the value of the exemptions the government had granted them on their imported goods. As Gumersindo Torres said, "The companies exploited the petroleum, and the government paid them for carrying it away" (Vallenilla 1973: 89; also Betancourt 1975: 23).

Gómez's liberal treatment of the oil companies was also a consequence of the mercantile relation which existed between the ruling elite and the oil industry. For this elite the commerce in oil concessions was the principal source of gain from the oil industry. According to an observer, throughout the Gómez regime, the concessions policy was characterized by transactions of an unparalleled corruption. Thousands of concession lots were acquired by more than a hundred companies through an intermediary system. Gómez granted leases to his favorites, probably for a "consideration"—and the favorites then sold them to the companies at exorbitant profits (Karlsson 1975: 73).

These lenient regulations reflect Gómez's reliance on the oil companies for political support. Backed by these powerful firms, he used the state as a private government. Gómez became the largest landowner in Venezuela and one of the wealthiest men on the continent. He "took exclusive control of the soap, paper, cotton, milk, butter and match industries; he became the only meat supplier for the port of Puerto Cabello and other urban markets, and was the major shareholder of the Compañia Anónima Venezolana de Navegación" (Sullivan 1976: 266).

THE PRIVATIZATION AND CENTRALIZATION OF THE LANDLORD STATE

As a consequence of this private system of commerce there developed a close connection between the growth of the oil industry and of Gómez's fortune. A historian points to "one advantage" in this close association: "Now the development and monitoring of the country's oil and mining industries would be linked directly to the personal gain of Gómez's family, thus ensuring that the head of the country was intimately informed on the progress and problems of the industry" (MacBeth 1983: 17). For most Venezuelans, however, this advantage did not translate into their individual benefit but instead heightened their sense that national wealth was being monopolized by a small clique. As this historian acknowledges, the "greater awareness of the country's oil potential had the pernicious effect of increasing the corruption and intrigue amongst Gómez's family and entourage, the consequences of which would be felt until 1935" (1983 : 17).

As oil production expanded, the center of gravity of the economy shifted from the cultivated soil to the naturally existing subsoil, from private agricultural producers to the state as landlord. Agricultural ground rent, which was distributed through economic competition among regional coffee and cacao producers, was now displaced by mining ground rent, which was monopolized and distributed at its own discretion by the central state. With this shift, political power, once fragmented among contending regional caudillos, became centralized in the state. Backed by the power of oil wealth, Gómez consolidated his own political power and decided on key appointments, distributed rewards and punishments, and came to exercise personal control over every branch of his government.

As the oil industry expanded in a society whose state had very limited institutional capacities, it promoted the concentration of state powers in the figure of the president. The collusion between foreign oil companies and a regional caudillo brought together the most dynamic corporations of the capitalist world and the most characteristic form of rule in nineteenth-century Latin America. As in many other instances in Latin America's history, the paradoxical result of the region's engagement with modernity was to reinforce practices and institutions considered to be traditional but which were the transcultural product of previous exchanges between European and American cultures.[15]

The more the state expanded institutionally and tightened its control over the body politic, the more Gómez appeared to be the source of its growth and the embodiment of its power. If on the public stage of politics Gómez played the role of a nineteenth-century caudillo, this stage was propped up by the oil industry. At a time when oil's presence began imperceptibly to permeate the body politic, the state, personified in the figure of Gómez, expanded its role as mediator between the national and

15. Ortiz's notion of "transculturation" (1995) highlights the "constructed" dimension (Poole 1994 : 126) of "invented" traditions (Hobsbawm and Ranger 1983). Manuel Moreno Fraginals provides a dramatic illustration of the collusion between "modernity" and "tradition" in his extraordinary historical interpretation of Cuba's sugar industry in *The Sugar Mill* (1976). He shows how the introduction of such modern technologies as steam engines at the point of production in the sugar mill intensified slave labor in the cane fields. Needless to say, while by the nineteenth century slave labor had come to be seen as a traditional aspect of Cuban culture, its development in the Caribbean during the previous centuries was construed as an aspect of Europe's civilizatory mission.

the international domains and between the social and the natural orders.[16] Through the effects of this double mediation, the powers of numerous social actors and institutions were condensed in Gómez. His figure, and the state he represented, was elevated above society as a transcendental agency, and its sacralized appearance was projected as the original source of these powers and the single expression of the national will.

To the extent that the state gained new capacities, its form and function came to matter as never before: it mattered how it was organized, what kind of access (some) people had to it, what decisions were made and who benefited from them. The growing public recognition of the importance of oil wealth as a collective patrimony focused attention on the state as the agent responsible for regulating the oil industry and allocating oil income. Whether positioned inside or outside the institutional structures of the state apparatus, Venezuelans learned to take the perspective of the state when they addressed their nation, to recognize themselves as citizens of an oil nation, and to assume the totalizing viewpoint normatively ascribed to the state as the nation's representative. This unified perspective facilitated the construction of the state as a single representative of a unified people.

With the state transfigured into the national landlord, political struggles came to center on the state's role as the representative of an oil nation. Since the 1930s, oil became a necessary reference point in the articles, political programs, and books written by Venezuelan politicians. As new social sectors sought to change the state, not just to replace its leaders, political struggles became more properly struggles about politics—linking contests over rulers to competing visions of rule. Oil was at the center of these visions. As the oil business became a state business, the politics of oil became the business of politics.

FROM CLASSICAL LIBERALISM TO RENTIER LIBERALISM

As I have argued, the unprecedented duration of the Gómez dictatorship was conditioned by the political support and economic resources given to his

---

16. Gómez made good use of modern technologies and resources. For instance, he used the expanded telegraph system as an intelligence resource to monitor his adversaries through a vast network of well-placed informants. His ability to defuse his enemies' plans added to the mysterious aura constructed around his public persona and enhanced his image as a powerful caudillo. Oil money, of course, was one of his most effective modern resources. According to Rourke, money was for Gómez "the golden key." "Money was always, to him, the greatest thing in the world, the only thing worth striving for. He thought that everyone felt the same way. He was convinced that that there was no real honesty of motive in the behavior of his enemies. They were simply out to overthrow him so that the money he enjoyed would become theirs" ([1936] 1969:192).

regime by the international oil industry. From 1908 until his death in 1935, Gómez managed to subdue local caudillos and concentrate power in the executive. He created a national army, built a road system that initiated the economic integration of the nation, developed an effective state bureaucracy and filled its top posts with his supporters, transformed rivals into allies by granting them status without power, and disposed of his enemies through exile, prison, or death. As a result, his regime achieved the nation's political and administrative unification and its first sustained political stability since independence in 1821.

Chronic political strife and the constant disruption of economic activities throughout the nineteenth century had made for unstable political regimes. The erosion of the economic basis of the landed oligarchy through war and civil conflict had turned the military into the major source of social and political power. "The landed aristocracy was decimated in the nineteenth-century civil wars: property and position depended heavily on political power, not the reverse" (Levine 1979:65). The expansion of the oil industry in the 1920s radically increased the extent of the state's power while intensifying its personal nature. In the context of a poor, agrarian society long torn by civil strife, this increase reinforced the prevailing tendency to view political power as the property of the ruler. Juan Vicente Gómez treated the state as a private government and depicted the nation as an hacienda writ large. In 1929, he told Congress, "Gentleman, managing the country is like managing an hacienda. I was a good 'hacendado' because I knew how to watch over my managers and foremen. My eyes were open. What we need now is not my presence, but a good administrator. If you want, I will choose him. You will leave me the command of the army, and we make an agreement to name a President" (Velásquez 1984:13).

Despite glaring contradictions, the official discourse of power was still nominally liberal. Gómez, while possessing absolute power, was concerned with preserving the appearance of legality. Figureheads from the social elite occupied the presidency, and Congress formally approved Gómez's legislation. Ever since the struggle for independence, liberalism had been the public language of the Venezuelan political elite; identified with the very origins of the nation, this language seemed untouchable. It was associated not only with the origins of the nation but with Bolívar's project of social emancipation and republicanism under the criollo elite's leadership. Thus, it had become an essential component in the legitimization of criollo rule since independence. The Liberal and Conservative parties, the main parties of the nineteenth century, shared the formal discourse of liberalism as well as an indifference to the effective organization of a liberal state. In this war-torn century, marked by shifting elite alliances and a succession of military rulers, "Liberals were Conservatives and the Conservatives were also Conservatives" (Velásquez 1983:23).

Since it was understood that liberal principles were fundamentally unrelated to the elite's actual practices, the elite could claim to represent them without visible political cost. An example of this was the National Constitution of 1864, drafted during the government of Guzmán Blanco. Formally "an ideal project for the transformation of Venezuela into a liberal and democratic state" (Carrera Damas 1980:138), it granted direct and secret suffrage for males over twenty-one to elect local and national legislators, and it established the separation of powers. In contrast to the constitution's democratic postulates, Guzmán Blanco exercised autocratic power. The gap between political discourse and practice reached unprecedented dimensions under Gómez, who eliminated political parties and rights of association but "who never thought of remaining as president without putting up an electoral show, without the appearance of alternation" (Carrera Damas 1980:139).

The Gómez regime came to an end with his death; it was not overthrown. Although under these conditions there was indeed understandable continuity because a fundamental realignment of social forces had not occurred, the extent to which *gomecismo* was collectively repudiated is striking. Even those who had worked under Gómez, such as his minister of war and successor, General López Contreras, felt compelled to distance themselves from gomecismo, for Gómez was now seen as the negation of the same liberal ideals that he had claimed to uphold.

How did it happen that gomecismo, despite a long-standing tradition of disparity between liberal discourse and autocratic practice, now came to be synonymous with autocracy and corruption? As far as I know, in Venezuelan historiography this question is not posed, for its answer seems self-evident: the façade was too transparent; it could not conceal the extreme autocratic character of Gómez's regime. While this is indeed true, the façade was transparent for another reason as well: as Gómez concentrated power, the gap between appearance and reality became so large that it became indeed a different kind of gap. Within this gap new social sectors found space not just to address the usual disparity between liberal principles and actual practices but to affirm liberal principles from a different standpoint.

In the opposition to Gómez the ideals of liberalism established roots, for the first time, in a fertile social terrain where they gained new significance. Liberalism ceased to be an abstract political notion, the substantive content of which was limited to the economic interests of an export-oriented oligarchy that saw in free trade a source of economic advantage, and came to inform and link the interests and convictions of wider social groups. The development of the oil industry during the Gómez regime transformed the relationship between dominant and subaltern sectors. The traditional agrarian oligarchy and the commercial bourgeoisie which once had shared a common interest in export agriculture now became oriented toward activities in urban commerce and real estate based on oil income and were challenged by the ascendant new commercial and manufacturing interests that had entered the economic space opened up by the expansion of the oil industry.

The international value of the bolívar reflected the financial weight of oil in the economy as well as the dominance of commercial over agricultural and industrial interests. A strong bolívar, whose value was unrelated to the productivity of domestic labor, raised the price of agricultural exports and made them uncompetitive on the world market and reduced the cost of imported goods, thus inhibiting local production and promoting imports. The internal circulation of oil revenues created a local market of consumers without its counterpart of producers. Imports became a crucial link in the circuit of the "realization of the oil rent" (Hausmann 1981), that is, by multiplying the goods available for purchase, they made possible the transformation of oil money into things. The concentration of financial resources in urban centers led to a rapid process of urbanization, giving rise to an incipient construction industry linked to the expansion of urban real estate development. The transformation of agricultural lands into urban real estate became a central path to wealth and the basis for the formation of major *grupos económicos,* that is, diversified conglomerates centered on one or a few families linked by ties of marriage, business, and friendship. This process did not set an emerging bourgeoisie against a traditional landowning class, as occurred in many countries. Landowners were quick to adapt to the new conditions and to shift investments to new activities.

A rapid process of urbanization began to signal the growing importance of urban sectors and the declining significance of the peasantry. Emerging middle sectors began to claim their own space within the national political system by appealing to the people as a collective subject that had been marginalized by oligarchic regimes. Universal suffrage became the emblem of liberalism's fulfillment. Thus, the ideals expressed and the interests advanced through liberal discourse were no longer the same. The remarkable historical continuity of the liberal "national project," noted by Carrera Damas (1980), conceals a less visible, but no less remarkable, discontinuity in the way this project was in fact interpreted.

This discontinuity has been less visible not because it was less real but because, from the outset, the new reality seemed so natural that its historical genesis and the economic interests it sustained were taken for granted. If one could take a bird's-eye view of this process, one might see this change as an emergent conception of Venezuela directly as an oil nation. During the Gómez period, the entity called Venezuela came to be seen as constituted not only by its people but also by its main source of wealth—not just by its social but by its natural body. Although the land and its products were celebrated in poetry as well as in the visual arts, music, and popular songs, agriculture did not provide a common source of national identification in Venezuela. In contrast, as the oil industry expanded and Venezuelan society changed, a perceptible shift occurred. Not only was oil included in the conception of what Venezuela was as a nation, but it came to define Venezuela as an oil nation. The opposition to gomecismo reflected not just a rejection of the familiar gap between ideals and practice but a revalorization of liberal principles that reflected a significant change in Venezuela's economic structure and social relations.

Ironically, the new social basis of liberalism came to be grounded in nature—in the collective interest in the nation's commonly owned subsoil, rather than in the atomized interests of private individuals: common landed property, not individual labor, became liberalism's new ideological and material foundation. The citizen was construed as a member of a corporate national body, not just as the autonomous agent of an atomized market or as the isolated bearer of formal rights. As before, the realization of the liberal national project required the democratization of political life. But now the social bearers of democratic ideals understood democracy as the extension of social participation not only in national politics but also in the nation's wealth. Democratic discourse presented the political and economic domains as two sides of the same oil coin.[17]

In an unexpected historical twist, this new liberalism shared a profound affinity with the original liberal ideas of Bolívar, which were modeled, as

17. In a lucid discussion of the relationship between the economy and the state, Keith Hart has shown how they function as two sides of the same coin, the specific properties of which have to be historically constructed.

Luis Castro Leiva has shown, after the republican ideals of Rousseau (1985) and thus found inspiration in the republics of the ancient world rather than in the contractual market societies of Locke, Smith, or Ricardo. In these ancient societies liberty meant, as Pagden notes, "not the freedom of their members to pursue their own personal goals unhindered but, as Constant phrased it, 'the sharing of social power among the citizens of the same fatherland'" (1982:142). In his famous 1819 Angostura speech, in which Bolívar expressed his vision of republican Venezuela, he underlined the ideal of a society in which "men are born with equal rights to all the goods of society" (1950:691). Paradoxically, a common interest in the nation's subsoil, itself the historical expression of the implantation in Venezuela of the most dynamic multinational corporations of the twentieth century, built upon a subterranean current of republican liberalism that had looked to the ancient past for its image of the modern future. As if Bolívar's specter hovered over Venezuela, this rentier liberalism fused the original liberal ideals of the founders of the fatherland, rooted in a communitarian conception of the republic, with the transfigured liberal ideals of social actors who imagined modern Venezuela as a community of citizens bound by a common link to their motherland's natural body. In Venezuela, "sharing social power" was beginning to mean sharing political rights and oil wealth among the citizens of the same land.

By restricting the social base of the regime and increasing its dependence on the oil companies, the centralization of power under Gómez limited not just the circle of beneficiaries of oil rents to his small clique but also the total amount of rents. Through pressure from below, the democratization of the state promised to increase the amount of state income, expand its beneficiaries, and most significantly, transform ephemeral wealth into permanent productive capacity, turning Venezuela into a modern nation. As the opposition construed the democratic state as the nation's agent, it assigned the state the historical task of uniting and developing the fractured nation by seizing control of the resources of the subsoil from foreign hands and using them on behalf of the collectivity as a united subject.

If the classical liberal view associated with the expansion of an atomized market supposes that national ends depend on the pursuit of each individual's own interests, in Venezuela's rentier liberalism, based on the expansion of the state's oil rents, each person's interests came to depend on the realization of the nation's own ends. Oil and politics had been linked by an autocratic regime. The new liberal project promised to break this link and to put another in its place: democracy.

THE VOICE OF DEMOCRACY

This discussion may allow us to listen to the voices that emerged after Gó-mez's death (his "last miracle"). Out of these voices Venezuela emerged as a an oil nation.[18]

The image of a ruler of unlimited political power who was believed to be "invincible and immortal" was re-created by Gabriel García Márquez in *The Autumn of the Patriarch*. The Patriarch—a synthesis of Latin American dictators in which Gómez's figure was prominent—returned from his presumed death, walked among the living, listening to their voices in order to destroy those who had conspired against him:

> [The Patriarch] saw through the smoke that all the ones he wanted to be there were there, the liberals who had sold the federalist war, the conservatives who had bought it, the generals of the high command, three of his cabinet ministers, the archbishop primate and Ambassador Schontner, all together in one single plot calling for the unity of all against the despotism of centuries so that they could divide up among themselves the booty of his death, so absorbed in the depths of greed that no one noticed the appearance of the unburied president who gave a single blow with the palm of his hand on the table, and shouted, aha! and that was all he had to do, for when he lifted his hand from the table the stampede of panic was over (1991 : 31).

After Gómez's death there were similar voices, attempts by traditional cliques "in one single plot calling for the unity of all against the despotism of centuries so that they could divide up among themselves the booty of his death." But during the Gómez regime not only the abrupt expansion but also the very nature of these "spoils" had heightened the contradiction between the public nature of the state's wealth and its private appropriation. By monopolizing both political power and the nation's wealth, Gómez had invalidated the legitimacy of his own voice—he could have no formal or acknowledged continuity; even his followers had to distance themselves from him.

18. In this section I have focused on materials written during the liminal period following Gómez's death, for they eloquently reveal how a new vision of the nation was defined. Whenever possible, I have referred to the compilation of some of these documents edited by Suárez Figueroa because it is readily available in Venezuela. The Venezuelan National Congress has published a multivolume collection of Venezuelan political thought throughout the republican era which includes materials covering the period I examine here. These useful volumes bring together primary sources and introductory essays by Venezuelan scholars. Particularly relevant for the issues discussed in this chapter are volumes 14 and 15, "El debate político en 1936" (1983).

In effect, his successors, General Eleazar López Contreras (1936–41), his minister of war, and General Isaías Medina Angarita (1941–45), López Contreras's minister of war, prompted by a changed public climate and pressure from below, distanced themselves from gomecismo and took ever larger steps toward the establishment of a democratic regime in Venezuela.

While many tough caudillos and prominent intellectuals had fought against Gómez, the students in Caracas undermined gomecismo and redefined the terms of public discourse. These students, known as the Generation of 28 because in 1928 they had participated in the most significant public protest against Gómez, Student Week, became after Gómez's death the founders of the nation's major political parties and were the leading figures in national politics until the 1970s.[19] Between 1928 and 1935 they articulated a new discourse about Venezuela whose importance cannot be underestimated.

According to Maza Zavala, "The controversy that was developed in exile between 1930 and 1935 about the nature, reach, route, and strategy and tactics of the Venezuelan revolution is, without doubt, the most important one in the contemporary history of Venezuela" (1991 : iii). There were certainly divisions within the left (mostly centering around the role of class struggle in the context of Venezuela's distinctive social formation), but there was a consensus about the need to overcome feudal structures, free Venezuela from the grip of imperialism, and democratize the political system. In the play of politics after 1936 these aims achieved more specific meaning, often losing their radical edge. The very centrality of the state and of its immense financial resources focused attention on the expansion and control of these resources, inhibiting demands for more radical social transformations not only in agriculture and industry but also within the oil industry itself. The main goal was to maximize oil income; the nationalization of the industry remained a distant dream.[20]

When Gómez died and there was an opening for free expression, the voice of this young generation achieved public recognition; for others to be heard, they had to echo its words, whose repressed presence had already

19. During Student Week, university students took advantage of carnival celebrations to launch a veiled critique of the regime; for an analysis of the symbolism and political significance of these events, see Skurski (1993).

20. The basic division was between the Marxists (whose leading figures were the brothers Gustavo and Eduardo Machado, Salvador de la Plaza, Miguel Otero Silva, and Juan Bautista Fuenmayor), and the Social Democrats (led by Rómulo Betancourt, Raúl Leoni, Valmore Rodríguez, and Luis Troconis Guerrero). The Marxists were more prone to emphasize class struggle and therefore to favor agrarian reform; but even they were cautious concerning oil and emphasized the distribution and use of oil resources, not the nationalization of the industry at this point.

permeated public discourse. Rómulo Gallegos, the teacher of many of these students, had finished in 1928 a draft of a novel tentatively entitled *La Coronela*. Inspired by the example of these students, he transformed it into *Doña Bárbara* (1929), an internationally acclaimed novel that became the mythic charter of Venezuela's democracy. Santos Luzardo, a young lawyer from Caracas, returns to his roots in the plains, where he defeats the forces of backwardness, represented by Doña Bárbara (an emblem of Gómez) and her ally Mister Danger (an agent of foreign interests), and brings the promise of civilization through his union with her daughter, Marisela, the embodiment of the people (Skurski 1993). As Skurski has shown, while the students had inspired Gallegos's novel, the novel shaped their orientation to politics and provided in Santos Luzardo a model that was widely emulated. Freer to express themselves at this historical opening, what these students said in 1936 marked the terms of political discourse in Venezuela for years to come. They no longer spoke as students but as aspiring national political leaders. Although their student organization (Federación de Estudiantes Venezolanos, FEV) remained an important association, they concentrated their efforts on organizing broad sectors of the population. As Levine has aptly noted,

> The most notable aspect of the political changes following Gómez's death is precisely the growth of organizations with a broad social base—unions, civic leagues, political parties, etc. Although these groups were generally founded and led by returning exiles of the 1928 generation, the organizations themselves were general in scope and not limited to students. Students as a power group per se soon faded from the scene. They provided the catalyst for party organization, but never again would they wield autonomous power. In 1936, power began to pass to those who could organize the masses. (1973:23.)

The year following Gómez's death was marked by important popular mobilizations and active political debate. A remarkable feature of this period was the emergence of a hegemonic discourse of democracy which developed in response to Gómez's privatization of the state. Democracy was identified with social harmony. While those associated with the Communist Party did not disregard class conflict, they did agree that the main opposition in Venezuela was between the foreign oil companies, and their allies within the domestic arena, and the unified population. Most of the young political leaders preferred to organize movements rather than parties, as the latter were associated with a history of political division and strife.[21]

---

21. López Contreras forced political movements to become political parties through the so-called Ley Lara, promulgated in 1936 in order to increase state control over political activity and dismantle

They encountered little ideological opposition from the right or from the state. As Velásquez has observed, only the Partido Acción Nacional (PARNAC) expressed the views of the right; but its action was limited to attacking members of leftist organizations as communists; it represented no ideological challenge. The president, General López Contreras, adapted to the pressure from below with great flexibility and "ideological mimetism" (Hermoso 1991:152). In his day-by-day account of events marking the dramatic year following Gómez's death, Hermoso has shown how the adaptability of left and the state to each other created an ideological consensus at the center: "The fact that there were no confrontations between extreme positions strengthened the 'political center.'" Standing at the center and buttressed by its institutional power, the state could emerge as a mediating figure: "López became an imaginary arbiter of the supposed confrontation between two ghosts: the nonexistent communist danger and the 'threat' of collapsing gomecismo" (1991:153). But the condition of possibility of this mutual convergence at the ideological center was the very centrality of the state as the manager of the nation's wealth.

MANIFESTOS OF THE NATION

The political literature of the period following Gómez's death eloquently articulated the new vision woven around this center. One of the earliest manifestos that circulated in December 1935, just after Gómez's death, was signed by a large number of intellectuals, politicians, professionals, and businessmen who proclaimed very cautiously their commitment to constructing a different Venezuela. "We are convinced there is a new Venezuelan reality in which the diverse expressions of civic life may be inspired and stimulated by a renewed spirit" (Suárez Figueroa 1977:111).

With the growing assurance that General López Contreras was not going to follow Gómez's procedures, the manifestos explicitly endorsed democratic goals in terms which linked the pursuit of political rights to the recovery of the nation's wealth appropriated by Gómez. Gomecista wealth was seen as an illegitimate and dangerous—"unhealthy"—source of power. The Bloque Nacional Democrático, founded in 1936 in Maracaibo, the center of the oil industry, criticized the fact that gomecistas continued to occupy a privileged position:

Communist organizations. For a discussion of changes in political discourse in this period, see Velázquez (1983); for a succinct description of the growth of civil society–based organizations between 1900 and 1945, see Margarita López (1984).

The nation faces, after the death and collapse of the Juan Vicente Gómez dictatorship, a situation of anxiety created by the fact that the important personalities who accompanied the dictator in the ominous task of plundering public and private coffers continue, inside and outside Venezuela, to enjoy their accumulated wealth in a defiant and rebellious posture, conspiring against our democratic institutions and threatening to become a constant danger to the health of the Republic. (Suárez Figueroa 1977 : 148.)

On 14 February, leaders of the Generation of 28 organized a mass demonstration in Caracas against gomecismo. As popular sectors confronted government forces, the police responded by killing several demonstrators. At this critical transition, this state action was read collectively as a sign that the new leaders were reverting to forms of violence identified with Gómez. In prompt response, a week later López Contreras presented the government's February Program, an analysis of the nation's major problems and a plan of national development which some regard as "the first large project of reform of the modern State in Venezuela" (Peña 1988 : 248). By incorporating criticisms produced within civil society, the state neutralized its opposition but also legitimated a reformist discourse which intensified the social pressure to democratize the polity.

Among the many reactions to the February Program, Miguel Otero Silva, who became one of the most influential intellectuals of this generation, published an article, tellingly entitled "Money, Money, Money," in which he reminded the public that money was required to finance the state's February Program.[22] I find revealing his didactic insistence that in Venezuela this money should come from the nation's two main sources of wealth: Gómez's personal wealth, which should be nationalized, and petroleum, which should yield larger benefits to the country through increased taxation (the idea that state's programs could be financed at least in part by citizens' taxes was simply absent). Otero Silva countered the fear that oil companies would leave Venezuela if the state imposed stricter conditions on them with the argument that they obtained oil at such bargain prices that they would never leave the country. Invoking the authority of Gumersindo Torres, Gómez's minister of development, who had pioneered the state's nationalist oil policy, Otero Silva reiterated his view that Venezuela sells its oil so cheaply that the state would

---

22. Miguel Otero Silva (1908–1985) was a leader of the Generation of 28. In 1936 he was affiliated with the Communist Party (he gave up his membership in 1951 but remained identified with the left). He later became a noted novelist, humorist, and journalist. As senator after 1958 he promoted the development of cultural institutions in Venezuela.

obtain more income if it simply gave oil freely to the companies but did not exonerate them from paying duties for their imports.

Obtaining more state income, however, was not enough. Otero Silva warned that the expansion of state income could not by itself assure that these financial resources would be used to implement social reforms, for in Venezuela state officials had made a habit of robbing the nation. Thus, he called for the democratization of the state and the imposition of strict controls over public functionaries. Otero Silva concluded his article by insisting that the "democratic revolution" begun in Venezuela on 19 December 1935 would have to finance its social programs by drawing on these two sources of national wealth. Gómez's biological death opened up a political space in which it became possible to link the demand to expand political rights to the demand to promote social welfare. Otero Silva did not hesitate to define as a "democratic revolution" this marriage of political rights and oil-financed social reforms.

In 1936 members of the Generation of 28 founded ORVE (Movimiento de Organización Venezuela) to promote a moderate program of political and social reform for the transition from "autocratic rule" to a "democratic regime." Its members included Alberto Adriani, who became López Contreras's minister of agriculture, and Rómulo Betancourt, who, along with other ORVE members, later founded the Partido Democrático Nacional (PDN), which was a precursor of Acción Democrática (AD), founded in 1941. ORVE's program established a stark contrast between the "barbarous" Gómez regime, which had denied the collective existence of the nation, and the promising new political situation:

> Under the previous regime there was no national existence. The state served interests opposed to those of the nation: it served the foreign penetration of the nation and provincial caudillos. A group of caudillos, seizing the country, subjected Venezuelan honor to powerful foreign interests and made the public administration a tool of public plunder. (Suárez Figueroa 1977: 142.)

The present was promising, however, because of the project of establishing a new relationship among state, nation, and public wealth:

> We want a Democracy, but a responsible Democracy, where the state would not be captured by the power of money . . . We want to unite, not divide Venezuelans. We want to transform politics, which before was a business of small oligarchic circles, into a national will and spirit which will permeate all the expressions of collective life with discipline and reveal permanently the creative will of the Venezuelan soul. (Suárez Figueroa 1977: 143.)

Money in Venezuela was beginning to be understood as oil money. A state freed from the power of money was one that controlled oil money rather than being controlled by it. While in the past politics had also been a "business of small oligarchic circles," money had now "captured the state" and made the business of these circles depend on the oil business. The task was to forge a national will that would domesticate the powers of money on behalf of the collectivity.

Nationalism, which had been identified with the achievement of political independence and the unification of the state, was now linked to the pursuit of economic development and collective prosperity. The political program of the Partido Democrático Nacional connected the change from Gómez's "autocratic state" into a "constitutional democratic state" to the use of national resources on behalf of all the people in order to promote national development. As the document stated, "Nationalism is for us the creation and defense of national industry and the exploitation of our large natural resources on behalf of the totality of the Venezuelan people" (Suárez Figueroa 1977:184).

Democracy came to mean a system of popular participation not only in national political life but also in the nation's natural wealth. One of the earliest expressions of this view appeared in a document of the Partido Republicano Progresista, an organization founded in 1936 by members of the Communist Party and socialist leaders (the Communist Party had been illegal since its foundation in 1931) designed to function as a popular front party. Its program affirmed the principle of popular sovereignty and demanded that the state not only represent but defend the interests and be the expression of the popular majority:

> The state should avoid being allowed to become, for any reason, a tool of domination and oppression against the popular majority by a minority protected under restrictive social and economic conditions . . . The state should be, then, a tool for the defense of the people by the people. (Suárez Figueroa 1977:136.)

Public sentiment against the legacy of gomecismo made it possible for this generation of politicians and intellectuals to present as a given the demand to democratize political life in conjunction with the demand to democratize the nation's wealth. Their conception of a prosperous democratic state was counterposed to the reality of the autocratic state under Gómez; they gave meaning to democracy by contrasting it to the personalistic regime whose rule they defined as both onerous and anachronistic:

Because Gómez and his relatives and close accomplices monopolized most of the wealth of the nation, both its land and its industries, and because the nation, as an entity which includes all Venezuelans, has been the most damaged of all both in the present and in the future, we have to struggle to make the state confiscate all the assets of Juan Vicente Gómez, his relatives and close accomplices. (Suárez Figueroa 1977 : 136.)

Arguing that all those who had "suffered personally" under Gómez (meaning political as well as economic hardship) could not be compensated legally as individuals, the document urges that Gómez's wealth be nationalized. The aim was to collectivize oil wealth through the state rather than to atomize it by distributing it to a few people. "Only by transferring this wealth to the state and using it on behalf of the nation will all of us Venezuelan workers feel partially compensated for all the personal harm we have suffered" (Suárez Figueroa 1977 : 136).

Foreign companies were associated with the transformation of the state into a tool of domination and of natural resources into money; the companies capable of effecting this alchemy held the key to real power. Rómulo Betancourt, in a speech at the first mass meeting of ORVE on 1 March 1936, depicted Venezuela as a captive country because its subsoil was controlled by foreign interests:

It is a country without an external debt, it is true, but its economy has been intervened by the most aggressive and bold sector of international finances: the oil sector. It is true that the Venezuelan state does not have foreign creditors, but, on the other hand, our subsoil has been distributed among the oil companies. (1975 : 25.)

In 1975 Betancourt claimed that this statement was "the first public discussion of the oil problem in Venezuela" (1975 : 25). It was not, but it was one of the first attempts to bring to a broad public a view which Gumersindo Torres had expressed in the 1920s: oil was a national resource that should belong to Venezuela. The new political parties made this idea the basis of their mass-based politics. "Our subsoil" was an image without public currency in 1920, but after Gómez's death it condensed new assumptions concerning the nation. Through democratic discourse, the wealth of the nation came to be identified with its natural body. Gómez had paid Venezuela's foreign debt but had sold the nation's subsoil ("distributed it among the oil companies"). Democracy promised to unify the nation, to use the nation's natural wealth on behalf of the nation's people.

In response to popular pressure, which included mass demonstrations in

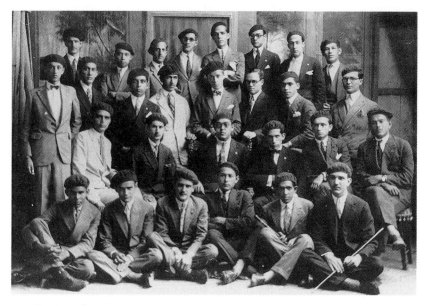

Students from the Generation of 28, including Rómulo Betancourt (in the back row) and Jóvito Villalba (center). (Fundación Andrés Mata.)

Looting in Caracas following General Juan Vicente Gómez's death on 17 December 1935. (Instituto Autonomo Biblioteca Nacional.)

June involving several thousand participants (thirty thousand according to ORVE), the government decided to confiscate all of Gómez's personal property. An editorial in ORVE's newspaper presented this decision as a victory of the June popular mobilization. It emphasized its popular character by referring to it as "Juan Bimba's" first "great triumph" and his "first justification for having collectively abandoned the workshop and the factory, the industrial enterprise or commercial establishment, in order to demonstrate in the street his will" (1983:265).[23]

The term *Juan Bimba,* which became popular in this period, refers not just to everyman, the Joe Blow of the United States, but to the virtuous poor man—typically in this era the rural worker, abused by oligarchic rulers. I have not seen Juan Bimba used as an emblem of the pueblo when *pueblo* is employed as an inclusive term to address the whole population as a unified community of values and goals, including its intellectual and professional elites. Thus, while pueblo is potentially a totalizing category which may include the middle-class leaders who speak on its behalf, Juan Bimba is a more restrictive category which refers to an archetype of the nation's neglected majority. The document defines the confiscated properties as part of the "immense wealth" stolen by the "Benefactor thief" *(Benemérito ladrón)*[24] from the people *(el pueblo).* Not only the opposition but the state presented this measure as an attempt to return to the people, as its rightful owner, the collective wealth that Gómez had appropriated. In order to guarantee that this collective property would remain in the hands of the state and at the service of the people, ORVE's editorial concluded by asking el pueblo to remain alert so as to avert the reprivatization of the confiscated property: "Gómez's lands and factories must not be sold to national or foreign capitalists. They should be exploited on behalf of the people" (ORVE 1983:266).

According to a Venezuelan historian, "This has been the most important sanction, in terms of its severity, that has been decreed since 1830" (Velásquez 1984:15). The administrative consequences of this measure were immediate: the state became an entrepreneur, acquiring banks, a vast array of industries

---

23. It is interesting to note that this mention of Juan Bimba presents the June 1936 actions as his first historical victory, thus indicating the relative "modernity" of Juan Bimba and the masses represented by him. Cartoonist Mariano Medina Febres (Medo) has been credited as the creator of this character (Febres 1990). It should be noted that in this case its sociological referents include only low-level urban occupations, not the professional and middle-level leadership which also participated in the June mobilizations. Perhaps the urban nature of this mobilization explains why in this case peasants are not mentioned. The graphic image which came to identify "Juan Bimba" in AD's propaganda depicts him as a (stereo)typical peasant dressed in villager's crude pants and shirt and *alpargatas* (rustic sandals).

24. Benemérito was an official title Congress bestowed on Gómez.

(paper, electricity, meat packing, soap, milk, matches), and large haciendas in up to fifteen states. This marked the beginning of the state's direct participation as a capitalist in the economy.

This measure created conditions which intensified the demands for democratization. Democratization was understood not just as the establishment of universal suffrage and a competitive party system but also as the expansion of the state's involvement in the economy. The creation of state-owned economic enterprises was seen as a means to ensure that the nation's wealth would be used for the benefit of the collectivity. Enterprises established with state money should not be privately appropriated but managed by the democratic state for the benefit of society as a whole. It was this reasoning which allowed ORVE to present this measure as Juan Bimba's "first great victory."

Those who articulated these demands increasingly appealed to el pueblo as a collective subject or to Juan Bimba, the prototypical common man, as the rightful beneficiary of state policies and as the embodiment of the desire for the democratization of the political system. While el pueblo had been addressed throughout the republican era as the sovereign of the liberal republic, now it was invoked as the legitimate heir of the nation's wealth who had been unjustly deprived of it. Popular sectors excluded from previous discourses about the nation articulated by educated urban men were now presented as citizens of an oil nation entitled not just to political rights but to the nation's wealth.

Demands to protect the nation's wealth focused on the need both to recover what Gómez had taken and to regulate the activities of the oil companies. Thus, the Partido Republicano Progresista also proposed that oil concessions to foreign companies be modified because the companies had already repatriated in profits more than their investments. It justified this demand by arguing that "in the hands of the oil companies lies the fundamental wealth of the country, petroleum" (the inclusion of the word *petroleum* here to designate the nation's wealth would be superfluous in a few years), but "the Venezuelan nation does not participate in this wealth except in a minimal proportion" (Suárez Figueroa 1977:136).

The nature of the state was publicly debated in newspapers and political meetings. On 18 March 1936 ORVE published a memorandum in which it stated its conception of the state. That document emphasizes unity, underlines the dangers of class struggle through reference to nineteenth-century civil wars, and focuses on the need to promote the idea of the state as a representative of the common interests of the nation:

We have to support and strengthen in Venezuela the idea of the State as the organ that conciliates social dissension and as the tool of collective discipline.

ORVE's document establishes a sharp contrast between the exclusionary and personalistic Gómez state and ORVE's image of the inclusive national state:

> In opposition to the personalist state monopolized by a group as was the case with the Gómez State, ORVE seeks a State in which all leading sectors of the nation *(todas las fuerzas vivas del país)* could participate, overcoming through just and unifying national policies regional polemics and resentments. (Velásquez 1983:49–50.)

In response to a request that it explain further its conception of the state by the assembly that approved the memorandum, ORVE's Committee of Political Orientation offered the following definition, which again was cast in opposition to the Gómez state:

> We understand by the State not the tool of domination and personal exploitation which was the state under the Dictatorship, but an administrative and political machinery, conscious and ordered, capable of fully developing, without residues of the traditional vices of corruption and theft, a coherent process of national reintegration and social justice. (Velásquez 1983:51.)

In order for the state—"as an administrative and political machinery"—to exercise its power on behalf of the collectivity, it would have to be accountable to it—it had to be a democratic state. Corruption was identified with autocratic rule; democracy was presented as providing a check against the possibility of corruption in a vastly expanded state possessing growing financial resources.

ORVE's political statements reflected basic postulates that had been outlined in the Barranquilla Plan written in 1931 by Betancourt and other exiled members of the opposition group ARDI (Agrupación Revolucionaria de Izquierda). This document defined the terms of political thought which prevailed among the non-Communist members of the Generation of 28. Since its foundation in 1931, the Communist Party had been very influential among members of this generation. It applied the theory of the international communist movement to Venezuela, arguing that in Venezuela conflicting class interests placed workers in opposition to capitalists. ARDI, in contrast, claimed that Venezuelan society was set apart by its distinct features: its weak proletariat and peasantry, rising middle class, powerful oil enclave, and strategically positioned state. Class, therefore, was not the determining factor in

Venezuela's political struggles. All classes had a common enemy: imperialism and its local allies, the "feudal structures embodied in gomecismo." These premises became the center of AD's self-definition as a multiclass nationalist party whose mission was to unite the Venezuelan people via the state against the foreign powers that had appropriated the resources of its subsoil. Thus, AD was to return sovereignty, dignity, and wealth to the nation.

This conception of nationalist politics animates a speech Betancourt gave in September 1936 in a meeting called to unify the left within a single party (five years before the founding of AD). Betancourt decries the fact that oil legislation in Venezuela has been written by the oil companies in collusion with local lawyers. The oil companies "take out of our country fabulous profits of no less than Bs. 500 million yearly" which could be used to solve urgent social needs, such as providing school for over 420 thousand children in Venezuela who did not receive any kind of formal education (1983 : 300). Betancourt appeals to the collectivity as a unified entity endowed with a single will and links plans to nationalize oil in the future to the nineteenth-century battles for political independence:

> Everyone is interested in achieving some day the nationalization of the enormous wealth of our subsoil, even though in order to achieve this aim we may have to wage another Ayacucho, making it possible in this fashion for Venezuela to be for Venezuelans. (1983.) [25]

For Venezuela to be effectively "for Venezuelans," the country had to reconquer the subsoil that had been appropriated by foreign powers. Only by uniting its body politic and its natural body would Venezuela be able to achieve full sovereignty; political independence without economic autonomy remained an insidious form of dependence. In the same speech, Betancourt summarized the political program of the unified leftist party in terms of two objectives: the struggles for democratic liberty and against imperialism. By democratizing the polity Venezuelans would regain control of the national

---

25. The battle of Ayacucho (9 December 1924) marked the independence of Peru and culminated the independence of northern South America. It was led by Antonio José de Sucre, Bolívar's most loyal officer. Betancourt's reference to Ayacucho rather than to Carabobo (Venezuela's battle of independence in 1821) is intriguing in part because it is uncommon. Ayacucho is invoked in Venezuela when the accent is placed on Latin American, rather than Venezuelan, independence or on the international dimension of Venezuelan independence struggles. Ayacucho is also associated with Sucre's loyalty to Bolívar, and thus to the nation. The scholarship program developed by Carlos Andrés Pérez during his first administration (1974–79), which sent thousands of Venezuelans to study overseas, was named after Sucre as the victor at the battle of Ayacucho (Programa de Becas Gran Mariscal de Ayacucho).

subsoil and achieve the nation's economic independence. The concept of "Venezuela for Venezuelans" powerfully joined both goals.[26]

In public meetings and writings, the young political leaders, writers, and activists seized for themselves the role of democracy's spokespersons for a general public. They informed this public about the meaning of democracy in Venezuela, emphasizing its economic foundation in the oil economy. "In a democracy," wrote an activist, "everyone believes that the *national economy* is everyone's affair (*es la cosa de todos,* literally, everyone's thing), each one expects benefits from its prosperity and is prone to suffer with its decline or its ruin" (Morales 1983 : 346; emphasis added).

The extent of the appropriation of this collective affair or thing by foreign powers was often quantified, and its vast magnitude was construed as the cause of prosperity abroad and poverty at home. This loss of the nation's patrimony was presented, as in the writings of Antonio Arráiz (a young Venezuelan intellectual who had lived in the United States) as a source of both intimate personal pain and love of nation. Arráiz argues that since agricultural products represent only 8 percent of the value of total exports (oil accounting for the remainder), Venezuelans own only one-twelfth of their exports.[27] He calculates the oil industry's daily profits at Bs. 1,360,000 and argues, through fictional characters, that this money supports the standard of living of the U.S. owners of the oil industry: Mr. Thus, or Mr. Such, the oil magnate, Molly, his wife, Ted, the spendthrift son, Mildred, the spoiled daughter ("who only knows of the art of making cocktails and of the skillful art of loving and being loved without consequences"), all of whom live in affluent homes (with "silver plates, Louis XV furniture"). In contrast, the masses in Venezuela remain trapped in miserable conditions.

For Arráiz, the laughable ease with which oil money could be drained from Venezuela was a sign that Venezuela was treated as a primitive nation of unreasonable people, who he figured in his writing as "monkeys" and "blacks" incapable of exploiting their own resources:

> One million three hundred sixty thousand bolívares go to them from Venezuela; from the poor, obscure, remote, and diffuse Venezuela. A little republic

---

26. This notion became one of the most popular slogans of his party, Acción Democrática (founded in 1941).

27. Although Antonio Arráiz was not a student at the time, he participated in the Student Week activities of February 1928 as well as in the assault on the San Carlos military garrison in April of the same year. He was imprisoned by Gómez, tortured, and exiled in 1935. He returned to Venezuela in 1936 and became a noted writer, poet, and journalist.

(una republiquita), populated by monkeys and blacks, a hot place where coconut trees grow and where these people have, poor souls!, this rich thing that is petroleum, which they allow to be exploited. (1983:195.)

According to Arraíz, Venezuelan oil in effect did not belong to "the poor Venezuelan man" but to the "blond mister" who came "attracted to its smell like flies to honey." Yet the "blond mister" obtained oil because "we had a General Gómez, who gave away even the subsoil, without pity." Arraíz concludes his article by making a direct link between his love of nation—"that rises up from within my interior . . . pathetic, almost painful"—and his nation's exploitation—"A suffering motherland (*Patria*)," which is "most loved" when it "suffers most, when I remember that one million three hundred sixty thousand bolívares of our national wealth leave us every day never to return again" (1983:196).[28] In his highly feminized image of the nation as weak, prostrate, and lacking in will, "love of nation" is identified with the male defense of the exploited nation's subsoil—the source of collective wealth, *la cosa de todos* (everyone's affair or business).[29]

Oil policy was made synonymous with a nationalist economic policy that should seek to defend the nation's subsoil, not just to maximize oil income. Since the blind pursuit of oil income would deplete the nation's subsoil, a nationalist oil policy should seek to make productive use of oil revenues. While the foreign oil industry exploited Venezuela's docile and wild nature, the (male) Venezuelan state would transform it into a domesticated and productive force. The need to transform ephemeral and corrupting oil money into permanent wealth was compellingly articulated in a newspaper article by Arturo Uslar Pietri, one of Venezuela's most influential public intellectuals:[30]

More than a third of Venezuela's public wealth now rests on the destructive utilization of subsoil deposits whose life is limited not only by natural condi-

28. The image of a "nation of monkeys," which has currency to this day, refers to a nation of primitive people who cannot defend themselves or their resources; "monkeys" can serve as an euphemistic metaphor for blacks, Indians, and even mestizos or Venezuelans in general. "Blacks" too can be a metaphor for all these categories, including "monkeys." The juxtaposition of these two terms helps blur the boundaries of the cultural and the natural, the social and the savage. (I am grateful to Aims MacGuiness for helping me see the multiple associations evoked by these terms).

29. As I indicated earlier, *cosa* literally means thing. In this context, this multivocal term brings to mind not only affair or business but also female genitals.

30. Arturo Uslar Pietri is a leading public intellectual of upper-class origin who articulated the bourgeoisie's emerging economic and political ideology. He became one of Venezuela's most influential public figures, occupying public office under various administrations and authoring texts ranging from economics and history to fiction.

tions, but also by the fact that their productivity depends entirely on factors and decisions that are alien to the national economy. This great proportion of wealth of destructive origin will doubtless grow when the day comes that the mining taxes are made more just and remunerative, bringing nearer the suicidal dream of those naive people who feel it would be ideal if the Venezuelan treasury could pay for the entire national budget out of mining income alone, which would simply mean the following: Venezuela would become an unproductive and idle nation, an immense petroleum parasite, swimming in a momentary and corrupting abundance and impelled toward an imminent and inevitable catastrophe. (Suárez Figueroa 1977 : 163.)

The proposed solution to the disturbing prospect of becoming a rentier nation, vividly conveyed by his image of the nation as an "immense petroleum parasite," was to use oil revenues to create "a reproductive and progressive economy." Uslar Pietri claimed that it was urgent to use the "transitory wealth" of the present "destructive economy" to create the healthy and broad foundations of a "progressive economy that will be our true declaration of independence." If political independence had been Simón Bolívar's heroic achievement, full independence would now be the task of those capable of transforming ephemeral wealth into permanent productive capacity. The editorial ended with a call to action:

If we were to propose a motto for our economic policy, we would suggest the following one, which dramatically sums up the need to invest the wealth produced by the destructive mining system in order to create reproductive and productive agricultural wealth: "sow the oil *(sembrar el petróleo)*." (Suárez Figueroa 1977 : 165.)

"Sow the oil" resonated widely in an agrarian nation that could no longer feed itself and whose economic elite sought new areas of profit making; it expressed the problematic of production, distribution, and reproduction in an oil nation. This phrase became the central slogan in the political discourse of democratic development.

OIL LEGISLATION: OIL NATION

Except for Gumersindo Torres's efforts to define a nationalist oil policy, under Gómez the state had essentially acted toward the companies primarily like a private party that benefited from the sale of national property. Gómez had made limited provisions to secure for the nation long-term revenues from the production of oil itself and had profited personally from the sale of oil concessions to the oil companies. This situation was to change after 1936, when public debate sought to establish a different relation between the state (as landlord) and the oil companies (as capitalists).[31]

The negotiations between the state and the oil companies followed a typical pattern that characterizes the relations between host nations and multinational corporations involved in the exploitation of natural resources. After an initial period in which terms are favorable for the foreign companies, states manage to obtain increasingly better conditions, a process that Vernon calls "an obsolescing bargain" (1971).

A central confrontation between the Venezuelan state and the oil companies occurred over the issue of taxation. Since Gómez had granted the oil companies long-term contracts (which specified the small and unchanging payment the companies would give the state), President López Contreras sought to increase the state's oil revenues by modifying national income tax schedules and tariff exemptions. Accustomed to Gómez's liberal economic policies, the oil companies opposed this attempt to reduce their profits and restrict their privileges. Arguing that income taxes and tariff exemptions had been agreed upon contractually, they took this matter to court in Venezuela and won the legal battle.

For the government, this setback had an important consequence. Development Minister Manuel Egaña (1938–41), after studying U.S. mining regulations, applied in Venezuela the same criteria that existed in the United States, where a distinction is made between the contractual rights of private parties and the government's rights as a sovereign state. Thus, in the United States, the government can lease public lands to private parties, establishing through a contract the level of its revenues. At the same time, as a sovereign state, it can impose—and change at will—an income tax, thus modifying the size of its revenues in accordance with the private parties' earnings. Although the companies accepted this principle in the United States, they strongly opposed it in Venezuela. This inconsistency was considered to be a serious affront to Venezuelan sovereignty.

World War II underlined the strategic importance of Venezuelan oil and in so doing also increased the bargaining power of the Venezuelan government. Since the oil companies had systematically refused to recognize the Venezuelan state's fiscal sovereignty, President Medina wrote a personal letter to President Roosevelt asking him to intercede on behalf of Venezuela's

31. This discussion of oil policy in Venezuela draws mostly from Mommer (1983, 1986), as well as from Lieuwin (1959), Tugwell (1975), and Vallenilla (1975).

claims. President Roosevelt responded by requesting that the oil companies accept Venezuela's demands. In exchange, Venezuela promised to become a stable supplier of oil for the United States.

A new oil law was passed in 1943 that fundamentally altered the state's relation with the oil industry. It assured the long-term presence of the oil industry in the country by validating many early concessions granted through illicit means under Gómez and, most important, by granting the oil companies large new concessions for a period of forty years. In turn, it created a capitalist tie between the landowning state and the tenant-producer oil companies. The new law considerably increased the state's participation in the industry's profits, both by fixing contractually a higher royalty and by establishing an income tax on the oil sector. It was believed that the royalty, which was set at 1:6 (meaning that one out of six barrels belonged to Venezuela), together with other fixed taxes, would yield an even, fifty-fifty split in the distribution of profits between the corporations and the state. In addition, in 1945 the state sought to raise its participation to 60 percent by imposing an income tax of 12 percent on this sector.

This income tax was justified on both theoretical and practical grounds. The theoretical argument was that surplus profits in a public interest sector should be seen as excessive profits: they should not be privately appropriated but should revert back to the nation. Accordingly, oil companies' profits should not rise above a fair percentage of return on capitalist investment—a principle that was accepted by OPEC twenty-five years later, in 1968. Thus, the ostensible purpose of this income tax was to transform private surplus profits into state revenues. In effect, by establishing the state's sovereign right to modify the income tax schedule, this law gave the government a tool to appropriate all surplus profits in this industry, that is, to capture an increasingly larger proportion of international ground rent (Mommer 1986:83).

A practical consideration facilitated the oil companies' acceptance of the Venezuelan state's position. Since the U.S. tax code does not recognize the principle of double taxation, their Venezuelan income taxes would simply be discounted from their U.S. income taxes. That is, the loser was the U.S. government (and U.S. consumers), not the U.S. oil companies. The law also included an important clause: it obliged the oil companies to build refineries in Venezuela. In sharp contrast to Gómez—who had asked the oil companies to establish refineries overseas, such as the island of Curazao, in order to avoid creating large concentrations of workers with their attendant labor problems—the Medina government sought to diversify the Venezuelan economy. The government's task was not solely to extract more revenues from the oil industry but to promote the industrialization of Venezuela—"to sow the oil." AD supported the goals of this policy but objected to it on technical and political grounds. It argued that the policy's specific methods of measuring profits did not enable the Venezuelan state to obtain even 50 percent of the industry's profits, not to mention the higher goal of a 60-40 distribution (Betancourt 1975:161–97).

The 1943 Oil Law is thus a landmark in the transformation of Venezuela into an oil nation. It fully recognized that the subsoil was national property and that the role of the state was to safeguard this property on behalf of the collectivity. The law confirmed the state's dual role as a sovereign power and as a landowner. The recognition of these roles legitimized an oil policy of incremental tax increases and an economic policy of state-promoted economic development.

HISTORICAL AMNESIA AND OIL'S SOCIAL INVISIBILITY

Oil's social invisibility has heightened the historical amnesia concerning the origins of Venezuela's transformation into an oil nation. This imperceptibility may be traced to the industry's origins as a transplanted foreign enclave, to its capital-intensive productive structure, and to the diffuse effects of the circulation of oil money throughout the body politic. Clearly, the *foreign* enclave character of the oil industry initially contributed to creating a sense of oil's unfamiliar presence in Venezuela. But as an *oil* enclave the industry became both extraordinarily tangible—a direct expression of a foreign presence—and yet so isolated and so clearly demarcated that it remained an isolated presence beyond its location.

As an export activity, oil extraction contrasts with labor-intensive agricultural export activities which involve large sectors of the population in seasonal cycles of planting and harvest or livestock reproduction, as well as with most mining operations, which require massive labor inputs. Oil extraction—often defined as oil production—is capital-intensive. After its exploration phase, the jobs that oil extraction creates tend to decrease. Carried out in relatively isolated areas of the country, forming separate pockets of economic activity, it never occupied a large percentage of the Venezuelan working population. Historically, most oil has been shipped out of the country, some of it after local refinement, without the involvement of most of the population or tangibly affecting their lives. Buying gasoline from Shell or Creole (Exxon) gas stations made evident the fact that the nation's basic resource became available to Venezuelans only through the mediation of foreign companies. With the aging of the industry, abandoned oil camps and decaying oil towns scattered throughout the states of Zulia, Portuguesa, and Anzoátegui have added a ghostly aura to oil's former presence in Venezuela.

The isolation of the early industry rested on its dependence on imported supplies for its operations and employees' consumption, the divorce of its production decisions from domestic considerations, and the absence of the local bourgeoisie from its control and management.[32] During the first decades of its existence, the industry's managerial and professional positions were almost entirely staffed by foreigners, with Venezuelans hired only as unskilled workers. Fenced oil camps re-created foreign comforts and conditions for the foreign managerial elite. "If ever could a white man live happily with his wife and children in a hot climate," remarks an observer in a memoir published in 1931, "that was in Mene Grande (a U.S. oil camp)" (Lady Mills 1931). As veritable enclaves with private roads, schools, stores, and medical supplies, these camps constituted, as a Venezuelan noted in 1936, "a State apart from the Venezuelan State" *(un Estado aparte del Estado Venezolano)* (Cabrera 1983:388).

With the passage of time, as the fences separating these two states were literally and metaphorically torn down, the Venezuelan state consolidated its sovereignty over the national territory. Yet to the extent that the Venezuelan state took up functions previously performed by the oil companies, the two states in effect merged into one, at once increasing the national state's apparent unity and intensifying its internal conflicts. While the oil companies' home offices always managed to retain decision-making power concerning a number of key issues (such as investment, technology, marketing, and prices), the national state increasingly tightened its control over the industry. In part through government pressure, but also through the industry's own policies, Venezuelans came to occupy some of the industry's top technical and managerial positions. No longer a separate enclave, the oil industry in effect became a school[33] that set standards of business practice within and outside the oil sector. Given the oil industry's international structure, the local subsidiaries necessarily remained foreign implants; yet with the passage of time they grew roots in the local terrain, generating a technocratic ethos among its

32. For a classic discussion of the significance of enclaves in Latin America, see Cardoso and Faletto (1979).

33. This term *(escuela)* was widely used by automobile, steel, and petrochemical industrialists whom Julie Skurski and I interviewed during our fieldwork in Venezuela. Many of the managers, technicians, and engineers who worked in the metalworking sector had previously worked in the oil sector and spontaneously remarked on the impact the industry had on their own formation. Although it is evident that the oil industry was a model of corporate rationality and organization in Venezuela, as far as I know no study has analyzed how the oil industry affected the development of business practices in other areas of the economy.

managerial staff which facilitated its identification with the oil industry's entrepreneurial rationality. By 1976, when the administration of Carlos Andrés
Pérez nationalized the oil industry, highly trained Venezuelans who ensured
its smooth operation as a national company occupied most of the industry's
managerial positions. After 1976, conflicts over distribution of resources and
profits which had previously set the Venezuelan state and the foreign oil
companies against each other were now played out within the Venezuelan
state itself.[34]

As the work of several Venezuelan scholars has shown, despite the limited space occupied by its productive structures, the oil industry reconfigured
space nationwide.[35] The oil industry destructured the social and economic
relations associated with Venezuela's agricultural past and structured the
urban-commercial organization of space of contemporary Venezuela (Santaella 1985:622). Calling it an "oil structure," Santaella argues that oil,
through its impact on urbanization, production, commerce, and consumption, as well as on systems of communication and service, had a "considerable
qualitative weight with regards to the occupation of space." As he says, "All
spaces become coherent within the Venezuelan territory through the dominance of the oil structure" (1985:622).[36]

Oil's effects on Venezuelan society are most pervasive not in its form as
a commodity with specific physical properties but in its form as money, not
as a use value but as an exchange value. In this respect, oil's social impact
occurs after it has been sold in the international market. At the surface level
of market exchange, the transformation of oil into money and of money into
goods and services takes on the appearance of a natural process; in exchange
for oil Venezuela receives its monetary equivalent in dollars which are then
spent at home and abroad. Yet these transformations involve as well the transfiguration of the social agents that participate in these processes. Thus, if oil
permeates Venezuelan society through its metamorphosis into money, it is
by metamorphosing society that oil money is fully incorporated into it and
achieves its multiple effects.

I refer to the incorporation of oil into society as the domestication of

---

34. For an informative report of this conflictive relationship, see the detailed, almost confessional
account of Andrés Sosa Pietri's experience as president of Petroleos de Venezuela (1993).

35. I have in mind Arcila Farías pioneering study of the Ministry of Public Works (1974), and Martín
Frechilla's monumental examination of plans to transform Caracas during the first half of this century
(1994).

36. For a similar argument and more extended discussions of the impact of oil on patterns of urbanization, communication and organization of space, see Arcila Farías (1974) and Frechilla (1994).

value. The construction of Venezuela as an oil nation was a part of this process of domesticating value. Conceptualizing Venezuela as an oil nation became a way of coming to terms with changed habits and expectations, of recognizing oil's potent presence within the body politic and thus of taming its effects. Through the old alchemic magic of money, "who makes a courtesan a slave, a slave a courtesan,"[37] oil pulled off the trick of putting a "primitive" Venezuela into a hat and taking it out in the form of an "oil nation."

THE NATION'S TWO BODIES AND DEMOCRATIC THEORY

Around three quarters of a century ago, the exploitation of the Venezuelan subsoil by foreign companies came to be interpreted in Venezuela as a loss of sovereignty. Because the foreign oil companies took oil from the country and left behind little in exchange, the nation's wealth, it was asserted, was "sucked away." A political consensus developed that Gómez had in effect "given away our subsoil." Yet this loss of the nation's physical wealth was the condition for the articulation of a democratic political project in terms of which the nation was constructed as a unified community of citizen landowners.

As Venezuela was represented as an oil nation in these terms and as the landlord state was transformed into the nation's agent, the state became the focus of social demands leveled against the internal and external forces that had "rapaciously" privatized the nation's collective subsoil. In the repeated call "to safeguard our national wealth" (originally enunciated, as we saw, by Gumersindo Torres's 1920 oil policy) and in the insistence on using this wealth on behalf of the collectivity that rightfully owned it (a demand that was forcefully articulated by the Generation of 28), particularistic interests were subsumed within the universal interest of the nation as a unified subject. Out of the struggle against gomecismo and foreign oil companies, a nationalist language developed that addressed Venezuelans as members of a national community sustained by the collective ownership of the common subsoil. The state's task, it was asserted, was to reintegrate the split nation that it represents by safeguarding the nation's vanishing physical body on behalf of the nation's eternal political body.

This image of a sovereign nation split into a mortal natural body and an

37. This expression comes from Juan Ruiz, the medieval poet known as the Archpriest of Hita, cited by Fernando Ortiz in his discussion of the effects of sugar export earnings on Cuban society (1995:81).

immortal political body resonates with medieval representations of theological and political power which still saturate the secular language of politics in the West. As Ernst Kantorowicz shows in his classical study of medieval political theology, the legal fiction of the king's two bodies developed in England during the sixteenth century as part of its process of nation-state formation. According to this fiction, the king has a natural body as an idiosyncratic mortal man and also a supernatural body as the embodiment of the immortal and omnipotent kingdom.

While Kantorowicz treats this legal fiction as an "offshoot of Christian thought" (1988:506), Claude Lefort asks whether we should not view it instead as a "theological-political formation" in which the integration of the religious and the political appears "logically and historically, as a primary datum?" (1988:249). The exchange of properties or "chiasmata" that for Kantorowicz obtains between the theological and the political for Lefort occurs "between the already politicized theological and the already theologized political" (1988:250). Thus, Lefort sees the representation of the king's two bodies not as the displaced product of successive social stages (Christocentric, juridico-centric, politico-centric, and humano-centric kingdoms) but as a multilayered cultural formation in which "what is displaced on each occasion is not eradicated, and proves to contain the kernel of a future symbolic configuration" (1988:250). Through his reinterpretation of the king's two bodies as a theological-political formation, Lefort seeks to place us in a better position to detect how "certain schemata of organization and representation survive thanks to the displacement and transference onto new entities of the image of the body and of its double nature" and, thus, to enable us to ask "whether democracy is the theatre of a new mode of transference, or whether the only thing that survives in it is the phantom of the theologico-political" (1988:249).

According to Lefort, while in the premodern world political authority was invested in the sacralized body of the king, thus giving society a body (1988:17), in modern democracies political power is totally disincorporated, thus abstracting it from any particular location or embodiment: power, by belonging to all, belongs to none. As Lefort put it, in modern societies "the locus of power is an empty place, it cannot be occupied—it is such that no individual and no group can be consubstantial with it—and it cannot be represented" (1988:17). Without the kind of natural foundation that sustained the monarchical model of the ancien régime, a "democratic society is instituted as a society without a body" (1988:18). As such, it emerges as "a purely social society" in which "the people, the nation, and the state" take on the status of "universal entities" which do not, however, "represent substantial entities" (1988:17). Without natural markers of certainty, modern democracy becomes a postfoundational society in which "people experience a fundamental indeterminacy as to the basis of power, law, and knowledge" (1988:19).

These considerations throw some light upon the transition from the rule of Gómez, whose quasi-sacral personal figure came to embody the state (and whose spirit is now invoked in popular religious practices to heal the wounded body and soul of citizens and nation alike), to the rule of democracy, whose representatives, as we shall see, have had to justify the claim that they rightfully occupy, rather than usurp, a sovereign space that in principle belongs to all. Yet this shift in the formal representation of sovereign power "from the body of the king to the body of nobody" (Turner 1989:331) should not be interpreted as the dematerialization of power or the erasure of its material foundations, but as a change in the form in which power is materialized and represented in modern societies. The theological image of the body's double nature, with its multiple religious and political resonances in the Christian West, may be displaced, as I have shown, to secular political leaders or to the nation's natural body. Lefort's notion of modern democracy as a "society without a body" or as a "purely social society," depends upon the acceptance of fetishized conceptions of power in premodern societies. Instead of examining these conceptions as ideological constructs, Lefort endorses their fetish-meaning ("he knows that the king really doesn't have two bodies, but still . . ."), reinscribing the mystified separation of the material and the sociocultural which they both reflect and express. By reinscribing rather than accounting for the separation between material practices and cultural constructs, Lefort's discussion instantiates a discursive approach to the demystification of state power that obscures from view the worldly relations of exploitation and domination within which political power is exercised and achieves its mystifying effects.[38]

For example, building on Lefort's elaboration of Kantorowicz's work, this separation makes it possible for Slavoj Žižek to discuss state dominance in terms of psychoideological operations that reduce the state to an idea and make its subjects responsible for their subjection: "It is the subject himself who, by behaving toward the Master in a subject-like way, makes him a Master" (1991:263). Similarly, Philip Abrams treats the state as a fiction that

---

38. For a lucid materialist critique of semiological approaches to power that includes a discussion of Žižek's work, see Pietz's important article (1993).

The Gómez family mausoleum in the cemetery of Maracay. (Photo: Julie Skurski.)

conceals the real practice of political power: "The state is not the reality which stands behind the mask of political practice. It is itself the mask which prevents our seeing political practice as it is" (1988:82).[39] Abrams argues that what exists—and what should be the proper object of study—is both the state's real institutional disunity ("the state-system") and the ideological message of its unity ("the state-idea") (1988:82). While he recognizes that the state is "an ideological artefact" (1988:81) that should be studied historically, by separating (fictive) mask from (real) practice and privileging the latter, he misses the opportunity to conceptualize the practice of masking and the masking of practice as dual aspects of the historical process through which states are constituted. The process of masking is active—it entails not concealing a preexisting reality but trans/forming it. Turning his own mask both

---

39. Abrams's provocative article has had considerable influence among scholars working on Latin America; for instance, see Joseph and Nugent (1994).

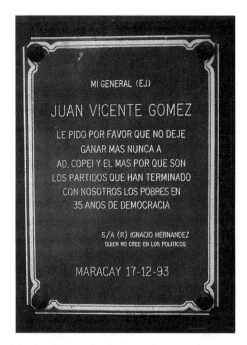

Plaque placed in the Gómez family mausoleum in the cemetery of Maracay: "My General (EJ) Juan Vicente Gómez. I ask you please never to let AD, COPEI, and MAS win because these parties have destroyed us poor people in 35 years of democracy. S/A (R) Ignacio Hernández, who does not believe in politicians." (Photo: Julie Skurski.)

into a defining feature of his political face and into a means to unmask politicians whose faces *are* their masks, "Superbarrio," the Mexican political activist who appears as a masked wrestler told his Harvard University audience: "Distrust all politicians who wear masks and don't show their true faces."[40] Analysis too should unsettle rather than confirm the separation between false mask and true faces. The state is not the mask that prevents our seeing political practice for what it is; it is the mystifying unity of the mask and the masked in terms of which political practice is constituted.

Rather than adopting a limiting view of the state that focuses on the belief in its power (as in Žižek) or regards it as a fetish idea that must be

---

40. Superbarrio's statement came during his response to my question: "Are you going to remove your mask some day?" at the conference Performance and Politics, Harvard University, 10 May 1996. His presentation took the form of a campaign speech as a candidate for the presidency of the United States.

disbelieved (as in Abrams), I suggest we analyze the historical production of the state as a mystifying complex of practices and beliefs. If a multiplicity of particularities produces the appearance of the state as a single general form, this Foucaldian "state effect" is always already present in each of these particularities as its condition of possibility. The state's reification is both the effect and the condition of its manifold objectifications. What could be called the "state form" works by establishing a relationship of equivalence between the general and the particular, the abstract and the concrete. Like money and capital, the state is not just a thing or an idea, but a complex ensemble of social relations mediated by things or thing-like objectifications of social practice. These objectifications are neither independent entities with inherent properties nor solely symbols of social relations, but are the medium through which these relations are constituted. "Social production relations are not only 'symbolized' by things, but are realized through things" (Rubin 1973: 11). Thus, it is by examining the historical objectifications of the state that we can understand its configuration in a given society—its particular general form.

By revisiting traces of the past and of its broken memory, I have sought to offer a view of state policies and contests over state rule that led to the mutual construction of Venezuela as an oil nation and to the reconfiguration of its state. As an oil nation, Venezuela was imagined as having two bodies, a natural body (the material source of its wealth) and a political body (its citizenry), both of which were represented by the state. When today Gómez's spirit is invoked in his mausoleum or incorporated in a *materia* (spiritual medium) and speaks to followers in the mountain of Sorte, the authority of his words is inseparable from the long-buried foundations of his power as representative of the nation's two bodies. The democratic state's power also lies on these foundations. As we shall see, if those who represent the democratic state appear as state usurpers (as is the case with Carlos Andrés Pérez, who was deposed and imprisoned between 1993 and 1996 for the illegal use of state funds), it is not only because they occupy a space that formally belongs to all but because their performance is collectively repudiated in terms of substantive criteria—of historically evolved expectations and standards concerning the state's role as representative of an oil nation. As both democratic and dictatorial states have been formed and evaluated in terms of these criteria, there has developed a counterpoint between dictatorship and democracy that continues, as the haunting presence of Gómez's spirit reveals, to this day.

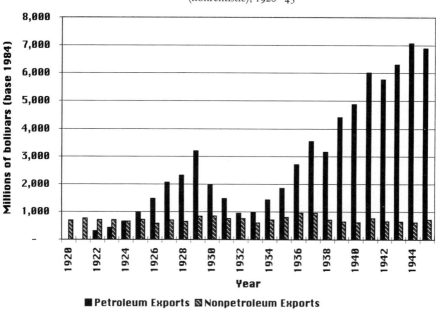

Figure 1
Relationship between nonpetroleum exports and petroleum exports
(nonrentistic), 1920–45

SOURCE: Baptista 1991: 118

Table 3
Share of agriculture in gross domestic product,
1920–45
(in millions of bolivars, base 1984)

Year	GDP (non rentistic)	Agriculture	% of Agr. in GDP
1920	7,324.4	1,985.8	27
1925	14,587.3	2,929.0	20
1930	21,334.5	3,357.5	16
1935	20,090.3	3,627.2	18
1940	30,121.6	3,716.0	12
1945	40,733.9	3,870.7	10

SOURCE: Baptista 1991: 114

Table 4
Share of petroleum in total exports, 1920–45
(in millions of Bolivars, base 1984)

Year	Total exports	Petroleum exports (nonrentistic)	Non-petroleum exports	% of petro-leum in total exports
1920	677.2	—	677.2	0
1925	1,690.2	980.9	709.3	58
1930	2,803.6	1,964.3	839.3	70
1935	2,635.5	1,846.5	789.0	70
1940	5,484.3	4,871.6	612.7	89
1945	7,594.5	6,882.0	712.5	91

SOURCE: Baptista 1991: 118.

Table 5
Urban/rural population distribution, 1920–45

Year	Total population	Urban population	Urban/total population (%)	Rural population	Rural/total population (%)
1920	2,992,468	490,765	16	2,501,703	84
1925	3,114,434	588,398	19	2,526,036	81
1930	3,300,214	749,844	23	2,550,370	77
1935	3,464,993	890,290	26	2,574,703	74
1940	3,783,780	1,169,188	31	2,614,592	69
1945	4,223,014	1,541,400	36	2,681,614	64

SOURCE: Baptista 1991: 21, 22.

PART TWO

Debut

VENEZUELAN COUNTERPOINT: DICTATORSHIP AND DEMOCRACY

General Pérez Jiménez, in front of his home in Spain.

3

THE EIGHTEENTH BRUMAIRE
OF DICTATORSHIP

The defining characteristic of Venezuela—as that of most Latin American countries in the nineteenth century—was the tragic contrast between social reality and the false covering of laws, constitutions, and institutions imported or translated from Europe through which we mask, more than remedy, our backwardness and our neglect.

Mariano Picón Salas

The tradition of all the dead generations weighs like a nightmare on the brain of the living.

Karl Marx

IMAGES OF HISTORY

The relationship between dictatorship and democracy figures in Latin America's political imagination as yet one more manifestation of the pervasive Manichaean confrontation between barbarism and civilization which has defined the continent's ambiguous identity since the conquest. Works of fiction and scholarly accounts typically depict Latin American nations as hybrid societies caught between a primitive and a modern order. Saturated by colonial visions and by republican ideals, the opposition between these two models of rule is underwritten by imperial images of a backward people in need of tutelary control as well as by nationalist imaginings of Latin America's distinctive identity.

This tension between the impetus to catalogue once again Latin America's ancestral deficiencies and the desire to celebrate its historical uniqueness energizes representations of Latin American politics. While fiction writers tend to focus on the distinctive character of the many emblematic caudillos and dictators that have come to distinguish Latin American political culture, social scientists generally concentrate on the modernizing construction of democratic institutions and analyze dictatorships as obstacles to progress.

Thus, if we were to look at the continent's stormy political life through the combined gazes of novelists and social scientists, it is likely that we would suffer from split vision. On one side we would see an elusive continent where history unfolds as the wild offspring of a unique merger of the real and the magical.[1] On the other we would recognize pale replicas of canonical first-world nations,[2] societies not so much different as incomplete, whose history, while traversing thwarted paths, is supposed to evolve toward familiar ends.[3] The clash between these images points less to two different ways of seeing the same reality than to the entanglement of even the most intensely inward-looking account of Latin American history with the view from the Empire. If a more compelling vision is to be achieved, a perspective must be sought that avoids both the tantalizing lure of a cultivated exoticism and the comforting appeal of an assumed familiarity—one capable of grasping the extraordinary within the quotidian making of a history that still remains to be written.

In pursuit of this aim, I focus here on several coups d'état that offer a glimpse into the terms in which struggles over the state were waged in Venezuela. In these struggles, competing images of democracy and dictatorship appeared as the main adversaries in a redemptive drama. Yet these models of rule were so bound up with each other, so conditioned by the oil economy which sustained them, and so deeply saturated by a colonial eschatology that in some respects they came to share attributes and to resemble each other. As in Fernando Ortiz's classic counterpoint between tobacco and sugar, in which the sharp contrasts that originally distinguished the production of the two main agricultural products of Cuban society became blurred as they came to be produced under similar conditions (1995), in Venezuela the Manichaean opposition between democracy and dictatorship has obscured the extent to which these political formations are the product of common circumstances and share features which blunt their opposition.

The construction of Venezuela's democracy is conventionally represented in political discourse as well as in textbooks and the media as an evolutionary process, the initiation of which coincided with Juan Vicente Gómez's death. As the previous chapter indicated, the dictator's death in December 1935 brought the end of his twenty-seven year rule and the beginning of the liberalization of the political system. Under the regimes of

1. The literary references are numerous, but perhaps the essential texts are Sarmiento's *Facundo* (1845), Rulfo's *Pedro Páramo* (1955), Asturias's *El señor Presidente* (1946), García Márquez's *El otoño del patriarca* (1974), Carpentier's *El reino de este mundo* (1949) and *El recurso del método* (1974), and Roa Bastos's *Yo el supremo* (1974).

2. I use this term with the necessary caveats. For a historically informed and culturally sensitive critique of the taxonomy of three worlds, see Pletsch (1981).

3. In different ways, this view permeates the works produced from the otherwise competing frameworks of modernization, dependency, and Marxist theories.

generals Eleazar López Contreras (1936–41) and Isaías Medina Angarita (1941–45), changes in the institutions of the state reflected and facilitated the increasing participation and representation of social groups in national politics. This process was accelerated by Acción Democrática (AD) after the 1945 coup that launched it into power and the election of its leader Rómulo Gallegos in 1947, the first president elected through universal suffrage in Venezuelan history. On 24 November 1948, nine months after Gallegos's election, the military coup that interrupted this process led to a ten-year dictatorship which was consolidated by a palace coup on 2 December 1952. On 23 January 1958 the dictatorship, in turn, was ended by another military coup, this time backed by massive popular support. Since 1958, Venezuela has experienced democratic rule, including several transfers of power between competing political parties. The prevailing view is that democracy was consolidated after the 1948–58 dictatorship, which figures as an interruption of democracy's evolution.

During the same period that saw the consolidation of Venezuelan democratic institutions, older Latin American democracies abruptly ended in violent coups. Between 1964 and 1976 the democratic regimes of Brazil, Ecuador, Peru, Uruguay, Chile, and Argentina fell to the military. Recently this trend has been reversed, and a process of redemocratization has begun throughout the region: in Ecuador (1979), Peru (1980), Argentina (1983), Brazil (1985), Uruguay (1985), Chile (1989), and, with constraints, in some Central American and Caribbean nations (El Salvador, Panama, Guatemala, Honduras, Nicaragua, and Haiti). Venezuelan democracy, which had struck foreign observers as an enigmatic exception during the authoritarian phase of Latin American politics, has been hailed as a potential model for the democratic regimes that have emerged from military dictatorships which failed to achieve progress through the harsh medicine of political order and economic orthodoxy. Until now regarded as an exception, Venezuela has come to be seen as an example:

> For me, then, the key issue is this: to what extent do the conditions which made for the restoration (indeed, virtually the creation) of bourgeois hegemony in Venezuela exist in these countries today? What we have at present is perhaps no more than a situation which makes such an outcome possible, and the beginning of the emergence, from country to country, of the elements of the "Venezuelan syndrome": restored legitimacy for bourgeois politicians, elite consensus, the definition of democracy in procedural terms, the shelving of conflictive issues, the marginalization of the left, and the deliberate strengthening of the executives over legislatures, and leaders over parties . . . There is

a discernible trend, in other words, toward "self-limiting democracy" of the Venezuelan type (Cammak 1986:1944).[4]

For Venezuelans accustomed to almost four decades of political stability, it is not the democratic period but the dictatorship from 1948 to 1958 that seems anomalous. Most analysts reproduce this view and regard the dictatorship as a dark parenthesis: the understanding of democracy is sought by studying the democratic period itself. Yet, as revisionist literature shows— the recent development of which is related to the renewal of interest in Gómez as part of the present crisis of the democratic system—the dictatorship from 1948 to 1958 was a time of fundamental changes which conditioned the reemergence and consolidation of democracy after 1958. In this section I explore the making of Venezuela's singular democracy in light of this dark dictatorship.

I approach the dictatorship tangentially, through some of the key constitutive moments of its making and unmaking; my focus is on a series of coups d'état that took place between 1945, when AD came to power by a coup and established a democratic regime (1945–48), and 1958, when the dictator was overthrown. Thus, the following interpretation does not pretend to be a comprehensive analysis of this period. Rather, this is a study of the orchestration of coups d'état seen as historical ruptures which allow us to observe the formation and transformation of cultural forms and political institutions during this period.

Although coups generally initiate the establishment of a new political order, like the liminal phases of rituals in relatively stable societies (Turner 1967:95–106), they are reflective and transformative occasions, moments betwixt and between ordinary times, when axiomatic values are invoked even as they are questioned and reformulated. In expressing and rearticulating basic values, these interstructural situations illuminate a society's sustaining principles and cultural forms. While my analysis is necessarily fragmentary, I try to place these coups d'état in their immediate context as well as within the longer process of Venezuela's transformation into an oil nation.

By illuminating distinguishing features of the construction of democracy in Venezuela, I hope to contribute as well to the large body of work devoted

---

4. Cammak's insightful characterization of Venezuela's democracy is at once a succinct description of its accomplishments and a sobering—and unusual—critique of its limitations. His understanding of its potential significance for other Latin American countries seems to be based on Levine's interpretation (included in the journal issue edited by Cammak) which minimizes the role of oil resources in the making of Venezuelan democracy (1986:52).

to the study of processes of democratization in Latin America in which Venezuela often figures as a successful example of transition to democracy.[5] If the rise of authoritarianism in the sixties led to studies which sought to show, in Albert Hirschman's words, how a "specific turn of the political tide" originated in "a precise feature of the underlying economic terrain" (1979: 68),[6] the reemergence of democratic regimes since the mid-seventies has stimulated two distinct areas of research, one focusing on politics or action and the other on culture or meaning, which share a tendency to approach each area as a relatively independent realm. From different perspectives, these lines of inquiry mark a shift from the study of interactions between levels, instances, or domains within society, to that of political action—from the problematic of society to that of the human subject.

While they are a welcome corrective to the one-sidedness of earlier frameworks (which left little place for human agents as political actors or as culturally constituted subjects), these lines of inquiry in turn show a tendency to re-create the old one-sidedness at another level by failing to locate actors in their formative social contexts.[7] Perhaps against the grain, this study persists in seeking significant relations among the production of material life, the creation of cultural formations, and the exercise of power. In focusing on these mutually conditioning relations, I seek to show the reciprocal constitution of cultural, political, and economic domains rather than to consolidate their appearance as independent orders.

ELECTING VIOLENCE, PEACEFUL ELECTIONS

During Gómez's twenty-seven-year rule, no mass organizations were allowed to exist. Yet only twelve years after his death, a national election was

5. There is a vast literature on democracy. In addition to the sources cited in this chapter, I have found particularly useful the work by Markoff (1996) as well as the body of literature on transitions to democracy. For reviews of this literature, see Mainwaring (1992) and Cammack (1986); for a discussion of its underlying assumptions, see Coronil (1997). Most references to Venezuela in this literature focus on the post-1958 period. For specific works on Venezuelan democracy, see Blank (1973), Batista Urbaneja (1992), Levine (1973), Hellinger (1985), and Rey (1988).

6. Hirschman was of course referring to the seminal work of Guillermo O'Donnell (1973; 1975).

7. These remarks refer only to *tendencies* in the contemporary literature. The focus on politics can be seen in the recent work coordinated by O'Donnell, Schmitter, and Whitehead (1986), who privilege political conflict within authoritarian regimes in their explanation of the forces leading to the transition to democracy. For a criticism of this view, see Cardoso (1985:5). The emphasis on discourse in the study of the constitution of political identities characterizes some of the work on Argentinean democratization, for instance Portantiero and Ipola (1981).

held to elect the president and Congress by direct and universal vote. All adult Venezuelans, without restrictions based on gender, property, or literacy, were allowed to vote in the election of 14 December 1947 and select the president among various candidates. Universal enfranchisement was established in Venezuela earlier than in eleven other Latin American countries and just one year after Italy and France (Therborn 1977:11; 1978:78). How can this relatively rapid turn to electoral democracy be explained?

Scholars agree that Venezuela's transition to democracy at this time was part of a post–World War II movement toward democratization that intensified a domestic process of liberalization that had begun after Gómez's death. Under Gómez, voters were in principle three times removed from electing the president. The constitution stipulated that all males twenty-one and over would elect representatives for municipal councils and state legislatures, who then selected national legislators, who in turn elected the president; in practice, Gómez was appointed president. In the aftermath of Gómez's death, his successor, General López Contreras, took steps to liberalize the political process in response to a collective rejection of the Gómez dictatorship.

When a peaceful demonstration in Caracas on 14 February 1936 was violently suppressed and protests throughout the city against state violence made evident the presence of new urban actors, President López Contreras established his position as a moderate by removing the governor of the Federal District, the person responsible for repressing the demonstration, and by restoring constitutional guarantees. He also announced his February Program, the first comprehensive development plan in the nation's history, a wide-ranging reformist program drafted by some of the nation's leading intellectuals directed to the modernization of the economy and polity. In April 1936 the National Congress ratified López Contreras, who promised to implement this reformist program, as constitutional president until 1941.

As these emerging urban actors became a more organized political force, their demands for fundamental social reforms and direct universal elections gained a wider audience and began to include the more radical workers of the oil sector. In December 1936, oil workers in the Zulia state organized a major strike that became a landmark in Venezuelan history. Their demand for better pay and working conditions and for the right to establish a union galvanized people into forming a movement of national support. In an effort to defuse this movement, López Contreras agreed to meet partially workers' demand for higher wages but promptly used the Ley Lara, a law against communist organizations passed in 1936 by the Congress dominated by gomecistas, to dissolve all leftist organizations, forcing them underground and exiling their main leaders.

Congress also revised the constitution's electoral regulations (which under Gómez had only formal significance). The constitution now restricted the vote to the very small portion of the population comprising literate males twenty-one years of age and over. According to a historian, "This behavior, the liberalization of politics and then the suppression of the political action that resulted, illustrates a pattern in post-Gómez Venezuelan politics," not "the insincerity of López's commitment to democratic or participatory political systems" (Lombardi 1982:221). Independently of López Contreras's motivations, this restriction clearly did not represent a turn toward autocratic rule, although it did reflect the ruling elite's effort to limit the extension of democratic rights and its anxiety concerning changed circumstances.

This integration of popular and elite interests around a reformist center came to characterize hegemonic political projects in Venezuela. If populism sustains the fantasy of national unity through the identification of people and nation, in Venezuela the expectation that collective well-being would be achieved through oil-financed national transformation turned this fantasy into an illusion of collective harmony. But from the outset, the construction of this illusion of harmony was premised on reformist control over the oil industry and the forceful exclusion of radical demands made by both elite and popular sectors.[8]

At the end of his regime, López Contreras allowed the suppressed groups to participate in the presidential election. Given the restrictive electoral franchise, these groups knew López Contreras would be able to impose his candidate. Instead of competing against each other in an electoral contest they could not win, the left readily united around a symbolic candidate, Rómulo Gallegos, the famous author of the novel *Doña Bárbara*. As expected, Congress elected the man López Contreras had chosen as his successor, his minister of war, General Isaías Medina Angarita (only around forty thousand people voted in this election).

General Medina, younger than López Contreras and not personally associated with the Gómez regime, had a stronger commitment to the liberalization of the political system and allowed political parties to organize more freely and to run in the 1942 municipal and state elections. Under his rule, a constitutional reform allowed women to vote in municipal elections and literate men to vote directly for congressional representatives, who in turn elected the president (rather than indirectly through municipal representatives who elected the congressmen).

8. I am borrowing the concept of "illusion of harmony" from the title of a book edited by Naím and Piñango that discussed different aspects of this illusion after it had begun to dissolve (1985).

Since 1936, the leaders of the Generación del 28 who claimed to represent the post-Gómez nation had demanded the establishment of direct election of the president and Congress by universal suffrage. By the time Medina came into power, their attempt to form a united leftist party, the Partido Democrático Nacional (PDN), had broken down. The Communists separated from the PDN in 1938 and formed the Partido Comunista de Venezuela (PC), leaving Betancourt in control of the PDN. While the Communists supported Medina as part of the United Front policy to combat fascism, the PDN leadership founded Acción Democrática in 1941, which made the reform of the electoral system one of its principal political goals.

When General Medina's term drew to a close, AD assented to Medina's selection of the civilian Diógenes Escalante as his successor, for Escalante promised he would establish universal suffrage. However, illness forced Escalante to withdraw, and Medina selected another civilian candidate, Angel Biaggini, who failed to make a similar commitment and was mistrusted by AD. The party's political ambitions suddenly appeared frustrated: it was difficult to imagine that AD would be able to win an election as long as the circle of voters remained restricted to a small minority. AD grew impatient.

At this time AD found an unlikely ally which was restless with the slow pace of change within the military establishment. A group of middle-level officers, many of whom had been trained outside the country and had been schooled in developmentalist ideologies which assigned the military a leading role in projects of national development, felt marginalized by the army's cliquish leadership and sought a more rapid pace of political reform and professional promotion. Led by Major Marcos Pérez Jiménez, a highly ranked graduate of Venezuela's and Peru's military academies, these officers formed a movement, the Unión Patriótica Militar (UPM), with the stated goal of taking over the government in order to bring "decency" and "patriotism" to the state, establishing democratic institutions and promoting the nation's development.

One of the UPM's secret documents illustrates the vague mix of patriotic rhetoric and military nationalism that informed its plans. Portraying themselves as democrats, in this document the UPM's leaders stated that their goal was to renew institutions and methods of rule and to include in government "men and norms with a true sense of patriotism and decency who would promote the Nation's progress and take it to the leading position to which it is entitled because of its glorious past" (Krispin 1994:62). They affirmed their commitment to democracy, which they defined as the expression of national unity through universal elections: "We do not defend personal or class interests, and seek the formation of a government founded on free and universal elections of all Venezuelan citizens, a constitutional reform that represents the national will, and the creation of a truly professional army." The military, they asserted, had to be "cleansed" of old and incompetent elements that caused its backwardness. Their statement concludes with their sworn commitment to conspire secretly to achieve their "sacred mission."

Although these military officers felt confident that they could overthrow General Medina, they had doubts about their ability to control the state given their narrow political base and their isolation from major social groups. While Major Pérez Jiménez proposed first to take over power and then to invite "distinguished" civilians to participate in the government, most officers agreed with Lieutenant Horacio López Conde's proposal to invite AD to participate in the coup from the outset.

The rebel officers worked out the alliance between UPM and AD in several meetings attended by representatives of both groups. Rómulo Betancourt and Raul Leoni participated in the first meeting and were joined in other planning sessions by Luis Beltrán Prieto and Gonzalo Barrios. These men decided to keep secret their decision to join the coup, ostensibly in order to take exclusive blame for the coup if it failed; reportedly, neither Rómulo Gallegos nor Andrés Eloy Blanco, the president and vice president of the party respectively, knew about it.[9] After several meetings, it was agreed that AD would lead the junta and that only two of the officers, Mario Vargas and Carlos Delgado Chalbaud (of higher military and social status) would participate in it.[10]

AD was a small but expanding mass-based party that had sought to gain power through elections since its foundation in 1941. In pursuit of this strategy, its leaders had done extensive grassroots work. While in the rural sectors they established a leading and long-lasting foothold, in the urban sectors they achieved significant support among white-collar workers,

9. It is likely that an additional reason for keeping this decision from Gallegos and Blanco was to avoid meeting their likely disapproval, given Gallegos's principled objection to violent illegal political actions and Blanco's own inclinations and enormous respect for Gallegos. Gallegos held AD's top position because as an internationally famed novelist and educator he was seen as a nonpartisan, national figure. Andrés Eloy Blanco, a well-known poet in Venezuela, shared with Gallegos a national presence as a nonsectarian person of wide appeal. However, real control of the party rested with Rómulo Betancourt, its general secretary. In these meetings, UPM was represented by Marcos Pérez Jiménez, Carlos Morales, Martín Márquez Añez, Horacio López Conde, and Francisco Gutiérrez Prado.

10. I draw on Krispin's work, which offers a detailed account of the 1945 coup (1994: 51–74).

teachers, and middle-level professionals but competed with the Communists for control over oil workers and the organized urban proletariat. AD's major obstacle, however, was what it perceived as the slow pace of electoral reform. When Escalante became ill and Biaggini did not promise that universal suffrage would be quickly implemented, AD's leadership came to accept without delay the offer of a nondemocratic path to democracy. The rapid pace of urbanization and economic expansion spurred by the growth of the oil economy created conditions which fostered a sense that progress was around the corner; it could not be made to wait.

On 16 October 1945, UPM leaders and Rómulo Betancourt met in secret for the last time before the coup. Each side assumed specific responsibilities. While the military would control the key garrisons and the heavily armed Palacio Presidencial de Miraflores (the presidential building), AD would secure support for the coup from the civilian population. In a highly centralized country with a relatively small elite united by links of family, friendship, and business, however, it was hard to keep secrets. General Medina was forewarned about the conspiracy by his nephew, Captain Elio Quintero Medina, who learned about it through his friend, Captain Wolfang Larrazábal.

In order to prevent the coup, on the morning of 18 October 1945 General Medina arrested Major Pérez Jiménez. Yet other UPM leaders proceeded to implement the coup as planned. The rebel officers took over the Military Academy and the Palacio Presidencial de Miraflores and arrested Medina's ministers. President Medina and loyal officers battled the rebels from the Ambrosio Plaza military garrison. The loyal head of the Caracas police asked President Medina for permission to attack the Military Academy, but he refused, explaining that he had been a captain of the academy's cadet company during seventeen years and did not want to be responsible for the death of young military officers.

Reportedly, President Medina believed that the rebellion was limited to Caracas and assumed that it would be subdued soon. Yet on 19 October he learned that rebel officers also controlled Venezuela's most important military garrison, the Cuartel Maracay. Airplanes from Maracay attacked loyal garrisons in Caracas, including the Cuartel San Carlos, which was defended by the Caracas police. When these planes hit the San Carlos garrison, the police deserted it, fearing that the bombs would set its arsenal on fire. In the ensuing confusion, popular sectors, resentful of long-standing police abuse, sided with the military and looted the San Carlos garrison. Reportedly, President Medina, worried about these developments, and seeking to avoid a blood-

The "Junta Revolucionaria de Gobierno," 19 October 1948. From left to right, Luis Beltrán Prieto Figueroa, Raul Leoni, Carlos Delgado Chalbaud, Rómulo Betancourt, Mario Vargas, Edmundo Fernandez, and Gonzalo Barrios. Next to the microphone, Valmore Rodríguez. (Fundación Andrés Mata.)

bath, decided to concede defeat. Soon thereafter, the police surrendered to the military. The coup was over. The new ruling junta comprised AD leaders Rómulo Betancourt (president), Raúl Leoni, Luis Beltrán Prieto, Gonzalo Barrios, and Edmundo Fernández, and two military officers, Carlos Delgado Chalbaud and Mario Vargas. This coup, orchestrated in secret at the top, was soon glorified by AD as Venezuela's "October Revolution."

UNIVERSAL ELECTIONS: PURIFYING THE NATION

Since independence, the language of revolution had magnified the importance of the repeated realignments of state power in Venezuela. After Gómez's death, as part of the hemispheric struggle against fascism and communism but also as a result of domestic efforts to build a broad progressive coalition, the state and the left had gravitated toward the political center, and the language of reformism had come to frame political discourse (Dávila 1992:101).

The 1945 coup against Medina provided a historical opening for the rearticulation of the language of revolution. By defining the coup as a revolutionary event, AD divided Venezuelan history into two periods and constructed itself as the agent of the nation's progress. Suddenly, the birth of modern Venezuela was shifted to 1945, turning that date as well into the moment of Gómez's "historical death."[11] Paradoxically, in the name of establishing democracy, AD gained control of the state by means of a violent coup against a constitutional regime that was widely acknowledged to be making steps toward democracy. AD emphasized that this coup was a means of establishing universal suffrage and therefore true democracy, thus differentiating it from coups that only changed the group in power. Compelled to legitimate its action but also caught up in the spirit of the times, AD presented universal suffrage as an epoch-making event that justified the coup as a means to implement democracy. A noted Venezuelan historian closely aligned with AD claims that "all Venezuelans of 1945 believed in universal suffrage as the miracle that would purify the nation" (*como el milagro de la purificación nacional*) (Velázquez 1979:75–76; Dávila 1992:39).

Once in power, AD moved quickly to establish universal elections. First, a new national Congress was elected by universal vote in 1946. This Congress then wrote a new constitution and electoral law. The long-sought goal was achieved: the constitution granted suffrage to all citizens eighteen years old or older, eliminating the literacy requirement and the exclusion of women, and established the direct popular election of the president, Congress, and municipal representatives. On 14 December 1947, Rómulo Gallegos, known as *el maestro* (the teacher), was elected president with almost 75 percent of the vote.[12] With this election AD sought to legitimate its ascent to power through a coup and established the equation between universal suffrage and democracy.

11. In AD's historiography, the year 1936 is kept as a modern landmark in the sense that it signals AD's origins through the foundation of ORVE (Movimiento de Organización Venezuela), the organization that gave birth to AD (Dávila 1992:56). This view is also present in fictional accounts, as in Gallegos's novel *Cantaclaro,* in which Juan Crisóstomo Payara, modeled after the caudillo Roberto Vargas Díaz, refers to the 1945 coup as the real origins of Venezuelan modernity—the date when "'Gómez really died.'"

12. In the 1946 congressional election AD obtained 78.4 percent of the votes (1,100,000); COPEI, 13.2 percent (185,000); URD, 4.2 percent (59,000); and PC, 3.6 percent (50,000). In the 1947 presidential elections, AD obtained 74 percent; COPEI, 22.4 percent; and PC, 3.1 percent (Parra 1968: 58–71).

THE TRANSITION TO DEMOCRACY

It is difficult to account for this relatively rapid and smooth transition to democracy in Venezuela. The conditions associated by most analysts with the emergence and establishment of bourgeois democracy were only partially present in the country. For many theorists, the development of capitalism and the formation of competitive social groups is a primary condition for the rise of democratic institutions (Therborn 1977:28). Yet in Venezuela, an expanding but state-dependent middle class, a combative but small and isolated proletariat, and a declining peasantry lacking in political organization appeared to be weak forces behind the push for democratization.

One explanation for the rise of democracy emphasizes the impact of World War II on Venezuela's domestic politics (Carrera Damas 1980). The international struggle against fascism was linked to promoting political forces of democracy within the hemisphere. Both the United States and the Soviet Union backed the establishment of reformist regimes. As a source of a strategic wartime commodity to the United States, whose supply was threatened by Germany, Venezuela became particularly important during that war. The U.S. government sought to counter both German and communist influence in Venezuela by promoting democratic reforms and closer economic and cultural ties with the United States. From this perspective, democracy was also promoted externally rather than generated solely from within.

Clearly, one should not expect to find in Venezuela a replication of the domestic conditions within which democracy rose in advanced capitalist nations. Undoubtedly, external factors related to the worldwide struggle against fascism during World War II played a crucial role in establishing universal suffrage in Venezuela at this time. But external conditions had an impact because there were also internal social forces which had a stake in democracy. In Venezuela, the struggle for democracy developed as a struggle against gomecismo and against communism. After Gómez's death, the opposition to gomecismo argued effectively for a radical redefinition of the state and established the terms which defined national political discourse ever since. In mainstream public discourse, gomecismo came to be equated with the denial of political liberties and with the privatization of state power and wealth.

The achievement of democracy, by contrast, was identified with the participation of the citizenry in both the nation's political system and in its wealth. While Gómez had used the state to enrich himself and to advance his personal goals, it was claimed that a democratic regime would invest the nation's wealth in projects that would benefit the collectivity and bring Venezuela into the modern world. The idea of democracy acquired specific content and sparked the national imagination in Venezuela through the alluring promise that a democratic system would offer people the right to participate in the political system and to benefit from the nation's immense wealth. This union of power and wealth, of political rights and economic entitlements resulting from the state-mediated union of the physical and the political bodies of the nation, gave Venezuelan democracy its distinctive form.

SOWING OIL: ERODING DEMOCRACY

Although Arturo Uslar Pietri, one of the victims of AD's 1945 trials against those enriched by the Gómez regime, had coined the slogan "to sow the oil" in 1936, AD embraced it as its own and made it into the guiding principle of its economic program.[13] "To sow the oil" was an appropriately ambiguous metaphor. The notion of *sembrar* (to sow) conjoined a known agricultural practice to the task of embarking on new productive ventures. It thus imaged in familiar terms—without specifying the form or direction this should take—the relatively new idea that oil income should be used to develop modern enterprises. As a key metaphor in narratives of national progress and affluence, it helped to circumvent conflictual issues of class or privilege by bringing to mind images of collective fecundity through the productive union of oil and agriculture—separate realms that Venezuelan school children learned to call *el reino mineral y el reino vegetal* (the mineral and vegetable kingdoms). Presiding over these kingdoms of nature, the state appeared as the great alchemist in charge of turning oil money into productive agricultural and industrial investments and, thus, of transforming Venezuela's vast but exhaustible oil wealth into permanent social wealth.

If we look at state spending between 1936 and 1948, we observe that this goal led to a gradual shift from military and administrative to social spending—especially in education and health—and to the growing promotion of national industry (Hausmann 1982:313–56). But during AD's triennium, a

13. Because Arturo Uslar Pietri had worked under President Medina, after the 1945 coup he was accused of corruption by tribunals created by AD to punish individuals who had benefited from their association with Gómez and his successors. These unfair trials were one of the sources of collective discontent with AD's "sectarian" policies. In response, Uslar sharply criticized both AD and Betancourt. Yet AD not only adopted Uslar's phrase as its slogan but placed it in the logo of the Corporación Venezolana de Fomento, a state agency founded in 1946 to promote industrial and agricultural enterprises.

Novelist Rómulo Gallegos during the 1947 presidential campaign. (Instituto Autónomo Biblioteca Nacional.)

significant change took place. Bolstered by a budget increase of 240 percent between 1945 and 1948, the government sought to link its plan for national development—democracy plus industry—to the consolidation of AD as a party.

During the Trienio, AD devised policies to promote economic diversification and to establish social welfare programs for the working population. However, its failure to include other nascent parties in the administration or policy process and its use of government programs to strengthen its own base resulted in its estrangement from these groups, which accused it of sectarianism and favoritism. Using the state to increase its support among peasants and workers, AD legislated wage raises and subsidies for basic consumer goods and promoted their political organization. The average daily wage increased from Bs. 7.15 in 1944 to Bs. 11.71 in 1948 in real terms (Hausmann 1981:323). The number of urban trade unions increased from 215 with a membership of almost 25 thousand in 1945 to 1,047 with almost 140 thousand members in 1948; in the rural sector the expansion was from 53 unions with fewer than 4 thousand members in 1945 to over 500 unions with over 40 thousand members in 1948 (Powell 1971:79).

AD also supported the development of a local entrepreneurial sector by establishing close links with their leaders and organizations, promoting policies that favored the expansion of private business in industry and agriculture, and granting low-interest credits through the Corporación Venezolana de Fomento (Venezuelan Development Corporation, or CVF), founded in 1946 as an autonomous institute linked to the Development Ministry. The budget of the Development Ministry increased 700 percent during this three-year period, reflecting the importance that the government gave to the promotion of industry. Its most dynamic agency was the CVF, which in close cooperation with private capital initiated studies for the development of basic industries in steel, petrochemicals, and hydroelectric power.

The expanding influence of the state and the use of its ample resources in a number of areas, however, created fears that AD was monopolizing political power. The most telling expression of this fear took place in response to Decree 321, an executive order through which the state sought to raise and homogenize educational standards. This measure affected in particular parochial schools attended by middle- and upper-class children and was widely seen in those circles as a threat to their social power and to the power of the Church. Issued on 30 May 1946 on the eve of final examinations, this decree established that teachers from the public school system would evaluate the final examinations in private schools. This decree ignited such an intense collective protest by the Church, students, and parents, that the government decided to reverse its policy; and the minister of education, Humberto García Arocha, resigned from the post.

Overall, however, AD responded to what many regarded as its monopolization of power by further concentrating power in the ruling junta itself. In a marked shift of its own program that specified that governors would be elected by each state, AD now gave the president power to name state governors. Concerned about ongoing conspiracies, and buttressed by the elected support it had received, the government passed a decree that strengthened the powers of the executive and temporarily limited constitutional guarantees. Acting in a fashion that came to typify the conduct of the petroleum state, AD countered the possible unpopular effects of this measure, which removed substantive political rights, by manufacturing the illusion of collective progress through the transformation of oil money into concrete achievements. At the May Day celebrations of 1947 Betancourt offered to give three thousand houses to workers across the nation and to provide Bs. 5 million in housing loans for the middle class (Dávila 1992:118).

Perhaps the most telling instances of a gap between rhetorical claims and substantive achievements took place in the oil sector. The 240 percent increase in state income between 1945 and 1948 reflected the conjunction of a post-Gómez policy of increasing taxation of the oil companies and the sharp rise in oil company profit as a result of the post–World War II expansion of the world economy. Taking advantage of this boom in oil profits, Betancourt, as president of the provisional government after the 1945 coup, used Medina's 1943 oil law to obtain 58 percent of profits by increasing the income tax to 28.5 percent. At the time, this step was proclaimed as a nationalist triumph. But with the continuous rise in oil prices, the oil company profits continued to increase while Venezuela's share of profits declined to 53 percent in 1946 and 52 percent the following year. The state could obtain more revenues—the aspired goal of 60 percent of oil industry profits—only by further increasing the income tax on the oil industry. But a ceiling had been reached; the local level of the income tax now matched the U.S. tax level (28.5 percent). Any further increment would have directly reduced the oil companies' profits.

The oil companies began to exert considerable pressure on the government. Oil production in the Middle East—characterized by low production costs and small rent payments—was expanding at a fast rate, while in Venezuela it was stationary. The oil companies, which had begun to direct their investments toward the Middle East, threatened to disinvest in Venezuela. In response to these pressures, AD modified the income tax regulations in 1948 but presented the new code as an advance for the state. It established the fifty-fifty principle, the equal sharing of profits between the state and the oil companies.

The new code was a triumph of nationalist rhetoric. The 1948 oil law established the fifty-fifty principle by erasing the distinction between royalties and income tax: Venezuela's 50 percent participation in the industry's profits was to be determined by adding royalties and income tax. The income tax, which had been designed by Medina's 1943 law as a tool to capture for Venezuela all surplus profit, now became tied to a formula that obliged the state to share it with the oil companies. As Mommer has shown, this regulation in fact reduced the power of the state to transform surplus profits into state revenues. According to his revisionist interpretation, the proclaimed nationalist victory of AD's fifty-fifty agreement conceals a significant "quantitative" and "qualitative" setback (1983:32).[14]

14. On the basis of careful archival work, Margarita López Maya highlights the exceptionally favorable conditions under which Medina's 1943 oil legislation was approved, and the opposition that AD faced when it sought to expand the state's oil income after 1945 (1994:159–221; 387–89). Unlike Mommer, for her AD's 1948 fifty-fifty agreement was a significant nationalist achievement. While this issue requires further investigation, in my view her data about the 1945-48 relations among the

Maximizing oil revenues had been the central aim of Venezuela's oil policy. This goal united most domestic groups against the foreign oil companies. But the oil coin had another side: given the enormous weight of the oil revenues in the economy and the conflicting demands for access to them, the use of oil revenues proved to be inherently divisive. Local groups actively conspired against the government. Oil companies, concerned as they were about the ongoing pressure to increase the state's share of profits in the oil industry, were not insensitive to the significance of the growing opposition to AD's rule.[15]

THE 1948 COUP: A TERRIFYING SOLITUDE

The administration of President Rómulo Gallegos lasted only nine months. Although AD had managed to thwart several plots against the government

---

oil companies and the Venezuelan and U.S. governments does not contradict Mommer's interpretation, which is based on distinguishing rents and taxes as sources of state income (1986:74–96). For an interpretation that supports Mommer's argument, see Espinasa (1989). I am grateful to Margarita López Maya for sharing her views on this matter with me.

15. Valero has argued that the oil companies and their respective home governments (particularly Standard Oil and the United States) were attentive to political developments in Venezuela and played a cautious role in the 1945 coup (1993); rather than favoring any one of the contending groups, they covered their options. Their role in the 1948 coup is still being debated. It is well known that Gallegos accused the U.S. government of endorsing the coup on the basis of the presence of the U.S. military attaché in Venezuela, Colonel Adams, in the Palacio de Miraflores (the seat of government) on 24 November 1948. President Gallegos wrote President Truman and accused the United States of having promoted the coup. In his reply, President Truman assured Gallegos that his government had not taken a role in the coup. His ambassador in Venezuela had informed him that Colonel Adams had acted on his own accord, that he had gone to the Presidential Palace only to get information firsthand. This delicate matter came to a rest, and no definitive light has since been shed upon this dark episode. For a carefully researched but still inconclusive discussion of this issue based on U.S. Embassy and State Department materials, see López Maya (1994:361–77). Krispin has argued that Colonel Adams's presence was circumstantial. On the basis of reports from the U.S. Embassy as well as accounts by observers, including Rómulo Betancourt, he discounts the United States' role in the coup (1994:103–20). Bravo presents a different interpretation that highlights the existence of conflicts between U.S. companies that resented AD's preferential treatment of Rockefeller's Standard Oil and the presence of differences between Colonel Adams and the U.S. ambassador, Walter Donnelly, who sympathized with the regime (1984). On the basis of the evidence presented by Bravo, Ocarina Castillo notes the extent of the connections established in Venezuela by the U.S. Embassy and the U.S. Military Mission, the presence of a hidden network of common military-economic interests underlying programs directed at the standardization of armies in Latin America and the defense of hemispheric security, and the overriding priority assigned by the United States to the struggle against communism and the control of strategic resources (1990:24–28). López Maya argues that oil companies played no role in the 1945 coup, and that in 1948 the large oil companies, particularly Exxon's subsidiary Creole, did not want to destabilize the modus vivendi they had achieved (1994).

after the junta took power in 1945 and although its leadership was aware of a growing conservative conspiracy, by the end of 1948 it failed to control the antiregime forces.[16] On 24 November 1948 the military coup took place. Surprisingly, it met no significant opposition. The standard interpretation of these events is that a politicized populace saw no effective way of resisting the coup or that it somehow acquiesced to its own demobilization. A closer examination suggests that by the time the military took over, the people had already been demobilized by AD's top leadership.

As promised, AD had not taken power in 1945 to hold it by force but to establish a democratic system. Yet the government's achievements in collective welfare—unionization, wage increases, public health programs, educational reforms, economic diversification—were appropriated as triumphs of AD, not of a modernizing Venezuelan state or of popular political battles. Even some of the groups that had supported AD's nondemocratic route to democracy were alienated by AD's monopolization of political power. When in 1948 three out of four Venezuelans elected Gallegos president of Venezuela, many came to fear that state power would be the monopoly of a clique in a new guise, that through the electoral system AD would replace the rule of one man by the rule of one party. Even conservative forces drew on the democratic discourse AD had helped promote—its critique of exclusionary governments—to counter AD's sectarian rule.

In this context, the focus of both political struggles and economic competition, for those who felt excluded from power, shifted toward gaining control over the government itself. Despite AD's significant concessions and overtures to the private sector, many local businessmen felt threatened by its social reforms and support of workers and peasants; for them, the party's socialist origins and rhetoric resurrected the specter of an uncontrolled popular onslaught on property and order. The Church, already alienated by the Decree 321, was concerned by AD's secular orientation in education. The Christian Democratic party (Comité de Organización Política Electoral Independiente, COPEI) and social democratic party (Unión Republicana Democrática, URD) feared that they would not be able to compete electorally with the party that controlled the powerful state apparatus.

Despite the massive flow of money that AD poured into the military, the military leaders who had engineered the 1945 coup against Medina resented

---

16. According to Krispin, there were eight unsuccessful coups after 18 October 1945. Some of these were carried out by lopecistas, medinistas, and gomecistas, but some by members of the younger generation associated with the UPM (1994:93–94).

being excluded from power and wanted a larger role in government. In this context, the military, the ultimate locus of state force, once again became the agent of political change. From the outset, the military had felt that it had been displaced by AD. Although the 1945 coup against Medina was planned and executed by military officers, AD gained exclusive control of the state and imposed its vision of politics. In response to attempts by the military to overthrow the government after 1945, AD sought to control the military by surrounding itself with trusted officers (which it included on what it called its white list), to control those who opposed it (which it placed in its black list), and to infiltrate the military with its own cadre. However, AD failed to control the UPM leaders organized around Major Marcos Pérez Jiménez.

Initially, following their preferred practice of negotiating settlements from above, the UPM leadership sought a compromise by appealing to Rómulo Gallegos as president of all Venezuelans. Acting as representatives of excluded interest groups, they asked President Gallegos to include non-AD civilians as well as military leaders in the cabinet and to exile Betancourt, who was seen as the main architect of AD's sectarian policies. AD would still have a majority in the Congress. Betancourt was willing to compromise, for he believed that in time AD would regain control over the executive.

But President Gallegos, who was fundamentally a novelist and an educator, not a politician, thought of politics as the play of principles, not the battle for power. At this critical juncture, he saw himself in the role of Santos Luzardo, the principled character of *Doña Bárbara* who combats barbarism in Venezuela's plains and brings civilization to the nation by establishing the rule of law. Objecting to any form of unconstitutional participation of the military in politics, he sternly refused to compromise, arguing that if he acceded to the demands of the military, he could not go home and face his wife, Teotiste. While Gallegos denied the political existence of the military in the name of what Marx once called "forceless principles" (1981:88), the same men who had thrust AD into power in 1945 were ready to gain control over the state by resorting, once again, to the principle of force.

In response to this military conspiracy against Gallegos, some middle-level AD leaders attempted to prepare for resistance on their own. Against the menace of a coup, they sought to present the threat of the organized masses. According to their plan, while a national strike involving over three hundred thousand workers would paralyze the nation, party militia would directly confront the military.[17] AD's top leadership, however, wanted to

17. They were armed with weapons captured from military garrisons during the 1945 coup against Medina Angarita.

avoid social conflict by all means. In their view, AD had organized the masses in order to obtain electoral support, not to unleash a process of radical social transformation. Once in power, they sought to build AD as a multiclass, reformist national party, to control the popular sectors through the state, and to forge an alliance with local and foreign propertied interests. Within the most conservative sectors of the local bourgeoisie, AD was still perceived as a radical party and its leaders as disguised communists, despite the fact that Rómulo Betancourt had included leading members of the national bourgeoisie in AD's cabinet and had sought to promote the formation of a national entrepreneurial sector. He also cultivated a close relationship with Nelson Rockefeller, who was interested in making Venezuela into a testing ground for U.S. corporate investments in agriculture and industry.[18]

When Gallegos refused to meet the military's demands, rumors of a conspiracy intensified. Although in October Betancourt invoked the threat of a strike of oil workers if a coup were ever attempted, he and AD's upper echelons strongly discouraged attempts by middle-level party leaders to mobilize AD's membership. AD defined itself as the Party of the People (*El Partido del Pueblo*), although by the people its leaders increasingly meant the popular sector controlled by the party's top leadership. Given their concern with strengthening this reformist alliance, AD's top leaders sought to neutralize the plot by negotiation from above, not mobilization from below. In this respect, AD behaved like the military conspirators, for the coup was planned at the top and did not involve the popular sectors. To avert the coup, AD relied on the support of key military figures, including Minister of Defense Delgado Chalbaud, a friend and former student of Gallegos's, who regarded him as his "spiritual son." Although Gallegos was informed of Delgado Chalbaud's conspiracy against him, he trusted his promise of unswerving loyalty.

Gallegos's secretary and friend, Napoleón Ordosgoiti, a journalist and filmmaker, was with Gallegos during the morning of the coup and provides an insider's account of Gallegos's response to Delgado Chalbaud's betrayal. Ordosgoiti reports that before the coup, he (Ordosgoiti) had been instrumental in arranging a meeting between Gallegos and a loyal officer, Carlos Méndez Martínez, who informed the president about the existence of a military conspiracy involving his defense minister, Delgado Chalbaud. According to Ordosgoiti, Gallegos decided to keep this information confidential in order to talk privately to Delgado Chalbaud, his minister and spiritual son.

On the morning of the coup, Gallegos invited Delgado Chalbaud to

---

18. Leading members of the bourgeoisie occupied key positions in the state during the Trienio, including the agriculture ministry and the Central Bank.

discuss rumors of military conspiracy at his house, "Marisela" (named after the character of his novel, the innocent daughter of Doña Bárbara). Reportedly, Minister Delgado Chalbaud promised the president his personal loyalty and assured him that he would arrest the main officers involved in the conspiracy, Marcos Pérez Jiménez and Luis Felipe Llovera Páez. Instead, soon after the meeting Gallegos received a phone call informing him that the presidential palace had been taken by the military and that all his ministers, except for Delgado Chalbaud, had been arrested. Ordosgoiti, who was in Gallegos's home at the time, reports that the president was visibly shaken and saddened by the betrayal. Minutes after the phone call, the head of the Military Academy, Lieutenant Colonel Castro Gómez, arrived at Gallegos's home and informed the president that "his regime had fallen." He asked Gallegos to which country he wanted to be exiled. Gallegos answered: Cuba (1984:96–103). The coup was over.[19] When Delgado Chalbaud and other military officers turned against Gallegos, AD was left defenseless. Domingo Alberto Rangel, one of AD's youthful leaders at that time, later referred to Gallegos's overthrow as a "golpe de teléfono"—a coup by phone—whose implementation was "no more difficult than a military parade" (1966:9).

Having sought to secure "social peace" by all means, AD was not prepared for war. As an analyst of this period has noted, AD's strategic priority had been to avoid any social confrontation:

> Maintaining "la paz social" constituted the main tenet of AD's political strategy during the Trienio. The idea that national economic development depended on the elimination of social conflict was embedded in the party's rhetoric. Acción Democrática was especially proud of its success at having reduced strikes to a minimum. Its leader were constrained by this strategy during the decisive months of 1948. They decided not to rely on the party's massive popular support out of fear of igniting social tensions. Instead, they sought a

---

19. Ordosgoiti also reports that Delgado Chalbaud used him as an intermediary to explain to Gallegos why he had acted as he did and to seek his forgiveness. Ordosgoiti traveled to Mexico to deliver Chalbaud's personal letter to Gallegos, who had left Cuba to Mexico after Prío Socarrás recognized the military regime in Cuba. After reading it, Gallegos tore the letter up and said: "These are all lies. He is a Judas." Reportedly, however, Gallegos allowed Ordosgoiti, who was afraid of the consequences of the failure of his mission, to give presents in his name to Delgado Chalbaud and his wife which Ordosgoiti had purchased: a black knife for Delgado Chalbaud ("black like his conscience") and a white scarf for his wife ("white as the color of AD") (1984:116–17). Ordosgoiti's figure reveals the dense and close-knit network of relationships binding the political elite. Although he was closely identified with AD and had supported AD's struggles, he also sought to remain on good terms with the new leaders.

solution from above, negotiating with military figures who had no interest in maintaining Venezuelan democracy. Thus, when the conspirators gave their coup, the streets were empty for the military troops; a popular government was overthrown for lack of popular resistance (Ellner 1980:141).

Unlike the previous attempts by the military to overthrow AD after 1945, the November 1948 coup was better organized and occurred at a time when AD's control of state power had alienated its political rivals. It was led by the same young officers who had overthrown Medina in 1945, and it included respected senior officers identified as AD supporters, such as Delgado Chalbaud. When the coup took place, President Gallegos made an abstract appeal to the masses to "fulfill their duty." The threat of a general strike was spread by a radio announcement and rumors, but no steps were taken to organize the strike. An attempt by some AD leaders to set up a provisional government in Maracay ended with the arrest of its leaders. In essence, AD's top leadership accepted the coup as a fait accompli that could not be altered by popular resistance.

Symptomatically, Betancourt chose political asylum by hiding in the Colombian Embassy but still felt—as the leader of the Party of the People— that he had to explain his escape from the field of battle if he were to maintain his image as a combative popular leader. He asked his party, in a letter written from his diplomatic haven, to present publicly his flight from the country as an order from the party so that from exile he could organize the masses in opposition to the government. His request was accompanied by a veiled threat: if the party refused, he would never come back to Venezuela. The party complied (Fuenmayor 1982:42).

Left on their own, the party members did not occupy the political space their leaders left vacant. There were no spontaneous social protests, no riots, no strikes, no public demonstrations, and therefore no repression.[20] Not a weapon was fired. Thus, the first democratic regime in Venezuela established through universal suffrage passed away without protest in streets, factories, or fields. In the words of Guillermo García Ponce (who became a major leader of the communist underground resistance against Pérez Jiménez) and Camacho Barrios: "The Government fell without a shot, without serious resistance, without a massive protest in the streets, in the midst of a terrifying solitude, before a country that turned its indifferent back to everything that happened" (García Ponce and Camacho Barrios 1982:37).

---

20. Bergquist notes that in the oil fields "protest was fragmentary and easily suppressed" (1986:268).

THE FORCE OF ARMS, THE FORCELESS PEOPLE

The military had feared popular opposition and took steps to suppress civil resistance. It occupied the main streets of Caracas, restricted movement within and between cities, and proclaimed in the media that it held the nation under control. But the show of force alone was enough to make its claims true; in hours the military effectively controlled the nation. An editorial entitled "Thank God" and published in a Jesuit-sponsored magazine ridiculed AD's announcement that three hundred thousand workers were going to strike in support of the party of the people. "Which people? The 300,000 brave ones that were going to fight in the streets against the army? What naiveté! That was five zeroes too many. There were 300,000 people ready to demand higher wages, to participate in a parade, not to work" (*Sic,* vol. 11, no. 110, December 1948, pp. 485–86).

In February 1949 AD called for a general strike, but "it was poorly organized, indifferently obeyed, and promptly crushed by military force" (Bergquist 1986:286). The junta responded to the strike by dissolving all of AD's unions. Reportedly, government officials told U.S. officials that they were surprised at the "weakness of the Acción Democrática unions, and the docility with which most oil workers accepted the new political order" (Bergquist 1986).

From AD's perspective the 1948 coup signals the beginning of a counterrevolution, for after 1948 most trade unions and grassroots organizations were dismantled. Yet in some respects these popular organizations had already been demobilized by AD after 1945. The price of "social peace," as Ellner noted, was the tight control of the labor movement through the party. AD had begun this control during President Medina's administration, when it pushed Medina to dissolve the communist unions which had achieved dominance over the labor movement, including the oil workers. As a result of this measure and of the Communist Party's own changes of policy and divisions during the Browderist popular front period, AD displaced the Communist Party as labor's leading party.

Once in power, AD used the state's political and economic resources to expand its hold over the labor movement. Trade unions in the oil sector that had begun as relatively independent and combative organizations under Gómez became, according to an analyst, a mere "tool of machine politics" (Tennassee 1979:306–7).[21] While the bureaucratization of combative trade

21. For excellent discussions of the struggle over the labor movement between AD and the Communist Party during this period, see Ellner (1979), Tennassee (1979), Lucena (1982), and Bergquist (1986).

unions is a rather common consequence of corporativist trade unionism, in Venezuela it was achieved with exceptional ease. Bergquist notes that Venezuela, "molded by its extraordinary petroleum economy, adapted to the logic of corporativist liberal policies and 'bread-and-butter' unionism far more readily and permanently" than Chile, Argentina, and Colombia, the other countries included in his pathbreaking comparative study of the politics of labor in Latin America (1986:262).

The rapid construction of AD as an electoral party had required the creation of an electoral mass. Rómulo Betancourt has described how he sought to reach the unorganized masses. His much-repeated slogan guided the party's policy in the early 1940s: "Not even one district, not even one municipality without a party office" (*Ni un solo distrito, ni un solo municipio, sin la casa del partido*) (Betancourt 1956:135). A Venezuelan analyst has noted that this political slogan, "which covers from top to bottom the geographic and political and administrative map of the country," has to be complemented with another slogan which was "practiced rather than formulated." This implicit slogan, according to this analyst, "covers from side to side almost the whole nation's social map: 'not even a trade union, guild, and peasant organization without its party office'" (Bautista Urbaneja 1992:142). He notes the difference between the stated slogan goal and the implicit practice: the former refers to the already existing political map of the nation—it is a call to bring the party's presence to even the most remote rural town in Venezuela. The latter addresses a social map that had to be created for the most part: the formation of trade unions, guilds, and peasant organizations controlled by the party.

This social map, which had been drawn fundamentally with state resources, was largely erased once AD was displaced from the state. AD's social reforms and unionization of labor were not sufficient to establish an autonomous grassroots movement that could act independently in AD's defense. According to an analyst, "AD's much-vaunted attack on the country's basic social and economic problems did not represent a fundamental 'social revolution,' as Adecos and pro-AD writers have insisted but, rather, represented an invigorated and expanded policy of domestic reform that had already been accelerating over the 1936–1945 decade" (Burggraaff 1972:81). For this observer, "the real revolution was political: for the first time in Venezuela the political base of the ruling party now resided in the middle and lower classes, not in the elite" (1972:81).

If AD's rule constituted a political revolution in this sense, the 1948 coup represented a shift of power from the civilian to the military middle-class leadership. While the former claimed that state power was founded on the authority of votes, the latter argued that it was based on the force of arms. According to Pedro Berroeta, a Venezuelan writer and supporter of democratic institutions, after the 1945 coup Betancourt was caught by the "illusion of the moment" and was "unable to measure the relative strength of the contending forces." At this historical juncture, "He believed that he had attained power when in reality he had only had it as a loan, for a brief transition, while those who really had power came to develop an awareness of their strength" (1987:210–11).

It is true that after the 1945 coup the lower and middle classes occupied the expanded political space opened up by AD; nevertheless their political force was increasingly defused by a centralized and hierarchical party which monopolized control over these emerging political actors. The state acted as the center of gravity for political life. For AD's top leaders control over the government granted mastery over the party as a whole. While during the Trienio AD's social base expanded dramatically, its political power came more and more from the top—from AD's control over the state apparatus itself.

Paradoxically, AD built upon and promoted the presence of new political sectors in national politics but harnessed their force through tight party dominance that rested on its control of the state. Thus, this political "revolution," made in the name of the people but only partially achieved by them, remained the illusion of a revolution, a party-controlled movement that corralled and protected a dependent populace. Since political power was concentrated at the top of the state apparatus, it was possible for the military to gain power by controlling the state.

Carved by the flow of oil wealth, an unusual social edifice was being built in Venezuela, one modeled after the Western ideals which Venezuela sought to attain: a productive civil society and a representative state, although with inverted structural elements in which the top supported the base. With the continuous expansion of the oil industry, an increasingly wealthy state, financially independent from domestic agents, was making the people dependent on it. The middle and lower classes, possessing limited economic strength and rudimentary political organization, were transformed from AD's source of power into a vehicle for legitimating it. Once in control of the state apparatus, AD expanded its political base and popular support by making ample use of state institutions and resources. After the 1947 elections, its rule was legitimated by massive electoral support, but this support was eroded by its monopolization of state power. In 1948 the military overthrew AD by dislodging AD from the state, its new source of power, not by disarming the masses. As soon as it seemed clear that the junta controlled the state, its rule was uncontested; the masses were immobilized because AD had not mobilized them.

1948: IN THE NAME OF DEMOCRACY

The same officers who had participated with AD in the 1945 coup against Medina to install a civilian government this time established an all-military three-man junta: Commander Carlos Delgado Chalbaud and Lieutenant Colonels Marcos Pérez Jiménez and Carlos Llovera Paez. On 25 November the newspapers carried the junta's first statement, in which they depicted the Gallegos government as incapable of solving the "national crisis" or control-ling "extremist groups"—a clear reference to Betancourt's influence in Gal-legos's government. AD's incorporation of popular sectors in national politics was presented as a source of chaos. The coup was justified in the name of securing order: the armed forces had taken "total control of the situation" so as to achieve the "final establishment of social peace in Venezuela" (*El Uni-versal*, 25 November 1948).

Carlos Delgado Chalbaud emerged as the head of the new junta. Re-portedly, Delgado Chalbaud had expressed discomfort at being both the ex-defense minister of the old regime and a prospective ruler of the new one. But upon being urged by Pérez Jiménez he agreed to join the junta on the condition that he be named its president because of his superior rank. Pérez Jiménez agreed. As Gallegos's defense minister, Delgado Chal-baud was already invested in the public eye with a certain degree of legiti-macy, while the Caracas social elite considered him one of its own and trusted him.[22]

The coup was presented by its leaders as an attack against AD's perver-sion of democracy. From the outset, Delgado Chalbaud identified himself as a supporter of democracy. On 25 November he told foreign journalists in Caracas that the armed forces did not intend to suppress political parties, that they "had not acted against AD, but against its leaders," and that they had taken over power "not to act against democratic principles, but to preserve these principles" (*El Universal*, 26 November 1948). On the evening of 26 November, when he addressed the nation for the first time, Delgado

---

22. In addition, it has been claimed that he was also the favored candidate of the U.S. military attaché, Colonel Adams, who on the day of the coup had been observed in the Presidential Palace busily conferring with various military leaders (García Ponce 1982:34).

Chalbaud reiterated the junta's commitment to what at that time was regarded as the only system imparting legitimacy:

> The Military Junta wants to state categorically that this movement is not in any way directed toward the restoration of a military dictatorship either openly or underhandedly . . . Power has been taken over not so as to violate democratic principles, but to obtain their effective application and to prepare an electoral contest where all can participate on equal terms (*El Universal*, 27 November 1948).

The following day, the front-page headline of the conservative newspaper, *El Universal*, reported Delgado Chalbaud's announcement under the large headline, "It is not directed toward any dictatorship."

After the coup, AD's limited opposition to the regime was swiftly repressed. News of the arrest of AD's leaders, often presented together with photographs of arsenals of weapons and bombs, were prominently displayed in the media as part of an ongoing process of "actively cleaning up the city" (*El Universal*, 28 November 1948). The preceding regime's social mobilization was presented as having polarized society and threatened the consolidation of democracy by creating "chaos" and "disorder." AD's call to a general strike on 24 November (which never materialized) was portrayed as proof of AD's disruptive tactics. The imposition of "order" was presented as a condition for a democratic restoration.

Since at this time extremism was identified with AD's efforts to organize the labor sector, the junta did not claim that the Communist Party had influence in the fallen government, as AD had done when it overthrew Medina in 1945. Immediately after the coup, when foreign journalists asked him about his position concerning the Communist Party, Delgado Chalbaud replied laconically that the party had a "legal existence in Venezuela" (*El Universal*, 26 November 1948). At this point the Communist Party did not oppose the coup. The junta presented AD as the only extremist party and the sole source of "chaos" and the armed forces as the natural guarantor of peace and order.

There was an exceptional acceptance or at least tolerance of the coup by non-AD supporters. During the Trienio, a sharp antagonism had grown between AD, which had sought to represent itself as the harbinger of democracy, and other political parties, which had also promoted democratic institutions but found themselves without influence over the new state. In order to legitimize its rule, the junta appealed to the general resentment against AD's monopolization of power.

While AD members were not sufficiently organized to resist the coup, nonadecos (*adecos* were supporters of AD) had been too alienated by AD to oppose the new rulers. Not just medinistas, who understandably resented AD, but also the leaders of COPEI and URD and leading "independent"[23] professional and intellectual figures supported the new rulers in the hope that the junta would open up the political system and promote the establishment of a less sectarian democracy. For them there was no contradiction between supporting democracy and backing the coup. As early as 25 November 1948, URD's Jovito Villalba declared his trust in the patriotism and selflessness of the armed forces and urged the civilian population to avoid acts of violence (*El Universal*, 26 November 1948). COPEI also chose to endorse the new rulers. According to COPEI's newspaper, *El Gráfico*, the junta had saved the state from the "chaos" and "horrible nightmare" identified with the "sectarian and hegemonic" rule of AD and of its leader, the "hooded" communist, Rómulo Betancourt (García Ponce and Camacho Barrios 1982:36).

For Mariano Briceño Iragorri, a respected man of letters, AD's sectarianism had left it alone in power. Many honest politicians truly believed in 1948 that "all the mistakes of the government rested on the shoulders of AD members" and that the new regime would promote the institutionalization of democracy blocked by the "sectarian politics of Acción Democrática" (1971:40–41). For them, the new regime was to be judged not by its origins but by its achievements. Just as AD had justified in 1945 the use of the military coup as an instrument to speed up the transition to democracy, the supporters of the 1948 coup against AD presented it as a means to put democracy on the right track. On the other hand, for Vallenilla Lanz, the fact that supporters of democracy were ready to embrace the coup confirmed his view of the opportunism of Venezuelan politicians. With evident glee he noted in his memoirs that URD's Jovito Villalba and COPEI's Rafael Caldera voiced support for the junta in 1948 and sought positions for themselves in the new government while their followers "filled the hallways of the government palace hunting for government jobs" (Vallenilla 1967:291).

However, many of those who initially supported the regime and even accepted positions in the government turned against it when the junta took no steps to restore democratic rights. Others, less able to reject public jobs or to take an open stand against the government, opposed it privately. When there was a crack in the mantle of control, this repressed resistance erupted

23. Independientes is a term used in Venezuela to designate individuals who participate in politics but are not affiliated with any political party.

into public view. For example, when General Isaias Medina died in 1953, thousands of *caraqueños* (inhabitants of Caracas), spontaneously and without partisan distinction, carried Medina's coffin from his home to the cemetery, in effect transforming his burial into an eight-hour political demonstration that at once honored a military leader who had respected the constitution and also protested the junta that had violated its promises to do so—an event eloquently described by Briceño Iragorri.[24] Underlying both notions—that the population acquiesced to the coup in the principled defense of true democracy or, alternatively, out of unprincipled self-interest—lies the reality of a society increasingly dependent on the state, in which the pursuit of individual interests was cast in terms of the fulfillment of the state's ends.

TRANSITION TO DICTATORSHIP: 1948 – 1950

Once the junta took control of the state apparatus, it declared AD illegal, accusing it of creating "a state within the state," and progressively dissolved the Congress, municipal councils, the National Electoral Council, and most trade unions. As in the initial stage of other Latin American coups, the dismantling of democratic institutions was presented as only a stage in the process of building democracy on stronger foundations.

In this case, however, there were significant differences of opinion within the junta with respect to the role of parties and of elections in Venezuela. Carlos Delgado Chalbaud, who headed the government, leaned toward an eventual return to democratic forms and sought to reinstitute general elections with the participation of most political parties. Pérez Jiménez, who controlled the armed forces, favored the consolidation of a military regime and wished to restrict the role of parties in politics. More than their political stance separated them. While Delgado Chalbaud belonged to an upper-class family, received his military training in France, and had wide support within the social and economic elite, Pérez Jiménez was brought up in a poor Andean town, was trained in Peru's military academy, and had a large following in the armed forces. Each needed the other and avoided a confrontation. They defined the junta's immediate tasks as the establishment of order and the promotion of major public works; their efforts converged toward this end.

Then on 13 November 1950 Delgado Chalbaud was mysteriously mur-

---

24. See in this regard the vivid description of Briceño Iragorri's own change of heart concerning the junta (1971:41).

dered, leaving Pérez Jiménez as the junta's strongman.[25] He decided to name a civilian as president. He did not wish to appear as a beneficiary of the murder of his fellow officer and sought to retain a representative of Delgado Chalbaud's social class and ideological position in the junta. Two of his civilian ministers refused to play the role of figurehead. Arnoldo Gabaldón, a widely respected public health doctor, who had greatly reduced malaria infestation in rural areas and was a political independent, accepted the post. But Gabaldón accepted the presidency because he mistook for drama what was only farce. Perhaps believing that the 1948 coup was indeed the midwife of an authentic democracy, he entered the political stage playing a part written for a different play. He behaved like the head of state even before he was proclaimed its nominal president. Without yet occupying the seat of power, he tactlessly announced his government program and his plan for elections and, most important, his cabinet appointments—creating either panic or hope among those who, like him, mistook appearance for reality.

Backstage, there was no need for a guillotine. Gabaldón's head fell with the stroke of a pen. He was told he no longer had the part. The role was given to Germán Suárez Flamerich, who understood the play for what it was. The ambassador to Peru, he was an undistinguished member of the Generation of 28 and therefore, as Vallenilla cynically commented, "even had a democratic background" (1967:325). With civilian Suárez Flamerich as president of the junta, Lieutenant Colonel Pérez Jiménez took command. Beneath the civilian cloak of its figurehead, the government took shape as a military dictatorship.

THE 1952 ELECTIONS: ILLUSIONS OF POWER

The men who had held power after 1948 were not politicians and in the following years acquired only limited political experience. They gained control of the state during a period of rapid expansion of the oil economy and were not compelled by economic and political conditions to seek support from other social groups. As a consequence of their sense of self-sufficiency, they grew distant even from the armed forces, their original base of support. They sought to avoid politics and to concentrate on visible achievements.

---

25. There is no definitive explanation for this political murder. Because Pérez Jiménez benefited, it was widely believed at the time that he was the mastermind behind it, but there is no evidence of his complicity. For a discussion of this issue, see Betancourt (1979:252–55) and López Borges (1971).

For these men the emphasis on public works became a way of eradi-
cating partisan politics and redefining political life: Through "the rational
transformation of the physical environment," the government proclaimed it
would bring modernity to Venezuela. The rhetorical emphasis on "rationality" and on the transformation of the "physical environment" expressed
a viewpoint held by nineteenth-century positivist thinkers in Latin America
which attributed the continent's backwardness to its natural habitat and assumed that, by changing the habitat, people would change. Politics was now
restricted to the management of the nation's resources by the state. Just as the
armed forces were entrusted with the defense of the national territory, it was
now in charge of safeguarding the "nation's wealth." Rather than allow the
"noisy" voices of political parties to speak in the name of the people while
pursuing partisan interests, they claimed the state would express the single
voice of the nation.

The ease with which they had carried out their coup, the concentration
of political power in their hands, their command of financial resources derived from constantly expanding oil rents, the presence of tangible accomplishments, the lack of significant public criticism—all combined to make
Pérez Jiménez and the junta leaders both overconfident and unrealistic. They
increasingly lost touch with political reality. In the context of silenced or
acquiescent political forces, the men in power came to hear only their own
voice. Thus, the junta came to believe its own rhetoric. By 1952 it thought
that by means of its public works program the "rational transformation of
the physical environment" had also successfully eradicated "the irrational
political sentiments" of the people (Vallenilla 1967:242). Therefore, the
junta felt there was no longer any reason to postpone an election. With
the reestablishment of constitutional rights, the small local opposition and
the bothersome foreign critics would be neutralized, and the government
could continue to fulfill unhindered its twin tasks of transforming the environment and uplifting the people. The rulers, convinced that the government's deeds had won the people over to their side, sought to transform rule
by force into rule by consent; the quiet legitimation of the vote was now to
be permitted.

The regime that had denied political freedoms now wanted to ensure
that every adult Venezuelan would vote so that it could claim to have full
support. In April 1951 a new electoral statute made suffrage compulsory for
all citizens age twenty-one and over. (Under AD's 1947 electoral law, voting
was a voluntary right of citizens eighteen and over.) According to this statute,
the electorate would choose a constituent assembly whose main functions

would be to elect a new provisional president within forty days and to write the constitution. The election of a constitutional president by universal suffrage would follow. In May 1951, a party was created to back Pérez Jiménez, the Frente Electoral Independiente (FEI). The electoral campaign would be allowed to start in May 1952.

AD was still illegal, as was the Communist Party. During this period, AD repeatedly attempted to organize a coup against the junta. But these efforts failed, bringing death or imprisonment to its leaders. AD's most serious loss was that of Leonardo Ruiz Pineda, who was murdered on the streets of Caracas on 21 October 1952. Widely respected as capable and courageous, he had been Gallegos's minister of communications and had secretly returned from exile to lead, together with Alberto Carnevalli, AD's underground movement.

The elections were scheduled for 30 November 1952, a month after the murder of Ruiz Pineda. Despite many instances of violent repression during the preceding year, the junta insisted that the election results would be respected. Most political leaders took for granted that the general state of repression and political restrictions forestalled the possibility of a fair contest; for them, "a government-perpetrated fraud in the election of November 30 was a foregone conclusion" (Kolb 1974:109). The standard set by the 1947 election, which took place in the context of ample democratic freedoms, made even more evident the limitations of the present one. While AD originally ordered its members not to vote,[26] COPEI and URD decided to occupy the political space opened up by the election in order to have a forum for their views, and hopefully to gain positions in the elected bodies of the state and to expand their sphere of influence.

The electoral campaign began on May 1952. The opposition organized successful rallies attended by people from a wide political spectrum opposed to the dictatorship. By contrast, the FEI failed to reach the populace; it had no organizational base or ideological appeal. The rulers attributed their failure in this field not to their politics but to their lack of experienced speakers. After giving a typically unsuccessful speech at an FEI rally, Laureano Vallenilla Lanz, always contemptuous of Rómulo Betancourt, confessed that for once he wished he had the ability to speak to the masses like AD's charismatic leader (who remained in exile) (Vallenilla 1967:313). The junta's typical response to the problem was to pour state money into it.

---

26. Reportedly, although AD planned to boycott the election, the murder of Ruiz Pineda a month before prompted its members to cast a protest vote against the government (Luzardo 1963:170–71; Kolb 1974:115).

Interior Minister Llovera Paez sent large sums of money and instructions to the governors of states and other local authorities for the enrollment of citizens in the regional parties allied with the FEI. Much of the money was passed out in small amounts as direct bribes for votes; in other cases, farmers were given credits for the purchase of agricultural equipment, or were presented with clothing, powdered milk, and other small gifts. Priests in rural towns were bribed to speak from the pulpit on behalf of the FEI candidates, some of them allegedly advising the country folk to remember on election that the regime's voting ticket was round "like the host in the Holy Sacrament" (Kolb 1974:110).

The opposition predicted electoral fraud; the government promised absolute honesty. In a sense, both were right. The junta, believing it had conquered the hearts of most of the people, was sure of its victory and saw no need to prepare a fraud. As Herbert Mathews reported in 1952, the government planned to hold honest elections because it believed it would win them (*New York Times*, 16 April 1952). The junta's optimism at that time was fed by reports that it received—echoes of its own voice—indicating that Pérez Jiménez could count on massive popular backing, and it predicted his landslide victory. For this reason, according to Vallenilla Lanz, they thought their triumph was certain.

On 30 November the government was unexpectedly proven right in its claim that it would hold an honest election but wrong in its prediction of the outcome. The first returns showed URD in the lead. The junta had made no provisions for altering the electoral results and had no plans for responding to a victory of the opposition. Certain of its victory, it was shocked by the indications of its imminent defeat.

THE EIGHTEENTH BRUMAIRE OF PÉREZ JIMÉNEZ

Events: The Golpecito (Little Coup)
Upon receiving news of the early vote count, Pérez Jiménez left a celebration with close friends at his home to attend an emergency meeting with his advisers at the Defense Ministry. There the mood was gloomy. As time passed, the electoral results indicated a clear defeat. The men in power found themselves at a historical juncture: they could either accept the results of the election or exercise force. Pérez Jiménez's top partners had believed their own rhetoric and were caught in the web of their words. Vallenilla's memoirs include an account—from an insider's partisan perspective—of how they broke free from this web, from the promises they had made, and from their commitment to resume the electoral process.

While at the Defense Ministry some argued that "all was lost, that the nation had rejected them," others felt that a compromise with URD's Villalba (who had won the election) had to be arranged (1967:346). But Colonel Carlos Pulido Barreto told the men around him, "All is not lost. We have *el Poder* and the arms. We are not going to turn them over" (Vallenilla 1967:343).[27] Then, meeting secretly in a bathroom, Colonel Pulido Barreto, Commander Tamayo Suárez, and Laureano Vallenilla agreed that "the result of the election does not matter. What matters is that we stay united and committed to retain command." They decided to overturn the election. Vallenilla, appealing to the traditional image of the caudillo, assured the officers that rule by force could easily be presented as just by manipulating the law. "The civil formula, the legal solution can be easily fabricated when we can count on the backing of machetes" (1967:345). They agreed that the military should remain in power, supporting Pérez Jiménez as the sole head of state. A coup was in the making.

However, at this turning point Pérez Jiménez "was filled with anxieties and doubts." According to an analyst, he was a "tireless schemer and meticulous plotter" but was "invariably assailed with fears and misgivings when confronted by unanticipated situations demanding immediate and decisive action" (Kolb 1974:113). Laureano Vallenilla claims to have swayed Pérez Jiménez by presenting a convincing justification for the coup. "This [is] a difficult, dramatic moment. We will have to choose between the electoral results and the development of the country. In a civilized nation there would be no dilemma." But in Venezuela, Vallenilla explained, if power were handed over to URD's Villalba, development programs would be dismantled, and "chaos" again would take over the life of the nation. General elections would be held, and Rómulo Betancourt, "the most astute" of all the party leaders, would win. Apparently possessing visionary powers, Vallenilla predicted, "less intransigent after his last exile, he would form a coalition government in order to distribute public jobs among adecos, *copeyanos* [COPEI supporters], and *uerredecos* [URD supporters]." He added that "bureaucracy would grow to satisfy the budgetary voracity of all parties. The junta's accomplishments would fall in ruins" (Vallenilla 1967:346).[28]

The next and decisive event was the arrival at Pérez Jiménez's office of a large group of military officers (between thirty and forty) who had been informed by Colonel Pulido Barreto of the decision to back Pérez Jiménez.

27. *El Poder,* "power," refers to the state, and in this case, in particular, the armed forces of the state.

28. It should be noted that this report was written in 1961, after Betancourt's 1958 coalition with URD and COPEI.

Reportedly, they urged him to remain in charge of the state: "You must keep el Poder, Colonel. We support you." They insisted that he should rule alone and attributed the present crisis to the lack of a unified leadership. "The problems and difficulties arose from divisions within the Executive" (Vallenilla 1967: 347). Vallenilla reported that Pérez Jiménez was moved. He told them, "If you support me, I'll stay . . . I could go abroad, but I think that Venezuela still needs me." Then he added, "I have no personal ambitions . . . If I decide to stay here it is because of the country, exclusively because of the country" (1967:347). With Pérez Jiménez now persuaded to play the role of national savior, the conspirators set out to ensure military support for the coup in the interior of the country, which they expected to achieve easily.

There was still uncertainty as to how civilian political forces would react to the coup. In order to reduce possible opposition to the "military solution," Vallenilla masterminded the "civil formula, the legal solution." Reportedly, he proposed it to Pérez Jiménez in the following terms:

> The junta, in a letter, should present its resignation to the Armed Forces since the power you exercise emanates from them. They accept it and choose you as Provisional President of the Republic until a Constituent Assembly meets. All that is needed is to write a certificate that will be signed by the heads of the different military branches. Then you occupy your post, designate a new cabinet, and deliver a radio message to the nation (1967:348).

The coup d'état was orchestrated in these simple terms on the evening of election day, 30 November 1952. The morning newspapers of 1 December reported the following returns as of 7 P.M. election day: URD, 294,573; FEI, 147,528; and COPEI, 89,095. These results were accurate. Since it had expected an electoral triumph, the junta had not taken precautions to censor the news or to alter the results. On the evening of the same day, the *New York Times* learned, from a telephone call, that URD was leading with 450,000 votes, followed by COPEI with 206,000; but the call was cut off before figures could be given for the trailing FEI. No more electoral results were allowed to be given or published.

But the coup's leaders were confident. Military support at regional bases had been secured. And equally important, the U.S. ambassador had also privately expressed his support for Pérez Jiménez (Vallenilla 1967:358).[29] Thus,

29. It is unlikely that without this support the coup would have taken place or that it would have taken the form it did. As the *New York Times* reported on 12 October 1955, "It is an open secret that if the United States had expressed its displeasure at the robbery of the Venezuelan election by partisans of Col. Pérez Jiménez in November 1952, the latter would have retreated, or at least would have

they turned their attention to ordinary affairs. Even as Vallenilla composed the junta's statement of resignation the day after the election, he noted that deposits had risen at the Industrial Bank, which he headed—all was normal. He felt that soon the nation too would return to normality, and he prepared to be back at work in his bank in two days. The assumption was that this palace coup would not be challenged, that in Venezuela, since the advent of Gómez, control over the state's administrative and military centers by a few leaders could bring control over the nation.

After approving Vallenilla's document, Pérez Jiménez informed him that the ceremony for the military to nominate him provisional president of Venezuela had to be postponed until the next day, 2 December. Vallenilla noted his satisfaction with this change, for it made Venezuelan events coincide with the chronology of European history—over a hundred years earlier:

> I am pleased. The second of December is a favorable date for coups d'état. Exactly a century and one year ago took place that of Louis Napoleon Bonaparte. Besides, the Great Napoleon thought that 2 December brought good luck. The battle of Austerlitz occurred on this date. I am superstitious, Colonel . . . and I have a hunch that things are going to turn out all right for us (1967:350).

The legal formula was framed without much effort to make it convincing or coherent. This façade was designed to induce compliance not through the power of persuasion but through the persuasiveness of power. On 2 December 1952, Pérez Jiménez sent a telegram to URD leaders accusing them of having worked in alliance with outlawed parties. Clearly, this accusation was only an excuse to attack both URD and the electoral results. In this telegram, Pérez Jiménez, indifferent to inconsistency, acknowledged URD's electoral victory, revealing once again that power, not truth, was the issue:

> The Armed Forces, so ill-treated by you, are not disposed to permit the damaging, through vile agreements, of the prestige and progress of the nation, seriously compromised by the *electoral triumph* of Acción Democrática and the Communist Party, which URD has propitiated (Kolb 1974:114; emphasis added).

Thus, Pérez Jiménez recognized that URD (backed by AD and the PC) had won the election but asserted that it had done so only through an unacceptable alliance with illegal parties. Hours later, however, when Pérez

---

come to an agreement with the opposition. By keeping ourselves strictly outside the conflict, and quickly recognizing the Pérez Jiménez regime, we, in a certain sense, intervened."

Jiménez was proclaimed provisional president in a widely publicized ceremony, the Electoral Council proclaimed that the partial electoral results were sufficient to indicate a victory for Pérez Jiménez. According to the altered results, FEI led with 578,000 votes; URD followed with 463,708; and COPEI was a distant third with 138,003. Not having anticipated a fraud, the junta had earlier chosen an honest man as president of the Electoral Council, who refused to sign the electoral certificate. Yet for the new script in this play any signature would do, and another member of the Electoral Council signed it.

At this time, however, votes were not to be the source of Pérez Jiménez's legitimacy. According to the new script, since the popular vote had been polluted by the illegal participation of AD and the Communist Party in the elections, the armed forces, as defenders of the integrity of the nation, were the ultimate source of power. This fact, in accordance with Vallenilla's design, had to be represented ceremonially. Thus, the junta, presided over by Suárez Flamerich, submitted its resignation to the armed forces. And the armed forces then named Pérez Jiménez provisional president.

Vallenilla must have been pleased. Not only was the coup successful, but it took place on 2 December, as he had wished, 101 years after Louis Napoleon Bonaparte's coup. Fortune also favored him personally; he was appointed minister of the interior, the nation's second most powerful political post. From that position Vallenilla could also expect to expand his material personal fortune. He unabashedly relates that just after his appointment, a vendor tried to sell him a lottery ticket. A bystander dissuaded the vendor, commenting that Vallenilla "had already won the big one" (1967:359). It had become commonly accepted that the state was a source not just of power but also of wealth.

Analogies

The coup was elevated by the men in power into an epoch-making event. When the force of circumstances made them face an untrodden path, Vallenilla brought his knowledge of European history to guide them in their making of Venezuelan history. It is precisely in periods of change, when people "seem engaged in revolutionizing themselves and things, in creating something that has never yet existed," Marx noted, that "they anxiously conjure up the spirits of the past to their service and borrow from them names, battle cries and costumes in order to present the new scene of world history in this time-honored disguise and this borrowed language" (1981:15).

In summoning the spirit of Louis Napoleon Bonaparte, Vallenilla contrived to divorce the 1952 coup from its family of Latin America military *golpes* and to establish its affinity with France's coup of 2 December 1851. By the alchemic power of historical analogies, he sought to bring local events from the wings to the center stage of history, to transmute Marcos Pérez Jiménez and Louis Napoleon Bonaparte into kindred spirits enacting a common historical mission.

But Pérez Jiménez and Louis Napoleon were perhaps related to each other only by their shared banality and distance from the ancestor whose power they both invoked. "Hegel remarks somewhere," Marx wrote, "that all facts and personages of great importance in world history occur, as it were, twice. He forgot to add: the first time as tragedy, the second as farce" (1981 : 15). In his classic analysis of the Eighteenth Brumaire, Marx saw Louis Napoleon as the main actor of the farce of 2 December 1851 only because "the class struggle in France created circumstances and relationships that made it possible for a grotesque mediocrity to play a hero's part" (1981 : 8). He regarded the depiction of Louis Napoleon as the hero who saved France from the chaos of factional disputes as but a dramatic construct, the illusion of a society in crisis.

It is fitting that Laureano Vallenilla conjured up the spirit of this particular French savior, a phantasm in his own time, in an effort to transmute another grotesque mediocrity into a savior and his petty coup dans l'état into an epochal coup d'état. It is appropriate as well that a Venezuelan historian and ex−communist leader, Juan Bautista Fuenmayor, also turned the 1952 coup into an instantiation of the "general historical law" best expressed in the Bonapartist coup of 2 December 1851, according to which an autocratic ruler would come to govern with the support of the bourgeoisie and in defense of its general interests whenever this class proved incapable of exercising direct political rule.

Writing Venezuelan history from a Marxist perspective in the shadow of European history, Fuenmayor hesitates: were local developments the outcome of their own laws, or simply the imitative product of the lawful evolution of European history? Since Fuenmayor knew that Vallenilla had modeled the Venezuelan coup after Louis Bonaparte's takeover, he feels he has to account not just for the inner determination of historical events in Venezuela but also for events that were engineered as the conscious imitation of another's lawful history. Unable to resolve this dilemma in his multivolume account of contemporary Venezuelan history, Fuenmayor asserts: "It makes no difference whether he [Vallenilla] devised Pérez Jiménez's strategy, or whether the historical process unfolded blindly, spontaneously, fulfilling historical laws. What is important is that events took place in this, and not another, way" (Fuenmayor 1982: 397).

These historical turns and their interpretations show that historical facts and personages may occur more than twice, that history may follow, as it were, the labyrinthine paths of Jorge Luis Borges rather than the spiraling dialectic of Hegel, that its stages are made up also of unending mirrors and props, not only of functional structures, that on occasion its characters may parade less as history's agents than as its impersonators. Or perhaps it shows that these historical twists occur more often when facts and personages are not assigned great importance when they occupy marginal spaces in the shadows of world history. They then appear to lack the power to become historical forces and find light not in original deeds but in their imitation, in Victor Hugo's "Napoleon le petit," not in the Great Napoleon of Austerlitz, in the nephew, not the uncle. Having the power only to imitate imitators, in times of crisis they conjure up the imitation.

But all imitators—whether of the original or of the copy—share a certain kinship. Unlike revolutionaries, they conjure up the dead not for the purpose "of glorifying the new struggles" but "of parodying the old," not of "magnifying the given task in imagination" but "of fleeing from its solution in reality," not of "finding once more the spirit of revolution" but "of making its ghost walk about again" (Marx 1981: 17).

Vallenilla knew that he was parodying the old. From his father, who as Gómez's ideologue had celebrated the virtues of the necessary gendarme for backward nations, Vallenilla received an elite upbringing as well as an interest in political power. A member of the Caracas upper class, he had obtained a classic education in Europe (in Germany, Switzerland, Italy, and France, where he studied philosophy, law, and political science). He returned to Venezuela at a time when, in the name of "the people," as he described it, middle-class politicians, younger military officers, and profit-seeking businessmen were replacing the old oligarchic order with democratic institutions.

Vallenilla distanced himself from what he felt were the unexamined convictions of his Venezuelan contemporaries. "I belong to that nihilist generation formed in France between the two world wars. I believe in practically nothing, but I am reflective" (Vallenilla 1967:97). He knew he had to settle for a life of compromise. "Contemptuous of both the lower classes and of professional politicians, he favored a Platonic government of philosophers, but settled for its vague Venezuelan approximation of lower middle class army officers and creole oligarchs" (Burggraaff 1972: 139).

In Europe Vallenilla also met many Venezuelan and other Latin American intellectuals, some of whom had been close friends of his father's. Vallenilla has written that he was deeply influenced by the positivist ideas of Cesar Zumeta, who encouraged him to contribute to work "next to those who want to build the nation, because our nation must be built and populated." "Do not forget," Vallenilla reports Zumeta told him, "that we are three million illiterate, or almost illiterate, sick, and naked people" (*Somos tres millones de analfabetos o casi analfabetos, desnutridos y enfermos*). He presented as Zumeta's idea a concept that became a legitimating principle of the Pérez Jiménez regime: "Votes, legality, freedom of press are luxuries for well-fed bourgeois; a modern city is not an ancient city, and democracy is not built on straw slums" (*ranchos de paja*). He depicted the transformation of the nation as a sacred task to be undertaken by the elite. "If God ever gives you the opportunity to deploy Power you must build roads, channel rivers, irrigate land, build schools, construct railroads."

Written in exile, Vallenilla's memoirs seem to adapt his memory of that conversation to his present situation: "If in order to accomplish these goals you must be strong, be strong, and if they take power from you and exile you, it doesn't matter. You will have the satisfaction of having fulfilled your duty. Of all our nineteenth-century rulers, only Guzmán Blanco escapes being forgotten because he built something. To construct, to edify, to grow, is the first obligation of leaders in this stage of the world" (1967:135–36). As in the conquest, a colonizing optic depicted the Americas as a land of naked and ignorant people to be civilized by the enlightened. During the colonial period, conversion to Christianity, however formulaic, was deemed to turn savages into rational beings. "In this stage of the world," according to Vallenilla, exposure to the external tokens of modernity, however mimetic, would bring a primitive people into modernity.

A few days after the takeover, the new minister of the interior told Pérez Jiménez that his knowledge of Venezuelan history and people allowed him to know what many Venezuelans thought "of this drama, or *sainete* [one-act farce], that you and I are representing in this sunny showroom that is Venezuela." Then he added, "Besides, I hope with all my heart that this is a sainete. I hate drama. I prefer the small genre" (1967:362). In this instance Vallenilla was proven correct, for compared to the farce of the 1851, that of 1952 could qualify only as an abridged approximation. Yet a brief comparison between both coups may help us understand the society whose rulers sought to model theirs after alluring European images.[30]

---

30. Since in this chapter I establish a rather playful counterpoint between events in Venezuela and French history as narrated by Marx in *The Eighteenth Brumaire of Louis Bonaparte* (1963), I base the comparison of Pérez Jiménez's 1952 coup and Louis Bonaparte's 1851 coup on Marx's account of the latter.

On 2 December 1851, Louis Napoleon took power after prolonged struggle within and outside parliament had produced a political stalemate among the basic contending social forces of French society: Legitimists (landed property), Orleanists (industrial capital), the proletariat, the lumpen-proletariat, the peasants, the middle classes, and the army. When the National Assembly rejected in November 1851 Napoleon's decision to restore universal suffrage because it was afraid that he would win with the support of the peasantry, it "once more confirmed the fact that it had transformed itself from the freely elected representative of the people into the usurpatory parliament of a class; it acknowledged once more that it had itself cut in two the muscles which connected the parliamentary head with the body of the nation" (Marx 1981:113). But just as through this refusal the parliamentary bourgeoisie had disowned the people it claimed to represent, the extraparliamentary bourgeoisie, through protracted conflicts, had come to disown its representatives in the National Assembly. By December 1851 it was ready to embrace, as were other groups, Louis Napoleon as its representative.

Thus, the 1851 coup came as the response to a stalemate of conflicting social forces. It could occur only because the alliance between different sectors of the middle and upper classes had fallen apart and the lower classes had been neutralized—workers, through repression (during the 1848 June uprisings more than three thousand workers were killed and more than fifteen thousand were deported); peasants, through their own disorganization and delusion (they saw in their ownership of smallholdings the key to their salvation and not a cause of their stagnation); and the lumpenproletariat, through their inclusion in the spoils of power (the Parisian lumpenproletariat had been granted material benefits through the 10 December movement). The National Assembly represented this fragmented body. In trying belatedly to gain power of its won, and recognizing the army "as the decisive state power" (Marx 1981:113), it attempted to form a parliamentary army. But "by debating its right to requisition troops, instead of requisitioning them at once, it betrayed its doubts about its own powers" (1981:112). Because of its fragmentation, "the National Assembly had become incapable of transacting business. Its atomic constituents were no longer held together by any force of cohesion; it had drawn its last breath; it was dead" (1981:114). It was in the context of a stalemate of competing social forces that Louis Napoleon took power.

The sainete of 1952 took place on the narrow stage of the Presidential Palace while the rest of the nation watched. The coup was the outgrowth not of the conflictual participation of social groups in political life but of their lack of participation; not of the fragmentation of political power but of its concentration. In Venezuela there was no National Assembly claiming to represent the nation by mediating its multiple and clashing interests but an autocratic executive claiming to embody the national interest of a silenced society. The coup resulted not from a social stalemate, a threat from below, or a conspiracy but from the delusions engendered by absolute state power. Pérez Jiménez had believed he would win a general election, and so he organized one. The coup was the response of those in power to the unexpected and intolerable reality of their electoral defeat.

True, the fact that the military government organized an electoral contest indicates at least the ideological pressure of democratic demands and the ruling junta's preference to present its rule within the accepted framework of democratic institutions. And the fact that the majority of the electorate voted against the government shows that the population was willing to take an oppositional stand in the public arena. But the ease with which the coup was organized and the electoral results were dismissed reveals the weakness of the bearers of democratic demands. The real locus of power remained in the state apparatus itself, not in civil society. The people had the power to vote, but their votes carried little power.

As the elections led to the coup, the opposition was proved right, but for the wrong reason. There was electoral fraud but only after the fact. Given the obvious evidence of fraud, the purpose of the fraud was less to forge the illusion that the ballot box was the source of legitimate power than to adorn military power with a façade of legitimacy. Once the coup was decided, Pérez Jiménez openly made a mockery of the elections. The initial tally was disregarded, the final count, altered, and the FEI, made into the winner. The electoral forgery left the marks of its own making visible. It was clear that Pérez Jiménez was in power by armed force and that the electoral votes were only an ornament for the rifle butt. In a menacing combination of elements, the choreographers of the coup re-created the procedures of legality but did not hide the signs of their crude manipulation, as if to communicate the warning that power could be exercised nakedly by those who controlled the state.

Vallenilla's response to criticism of the coup reveals the spirit of the coup as well as the cosmetic character of the electoral forgery. A few days after the coup a friend whose opinion he respected told him, "You should have thought things out before acting. Modifying the electoral results is something very serious" (Vallenilla 1967: 362). Vallenilla's own reply reportedly was:

> This accusation does not bother me. I know the worth of votes in Venezuela.
> Votes are obtained through deceit, falsehood, slander, or coercion. Each side

uses the means at its disposal. Demagogues appeal to suffrage. The others, [go] to arms in order to impose their will. In both cases the origin of Power is spurious and can be purified only by an efficient and intelligent government performance. I do not fear what is attributed to us, but the use that we will make of the Supreme Command. If during the next five years we accelerate the process of transformation of Venezuela and at the same time we create wealth and raise the standard of living, then blessed be the *golpecito* [little coup] of 2 December! (1967:362.)

Thirty years later, Pérez Jiménez reiterated this view, emphasizing that democracy was to be defined by the government's accomplishments rather than by its electoral origins: "For us, democracy was not a question of the popular vote, it was enough to reach the Presidency with the authority of that vote so as to be able to have free rein to do whatever one felt like" (Blanco 1983:186). Instead, "For us, democracy was the result of the government's actions, not of its origin" (1983:186). He insisted that he never cared about labels, only about deeds. "For me, it did not matter whether the government was called *dictadura, dictablanda, protodemocrático, predemocrático*. For the essential thing was that the government benefit the Venezuelan nation" (Blanco 1983:187). When Pérez Jiménez was asked about his government's apparent concern for respecting certain democratic forms, he explained that this concern was strategic:

Yes, we did that for appearance's sake, to fulfill that formality. But not because we gave it the full importance we gave to other things. The achievements of the government continued to be of capital importance. Since I understood that if the parties were once again given full powers, the exceptional undertaking the government was carrying out in Venezuela would be truncated, I decided to use a democratic form in order to extend my government for one more period. Just one more period, so as to then withdraw from the field because I knew that within this period of time it would be possible to accomplish a sum of works which have been impossible to achieve in twenty-five years of democracy. (Blanco 1983:187.)[31]

The Eighteenth Brumaire of Marcos Pérez Jiménez was staged at the top by men who held state power. These men could say, like Vallenilla, that "without bloodshed, with a few measures, we have twisted the course of

---

31. The question referred mostly to the 1957 plebiscite, but Pérez Jiménez's answer expresses his general attitude toward democratic forms as well as his position in 1952 concerning the electoral forgery and his decision to stay in power for five more years.

history and avoided a catastrophe" (Vallenilla 1967: 368). On this stage the army appeared as "the decisive state power." But if the force of arms controlled the state, the state controlled society with the force of money. With the violent expansion of this independently wealthy state, all major social groups had come to see it as the source of their security or fortune. More fundamental, their very identity was bound up with the state, for they had been formed or transformed by its expansion. Before it they stood in awe. To the extent that they were offspring of the petrostate, their historical formation as social forces was too recent, their political experiences too narrow, their reliance on the state's financial and political resources too great, for them to follow an independent course of action. True, there had been opposition to the regime before the 1952 coup—student unrest, labor strikes, constant political conspiracies. But these movements, not sufficiently rooted in society, ultimately sought support in the state itself; most civil opposition effort became entangled in a military conspiracy. There were no independent mass uprisings, no significant alliance of interest groups or social classes against the regime. Just as the 1948 coup that overturned President Gallegos occurred without significant resistance, the 1952 coup that overruled the November elections took place uneventfully.

The government was again surprised; its leaders had lived their illusions, even their delusive fears, as reality. When Vallenilla informed Pérez Jiménez that the coup was successful, that there had been no resistance, Pérez Jiménez reportedly asked, almost with disbelief, *"¿Entonces nadie se ha alzado?"* (Then nobody has rebelled?). Vallenilla's answer is revealing. "No, Colonel, but we cannot cry victory yet. The coups of force sometimes have unpredictable repercussions. A century ago in Paris all seemed to go well. Suddenly, problems started on 4 December. There were deaths. We will have to remain watchful" (1967: 358). Venezuelan events were again viewed in the light shed by French history. But in Venezuela, 4 December passed uneventfully. This was a sainete.

4

CONSTRUCTING THE NATION:
THE NATION AS A CONSTRUCT

I found this country as a house in ruins and built a solid house.

Juan Vicente Gómez

In this house I have poured all my disillusion. My house is the image of the country I wanted to build.

Marcos Pérez Jiménez

In 1958 the successors of the dictatorial government encountered a very solid foundation on which to construct a solid building.

Tomás Pérez Tenreiro

Once installed as the constitutional president for the next five years, General Pérez Jiménez no longer depicted his administration as a transitional regime leading toward the reestablishment of a party system and free universal elections. The junta, under his command since the murder of Delgado Chalbaud in 1950, had hardened. After the 1948 coup, repression had been severe against the leadership of trade unions and political parties, but it now increasingly affected the growing middle-class opposition to the regime's delay in restoring civil liberties. In Venezuela, journalists and scholars have often characterized the government's tougher posture as a change from the "soft" dictatorship of 1948–50 to the "hard" dictatorship that began after 1950—from *dictablanda* to *dictadura*.[1] After the coup, the legalized *dictadura* sought to appropriate democracy for itself by redefining it.

While in 1948 it presented itself as the defender of a betrayed democracy and after the assassination of Delgado Chalbaud still promised to restore a party system, by 1953 the military junta claimed to represent "true" democracy—not the pseudodemocracy of political parties and empty promises but the real democracy of political order and material deeds. Like his admired friend, Juan Domingo Perón, then the military ruler of Argentina (Portantiero and de Ipola 1981:14), Pérez Jiménez derided politics and its

---

1. In Spanish, *dictadura* means dictatorship, *blanda* means soft and *dura* hard. As in all distinctions, the concern to distinguish degrees may obscure fundamental changes in kind.

language of deceit, which only betrayed the people's interests. He offered instead material benefits, in return for which he asked for the acceptance of his authority as leader of the nation. Democracy was now to be judged by its deeds and practical accomplishments rather than by its origins or methods. Political activity was monopolized by the state; most parties and trade unions were outlawed. The stated aim of the regime—to rid Venezuela of the scourge of partisan politics in order to concentrate national energies on material progress—was to be carried out in an atmosphere of political stability (Burggraaff 1972: 130–31).

This concern to "build" the nation by constructing its material structure was expressed in terms of a modernizing discourse that combined a positivist emphasis on the formative power of the physical habitat with a conception of development as moving by stages toward a concrete end. State leaders treated some of the most visible manifestations of modernity as the source of modern society's progress rather than as their outcome. In their accounts, the effort to catch up with advanced nations entailed using rationally the nation's powers, which they identified with the riches of its subsoil, and controlling the cause of their wasteful use, which they attributed to the backward masses and the self-interested politicians who claimed to represent them. From the new leaders' perspective, the rational use of oil money entailed transplanting onto Venezuelan soil what they saw as the visible signs and sources of modernity. Under Pérez Jiménez, sowing the oil continued in a new guise.

The coup of 1952, so thinly disguised, was now depicted as the founding moment of a new era. Through the annual ritual inauguration of grandiose public works projects on its anniversary each 2 December, Pérez Jiménez attempted at once to validate the coup and to present his administration as the expression of the national interest. The deeds spoke for themselves; there was no need for political speech. As a spectator, el pueblo was invited to applaud them silently.

THE NATION AS A CONSTRUCT

As I sought to show in previous chapters, when the oil industry and state income expanded during the second quarter of this century, dominant discourse construed the nation as an entity made of both a social and natural body. The nation's wealth, which during the nineteenth century had been identified with its agricultural output, became defined as residing directly in the materials of nature. To this transformation in the locus of wealth, from the cultivated soil to the untransformed subsoil, corresponded a change in the social basis of political power, from regional caudillos and their armies to the oil-financed state and political parties representing the people. In the context of expanding oil revenues, the principle of national ownership of natural resources provided the material foundation for the institutionalization of popular sovereignty.

Just as the promotion of democratic politics had been bound up with a conception of the nation that fused such democratic rights as universal suffrage and free political expression to the collective entitlement to the nation's petroleum wealth, the demobilization of society under Pérez Jiménez entailed a reconceptualization of the relationship between the people and the state which polarized tendencies already present in the democratic project. The nation's social body became more marked as the passive beneficiary of its natural body, seen now as the main source of the nation's powers. This shift marked a subtle but perceptible displacement in the locus of historical agency from the nation's social body toward its natural body—from the people to nature.

As in the democratic narrative of nationality, nature appeared as a social actor not independently but through the mediation of the state. But the military state claimed to represent the nation directly, without the mediation of the people. As nature's agent, the state now proposed to transform the nation's natural body into its civilized material habitat. The assumption was that this modern dwelling would have the power to transform the people that inhabited it. Pérez Jiménez's fundamental belief was that a transformation in the physical habitat would change the Venezuelan people. Yet he also sought to facilitate this civilizing process by infusing this dwelling with Venezuela's spirit.

THE SPIRIT OF THE NATION

"The formation of a national consciousness," according to Pérez Jiménez, involved the development of what he called a "healthy nationalism," that is, one based on positive "facts" rather than on "negative and unachievable theories." While these facts for him were mostly associated with the material achievements of metropolitan societies, he also paid some attention to certain aspects of domestic culture, which he called the "spiritual" dimension of nationalism. According to him, "Our nationalism must imply the defense of the traditions that express what is positive in the Venezuelan spirit."

From the government's scattered actions and pronouncements, more than from any explicit program, one could deduce that these positive ex-

General Marcos Pérez Jiménez receives representations of himself as gifts. (Instituto Autónomo Biblioteca Nacional.)

pressions of the Venezuelan spirit had three fundamental sources: history, religion, and popular culture. The government sought to benefit from the energy flowing from these sources of collective identity while also attempting to contain and delimit their expression by reducing them to bounded and controllable manifestations. National history was treated as a cult of the heroes of the independence wars, Catholicism as the worship of a pantheon of saints identified with specific national regions, and popular culture as official folklore.

The main vehicle for the affirmation of national history was the Week of the Fatherland (*la Semana de la Patria*), a week of parades and ceremonies the stated aim of which was to revalorize the concept of the fatherland (*patria*), to honor the heroes of the independence, and to celebrate the values of the nation. Evidently, by linking the fatherland and the state the regime hoped also to establish a line of continuity between political and economic independence on the one hand and the founders of the nation and its present-day builders on the other, and thus to create the image of a unified collectivity embarked on a civilizational process. Like Guzmán Blanco and

Gómez, who sought to modernize Venezuela, Pérez Jiménez saw himself as the embodiment of Bolívar's spirit.

Established by governmental decree in 1953, the Week of the Fatherland culminated on 5 July, the date of Venezuela's declaration of independence in 1811. The main event took place in Caracas on this date when representative sectors of the population—workers, students, the military, professionals, and public servants—were obliged to attend a large parade that commemorated the heroes of independence; starting in 1955 this parade took place on the Paseo de los Próceres, an avenue built by Pérez Jiménez surrounded by monuments that honor those heroes. By furthering the deification of Bolívar that had begun with President Guzmán Blanco in the nineteenth century, the Week of the Fatherland continued as well the sacralization of the state as the ultimate source of national values.[2]

The sacralization of politics implied also the politicization of religion. In contrast to AD, which had alienated the Catholic Church when it tried to regulate Catholic educational institutions, Pérez Jiménez actively encouraged the Church's evangelizing efforts and promoted the establishment of regional patron saints throughout the country. The government promoted Catholicism and the cult of the Virgin Mary throughout the nation. Each year a different Virgin was named patron saint of the Week of the Fatherland, and pilgrimages and masses were organized to worship her in cities throughout the country. In 1952 Pope Pius XII accepted the government's request to designate the Virgin of Coromoto as Venezuela's patron saint.

As part of its support of the Catholic Church, the state sought to eradicate autonomous forms of popular religiosity. Its principal target was the so-called cult of María Lionza, a popular religion which combines indigenous, spiritist, African-American, and popular Catholic beliefs and practices and had expanding appeal among working and middle-class sectors (including the military) in urban centers. While the government sought to suppress its ritual practice as a form of witchcraft (*curanderismo*), it appropriated its mythical cosmology as an expression of national identity (Barreto 1995). Repressed as a religious figure, María Lionza was celebrated as a national myth. In this manageable form, she became a cultural figure who appeared as part of the nation's folklore in theatrical productions, paintings, sculptures, and accounts by writers and journalists. In 1953 an imposing statue of María Lionza by Venezuelan sculptor Alejandro Colina, which he had created years earlier,

---

2. For a brief discussion of the Semana de la Patria, see Castillo (1990: 120–24); for a discussion of the deification of Bolívar, see Carrera Damas (1969).

Statue of Maria Lionza by Alejandro Colina, placed by General Marcos Pérez Jiménez on the grounds near the Central University of Venezuela in 1953.

was placed next to the recently constructed campus of the Central University of Venezuela designed by modernist architect Carlos Raul Villanueva and sponsored by Pérez Jiménez. As Barreto has shown, through the state's efforts to regulate and control this popular religion, María Lionza's public image changed during this period (1948–58) from the pagan popular figure evoked by Molina's sensual and muscular sculpture to a chaste image that has an uncanny resemblance to the Virgin of Coromoto.

During this decade, for the first time in Venezuela's history, the study of the nation's popular traditions became part of the primary school curriculum. Officializing "folklore" as a component of national identity, the government institutionalized certain forms of popular dance and music, transforming them into the representative expressions of national culture to be taught in schools and performed at official events. At the same time, the government supported the creation of dance and theater companies which disseminated these official expressions of national folklore throughout Venezuela and abroad.

The most important of these groups was El Retablo de las Maravillas (The Shrine of Wonders) founded by Manuel Rodríguez Cárdenas, director of the Department of Labor Culture of the Ministry of Labor. According to Rodríguez Cárdenas, El Retablo de las Maravillas was a group formed, as its slogan indicated, by "the workers' children for the workers." A non-professional troupe, this artistic group claimed to represent "a youthful labor movement unified around art and directed at the spiritual education of the masses" (Rodríguez Cárdenas 1954:16; Castillo 1990:124–26). Its repertoire brought together stylized forms of dance from the nation's different regions.

Just as the state's physical constructs were intended to uplift but also to contain the people, the state's creation and promotion of selected national traditions were supposed to stimulate as well as to discipline popular creativity. The junta mistrusted popular sectors and yet saw them as a source for building a homogenizing national culture. While it exerted tight control of politics through censorship, dismantling parties and unions, and repression, the government stimulated the organization of culture as an apolitical realm celebratory of a harmonious and authentic nationality.

The dictatorship's ambivalent attitude toward the popular sectors rendered more visible a contradiction at the heart of Venezuela's democracy which is covered over by the state's celebratory discourse of the people: the construction of el pueblo at once as the foundation of the nation's sovereign identity and as a primitive mass to be shaped by the (more) enlightened state elite. While the democratic regime had sought to uplift the people by encouraging yet directing their political participation, the dictatorship attempted to shape them by restricting their activity and modifying their physical environment.

THE NATION'S BODY

Under Pérez Jiménez, the redefinition of state ideology, achieved in the context of restricted public discourse, occurred through deeds and brief pronouncements. Vague slogans such as the "rational transformation of the physical environment" encompassed state activities in vastly different areas.

Through practice, however, it became clear that the regime focused on those visible signs of modernity it regarded as the essence of capitalist development. These concrete embodiments of progress—luxury hotels, freeways, a steel mill, a modernist university campus—were seen at once as symbols of progress and as its cause. Upon being transplanted from metropolitan centers to the backward national soil, these fetishes of modernity were believed to carry the power to bring progress to Venezuela.

Pérez Jiménez avoided political rhetoric, which he identified with the parties he abhorred, and ideological discussion, which he distrusted. His vision of Venezuela was not articulated programmatically but enacted pragmatically. It was only in response to mounting foreign criticism that he attempted to formulate the goals guiding his government.[3] Although he now held constitutional power and still sought to build his identity as the restorer of order and an efficient administrator, he was called on to give purpose to his rule and to define the proper links between citizen and state.

As if faced with a distasteful assignment, Pérez Jiménez pieced together a doctrine and called it the New National Ideal, first introduced in 1955 at a celebration commemorating the tenth anniversary of the overthrow of President Medina. Government brochures articulated the doctrine in a laconic synthesis of ideas that had always guided the regime adorned with vague rhetorical expressions alluding to "progress" and "modernization." According to a Venezuelan scholar, the New National Ideal was an "ideological composite" of Venezuelan liberalism, positivism, traditional militarism, and democratic party rhetoric (Avendaño Lugo 1982:342). To explain the regime's purpose, this doctrine asserted that the military's higher "destiny" was to eliminate political strife and channel social energies toward the "material construction" of the fatherland: "A clear demonstration of our national consciousness is the materialization of the abstract concept of Fatherland in works of great scope, whose importance will be self-evident" (Pérez Jiménez 1956:27).

In "materializing the abstract concept of the Fatherland," the nation was turned into a visible construct, a concrete appearance. With nature understood as the physical environment and the people as the passive beneficiaries of a revolution in its physical geography, the nation was transformed into a mass to be shaped by the state. The notion of the "rational transformation

---

3. During the International Petroleum Conference held in Caracas in April 1955, the labor representative of the International Labor Organization (ILO) criticized the regime and demanded it permit a free trade union movement. Pérez Jiménez retaliated by expelling the delegate from the country, which led to a wider confrontation (Kolb 1974:149–53).

of the physical environment" was conceptualized as a means to mold and discipline the social body. Politics would no longer be a "disorderly" struggle among competing groups over the spoils of power but rather the harmonious "construction" of the nation by the state.

The discourse of material progress was employed to highlight not the technical complexity of development but its simplicity in the absence of partisan conflict. In this respect, the regime's ideological framework was closer to positivism as interpreted in Venezuela in the early twentieth century than to modernization theory after World War II. After the war, development ideology was influential in Latin America through the work of Raul Prebisch, one of the leading figures in the Economic Commission for Latin America (ECLA). Many countries accepted ECLA's evaluation of Latin America's basic structural problems—unequal terms of trade, domestic unemployment, and external dependence—and endorsed its conception of "inner-directed growth" as a way of countering them. ECLA assigned a central role to the state as the agent responsible for planning and promoting the development of integrated and relatively independent economies in Latin American nations. According to ECLA, by promoting the growth of domestic industry and agriculture through import substitution, the state would stimulate as well the formation of the modern social classes associated with modernity—the bourgeoisie and the wage-earning working class.

The Pérez Jiménez regime's economic policy developed, without much theoretical elaboration, along lines that had been laid since 1936.[4] Since some of its goals, such as the promotion of industry and agriculture, were common wisdom in Latin America and informed the formation of ECLA's project, it is difficult to discern influences and to characterize the ideological framework specific to the regime's economic policies. While the noted economist Domingo Maza Zavala dissociates Pérez Jiménez's economic project from ECLA's developmental program and links it to the military developmental ideologies of Perón in Argentina, Odría in Peru, and Rojas Pinilla in Colombia (as precursors of the military's more coherent bureaucratic authoritarian programs developed in Brazil and Argentina in the 1960s and Chile in the 1970s), historian Ocarina Castillo sees an underlying continuity in the economic policies of the regimes established in Venezuela after Gómez's death. According to Castillo, what differentiates Pérez Jiménez's economic

4. While the regime sought in 1957 the advice of one of CEPAL's leading representatives, Brazilian economist Celso Furtado, according to Venezuelan economist Orlando Araujo, the Furtado report was sought only to buttress the public image of the dictatorship and the government paid no attention to it (Castillo 1991:172–73).

project from those that preceded and followed it is not its content but "its leading agents" and therefore "the internal and external political conditions under which it would unfold" (1990:62–63).

I would emphasize the importance of a distinct legitimating framework as one of the conditions which helped give form to Pérez Jiménez's development plans. As Castillo's work on the regime reveals, its economic project was cast in the legitimizing discourse of enlightened military despotism, not of the modernization theory that AD formulated during the Trienio or after 1958, or of the bureaucratic authoritarian doctrines developed by the military in Brazil and Argentina.[5] Its discourse facilitated the concentration of decision making at the executive level and the silencing of public discussion about the state's development project. If politics was reduced to technique, technique itself was simplified to its allegedly self-evident tenets.

We can see the laconic terms in which the regime's most outspoken ideologue claims to have represented his conception of "material progress" through an unusual dialogue which reportedly occurred in 1953 between Interior Minister Vallenilla Lanz and his prisoner, Alberto Carnevalli, AD's top underground leader. When Minister Vallenilla visited his prisoner, they engaged in a heated exchange, made possible by their common social background, concerning the theories of Vallenilla's father, the noted positivist historian and ideologue of the Gómez regime, Laureano Vallenilla Lanz.[6] In *Cesarismo democrático,* Vallenilla Lanz *padre* (senior) had argued that Latin American countries were unprepared for democratic institutions because they lacked social development due to a legacy of civil strife, fragmented economies, racial mixing, and the lack of educational institutions. Consequently, these countries had to be ruled by democratic caesars, enlightened despots who would transitionally monopolize political power to reorder society and create the conditions for an eventual democracy.[7]

5. Castillo's work is the most complete discussion to date of the ideological foundations of Pérez Jiménez's economic project (1990); other works which include an assessment of this economic program within a more general discussion of the period include Bautista Urbaneja (1992), Manuel Rodríguez Campos (1991), Martín Frechilla (1994), and Stambouli (1980). The reference to Maza Zavala's evaluation of the regime's economic program is based on a taped interview (Castillo 1990:172). For a discussion of bureaucratic authoritarianism and its typical forms of discourse, see O'Donnell (1973) and Collier (1979).

6. Laureano Vallenilla Lanz *hijo* (junior) dropped his mother's last name in order to be named like his father, Laureano Vallenilla Lanz.

7. Although often dismissed as an apologia for the Gómez dictatorship, which he supported, his work constituted an innovative sociological interpretation of Venezuelan history whose merits have been widely recognized (Salazar 1966; Caballero 1966).

Vallenilla recounts that Carnevalli—whom he considered "the best of the adecos" (1967:381)—pressed him to explain how he planned to eradicate *cesarismo*. His answer was a formulation of the dictatorship's credo: "I am committed to achieving a program of vast scope, a revolution in the physical geography of Venezuela, which, if completely realized, will extinguish forever the causes of cesarismo" (1967:383). I believe Vallenilla Lanz felt no need to give details to Carnevalli or to the reader of his memoirs about this "revolution in the physical geography of Venezuela" because its tenets in all likelihood were accepted by contending parties. As Castillo suggests, what ultimately distinguished the new regime was the agents in charge of executing the program, not its basic content.

By claiming to rule according to rational principles, the military junta intended to underline the technical character of development and therefore to eradicate public debate about its means and ends. Such a strategy has often led in Latin America to the production of highly elaborated development programs, but the claim to rationality during this boom period in Venezuela produced minimalist proposals and ad hoc policies. From the junta's perspective, since AD had squandered the nation's wealth and social energies in partisan social reforms, the military regime could readily demonstrate its superiority and promote development by transforming oil money into physical accomplishments, visibly reincorporating into the nation the value extracted from its subsoil. Through the power of the state, the official ideological landscape changed; the physical geography advanced to the foreground of official discourse, while el pueblo receded to the background and was transfigured from a historical subject to a spectator of the military regime's physical revolution.

This focus on public works shifted attention from the valorization of the subsoil to the rational use of oil money. This shift was facilitated by the state's concern that it not alienate the oil companies. While the regimes of General Medina and AD had the support of a broad constituency and could thus seek to maximize the value of the nation's wealth through nationalist oil policies, Pérez Jiménez was content with the terms of the policy he inherited and sought legitimacy by emphasizing the transformation of oil money into public works. In this new political landscape, democracy meant not political rights but material deeds. As an analyst has observed, "Democracy in the political sense, involving freedom of speech and press, and the formation of political parties competing for the power to govern, is specifically excluded as prejudicial to the national interests" (Kolb 1974:153).

Although elements of earlier elite ideology were evidently present in the New National Ideal and were incorporated into its military develop-mentalist discourse by Vallenilla Lanz and others, Pérez Jiménez claimed personal responsibility for its formulation. During his rule he sought to con-trol the regime's doctrine as much as he did its actions and has since vehe-mently refuted the claim that he was persuaded by Vallenilla to adopt this program. Pérez Jiménez recently emphasized in an interview that "the pa-ternity of the philosophical ideas that guided the regime belonged exclusively to Marcos Pérez Jiménez" (Blanco 1983 : 347). Distancing himself from the traditional elite, he insisted that he wished to be identified only with his government's material accomplishments and not with abstract ideologies, saying of Vallenilla's doctrine of cesarismo that "I do not understand it now and did not understand it then" (1983 : 257). For Pérez Jiménez, his program of material achievements *was* the philosophical foundation of his regime. Having silenced the opposition, he sought to restrict political language alto-gether; the language of order was that of tangible deeds, not ephemeral words.

Twenty-five years after his overthrow, at the end of a book-length inter-view, he asked his interviewer to include in the book a photo of his home in Spain (see photo, p. 120), a house that he had largely designed, explaining that "in this house I have poured all my disillusion. My house is the image of the country I wanted to build" (Blanco 1983 : 410). His ideal image of the nation as the house he built—which was a monumental construction in a patchwork of several European styles—is emblematic of a patriarchal con-ception of politics and a fetishistic view of progress. By redefining politics as the activity of turning the nation into a physical construct and by treating the tangible tokens of modernity as potent civilizing forces, Pérez Jiménez sought to domesticate the barbarous populace that had occupied the public space, to discipline its movements, speech and opinions within the imposing walls of the nation yet to be built, the dictator's castle writ large.

OIL BOOM AND DICTATORIAL POLICIES

Without a clear program for economic development but having abundant monetary resources, Pérez Jiménez's government set out to purchase eco-nomic progress. Its shopping list had the coherence of what passed as com-mon sense in certain elite circles in Venezuela at the time and reflected the regime's assumptions about the character of development and the sources of modernity. A Venezuelan economist perceptively notes that "between 1950 and 1959 Venezuela was a case of a process without a plan or program, in which industrial policy is a mere reflection of the public spending policy" (Araujo 1960 : 15). Investments in infrastructure, in industry, or in the service sector were part of a development plan only in the sense that they fit into the regime's fetishistic vision of modernity as a collection of grand material achievements. The projects had in common the quality of spectacular display. Many of them also exhibited a disregard either for their utility or for their impact upon the social and natural setting.

The concern for appearance, coupled with the outward orientation of the regime, was typified by the government's goal of transforming Caracas into an international tourist center and conference site. The capital received a major portion of government income in the form of projects designed largely to attract and impress foreign businessmen and the diplomatic community, as well as the affluent traveler. For this highly commercially oriented regime, buttressed by foreign economic and political support, the transformation of Caracas into a glittering tourist and commercial center symbolized the regime's mediating role between the local, backward society and the international, modern world. Pérez Jiménez's pet project, the Humboldt Hotel (named after the nineteenth-century German author), a glass-encased skyscraper, was located on top of the Avila mountain ridge. Its perch above the capital was emblematic of the state's two-directional role in the circulation of oil rents. The hotel commanded a view of the sea to the north and of Caracas to the south, was equipped with an ice-skating rink, and could be reached only by a long ride in a funicular—small suspended cars which lifted the visitor out of the city until it became a scenic outline in the valley's landscape. Built without an adequate study of its viability as an economic concern, the hotel was never profitable and has remained shut since the Pérez Jiménez regime.

But luxury was for the regime an essential dimension of the ideal to be attained. It was a visible sign of social ascent and a means to achieve the public recognition so fervently sought by the military elite and its nouveau riche associates. Through the conspicuous display of luxury, the military regime sought to impress not just metropolitan visitors, who represented a superior external world, but also the traditional domestic elite, from which it felt excluded, and the people, whom it sought to control.

The government sought to buttress the military's sense of identity by building a social club for officers which was intended to surpass the luxurious settings that the Caracas elite enjoyed in its exclusive clubs. *Time* magazine found in this club a symbol of the oil-rich nation to which U.S. businessmen flocked:

Nothing in Venezuela—or outside of it, for that matter—can compete with the palatial Círculo de las Fuerzas Armadas, the social club for military officers and top government officials. It has a hotel (television in every room), restaurants, bar, cocktail lounge, nightclub, two swimming pools, stable, gymnasium, fencing court, bowling alleys, library, and theater. Some notably sumptuous touches: marble floors, blue Polaroid windows, Gobelin tapestries, Sèvres vases, Tiffany clocks, a glass-walled conservatory housing a living, blooming chunk of the Venezuelan jungle. To the grander dances at the club, some colonels' wives wear $1,500 Balmain gowns. (28 February 1955.)

Behind its spectacular appearances lay the unresolved tensions of a socially marginal but aspiring military elite unversed in the amenities of the upper class but also disconnected from, and contemptuous of, the popular classes.

Within this vague programmatic framework, political alliances and constraints helped define the government's economic policy. With the army as the basis of its power and businessmen (both local and foreign) as its primary allies, the government sought to contain el pueblo by neutralizing the middle class—led parties that in the recent past had manipulated the masses, captured the state, and upset the social order. The wealthy military government claimed to embody the national interest—to rule not in the name of the people but on its behalf.

For the rulers, having power meant being able to stand above particularistic interests, not to harmonize them; their capacity to resist demands confirmed their power. "The fact can be stated simply: the armed forces had no intention of responding to demands made by autonomous interests of any kind. The military seemed more confident about the possession of bureaucratic power than ever before in the country's history" (Taylor 1968:37). Pérez Jiménez treated his local allies not as partners in making policy but as subservient supporters. His policies required no discussion, negotiation, or compromise. Pérez Jiménez attempted to rule alone.

During this Cold War period, when conservative governments in Latin America were actively supported by the United States as allies in the struggle against communism, Pérez Jiménez presented Venezuela's economic policy strategically in terms of the defense of the nation's physical integrity. "The military officialdom that supported Pérez Jiménez's takeover of power firmly upheld the notion that Venezuelan development and defense must focus on its internationally strategic location and natural resources" (Skurski 1985:45). Within sectors of the armed forces, it was believed that the state should combine the defense of Venezuela's strategic interests with the promotion of a model of economic development based on natural resources (Rincón 1982: 73–78). The military included as state-controlled strategic activities not only the production of military weapons and supplies but also of electrical power and basic industries: steel and petrochemicals.

This general political framework helped orient the government's state-centered economic policy along the following lines: increased openness to foreign capital; repression of domestic labor; economic growth through state investment in infrastructure, services, and basic industry; and the promotion and yet containment of the local bourgeoisie. While this program at first consolidated the regime, its consequences eventually undermined it, paving the way for the regime's overthrow.

I will provide a context for the 1958 coup d'état against Pérez Jiménez by offering a view of the regime's economic program which summarizes major developments in these four areas. Within this framework, I will provide a glimpse of the inner dynamics of change through an account of the conflictual relationship between the private sector and the state concerning the promotion of a national steel industry that offers a vivid image of the regime's distinctive character—what historian Castillo calls "its leading agents." Yet this case also shows that these agents—some of whom were key figures in the regimes preceding Pérez Jiménez's dictatorship and came to play a leading role in the democratic administrations that followed it—did not come with fixed identities onto history's stage, but rather developed new roles under changing circumstances.

Openness to foreign capital. The regime's willingness to provide highly favorable conditions for foreign capital (low taxes, free currency convertibility, and profit remittances), evident in every economic sector, was most blatant in the oil industry. While it accepted the basic framework it inherited, these policies represented a retreat from the increasingly nationalist policies of previous regimes. The regime reaped the benefits of past policies, did not promote new gains, and in some areas simply undid them.

This was a period of rapid economic expansion. International conditions fueled the rising demand for Venezuelan oil: the rebuilding of Europe, the U.S. arms build-up, the spread of U.S. multinational corporations overseas, the Korean War, the attempted nationalization of Iranian oil, and especially the Suez crisis. During this boom period (1947–57), domestic oil production expanded at a stable yearly rate averaging 9.4 percent, prices at 7.4 percent, and exports at 17.4 percent (Hausmann 1981:208). Between 1949 and 1957, ordinary oil income increased at an annual rate of 11.6 percent, total oil income at 15.4 percent, and government income at 13.9 percent (1981:317).

In this context, the military government felt no need to pressure one of its major allies, the oil companies. On the contrary, it was particularly receptive to a campaign orchestrated by the oil industry and the U.S. State Department in which cheaper Middle Eastern oil was portrayed as a threat to Venezuelan oil exports in order to discourage the continuation of Venezuela's assertive oil policies (Rabe 1982: 122–24). In response to these pressures, the military government abandoned efforts to develop mechanisms of national control over oil pricing and the local capacity to manage oil industry affairs. It also dropped plans to develop a national petroleum company, did not encourage the oil companies to reinvest profits in the nonoil economy, and let them declare sales revenues beneath their real level. It has been calculated that between 1949 and 1954, the " 'tax adjustments' of the Pérez Jiménez regime cost Venezuela a whopping Bs. 4,508 million in revenue losses" (Baloyra 1974: 48). The 1955 Hydrocarbons Law, the only one decreed during this period, did not address fundamental issues, only minor technical details. "The oil policy of Pérez Jiménez was passive. The former aggressive tactics to increase the nation's share in oil profits were replaced by a policy of friendly cooperation" (Hassan 1975: 18). In short, the oil industry was treated simply as a source of immediate revenues.

Concerned only with expanding immediate government revenues without antagonizing or restricting the oil companies, the regime failed to develop a long-term oil policy. Since it was unable to interpret the significance of the shift in petroleum investment toward low-priced sources in the Middle East, the regime accepted the oil industry's interpretation of these changes. Pérez Jiménez reversed the policy of increasing the nation's income by raising taxes and instead expanded production. "Between 1950 and 1957, oil production rose from 547 million barrels a year to over one billion as predictions of a glut of oil on the world market proved premature" (Rabe 1982: 129). Taking a short-range commercial approach, the government rendered itself even more vulnerable to the industry's control of oil prices and production.

Thus, when the government needed additional revenues in 1956 as a result of administrative mismanagement and overexpenditure, it obtained them not by asserting its power as landowner and demanding more rent, but by commercial means—by selling concessions to oil companies. This reversal of AD's policy of "no more concessions" gave the oil companies 821,091 hectares of land and brought the government almost Bs. 2,115 million in extra revenues between 1956–57 (Vallenilla 1973: 219).

This policy shift corresponded to a change in the social basis of the dictatorial regime. The post-Gómez administrations, which increasingly relied on popular support to secure political legitimacy, had sought to maximize state income by augmenting the domestic share of oil profits, that is, by demanding more rent. The military men who took power in 1948, who relied on the support of private and foreign capital to buttress their power, sought to expand state income by increasing the total level of oil production. Not counting on popular support, Pérez Jiménez tried to maximize the backing of his foreign allies, and was satisfied with the level of revenues produced by his "low-risk" stance:

> The military, especially Pérez Jiménez, seemed to have followed a line of contentment with whatever level of resources were generated by a modest, "low risk" governmental share in the profits of the industry. Impressed with the argument that the industry had to remain "competitive" and that the companies could not shoulder a heavy tax burden, the military converted the arguments and protestations of the industry into government policy most of the time . . . In contrast, the adecos assumed that the companies would always find the business profitable and that, short of nationalization, they would resist but finally accept larger and larger tax rates and more governmental regulation. (Baloyra 1974:51.)

The military regime, as the guardian of the national territory, took the sale of concessions seriously. Bidding was competitive (in part because the new oil companies emerging in the United States were interested at this time in securing oil fields overseas), and the government obtained terms ten times better than in 1943 ($388 per hectare as opposed to $38).

The oil companies felt secure in Venezuela and reciprocated. During this period they expanded their activities considerably. The number of producing oil wells increased yearly, jumping from 6,031 in 1948 to 10,124 in 1957 (BCV 1977:69). The companies' total investment during the 1948–57 period, however, grew at a moderate pace, only 11.8 percent in real terms, equivalent to 1.2 percent average compound rate per year; but it represented over 20 percent of total investment during a period when nonpetroleum investment grew 70.3 percent in real terms (Salazar-Carrillo 1976:108). And in 1956–57 there was a considerable increase of investment, not only in oil production but also in transport, refining, and marketing. Between 1950 and 1957 oil industry profits in Venezuela amounted to $3.79 billion dollars; nearly half of the dividend income of Standard Oil of New Jersey (Exxon) came from its Venezuelan subsidiary, Creole Petroleum (Rabe 1982:129).

Pérez Jiménez also opened Venezuela's doors to foreign investors in the nonoil economy at a time when U.S. manufacturing corporations were expanding their direct investments abroad. Intending to make Venezuela a choice location for foreign investment, in the summer of 1953 he instructed consulates to promote Venezuela to business. Soon afterwards, *Time* magazine responded with this vivid description:

> One place where U.S. businessmen abroad can still flourish in a climate of high-riding free enterprise is the oil-boom republic of Venezuela . . . Since 1948, when the government and the foreign-owned companies . . . worked out a mutually satisfactory deal that calls, in effect, for a 50-50 split of all profits, production has shot up to 1,000,000 barrels a day, flooding the sparsely-populated country with $700 million in oil income. The gratified government has thrown the door wide open to foreign enterprise, and the biggest colony of U.S. businessmen overseas is happily at work making money in one of the world's most profitable markets. Venezuelan law lets the foreigner operate freely, and U.S. firms, which own two-thirds of Venezuela's $2.3 billion foreign investment, take their profit out in dollars, with no red tape. Yanquis residing in Venezuela pay no U.S. income taxes, and the Venezuelan tax is downright benign (cited by Kolb 1974:130).

Between 1951 and 1957 foreign investment more than tripled, with the United States accounting for almost 70 percent of the total (BCV 1958:81). In this period, foreign capital investment in industry increased from Bs. 165 million to Bs. 411 million—from 10.7 to 14.8 percent of total investments in this sector (Aranda 1977:163). Given Venezuela's delayed industrial development and booming economy, this flow of foreign investment into manufacturing did not displace existing local capital from industry. Nor did it discourage commercial activity. Trade between the United States and Venezuela also expanded during this decade, reaching a value of over $1 billion in 1957; with only seven million inhabitants, Venezuela became the United States' sixth-largest commercial market in the world (Rabe 1982:128). Thus, transnational capital paved the way for the movement of local capital into industry, either by the force of its example or by becoming its partner in joint ventures. Out of this convergence of interest in industrial development came a nascent alliance between the leading sectors of local and foreign capital in support of state-promoted industrialization.

Repression of domestic labor. During this period, trade union activity was curtailed, and strikes were not permitted. The Confederation of Venezuelan Workers (CTV) was dissolved on 25 February 1949, and after a 1950 oil workers' strike (protesting the regime's political restrictions), the government attacked the petroleum workers union. Since the Venezuelan labor movement had been primarily organized by AD and the PC, when these parties were repressed, the trade union movement was practically dissolved. In its place the government installed a captive organization named Movimiento Sindical Independiente, which orchestrated contracts favorable to the companies.

Given the strategic importance of the oil industry for the United States, the State Department and U.S. oil companies felt that control of Venezuelan workers could not be left in Venezuelan hands. The FBI and the CIA were allowed to conduct surveillance activities in Venezuela to help eradicate communist influence in the worker's movement:

> The oil companies cooperated by submitting their employees' finger-prints to the FBI to determine if they were communists or "fellow travelers." In addition, they increased surveillance of their property and accepted the offer of the Central Intelligence Agency to watch for subversives and saboteurs among Venezuelan oil workers (Rabe 1982:121).

By the end of the regime, "while some Pérez Jimenista unions continued to exist, the union movement had in effect been destroyed" (Fagan 1977: 177). Thus, despite the booming economy, labor demands—which never ceased—were blocked, and the steady expansion of real wages that had begun in 1945 came to an end.

A second element in the regime's labor policy that served to contain local labor was the promotion of European immigration. By encouraging selective immigration the government brought in relatively skilled labor—almost eight hundred thousand laborers of both urban and rural origin—mainly from Spain, Italy, and Portugal. Fleeing the effects of World War II and the Spanish Civil War, they came to Venezuela in pursuit of security in a booming economy. Thus, European labor, instead of exerting a radicalizing influence on the working class, as in other Latin American countries in the early twentieth century, helped demobilize it by displacing less-skilled local labor, by lending political support to the regime, and by opposing other workers' demands in their work sites.[8]

However, given Venezuela's capital intensive industrialization, most urban job creation took place in the commercial and service sectors; manufacturing employment amounted to only 18.1 percent of the total (and of this, one half was in artisan enterprises), in contrast to a Latin American

---

8. Before the 1957 plebiscite, Pérez Jiménez granted foreigners the right to vote after living in Venezuela for only two years. This measure was widely seen as opportunistic and fueled the growing opposition to the regime.

average of 27 percent by 1960 (Hassan 1975:87). From 1950 through 1957, agricultural employment declined from 44.1 percent to 38.3 percent of total employment (Aranda 1977:171). At a time when the channeling of oil-revenue expenditures to the major cities drew peasants and agricultural workers to migrate, factors such as a rural/urban wage differential of over 400 percent in many areas (Hassan 1975:82), worsening conditions for traditional agricultural production, and the expansion of commercial agriculture helped undermine already weak social ties in the countryside.

Thus, while the transformation of traditional agriculture in neighboring Colombia caused intense rural violence at this time, in Venezuela it took place without overt political conflict. In one of the most rapid processes of urbanization in modern times, the percentage of labor employed in agriculture shifted from 71.1 in 1936 to 36.5 in 1961 (Hassan 1975:81). The traditional hacienda declined drastically in response to the rapid growth of capitalist agriculture in the countryside (Hernández 1988:109). During this period most rural workers were employed by large commercial farms or they cultivated subsistence plots. During the fifties the control and repression of labor became fundamentally an urban problem; Venezuela had ceased to be a rural country.

Economic growth through state investment in infrastructure, services, and basic industry. As I have indicated, official historiography tends to treat the 1948–58 period as a dark parenthesis in Venezuela's progress toward modernity and thus to disconnect it from the democratic regimes that preceded and followed it. Yet, using budgets as indicators of policy priorities, Baloyra's close comparison of budgets under military regimes (1938–45 and 1949–57) and democratic administrations (1946–48 and 1958–69) has shown that they were strikingly similar in terms of percentage distribution among categories (Baloyra 1974). AD spent a somewhat larger share of its budget on health and education; and Pérez Jiménez, more on communications (largely as a result of the partial completion of highway construction and railroad plans initiated under AD)—but even here the differences are not considerable. At this macro level the basic difference is that AD actively sought to increase state revenues and spent more in every ministry (except Justice), while Pérez Jiménez spent what he had available but did not seek to maximize state income (Baloyra 1974:59–61).

The difference between democratic and dictatorial economic policies in Venezuela has been heightened by their contrasting positions toward planning. While democratic regimes made elaborate development plans and publicized them widely, Pérez Jiménez preferred to present development as a simple process that would follow from a rational use of the state's resources.

Scholars who have paid attention not so much to the stated programs but to Pérez Jiménez's investments in steel, petrochemicals, telephones, sugar mills, and electricity tend to interpret these investments as signs of the conscious development of a productive state, and thus to establish a line of continuity with democratic regimes (Aranda 1977:141). These investments reflected the militarization of the state during the Cold War period and the U.S. endorsement of conservative regimes in Latin America as bulwarks against the communist threat. Under this militaristic Cold War ideology, the regime's economic policy acquired some coherence along two lines: the production of goods considered strategic for the nation's military security, on the one hand, and the state's control of basic and related industries to the exclusion of the local private sector, on the other.

The state's move to production served to concentrate control of the state in Pérez Jiménez's hands, to prevent the creation of alternative centers of power within the private sector, and to enrich those associated with its promotion. Given the absence of careful planning, it is difficult not to conclude that these considerations played a key role in the way these projects were formulated and carried out (Skurski 1985; Luzardo 1963:177; Bigler 1980). The petrochemical plant was the most notorious case in point. Located in a remote and inappropriate area on land purchased from a military friend of Pérez Jiménez's, the severely flawed project (largely inoperative and still unprofitable despite repeated efforts to salvage it three decades after its construction) was directed by unqualified military cronies. But Pérez Jiménez and his friends were enormously enriched through their involvement in the construction of this industrial façade.

In light of the sharp separation that official historiography has established between democratic and dictatorial regimes, it is salutary to note continuities in their economic policies and to be skeptical about one-sided negative evaluations of the Pérez Jiménez regime. Yet a focus on apparent continuities may also obscure some of the distinguishing features of the regime's move to production. Many of these projects were conceived in the same spirit as its other nonproductive public investments: as spectacular works which were thought to have the power to buttress the regime and to induce with relative ease the nation's development. Not much care was put into the formulation of these projects, many of which originated in response to circumstantial or political considerations and were ill conceived either as profit-making ventures or as catalysts of growth. Thus Pérez Jiménez's distinguishing approach to modernity cannot be discerned at the level of statistical aggregates or the pattern of investment programs but requires a qualitative examination of his specific projects. My discussion of steel production at the end of this chapter seeks to illustrate this point.

Promotion and yet containment of the local bourgeoisie. In the period between 1945 and 1960, Venezuela experienced the highest growth rate in real GDP in South America and one of the highest in the world (Hassan 1975:10). In the period between 1950 and 1957, ordinary oil revenue grew an average of 11.6 percent and government income an average of 13.9 percent annually, while the total value of oil exports increased 250 percent and treasury reserves 400 percent (Salazar-Carrillo 1976:98). The money supply doubled, and demand rose sharply.

This was a period when local businessmen both expanded their investments in traditional areas—banking, construction, commerce—and diversified their activities in new ones—commercial agriculture and industry. But this expansion, the product of the oil boom, was limited by Pérez Jiménez's policies, which sought simultaneously to promote economic growth and to impede the development of an independent private sector, at once to encourage economic entrepreneurship and yet to contain it within crippling and often arbitrary limits, as the following discussion of steel production illustrates.

The banking sector grew rapidly during this decade in response to the explosive expansion of fiscal income, government spending, and commercial activity.[9] However, bankers were ill equipped to finance industrial growth, for they were legally prohibited from making loans with terms of over two years. There were also no investment banks or savings and loan banks as yet through which funds could be channeled for productive ventures. Consequently, local funds went toward commerce and short-term projects, and long-term financing was sought abroad.

In contrast to this explosive growth of the money supply and of the banking system, local production developed little, and prices remained stable. Given the availability of foreign exchange, the increased demand fueled by the injection of money was met by a sharp expansion of imports, from $557 million in 1947 to $1,776 million in 1957 (BCV 1978:238). "The high increase of Venezuela's imports up to 1957 reduced the inflationary pressure resulting from the increased quantity of money and of effective demand in a time when the productive capacity of the economy was limited" (Hassan 1975:66).

9. In 1947 private bank assets amounted to Bs. 779 million, their loans and investments to Bs. 445 million, and their deposits to Bs. 72 million. By 1957 these figures reached Bs. 5,386 million, Bs. 3,658 million, and Bs. 1,501 million respectively (Hassan 1975:55).

At a time when balance of payments constraints spurred local industrialization and inflation was an increasing problem in most of Latin America, Venezuela had the lowest change in the cost of living in the region, with an annual increase of only 1.7 percent in 1950–59 (Hassan 1975:66). Both these factors were to shape public policy as well as business and consumer expectations and behavior. A high level of imports became an essential element of Venezuela's economy and of state policy. At this early stage of industrialization, just as consumer demand was satisfied by imports, production requirements were met by imported material and equipment. But the facility with which consumer demand was satisfied through imports helped strengthen business interest in maintaining the existing low level of protection, thereby limiting the possibility of continued industrialization, particularly by local capital. In the name of defending the public's access to high quality and reasonably priced goods, the government sided with commercial interests and with U.S. exporting manufacturers. Thus, in 1952 the government signed a revised version of the United States–Venezuelan Commercial Treaty of 1939, which maintained highly favorable conditions for imported U.S. manufactured goods. The failure of nascent local industrial interests to gain tariff protection for products they sought to produce created a split between elite commercial and industrial interests, an event which was eventually to have political consequences.

But while they helped form a market of consumers, which stimulated commercial expansion, soaring oil revenues also created conditions which promoted some industrial production. The construction boom stimulated significant industrial growth among related industries having comparative advantages as the result of transportation costs—cement, paints, wood, and nonmetallic minerals, which made up 12 percent of industrial production by 1955. At the same time, the expansion of demand in the area of final consumer goods, encouraged by the domestic production of certain lines of textiles, shoes, and clothing that did not compete with foreign imports, increased local industrial production to 12 percent by 1960 (Hanson 1977:66–67).

In contrast to the experience of earlier "late" industrializers in Latin America during this period of expansion of transnational corporations into direct investments overseas, foreign capital did not displace less efficient local producers but rather encouraged the development of state protection and private investment in industry. Pioneering local capitalists began to discover that they could prosper behind the mantle of industrial protection and avoid the strong competition that prevailed in the commercial sector.

Without a coherent industrial policy, the state granted protection to industries in a piecemeal fashion, responding clientelistically to individual requests. Many of these industries were basically final-assembly operations that were given not only free access to imported inputs but also protection against imports, either through tariffs—when not in violation of the U.S. trade agreement—or through import quotas. Since only a few firms were given protection in each productive line, they were granted a virtual monopoly. This policy helped shape the oligopolistic structure that has characterized Venezuela's industrial production. When private capitalists sought to invest in large or strategic productive projects (as in the steel industry), the government appropriated these projects for itself. In practice, then, the dictatorial regime began to establish an import-substituting industrialization policy.

In the period between 1950 and 1957, gross fixed investment increased at an average annual rate of 8.4 percent and averaged 27 percent of gross domestic product (Hassan 1975:44). During the same period, government investment in the industrial sector increased fifteenfold from 1950 through 1957 (from Bs. 35 to Bs. 527 million). Total gross fixed investment doubled during this period, from Bs. 3,313 in 1950 to 6,041 in 1957. While public investment in industry almost tripled, from Bs. 1,054 to Bs. 2,748 million, private investment increased by 50 percent, from Bs. 2,259 to Bs. 3,293 million (Falcón Urbano 1969:101).

Industrial growth expanded at an average rate of 11.4 percent a year—a high rate, but approximately the same as the rate of expansion of the rest of the economy. Given the extremely low level of industrialization at the outset, this high-growth statistic is somewhat misleading; by 1957 the role of industry in the economy was still relatively low. This industrial expansion took place in areas where Venezuela had advantage—capital-intensive manufacture—or in relation to nontraded items such as construction, beer, and cement (Hanson 1977:69). Particularly telling of structural limitations was the slow increase in industrial employment, from 188 thousand in 1950 to 242 thousand in 1957 (Aranda 1977:160). Agricultural output lagged but still reached a moderately high rate of 4.5 percent a year during this period (Hanson 1977:69).

While these observations present a general image of socioeconomic trends during this period, a case study of the promotion of the steel industry offers a glimpse into the dynamics of these trends. Macroeconomic indicators show a significant continuity between democratic and dictatorial economic policies but obscure the extent to which under Pérez Jiménez leading businessmen found themselves isolated from the state and unable to influence national economic policy.

STEEL PRODUCTION: THE STATE AND THE IRON SYNDICATE

I will present a brief sketch of the three stages of the establishment of the steel industry in Venezuela: an initial phase, up to the 1930s, during which private entrepreneurs and state officials began to imagine the development of a national steel industry; a second phase (the 1945–48 triennium), when AD actively sought to promote the steel industry through the Venezuelan Development Corporation; and a third stage, during the 1948–58 dictatorship, when both the state and the private sector's Iron Syndicate pursued separate projects until the state took control over the steel industry.[10]

Origins

Early interest in iron ore deposits in the Guayana region grew out of a nineteenth-century gold boom in the area. At a time when the El Callao mine, deep in Venezuela's Amazonian region, became the world's main supplier of gold from 1882 through 1885 (Dodge 1968:38; cited by Skurski 1985:12), many local and foreign entrepreneurs were drawn into this region. Two U.S. citizens received concessions in the area which led to the discovery of iron ore deposits and to the beginning of iron exports in 1913, but these activities turned out to be unprofitable and the companies dissolved; consequently, interest in the Guayana region declined.

Among the Venezuelans who had gone to Guayana in search of gold were six members of the elite Zuloaga family, whose commercial and agri-

10. This section summarizes Skurski's work (1985). I participated with Skurski in the early stages of this research. Research included interviews with many of the leaders of the Iron Syndicate and state officials involved in the steel project, as well as as archival work in private-sector institutions (FEDECAMARAS), state agencies (Corporación Venezolana de Fomento), and official archives (Archivo Histórico de Miraflores). The Archivo Histórico de la Nación has a comprehensive record of the fundamental documents. For instance, Serie B, Caja 87 C26, contains a historical summary of the iron and steel projects; Serie B, Caja 45 1, information about technological processes produced for Pérez Jiménez by the Oficina de Estudios Especiales; Serie B, Caja 13 C3, a compilation of the various steel projects; Serie D, Caja 40 C8, minutes of meetings of state agencies concerning "basic industries"; Serie , Caja 56 C7, analysis of the links between the steel industry and the electrification of the Caroní River; Serie B, Caja 442 C6, and Serie C, Caja 3 C, documents concerning the proposals for the steel projects solicited by Pérez Jiménez. Documents about steel production and the Iron Syndicate in the Corporación Venezolana de Fomento are scattered in several folders and boxes, including a copy of the founding document of the Iron Syndicate (also available at the Registro Mercantil). After I wrote this account I had the opportunity to read Martín Frechilla's carefully researched discussion of the promotion of steel production in Venezuela (1994). I have sought to incorporate some of the superb information he provides. Both Skurski and Martín Frechilla point to continuities in AD's and Pérez Jiménez's steel policies, but while Skurski emphasizes the factors that marred Pérez Jiménez's steel project, Martín Frechilla underlines the technical care which each regime devoted to their formulation.

cultural enterprises had suffered significant losses during nineteenth-century civil wars. The Zuloagas did not find gold but developed a keen interest in the region. In 1939, at the request of the U.S. Steel Co., the Ministry of Development carried out a survey of the Guayana region which resulted in the demarcation of a large area rich in iron ore as a national reserve. A remarkable aspect of the government report was a recommendation that a steel industry be developed in Guayana in order to process the nation's iron ore and that the hydroelectric potential of the Caroní River be investigated. The two experts in charge of directing this report were Guillermo Zuloaga and Manuel Tello, upper-class Venezuelans trained as geologists in the United States. Zuloaga, whose family had established the Caracas Electricity Company, created the Development Ministry's Department of Mines and became a director of Standard Oil's Creole Petroleum of Venezuela. The Zuloagas and the Tellos were later to play an active role in the development of the Iron Syndicate.

Steel and AD's Trienio

While AD's policy of sowing the oil gave priority to the promotion of consumer industries through the Venezuelan Development Corporation (CVF), the CVF created in 1947 a Steel and Iron Department in order to plan steel production to supply local industry in the future. A year later, U.S. Steel discovered what at the time was the largest iron discovery of the century: an iron mountain of 400 million tons of 65 percent pure iron ore in proven reserves. Known locally as *la Parida* (the One that Gave Birth), the mountain was soon renamed and regendered as Cerro Bolívar (Mount Bolívar). As its strategic economic and political importance became evident, the iron mountain originally identified with generative Mother Earth came to be named after the Father of the nation and enlisted as a force in the battle for the nation's economic independence.

This discovery reflected U.S. Steel's change of policy concerning its iron ore supplies. As a result of the expansion of the world economy after World War II, this major U.S. corporation ceased to rely on its domestic iron ore reserves and sought to secure foreign iron sources. In turn, this discovery prompted the Venezuelan state to change its steel policy. Rather than waiting for the domestic development of consumer goods industries, the state decided to promote immediately the domestic production of steel. Not wanting to export yet another unprocessed natural resource, the government sought to advance its timetable for the domestic production of steel. The oil experience was not to be repeated.

Oil, however, exerted its influence in many ways. Through the CVF the government sought to link steel production to the nation's oil wealth and to make productive use of natural gas, a by-product of drilling for oil. As a result of its inquiries, the CVF learned of an innovative development in gas reduction technology, the patent of which was held by a U.S. company owned by William Brassert. Not wanting to venture alone in this new field, the CVF asked Nelson Rockefeller (with whom it had established close ties and joint ventures through the International Basic Economy Corporation, IBEC)[11] to participate in establishing a joint pilot plant with Brassert. Rockefeller agreed, for this plan matched his IBEC project to turn Venezuela into a model of U.S. corporate investment in Latin America's diversification through joint ventures of foreign, domestic, and state capital.

This alliance, however, proved conflictual in ways which revealed the gap between Venezuela's dreams of participating "as an equal partner of an international petroleum company involved in revolutionizing the steel industry" and the "close interconnections that existed within the U.S. corporate elite which would have priority over ties to Venezuela" (Skurski 1985:31). As it turned out, William Brassert was a college friend of David Rockefeller. When the CVF asked Nelson Rockefeller to participate in the Brassert project, he learned that it was the same project that his older brother David had been supporting. The Rockefeller brothers and Brassert negotiated among themselves, without informing the CVF, the terms of their agreement concerning the establishment of the pilot plant and issues of patents, ownership, and royalties.

At a time when the CVF thought it was participating as an equal partner in a pioneering economic project, it learned almost by accident that it was no longer wanted. In response to an inquiry about patents, Brassert wrote the CVF that it would establish the pilot plant without CVF's involvement. The CVF felt excluded from a technological breakthrough and betrayed by Nelson Rockefeller. Brassert's letter initiated a complex set of negotiations between the CVF and Rockefeller, who explained that his brother had prior links to Brassert and that he had planned to inform the CVF later about the results of their negotiations.

These events, together with tests with Venezuelan iron ore indicating that the Brassert process was expensive and unproved, plus negative reports about the Brassert patent from a group of lawyers (Martín Frechilla 1994:

11. IBEC was a development corporation created by the Rockefellers to diversify their economic investments in Latin America and thus reduce their identification with oil extraction. For a study of this corporation that emphasizes the role of Standard Oil in its promotion, see Broehl (1968).

224), led the CVF to explore alternative gas reduction techniques being developed in Sweden (the Wiberg process). CVF's Luis Alberto Roncayolo, stationed in New York since the end of 1947 in order to supervise gas reduction techniques being developed in the United States, including the Brassert technology, was now asked to go to Sweden to examine this new technology as head of a commission of Venezuelan officials and businessmen.

In a parallel development, in May 1948 the CVF learned of the great hydroelectric potential of the Caroní and Orinoco rivers from a preliminary study it had commissioned from Burns and Roes Inc. Although these results were positive, the CVF, shaped by the development model's focus on oil, did not seek to integrate its steel and hydroelectric projects. Perhaps it would have, but in November 1948 the military suddenly took power out of AD's hands and changed the context within which the steel industry would be established in Venezuela. The CVF's commission was left stranded in Sweden.

Steel, Dictatorship, and the Iron Syndicate

During the Trienio, AD made a special effort to invite domestic business leaders to participate in the state's economic agencies such as the CVF. After the coup the military junta assured private sector leaders that CVF's plans would be unaltered.

However, it was soon clear that the state had different plans. Once Pérez Jiménez took control after Delgado Chalbaud's murder in November 1950, relations between the private sector and the CVF changed: the CVF's steel department was transferred to the Ministry of Mines; the electricity department was reduced; the CVF's statute guaranteeing it from 2 to 10 percent of the state budget was eliminated; and the business representatives from FEDECAMARAS on CVF's board of directors were removed, a decision that its representatives learned of from the newspapers. With these gestures, the state sent a message to the private sector that it ruled alone; it effectively reduced the power of FEDECAMARAS and insulated itself from the influence of organized business (Bond 1975; Skurski 1985:35).

With the demise of the CVF project, a group of business leaders decided to undertake the promotion of a steel mill themselves. The main promoters of this project were the brothers Alberto and Gustavo Vollmer, and Eugenio Mendoza Goiticoa. They were associated with several prominent families, including the Zuloagas, the Machados, and the Boultons. United by ties of marriage, friendship, and business, these families had investments (often joint) in a large variety of industries, ranging from those linked to commercial agriculture, such as animal feed and rum, to urban-directed industries, such as electricity, cement, and construction materials. They sought to promote the domestic production of inputs for their expanding investments in the industrial sector. Shortages during World War II convinced them of the need to secure a domestic source of steel products for their construction and building firms as well as for the metalworking industries they planned to establish, such as industrial bridges and structures, tanks and water pipes, and automobile parts.

Their initial plan aimed to establish two companies: an iron mine and a steel plant. Aware that a move into basic industry was a politically sensitive undertaking, they formed the Sindicato del Hierro (the Iron Syndicate), a nonprofit civil association whose stated goal was to carry out studies to promote these companies, seek broad participation from local entrepreneurs, and gain state approval and support.

The Vollmer brothers, investors in agribusiness, construction, and banking, were the main force behind the Iron Syndicate, but they agreed that Eugenio Mendoza was in a better position to seek approval for the steel project from the military junta, given his links to both the Caracas social elite and the government, and his public image as an advocate of Venezuela's industrialization. As Medina's development minister during the war period (1942–44), Mendoza argued that Venezuela "had to produce what it consumed" and promoted domestic industry through the ministry's newly created Industry Division.[12] During this period Mendoza's own industries had prospered. Now his associates held high posts in the military government: Gerardo Sansón, a director of his cement factory, was the Minister of Public Works, and his friend Santiago Vera Izquierdo was Minister of Mines.

Mendoza first explored the terrain with Vera Izquierdo, who told him the government apparently had no plans to build a steel mill. Encouraged by this information, Mendoza approached Laureano Vallenilla Lanz (a childhood acquaintance), who as Pérez Jiménez's closest advisor and president of the Industrial Bank would have a decisive voice in this matter. Mendoza sought to sweeten his request for state support for the Iron Syndicate by offering the syndicate's presidency to Vallenilla's father-in-law, Adolfo Bueno, a physician from the elite who had made his wealth by selling an oil concession he received from Juan Vicente Gómez in gratitude for having successfully treated him.

Vallenilla, whoever, had no respect for Mendoza and his associates,

12. Interview, 1978.

whom he regarded as crass and opportunistic businessmen who sought to use the state for their own benefit. For him, the offer of the Iron Syndicate's presidency to Dr. Bueno was a transparent scheme to hide behind a respected figure and seek state support. Vallenilla, however, decided not to veto the project but only told Mendoza that he found the Bueno proposal unacceptable. He reminded Mendoza that, when AD had confiscated Bueno's goods in 1946 as part of its campaign against those enriched by the Gómez regime, Mendoza had removed Bueno from his post as director of Mendoza's cement factory rather than offering his support.

Pérez Jiménez was also critical of the Iron Syndicate's project but for different reasons. He distrusted the Caracas economic elite, was concerned about the power a steel mill would grant them, and was sensitive to demands within the military that the state establish control over basic industries. Yet Pérez Jiménez decided to allow the Iron Syndicate to continue its project in order to see what it would do. Thus the Minister of Mines assured its leaders that the state would approve their plans.

With the seeming assurance of state support, the Iron Syndicate sought to present itself publicly as the enterprise of a modernizing entrepreneurial class, distinct from the closed system of elite favorites enriched by the state under gomecismo. It initiated an unusual national, high-profile campaign to establish its image as a technically sound project with broad-based support. Its main leaders were men who had participated in investigating and promoting the steel industry since the Triennium and had expertise on the subject: Alberto Vollmer, Antonio Alamo Blanco, Luis Roncayolo, and Guillermo Machado Mendoza. Members of the Iron Syndicate met with business and political leaders throughout the country to gain political and financial support for the project and to counter the impression that it was the project of a small clique. By October 1952, the Iron Syndicate had 170 stockholders (109 subscribed in Caracas, 21 in Maracaibo, and 38 in other cities of the interior). Its president was Eugenio Mendoza, and its directors were representatives of Venezuela's leading business families, including Guillermo Zuloaga, author of the 1939 iron ore survey. It was officially registered on 4 June 1953, and in October it began exploring sites for the mill using a tractor shipped from the Vollmer's distant sugar refinery.

Iron Syndicate leaders also sought the participation of foreign capital in the project. They attracted the interest and support of German enterprises and of the two major U.S. companies that mined iron ore in Venezuela: U.S. Steel and Iron Mines. They also arranged in London and New York for contracts on two preliminary projects involving electric reduction Siemens-Martins furnaces; studies confirmed the Caroní River's great potential for supplying hydroelectric power and had led the project to shift from gas to electrical reduction technology.

For the private sector, the steel mill was a strategic investment. Given local capitalists' interest in obtaining a secure and economical domestic supply of steel inputs for their local industries, the Iron Syndicate felt that the mill had to fulfill certain technical requirements: it should use hydroelectric power and electric iron reduction furnaces; first produce "bar-mill shapes" (bars, concrete reinforcing rods, wire), with provisions for installing a rolling mill to produce flat products at a later stage; and be initially of modest dimensions (120 thousand tons–per–year capacity).

Pérez Jiménez followed these developments closely. After his 1952 coup, he changed course, establishing an executive office to plan the state's expansion into basic industry, including steel. The steel mill project was assigned to a committee under the Defense Ministry headed by Captain Victor Maldonado Michelena. A mechanical engineer trained in Argentina closely linked to Pérez Jiménez, he had been impressed by the Argentinean military's production of strategic supplies. As early as 1951 Maldonado Michelena became a proponent of the Venezuelan military's control of the production of military supplies and of the nation's basic industries (Rincón 1982:44–45).

In May 1953, Maldonado Michelena traveled to Germany, Switzerland, and Italy as a special officer of the CVF in order to explore steel production technologies. Maldonado brought several German technicians to Venezuela to evaluate existing studies, whose findings confirmed those of the Iron Syndicate concerning the kind of plant and technology that should be used in Venezuela. While some scholars believe that Pérez Jiménez decided to use hydroelectric power independently of the private sector findings, on the basis of Maldonado's work (Martín Frechilla 1994:227), others argue that the army adopted the project for itself only after the Iron Syndicate found that the existing technology could be used for the reduction of Venezuelan iron ore and that this process could utilize hydroelectric power (Skurski 1985:50; see also Dinkelspiel 1967:29; García Iturbe 1961:25–29). According to Dinkelspiel, Maldonado's evaluations were the only technical studies which the government had commissioned for the steel mill (1967:29).

The organization of the state's steel mill project came under the Office of Special Studies of the President of the Republic, which Pérez Jiménez created in August 1953 and which was headed by Lieutenant Colonel Llovera Páez, a trusted friend who had participated with him in the 1948 coup. In

November, Llovera Páez met with Eugenio Mendoza and informed him that "initially" the state would control the steel mill but that the state welcomed private sector investment in it. The mill would use electrical power and have a capacity between 120 thousand and 500 thousand tons. This signaled to the Iron Syndicate leaders that their project was in jeopardy.

Pérez Jiménez also established the Commission for the Study of the Electrification of the Caroní to direct the hydroelectric project. It was headed by Major Rafael Alfonzo Ravard, who had a degree in civil and hydraulic engineering from the Massachusetts Institute of Technology and had studied at the Superior War School in Paris; unlike most of Pérez Jiménez's associates, Ravard belonged to the Caracas social elite.

Pérez Jiménez publicly announced the state's decision to construct a steel mill on 9 January 1954 at an occasion which assured its impact: the inauguration of U.S. Steel's iron ore shipments from the Cerro Bolívar. This message had a double audience: foreign corporations and local capitalists. The foreign companies attending the ceremony, U.S. Steel and Iron Mines, hoped to develop steel mills themselves in Venezuela. However, the Iron Syndicate's directors were pointedly not invited to the event. Pérez Jiménez's announcement was a means of informing both foreign and local capitalists not only of the state's plans but also of its intent to formulate them without taking the private sector into account.

The following month the director of the Office of Special Studies, Llovera Páez, declared that the steel company would be open to minority participation by private capital. This kept alive hopes among the Iron Syndicate promoters that they would be able to influence state decisions by investing in the state company. Then in a sudden reversal, the government announced that the industry would be entirely state owned, and prepared a secret bidding for a plant whose design had not been made public.

In light of these developments, Iron Syndicate leaders knew they could no longer pursue their original project. Yet still intent on producing certain steel inputs for their industries, they bought Sivensa, a small manufacturer of steel reinforcing rods in Caracas, with the idea of expanding it and Alberto Vollmer made plans to establish yet another steel processing plant. However, Pérez Jiménez now dealt with these initiatives as a challenge to state power and ordered them halted or he would imprison Alberto Vollmer if he did not comply. Soon thereafter, in early 1955, Pérez Jiménez dissolved the Iron Syndicate and ordered its studies turned over to the government (Skurski 1985:53).

The government's handling of the steel project raised doubts about its aims and competence. The bidding process was marred by irregularities.[13] The contract was awarded to Fiat, which was in charge of design and engineering; then Fiat contracted the construction of the plant to the Innocenti Società Generale per l'Industria Metallurgia e Meccanica. After Fiat signed the contract on 31 December 1955, it withdrew from the project and left Innocenti in charge of it, despite the fact that it was primarily a seamless tube manufacturer without any experience in steel mill construction.

Fiat offered the least expensive project (approximately $101,553,000) but did not deliver as promised; the project cost more than three times this amount, was not completed on time, and failed to produce as projected. Secret contract revisions abruptly raised the mill's capacity to six hundred thousand tons a year and redesigned the plant, without technical studies, so that over half its production would go to seamless tubing used in the petroleum industry rather than to inputs for locally owned industries (Skurski 1985:55). The contract also specified that Innocenti would receive its payments in dollars at banks outside the country prior to its delivery of equipment. By the time Pérez Jiménez was overthrown, the contract had already cost the state $388,500,000 (Dodge 1968:76–77). Reportedly, Pérez Jiménez and Llovera Páez each received $7 million from Innocenti at the moment the contract was awarded (Dinkelspeil 1968:35). It took long and costly redesign under the following democratic regime to make the plant productive.[14]

In contrast, the Guayana hydroelectric plan was implemented effectively by Rafael Alfonzo Ravard. The dam was completed according to plan without signs of corruption or graft. Ravard envisioned the hydroelectric project as the heart of a potentially vast industrial complex in the Guayana region. Yet he shielded his plan from politics by keeping his project small and linked

13. In 1954 Llovera Paez traveled to Europe to invite proposals for the state's steel mill. The Office of Special Studies received eleven preliminary projects and in 1955 invited six companies to participate in a bidding round based on more detailed plant specifications.

14. Martín Frechilla, on the basis of García Iturbe's work (1961), offers a different interpretation. Their argument is that the Fiat-Innocenti bid was the most reasonable and that the steel mill was advancing according to schedule (1994:230). According to García Iturbe, the critique directed at the Innocenti project was a ploy to bring in the Koppers company, which had presented the highest bid but which was linked to members of the Iron Syndicate. Martín Frechilla singles out Antonio Alamo and Luis Alberto Roncayolo as individuals who in 1959 participated in the Venezuelan Institute of Iron and Steel, which was involved in the evaluation of the steel mill and who had an interest in the Koppers company (1994:230). The argument presented here draws extensively on the work of Skurski (1985), and also on Dodge (1968) and Dinkelspiel (1967) and numerous interviews with individuals who were involved in the steel industry in Venezuela, including Alberto Vollmer, Eugenio Mendoza, Antonio Alamo, and Hector Santaella. Needless to say, I offer this interpretation as a partial account of a complex issue which requires further research.

only to the state's steel industry. Having buffered his undertakings from political power, after the overthrow of Pérez Jiménez, Ravard was not regarded
as a collaborator of his regime and was given the presidency of the CVF
under AD (Skurski 1985: 56). In that capacity, he designed and then became
president of the Guayana Regional Development Corporation (CVG), a holding corporation which controlled all the major industries of the Guayana
region and became a model for the association between the state and local
and foreign private capital.[15]

CONCLUSION: DECONSTRUCTING THE DICTATORSHIP

This analysis of the Iron Syndicate's efforts to promote steel production in
Venezuela illustrates several processes that characterize the evolution of the
petrostate under Pérez Jiménez: (1) the construction of the state as the central
agent of national progress; (2) the identification of national interests with the
interests of the state, and therefore the exclusion of the private sector from
positions of political influence; (3) the definition of certain raw-material industries as "basic" industries of national interest to be developed by the state;
(4) the personification of state power in the figure of the president; (5) the
fetishization of modernity in large-scale economic projects as embodiments
of modernity to be implemented regardless of their overall social, economic,
and ecological impact; (6) the arbitrariness and unaccountability of state
power; and (7) the spread of corruption not only in the form of the private
appropriation of public resources by top government officials, but also in the
form of the massive misuse of public resources in unproductive projects that
require continuous and wasteful state support. Under subsequent democratic
regimes, as we shall see, some of these features of the petrostate were to
change, while others were intensified.

While the bourgeoisie grew in wealth and size during the economic
boom of the fifties, its expansion through new paths was blocked by limits
defined by an increasingly arbitrary and unresponsive state. Major entrepreneurs who had sought to go beyond these limits by investing in steel, metal
products, and petrochemicals and by securing more active state promotion
of industrialization encountered opposition from the military government.

15. After working for over two decades as head of the CVG, in 1974 Ravard became a director for
the Mendoza Group (a conglomerate headed by Eugenio Mendoza). In 1976, when the petroleum
industry was nationalized during the administration of Carlos Andrés Pérez, President Pérez chose
him to be the first president of PETROVEN, the state's new holding company for the national oil
industry (Skurski 1985: 56).

Having grown under the protection of the state and the support of the oil economy, they lacked independent economic strength and were not organized as a political force. But when in 1957 a set of political and economic factors converged to undermine the regime, these businessmen withdraw their support from the dictatorship and turned into advocates of democracy.

5

The Twenty-third of January
of Democracy

With a state of mind less influenced by fantasies the insurrection of January
23 could have achieved its plenitude.

Domingo Alberto Rangel

How to explain the fall of a military dictator who ruled during a period
of rising state income and rapid economic growth? Between 1945 and
1957, government income increased eight times and oil income eleven times;
by 1957 oil provided 70.7 percent of total fiscal income (Aranda 1977:141).
During the Pérez Jiménez dictatorship this unprecedented fiscal abundance
fueled business expansion and also wasteful overspending on the basis of easy
credit. But with a downturn of this expansive cycle by the end of 1957, a
spiraling fiscal contraction developed which left the business sector pressed
by creditors and many enterprises on the verge of bankruptcy. Even the construction industry fell into a slump. Most analysts have attributed the fall of
Pérez Jiménez to this "economic crisis."[1] But grave as this situation was, it
was all the more serious for being unnecessary, its severity caused less by
financial than by political factors.

Ever since the height of the boom in 1955 the government had made it
a practice to postpone paying its debts to the construction companies with
which it had contracted for projects. The government would issue notes that
could not be immediately redeemed in banks but could be used by these
companies in order to obtain loans, often from foreign banks. In effect, these
government notes constituted forced interest-free loans for the government
"that hard-pressed firms in need of cash were forced to sell . . . at a discount"
(Kolb 1974:167; see also Burggraaff 1972:144). By 1957 this practice had
escalated until government debt was estimated at over $1.4 billion (Alexander
1964:60), of which the domestic debt was only $150 million (Vallenilla 1967:
452–53).

In Pérez Jiménez's view, the private sector, not the government, had

---

1. Helena Plaza (1978) is critical of this view and highlights the political factors of the crisis.

incurred this debt. According to him, the private contractors had obtained financing on the basis of government contracts, including contracts with schedules that tied payments to the completion of distinct phases of the work. When they did not finish their work as planned, the contractors received delayed payments from the government, even though they had to pay their creditors on time (Blanco 1983:163). From this perspective, the debt resulted from the private sector's inability to meet its commitments on time.

Given the available evidence, it is difficult to assess the merits of these views. During the 1957 downturn creditors were more inflexible in their demands and contractors more hard-pressed to meet their financial obligations. What remains unclear and is "inexplicable" for some (Burggraaff 1972:144) is why Pérez Jiménez refused to pay government contractors, if only in order to buy political support. According to Vallenilla Lanz, sheer stubbornness was the basis for Pérez Jiménez's refusal to begin payments on the $150 million domestic debt (despite having a surplus of over $700 million in the national treasury), even after Vallenilla pleaded with him. Even when the military publicly expressed concern over his policies, Pérez Jiménez cut off dialogue by denying that the debts existed, asserting that "they are not debts, but obligations" (Vallenilla 1967:451).[2]

As the government's indifference to the private sector's demands aggravated the effects of the financial shortage and as the business sector, made increasingly uneasy by the economic climate, exaggerated its ailments in frustration with the state's unresponsiveness, an economic downturn was construed as an "economic crisis." If the difference between "economic problems" and an "economic crisis" is that "problems can be lived with" but a crisis questions "the viability of the system" and "entails inevitable change," as Smith proposes in his discussion of England's troubles (1984:12),[3] then at this time in Venezuela the crisis was not economic but political; it was the political system that no longer seemed viable.

These difficulties coincided with a political juncture that also was the product of governmental miscalculation. The 1953 constitution stipulated that presidential elections should be held every five years. Those who drafted that constitution anticipated that within five years the government's programs would have won popular support for Pérez Jiménez. Within four years, by 1957, it was evident that they had been overly optimistic: the gov-

2. Two decades later he maintained the same position (Blanco 1983:163).
3. Smith makes this argument in relation to England, but it is applicable to Venezuela.

Mobilization in support of the 23 January 1958 coup against General Marcos Pérez Jiménez near a housing project built by him. This housing project was named "2 December" after the coup that consolidated Pérez Jiménez's power and renamed "23 of January" for the 1958 coup that overthrew him. (Instituto Autónomo Biblioteca Nacional.)

ernment's public works had not produced sufficient public support. Reportedly, Vallenilla, as if sensing that power had been excessively concentrated in the executive, explained to Pérez Jiménez that public works were not perceived as belonging to the collectivity: "They were too much ours. They have a first and a last name, this is our greatest sin. They [the people] will not forgive us" (1967:449). Ironically, by 1957 the dictatorship faced the prospect of being forced by its own constitution to support an electoral contest it was likely to lose.

THE 1957 PLEBISCITE: ANOTHER COUP D'ÉTAT

Pérez Jiménez initially sought to organize an electoral contest between two parties, his own and COPEI, the only other legal party. Yet, afraid that COPEI could become a channel for other political groups to express their political opposition to the regime, as had happened in the 1952 elections, Pérez Jiménez pressured COPEI's leader, Rafael Caldera, to reject support from the illegal parties. Caldera refused and was arrested (Plaza 1978:82). This attack on a leader having intimate connections with the Church hierarchy and with the social and economic elite further isolated Pérez Jiménez.

Obsessed with retaining power, Pérez Jiménez felt he had no alternative but to create an electoral fiction. Once again he sought to illuminate the present with the light of the past. In 1952, taking his regime's claims for reality, Pérez Jiménez had held an honest election. In 1957, mindful of his former delusion, he sought to create the public illusion of popular support. Given his ideal conception of the polity as a passive and silent body, el pueblo would be given only the most restricted participation in constructing this illusion. Thus, on 4 November he announced that he had designed a plebiscite—a flagrantly unconstitutional move—which he defined as "a form of universality through which the opinions held about the current regime will be expressed" (Plaza 1978:66). On 15 December the question was presented to the people for a yes-or-no vote as to whether they accepted the regime's public works program and agreed that "the person presently occupying the Office of the President should be reelected" (Herrera Campíns 1978:94).

The president's public works were his record and his platform—he avoided political rhetoric. Words could only lead to the slippery terrain of interpretation, to the detachment of fact from opinion, and thence to the corrupt world of lies fabricated by politicians. But public works, he felt, spoke for themselves in the simple language of objective reality, a democratic language which met the authentic needs of the people. And votes, like public works, could be produced.

On 15 December, just when the first ballots were being counted, Laureano Vallenilla Lanz announced to the international press the results of the elections. The pretense was evident. The electoral returns, altered to an unknown degree, showed an 81 percent vote of support for Pérez Jiménez (the highest percentage of any president in Venezuelan history). Overnight, in an overproduction of appearances, Pérez Jiménez construed himself as a popular dictator.

Between 1952 and 1957 Pérez Jiménez had not become more realistic but had simply traded one illusion for another. In 1952 he thought he had the support of the people, in 1957 that of the military. In the first instance, support that existed only in the government's rhetoric was imagined to be real; in the second, support that was once real was imagined to be eternal. After five years of highly personalized power, Pérez Jiménez no longer held the illusion that he possessed or could ever easily obtain popular support. Having failed to win over the people, he had also come to treat his allies as if they, too, belonged to the ranks of the untrustworthy, the subordinate, those who must be ruled rather than rule. In this respect his regime represented a revival of caudillo repressive control over those regarded as possible challengers to power. Unlike traditional caudillo rule, however, repression was directed not against loose coalitions formed around rival military leaders but against members of the increasingly professionalized armed forces. This control also affected members of the business sector and professional groups, which had grown considerably under the stimulus of an expanding economy.

Counting perhaps on the elite's historic fear of popular mobilization, Pérez Jiménez dismissed signs of dissent from the Church, business, and even the armed forces, certain that these sectors would prefer to support him over facing the threat of the unknown. But above all, he counted on the adhesion of the armed forces to his continued personal leadership of the country. And it was about this that he was most seriously deluded.

THE LONELY DICTATOR:
FACING AN ESCALATING OPPOSITION

In reality, despite the much-claimed unity of the armed forces, by 1957 the military was deeply divided. Many factors had eroded its unity but underlying them all was the excessive centralization of power and benefits in the executive. The military hierarchy felt excluded from both the responsibility and the rewards of rule. Pérez Jiménez made arbitrary appointments on the basis of personal loyalty, not merit, often removing qualified officers he saw as potential rivals from positions of power. He favored the army (his own branch) over the navy and the air force; relied for internal security on Pedro Estrada's secret police (the dreaded Seguridad Nacional), which came to extend its control over the military itself; and blocked the advancement of junior officers who felt they were better qualified because they had been trained in the United States, the world's military leader after World War II. Pérez Jiménez had promised the modernization of strategically important sectors of the military and its involvement in different areas of the economy—from communications to industry—yet ascendant officers could not expect to have a role in the government's projects or trust the viability and realization of the projects themselves. In time, the very defense capacity of the country came to be questioned.

Moreover, for those officers outside the inner circle of power, the boom was largely a phantom. While they received fixed salaries of moderate size, civilian businessmen and professionals prospered, and government leaders— particularly Pérez Jiménez—flaunted lives of luxury (Rangel 1977: 58). A confidential report of the U.S. embassy on the military situation during 1957 stated that the problem was not that too much of the state's money was finding its way into Pérez Jiménez's purse but that not enough of it was trickling down to the pockets of the military hierarchy (Burggraaff 1972:150). Thus, the disparity between the benefits received by the ruling clique and the rest of the officer corps was accentuated by Pérez Jiménez's disdain both for sharing the spoils of power with his main supporters and for constructing the image of the selfless statesman.

But the breakdown of military support remained hidden in the barracks, waiting for an appropriate political juncture to emerge into public view. When during 1957 "the breakdown of political channels of communication" which resulted from the dictatorship's centralization of political power and decision not to have an open election "merged with a breakdown of market channels of communications" (the state's refusal to pay its debts; Skurski 1985:44), a series of escalating signals from multiple sectors, each reinforcing the other, began to converge in opposition to Pérez Jiménez.

In this context, the Junta Patriótica, a multiparty and multi-interest group sought to turn political disaffection from the regime into coordinated opposition to it. From its foundation in June 1957 by Fabricio Ojeda, a middle-level URD leader, and Guillermo García Ponce, a leader of the Communist Party, the Junta Patriótica's objectives were to ensure respect for the constitution and the conduct of free elections, to prevent the reelection of Pérez Jiménez, and to struggle for the establishment of a democratic regime.

The Junta Patriótica's many manifestos—which were printed by the hundreds of thousands and distributed throughout the nation—called on Venezuelans to set aside partisan interests and unite in a common struggle against the dictatorship. It defined the struggle against the Pérez Jiménez regime as part of a civilizing effort to bring Venezuela out of a state of barbarism. In its first manifesto, dated 10 July 1957, the Junta Patriótica stated that "the majority of Venezuelans of different ideologies agree that as a civilized nation Venezuela must prove to the world that it is a country politically and economically strong, one capable of exercising its sovereignty in its broadest democratic expression" (Plaza 1978:80). In another manifesto issued in August, it proclaimed that in demanding free elections it "neither sought nor defended power for the sectarian benefit of any one group" (Stambouli 1980), a statement that was a critique not only of Pérez Jiménez's rule but also implicitly of AD's.

When the plebiscite was announced by Pérez Jiménez on 4 November, the Junta Patriótica defined it as "another coup d'état" (Plaza 1978:84). In a manifesto addressed to the "National Armed Forces" dated 8 November, the junta denounced the government's violations of the constitution and asked, "Are the Armed Forces to protect the violation of the constitution, or to defend it? Is the military to act in a servile manner, like the Congress has done, made up of men without dignity and patriotic consciousness?" (1978: 84). After the plebiscite of 15 December, the Junta Patriótica called upon all Venezuelans to set aside differences and join in a united front in the struggle against the dictatorship.

Throughout 1957, the Church, sensitive to the changing times—both the growing local opposition to the regime and Pope Pius XII's call for a more socially responsible Church—and more protected from the regime's retaliation, took the lead in openly criticizing the government's social policies. On 1 May 1957, a pastoral letter written by Caracas Archbishop Rafael Arias was published and read during Mass throughout the nation. The pastoral letter restated in religious terms the basic tenets of democratic discourse elaborated by the youthful critics of the Gómez regime in the 1930s. It condemned the disparity between the wealth of the nation and the poverty of the people and attributed this disparity to the misuse of oil resources by the state:

> Our country is getting richer impressively quickly. According to a United Nations economic study, per capita production in Venezuela has increased to $540, which places Venezuela first among its Latin American sisters, and above Germany, Australia, and Italy. But then, no one will dare to affirm that this wealth is distributed in such a way that it will reach all Venezuelans, since an immense mass of our people live in conditions which cannot be regarded as human. (Plaza 1978:74.)

The letter criticizes unemployment, low wages, lack of social services, deficiencies in public welfare institutions, and even condemns the "frequency with which the Labor Law and the legal instruments created to defend the working class are violated" (Plaza 1978:74). This pastoral letter was not an isolated act. At this time the editorials of the Church's newspaper, *La Religión*, took to criticizing the regime, which resulted in the persecution of the paper's director, Padre Hernández Chapellín. This shift in the Church's position was read as a signal indicating a withdrawal of support from the regime at the highest levels of Venezuelan society.

Even the U.S. government, which in 1955 had awarded Pérez Jiménez the Legion of Merit medal, had grown concerned about the political unreliability of his personalized power, as exemplified by his proposal, presented to the 1956 Panama Conference of American Presidents, to develop a multilateral aid agency, a proposal the United States strongly opposed. A Venezuelan analyst suggests that a decline in U.S. support encouraged the business elite to change its position toward the regime by 1957 (Rangel 1977:42), but it is likely that these were converging and mutually reinforcing processes.

The turnaround of private sector leaders was a crucial factor in consolidating the opposition to Pérez Jiménez. In 1948, as well as in 1952, most business leaders, alienated by AD's populist policies during the Trienio, strongly supported Pérez Jiménez. Yet by 1957 members of the business elite, particularly those promoting industrialization, had become critical of the state's unresponsiveness to their concerns and mismanagement of the economy (Skurski 1985). Thus, by the end of 1957 they were conspiring with AD, URD, and COPEI (but not the PC).

While the Caracas Chamber of Commerce and Industry issued a public critique of the regime, in December two leading business leaders, industrialist Eugenio Mendoza (ex-president of the Iron Syndicate) and banker Mario Diez (a top executive of the First National City Bank's subsidiary), met with the leaders of these parties in New York to discuss the organization of the opposition and to set the ground rules for establishing an electoral regime (Blank 1973:25). Their agreement in the New York meeting "symbolized AD's recognition that majority electoral support could not justify a one-party government" (Lombardi 1982:229). Equally important, it symbolized AD's recognition that party rule could not justify the exclusion of the private sector from active participation in the government and the private sector's recognition that political parties may provide a reliable medium for the representation of their interests.

An essential catalyst in this chain of reciprocal transformations was the withdrawal of the military's support from the regime. Given the conspiratorial nature of military politics and the repressive character of the regime, unrest within the military was kept from public view—sanctions against officers who expressed differences with the regime were swift and often harsh. But in a small country it was difficult to keep the bright flashes of discontent in the dark. Already, in a manifesto of 10 September, the Junta Patriótica had informed the public of opposition within the armed forces to Pérez Jiménez's plan for reelection (Plaza 1978:81). After the plebiscite, rumors of a *golpe* (coup) circulated cautiously but ever more frequently. People with contacts anxiously offered *datos* or *bolas* (facts or rumors), whose source, it was generally claimed, was always a well-placed friend or relative, a captain or colonel "in the know." Through gossip, a crack in the military edifice had become visible.

THE TWENTY-THIRD OF JANUARY OF DEMOCRACY

While by the end of 1957 the soft murmur of gossip, quietly announcing discontent within the military, eroded a sustaining tenet of the regime's identity—the belief in the unity of the armed forces—it was the harsh sound of an air battle during the 1 January uprising that shattered this dogma. Still dazed by the firecrackers and parties of New Year's festivities, the Caracas population awoke to the startling spectacle of a battle between rebel air force planes and army artillery as the former attacked and the latter defended the Presidential Palace.

The defeat of the hastily executed uprising (originally planned for 4 January) was brought about by the leaders' failure to act at the crucial hour; the insurgents, "by an appalling lack of coordination" (Burggraaff 1972:155), failed to implement a planned chain of simultaneous uprisings in strategically located military garrisons. Without much effort, two loyal supporters of Pérez Jiménez, colonels Roberto Casanova and Abel Romero Villate, managed to subdue the insurgents. By the next day the government controlled the situation. Yet in shattering the myth of the unity of the armed forces this attack transformed the context of political action—it both intensified the opposition against the regime and undermined the regime's capacity to suppress it. It revealed that the crack in the military edifice reached its very foundations.

As if it were no longer contained by the regime's sustaining myth, opposition to Pérez Jiménez surfaced in the major urban centers, widening further the crack that this illusion had concealed. Intellectuals, professional associations, and interest groups began to voice publicly their opposition to the regime. Even one of its leading beneficiaries, the Engineer's Association, issued a statement criticizing the regime's chaotic public works program. In the streets of Caracas students clashed daily with the police, and several large demonstrations, including one by women in front of the Seguridad Nacional, took place in early January.

But the civil opposition leaders felt that only the military could overthrow Pérez Jiménez. Thus, in this escalating flurry of manifestos, an appeal was made to the military to pronounce the decisive word. In a manifesto issued in January, the Junta Patriótica praised the military for having taken up arms and urged it to overthrow the "'triumvirate' of Pérez Jiménez, Vallenilla Lanz and Estrada" (Burggraaff 1972 : 159). By reducing the rulers to three individuals—two of whom were civilians—the Junta Patriótica sought to dissociate the military as an institution from responsibility for the regime's debacle. In a belated response to appease the armed forces, Pérez Jiménez fired Vallenilla and Estrada, gave their key posts to military men, and increased the number of officers in his cabinet to seven. But this inclusion of military men in the highest government circle only brought the struggle for power closer to home.

After the abortive uprising, conspiracy within the military intensified; but without his trusted allies, Vallenilla and Estrada, the dictator could not easily identify and use loyal officers to police the rebellious officers. As he set one branch of the military against another—the army confiscated ammunition from the navy, the air force was held in check, suspect garrisons in the interior were disarmed—discontent within the military grew, fueling the hopes of ambitious generals. Pérez Jiménez's own minister of defense, General Rómulo Fernández, orchestrated an unsuccessful coup. Not trusting anyone else for this key post, Pérez Jiménez decided to take personal charge of the Defense Ministry, claiming that this step would "assure the maintenance of the unity of the Armed Forces" (Burggraaff 1972 : 161). Yet because this concentration of power in the presidency had been at the root of the division of the armed forces, it only heightened Pérez Jiménez's isolation and vulnerability.

On 14 January, major private-sector associations responded to this political crisis by issuing a manifesto that proclaimed the need for the government to guarantee the full exercise of constitutional rights in order to secure "the institutional and democratic restoration of Venezuela." The manifesto also stated that it was necessary "to regulate and dignify the administration of public moneys, so that our natural resources be channeled toward the benefit of the whole collectivity, without personal advantages derived from official action" (Stambouli 1980 : 131). The next day the Engineers Association demanded "the full restoration of human rights" as well as "a better and more honest investment of the nation's resources" and a "free and healthy critique" of the use of "public moneys" for sumptuous public works (1980:31). As in the struggle against Juan Vicente Gómez, the demand by the movement against Pérez Jiménez for the restoration of constitutional rights was inseparably linked to the right to benefit from the nation's wealth; political rights included the economic entitlement to the nation's collective wealth.

A committee created by the Junta Patriótica coordinated the civilian and military opposition to the government. It planned to topple Pérez Jiménez by combining a general strike with a military uprising. Once victory was achieved, a three-man provisional junta—headed by Navy Commander Wolfgang Larrazábal together with two civilians, economist Manuel Egaña and engineer Pedro Emilio Herrera—was to organize the replacement of the deposed dictatorial regime by a democratic state.

Although on 21 January a strike paralyzed Caracas, the military uprising failed to materialize. By the next day the insurgency seemed under control. On the eve of 22 January, Pérez Jiménez relaxed, playing dominoes in the Presidential Palace. "The public," he reportedly said, "had spent its fury and must now subside" (Kolb 1974:176). His playing dominoes was no mere distraction but symptomatic of his self-involvement and isolation as a ruler. Reportedly, he often played dominoes in social gatherings to deter people from engaging him in conversation (Bautista Urbaneja 1992:188). His self-involvement and disdain for public opinion proved to be costly. Two phone calls on the night of 22 January were enough to complete the turn of events. The first brought Pérez Jiménez from his reverie back to reality: Rear Admiral Wolfgang Larrazábal, in the name of the chiefs of staff of the armed forces, demanded his resignation. The civil insurgency had subsided, but the military had turned against him.

Larrazábal's unexpected move must have indicated to Pérez Jiménez the unsuspected scope of the military opposition. Larrazábal was known as a quiet man, more a conformist than a conspirator. Although the navy's top officer, Larrazábal had been relegated by Pérez Jiménez to the minor post of head of the officer's club, an affront that created discontent within the navy but one that Larrazábal seemed to have accepted with resignation. In fact, he joined the insurrection only when he failed to persuade younger officers to seek a compromise.

Hoping to negotiate an agreement, Pérez Jiménez asked to meet with the insurgent officers at midnight. Larrazábal agreed. While Pérez Jiménez went to his home to ready his family for any eventuality, colonels Roberto Casanova and Romero Villate, who had stifled the 1 January uprising and were regarded as his trustworthy supporters, stayed in the Presidential Palace to defend the government. The second phone call turned colonels Casanova and Villate from his loyal defenders of 1 January into rebel insurgents. When Larrazábal urged them by phone to join the insurrection, they agreed—on the condition they be included in the new junta. Larrazábal accepted their demand.

Thus, when Pérez Jiménez returned to the Presidential Palace, Casanova and Villate informed him that he had to leave the country immediately. In the end Pérez Jiménez was alone, without loyal supporters. He had no choice but to leave. Fighting was neither necessary nor possible. At 3 A.M. he left in the presidential plane to the Dominican Republic, which was ruled by his friend, the military dictator Rafael Leonidas Trujillo. A small group of his close relatives and friends escaped with him, in their rush accidentally leaving on the airfield a suitcase containing almost $2 million in cash and records of personal profits on government projects involving close to $10 million.

Once again civil resistance developed into a military conspiracy. Without the insurgence of the military, the civilian opposition would have been unable to topple Pérez Jiménez. Yet without the ever-increasing, broad-based civilian opposition to the regime, the military would not have turned against its leader. The 1958 revolution was neither a traditional military coup nor a mass uprising from below. Rather it was, in a peculiar but real way, the crystallization of collective discontent—from different classes, sectors, and bulwarks of power, including the military—against the increasingly arbitrary and personal rule of Pérez Jiménez. Peculiar, because these groups had not participated in common struggles and were not linked by interdependent sectoral interests. Real, because they were nevertheless united in their opposition to an unresponsive government and shared an interest in a state that would use the nation's fiscal resources on their behalf. Despite their sharp economic and ideological differences, these groups formed a community of interests and ideals on the basis of a shared orientation toward the state as the main source of collective and individual welfare.

Although the fall of Pérez Jiménez took place because there was general opposition to the regime, it was quickly interpreted to be a direct consequence of massive popular resistance—as if the overthrow were not a military coup but the collective triumph of a united people who rose up in unison against a tyrant. At this transitional juncture, on the public stage of national politics, differences among social groups—differences of interest, position, ideals—were subsumed ideologically within a common identity. The united collectivity, the people, was depicted as having reemerged as the active subject of the nation's history, acting with a single will to free itself from

Front page of El Nacional, 23 January 1958, announcing the overthrow of the dictatorship of General Marcos Pérez Jiménez. (Archivo El Nacional.)

oppression, continuing an exemplary heroic tradition initiated during the Independence Wars.

This interpretation of experience invested with new meaning the process of political democratization; it seemingly marked a disjuncture between the past—politics as self-interested elite maneuvers—and the present— politics as altruistic actions by state representatives on behalf of the people. If pacts and agreements were now made by democracy's leaders, they were no mere pacts but an expression of the Spirit of 23 January, a concretization of a transcendent collective accord. Thus the history of the popular overthrow of Pérez Jiménez became, even as it was lived, the origin myth of democracy's birth.

THE SPIRIT OF 23 JANUARY

On 23 January, while the nation's major newspapers celebrated the overthrow of Pérez Jiménez as a triumph of el pueblo and the Junta Patriótica published a manifesto comparing the victorious struggle of the people against the dictatorship to the Independence Wars of the nineteenth century, Wolfgang Larrazábal addressed the nation and stated matter-of-factly that the armed forces had taken over the "Public Powers of the State." Three objectives, according to Larrazábal, motivated this action: to save the "unity and institutional sense of the military"; to satisfy the "unanimous clamor" of the whole population; and to lead the republic to "a legal and political organization in accordance with the universal practice of democracy and law" (*El Nacional*, 24 January 1958). At dawn on 23 January, masses of people took over the streets of Caracas in jubilant celebration of the advent of a new political life. They attacked the jailers at the Seguridad Nacional, freed political prisoners, and looted the homes of the most hated *perezjimenistas* (such as Pedro Estrada and Luis Vallenilla). Each new victory became part of a drama that was acclaimed as a transcendent historical event as part of its enactment.

When it became known that day that the five-man military junta included colonels Casanova and Villate, who were closely associated with Pérez Jiménez, it suddenly seemed as if the democratic coup which many groups had organized had been overturned by the military's right wing, or more perversely, as if the drama that the people enacted in the streets as a democratic revolution was only the backdrop for an oligarchic restoration orchestrated at the top. In order to avert the threat of continued military control, the Junta Patriótica called for public demonstrations and pressured the new defense minister, Colonel Castro León (who had participated in the

I January military uprising against Pérez Jiménez), to remove the despised colonels, Roberto Casanova and Romero Villate, who had exchanged at the last moment their loyalty to Pérez Jiménez for a position of power in the new regime.[4]

Perhaps the "Public Powers of the State," as Rear Admiral Larrazábal had claimed, were in the hands of the military, yet the top military leaders responded to society's political expressions. In response to political pressure from above and mass mobilization from below, which included violent confrontations and numerous casualties,[5] the two colonels were replaced on 25 January by two civilians. These civilians were two business leaders, Eugenio Mendoza, the Iron Syndicate's Former president, and Blas Lamberti, both of whom had been among the first members of the economic elite to seek a broad-based alliance to overthrow the dictatorship. Ironically, the direct participation of the bourgeoisie in the junta was publicly represented as a triumph of popular pressure, as another confirmation that the junta embodied the nation's single will, the unified pueblo. Once again, the people seemed to have exerted their power. Probably at no other juncture in this century had so many Venezuelans been drawn together by the force of historical events and experienced, however illusorily, a sense of national community. This sense of the transformative power of collective unity came to be captured in the expression "the Spirit of 23 January," a slogan which was constantly invoked during the difficult days of institution building, when the contradictions concealed within this ideal threatened to tear the fragile fabric of a democracy in the making.

DEMOCRACY

Eugenio Mendoza, together with many people who had upheld Pérez Jiménez during his rule, now heralded the banner of democracy. Laureano Vallenilla recalled that in 1952, after Pérez Jiménez's coup, his childhood friend Mendoza had told him, "Business has never been better—keep it up, brother!" (Vallenilla 1967:376). Thus, it is with bitter irony that Vallenilla closes his memoirs by referring to a New Year's telegram from Mendoza he

---

4. The members of the Junta Militar were Rear Admiral Wolfgang Larrazábal, and colonels Roberto Casanova, Abel Romero Villate, Pedro José Numa Quevedo, and Carlos Luis Araque.

5. It is difficult to determine accurately the number of casualties during the violent conflicts that took place during 23 January. While the government declared that there were only 23 casualties, a newspaper reported that as many as 300 people were killed and 1,000 wounded in confrontations with the police and the Seguridad Nacional (*El Nacional,* 24 January 1958).

had found in his pocket as he began his exile in France, just as Mendoza had emerged as a representative of a bourgeoisie which had suddenly discovered its democratic vocation. It wished him and his wife "All the best for 1958" (1967:478).

But this political juncture was a crucible not only for democratic institutions but also for political actors. Individuals and institutions did not appear on the stage of national politics with fixed identities but were changed by the historical events in which they participated. Their transformation, including their shifts of loyalties, was accepted not just as a matter of fact but as a necessary condition for the construction of democracy. Only those who had been intimately associated with the regime's repressive apparatus or who had flaunted their power were ostracized. After 1948 leading members of the local bourgeoisie had turned against the party system and came to trust the military as a party of their own—the "party of the bourgeoisie," as Poulantzas once called the military (1978). By 1957, when it became evident that for Pérez Jiménez there was no party other than himself, they began to accept a party system within which they could operate and, perhaps, which they could make their own.

The challenge facing the democratic opposition to Pérez Jiménez was to turn generalized discontent with the dictator into support for democracy, given collective memories of AD's sectarian triennium. The solution devised was the orchestration from the top of a coalition of political parties and interest groups around a centrist populist program. Betancourt had been preparing for this strategy. In 1956 he had proposed to the party leadership in exile that AD cooperate more closely with the private sector as well as with the "democratic" parties, that is, COPEI and URD. This distanced AD middle-level leaders, many of them younger and ideologically closer to socialism, who had worked with the PC within the country during the resistance and who had formed the Junta Patriótica. Despite their opposition, at Betancourt's insistence the PC was excluded from the nascent alliance.

The exclusion of the Communist Party was justified by depicting it as a party committed to an eventual dictatorship (of the proletariat) and thus at odds with the construction of Venezuelan democracy. By this means the democratic parties could present themselves as moderate forces to the private sector as well as to the U.S. government. Thus, the PC's exclusion was depicted as an action directed at preserving, rather than fracturing, national unity. Although formally excluded from these pacts, throughout 1958 the PC was a major backer of the ruling junta and of the efforts by the new alliance to ensure unified support for the transition to democracy. This support was ratified at its 1958 national assembly, where the PC vowed to "give everything that it is capable of, to make all the sacrifices, to preserve this unity" (Plaza 1978:138). Although the PC defined itself as Leninist, it did not follow the principles enunciated by Lenin in his April 1917 thesis, when he argued that the struggle for socialism need not wait for the consolidation of bourgeois rule. Largely under the influence of Browderism (originating with the U.S. Communist Party), the Venezuelan PC accepted a staged conception according to which socialism in backward countries should occur after the consolidation of capitalism—a notion closer to the Mensheviks than to Lenin. Just as the war effort and the struggle against fascism in advanced capitalist nations had encouraged a politics of alliance among all democratic forces, the fight against Pérez Jiménez had led the Venezuelan PC to define post-1958 politics in terms of a conflict between the threat of a military dictatorship and the consolidation of democracy.[6]

By means of pacts and agreements, the major representatives of the democratic parties sought to avoid what its leaders regarded as the two major dangers facing democracy: the return of military rule, widely regarded as the "homicidal path," and the recurrence of sectarian party politics, which Betancourt called the "suicidal path." They decided to join efforts to secure a harmonious transition to a democratic regime by means of a free electoral contest, but one without absolute losers. All the parties (except the Communist Party), it was agreed, would have a share of power and of its responsibilities and benefits, regardless of which candidate won. The private sector would have significant participation in the government and voice in policy making. AD, the party most likely to win, was at the same time the one most interested in securing this agreement. In order to obtain and maintain power, it understood that it had to share its spoils.

The top military leaders endorsed these decisions. Immersed in this collective movement, and caught up in its momentum, they sought to restore the role of their institution as guardian of the constitution and defender of the nation's sovereignty. While much blame fell on the military and its image had been damaged during the dictatorship, it felt it had actually been excluded from its rightful role by Pérez Jiménez. In the opinion of Larrazábal, Pérez Jiménez had ruled alone. "We thought that he was not ruling in the

6. As early as 1959, the Communist Party became critical of its 1958 position. Plaza's pioneering exploration of the PC's position in 1958 and of its decision to join the armed struggle during the Betancourt regime (1959–64) remains an essential source on this controversial topic (1978). Ellner's work provides the most informative account of the influence of Browderism on the Venezuelan Communist Party (1980).

name of the Armed Forces, because he did not have military men close to him" (Blanco 1980:190).

In order to regain legitimacy and to dispel fears that the junta would try to remain in power, its leaders decided to hold elections promptly. The personal ambitions of military leaders were to be contained in the interest of the institution as a whole. Needless to say, it was understood that the interests of the institution and the well-being of its members—which had been so sorely neglected by Pérez Jiménez—would be well taken care of by the new democratic regime.

PACTS AND THE SPIRIT OF DEMOCRACY

The Spirit of 23 January took tangible form in several pacts and agreements. On 24 April 1958, all political parties (including the Communist Party) signed the Reconciliation between Labor and Capital (*El avenimiento obrero patronal*). This pact subordinated workers' demands to the need to create the climate of stability then deemed necessary for the consolidation of democracy and established collective bargaining as the only permitted mechanism to exert labor pressure. Predictably, by containing labor demands, this agreement made workers pay the price for political stability (López and Werz 1981:11–14). Despite its demobilizing character, Communist leaders endorsed this agreement, for they wanted to preserve the organizational unity of the workers movement (*el comité sindical unificado*), which AD and COPEI had threatened to disrupt (Croes 1973:175).

Two Venezuelan analysts have commented that "this highlights the top priority given to democratic stability as a common objective of all parties" as well as the "inconsistency or lack of strategic and tactical clarity of the elites of this party [the PC]" (López and Gómez 1985:80). But whether this pact was the product of inconsistency and political blindness or not, both aspects of this policy—the priority given to the support of democracy and the willingness to curb labor demands—were rooted in tacit assumptions about Venezuelan society: the notion that oil was the basic source of wealth in Venezuela, and the belief that workers would do better by supporting a regime that would redistribute oil rents than by demanding higher wages, thereby risking destabilizing the emerging democracy.

A second pact was perhaps even more fundamental, for it coordinated the relations of parties around a common political program. This pact followed the failure of negotiations, supported mostly by the Junta Patriótica, to produce a single national-unity candidate for the 1958 elections. By means of the Pact of Punto Fijo, signed by AD, URD, and COPEI on 31 October 1958, the parties agreed to respect the results of the elections and to form a coalition government whose program would be previously established and accepted by the contenders. Just before the elections were held, in December 1958 the outline of a Minimum Government Program and Declaration of Principles was signed by the presidential candidates.[7]

Essentially, this program defined a project of capitalist development, sponsored by a reformist democratic state and with the active participation of local and foreign capital. The Church and the military, through this pact and other formal and informal agreements, were given ample reassurance that their roles in society would be respected and supported; AD thus agreed that it would not repeat its attempt to exert control over educational institutions managed by the Catholic Church. This agreement has been seen as emblematic of the forms of solidarity that had evolved in the struggle against Pérez Jiménez. In Levine's apt words, the spirit of 23 January "took concrete form" in the Pact of Punto Fijo (1973:43).

As expected, AD's Rómulo Betancourt won the December 1958 election by a relatively wide margin. Betancourt obtained 1,284,042 votes, followed by Wolfgang Larrazábal (supported by URD and the Communist Party), whose 903,479 votes reflected not only the strength of these parties but his popularity as the public leader of the rebellion against Pérez Jiménez. In third place was COPEI's Rafael Caldera, with 423,262 votes. Once in power, Betancourt kept the preelectoral agreements and established a coalition government in which the reformist parties and the private sector were represented, thus initiating a period of uninterrupted democratic rule which, with some modifications in the original agreements, persists until today.

DEMOCRACY: THEORETICAL CONSTRUCTS AND HISTORICAL REALITIES

Most analysts have attributed a crucial role to politics in bringing about and maintaining democracy in Venezuela. According to the prevailing viewpoint, Venezuelan democracy is the outgrowth of a particular political style characterized by the avoidance of conflict and the pursuit of consensus around procedural forms rather than substantive issues. While this viewpoint

---

7. Ever since the 1930s Betancourt, influenced by European social democracy, had proposed the development of a minimum program, against the more anticapitalist position of the radical left (Sosa and Lengrand 1974).

may include the recognition that oil affluence in a small country without deep ethnic divisions and with a relatively small and homogeneous upper stratum created favorable conditions for democracy, it underlines the fact that democracy can be accounted for only by the political skills of Venezuelan leaders.[8]

Politics is thus treated as an elite activity that reflects the negotiating skills, flexibility, and, above all, learning capacity of Venezuelan leaders—mostly politicians and entrepreneurs, but also military officers, the Church hierarchy, and the representatives of other major interests, including labor. In a country bereft of democratic traditions and torn by a violent history, its leaders are seen as having been particularly receptive to the lessons of the recent past. Just as AD's Trienio taught them to avoid sectarian party politics, the dictatorship warned them of the dangers of personalistic military rule. The representatives of major sectors learned to circumvent conflictive issues, to exclude certain basic issues from political debate, to conciliate differences, and to trade disruptive ideological programs for the workable arrangements of incremental reform. It is as if a harmonizing ethos animated Venezuelan political actors.

While politics, construed as a style and as a set of skills, is invoked to explain the construction of Venezuelan democracy, politics itself remains unexplained, except tautologically. Instead of explaining the spirit or the skills and unusual learning capacity of political actors, their exceptional personal abilities or cultivated faculties are used to explain their actions. It is undeniable that Venezuelan politicians learned lessons from past experiences and managed to establish significant compromises. Yet this learning must itself be accounted for.

Typically, the next step has been to portray these democratic actors as setting in motion a process the basic dynamic of which is explained by recourse to theoretical schemes originally devised to account for the historical experience of metropolitan nations. Thus, the diversification of industrial production and the growth of the middle class are seen as processes that intrinsically generate opposition to authoritarianism and support for democracy. Since this interpretation coincides with that of the main local ideo-

8. This viewpoint is particularly present in works influenced by actor-centered conceptions of politics, for instance, Levine (1973) and Alexander (1964), but it also appears in the more structural interpretations of Stambouli (1980), Blank (1973), Karl (1981), López and Gómez (1985), and Urbaneja (1985). In the interpretations of Plaza (1978) and Hellinger (1985), the political cunning of elites is seen as setting in motion the structures shaped by the oil economy. For a review of interpretations of Venezuelan democracy, see Abente (1986).

logues, social theory and local ideology join hands in the representation of the turn to democracy as the outcome of the growth of a young capitalist nation which has matured to the point of revolt against dictatorial rule.

For instance, a widely cited interpretation portrays the turn to democracy in 1958 as the result of a combination of "structural" factors—the "ripening" of the "conditions" for democracy as a result of industrialization—and of human will or "statecraft"—the orchestration of a compromise through which the bourgeoisie, in a "classic exchange of 'the right to rule for the right to make money,'" supported the establishment of a democratic party system (Karl 1981 : 10–20). Two illusions are brought together in this explanation of Venezuelan democracy. The first is the chimera of modernization ideology as a theory of history, what O'Donnell has called the "optimistic formula: more economic development [equals] more likelihood of political democracy" (O'Donnell 1973).[9] While it is indeed true that Pérez Jiménez alienated important sectors of the private sector, it is not clear whether their conflictual relationship was structural and unavoidable rather than contingent and surmountable. Capitalist development is inherently conflictual but has taken place under both dictatorial and democratic forms. The growth of capitalist industry under the military dictatorships of Brazil, Argentina, and Chile in the sixties and seventies demonstrates that it is possible to have expanded industrialization under dictatorial regimes in Latin America. The crisis of these authoritarian regimes cannot be reduced to an inherent conflict between capitalist industrialization and dictatorship. Even if it could be demonstrated that democracy were capitalism's best political shell, the transition to democracy in Venezuela could not be deduced from this general principle but would have to attend to the distinctive historical formation of state and society in Venezuela at this particular juncture.

The second illusion conjures up once again the spirit of Bonapartism, "the classic exchange," as an analogy to explain the role of statecraft in arranging the alliances and pacts that led to Venezuelan democracy. As in France in the nineteenth century, it is assumed that in Venezuela in 1958 the bourgeoisie exchanged the right to rule for the right to make money. Understanding the origin and use of Bonapartism as a theoretical construct may

9. A classic formulation of the modernization view can be found in Lipset (1959). Therborn offers a sound review of the turn to democratic institutional forms in Europe and America (1977; 1979). For a thorough discussion of the relationship between development and democracy in Europe and Latin America based on a development of Barrington Moore's model, see Stephens (1987) and Stephens and Stephens (1988).

help us appreciate its scope and limitations as it is applied to the rather un-classical relationship between state and society in Venezuela.[10]

CLASSICAL AND RENTIER BONAPARTISM

The concept of Bonapartism was initially devised by Marx to explain the rise of Louis Napoleon's imperial rule. In this case, Bonapartism refers to a situation of class stalemate in which the bourgeoisie, unable to rule through its own representatives, exchanges the right to rule for the right to make money. Since then, Bonapartism has been extended not only to explain authoritarian regimes in general but also to define a general phenomenon reflecting the "relative autonomy" of all capitalist states.[11] Thus, Poulantzas argues that Marx's concept of Bonapartism should not be applied only to a "concrete form of a capitalist state." Rather, it must be seen as "a constitutive theoretical characteristic of the very type of capitalist state" (1973:258).

This extension of Bonapartism dissolves its original historical specificity but at the same time makes it evident that both its specific and general use assumes the existence of a universal-type capitalist state-society relation distinguished by a sharp separation between the political sphere and the domain of profit-making activities. From Poulantzas's discussion it is clear that by "the very type of capitalist state" he has in mind not every form of capitalist state but the state of societies in which the "dominance" of the capitalist mode of production—also seen as a homogeneous type—"is already consolidated." As he says, "we are concerned here with a political form belonging to the phase of expanded reproduction" (1973:260). Viewing them as universal types, Poulantzas is seeking to establish the general form of the relationship of *the* capitalist state to *the* capitalist society.

Yet in my view, Venezuela, like many other societies, does not fit either the restricted or the expanded concept of Bonapartism. An appreciation of the rentier character of the Venezuelan state suggests that the employment of the Bonapartist model to Venezuelan democracy exemplifies the recurrent theoretical misrecognition of a distinctive history. It also reveals the limits of

10. Karl uses the "classic exchange" formula to explain Venezuelan democracy, but unlike analysts who pay limited attention to the political and social effects of the oil industry in Venezuela, she attributes fundamental significance to oil money in the creation of the system of alliances and compromises she analyzes.

11. Schmitter has suggested that Latin American military regimes could be seen as forms of "Bonapartism" through which a bourgeoisie that has been unable to impose its hegemony upon society "exchanges its 'right to rule' for its 'right to make money'" (1973:187).

ostensibly universal theoretical schemes formulated on the basis of particular historical experiences.

Ironically, Marx, whose *Eighteenth Brumaire* has served as the foundation of the Bonapartist construct, cautioned in that book against the decontextualized use of theoretical categories. His work directly criticized the misuse of historical analogies and, in particular, of "Caesarism." Fashionable in France at that time, this notion attributed to isolated individual figures (in this case Louis Napoleon) a determining effect upon history.[12] "Lastly," Marx emphasized, "I hope that my work will contribute toward eliminating the school-taught phrase now current, particularly in Germany, of so-called Caesarism" (1981:7). He provides persuasive reasons against the transposition of the Caesarism concept from Rome to France:

> In this superficial historical analogy the main point is forgotten, namely, that in ancient Rome the class struggle took place only within a privileged minority, between the free rich and the free poor, while the great productive mass of the population, the slaves, formed the purely passive pedestal for these combatants. People forget Sismondi's significant saying: the Roman proletariat lived at the expense of society, while modern society lives at the expense of the proletariat. With so complete a difference between the material, economic conditions of the ancient and the modern class struggles, the political figures produced by them can likewise have no more in common with one another than the Archbishop of Canterbury has with the High Priest Samuel (Marx 1981:7–8).

A similar objection can be raised to the transposition of Bonapartism from France to Venezuela. In seeing the organization of a democratic regime after 1958 as an instance of Bonapartism the main point is also forgotten: that in Venezuela class struggle centered on the state, with the primary focus not on the appropriation of domestically produced surplus value but on the capture of state-mediated oil rents; that in pursuit of their interests classes sought less to use the state against each other in order to obtain revenues (although they of course also sought to do this) than to use each other to gain access to the state as the primary source of wealth. As crystallizations of the Spirit of

12. Earlier in this essay I indicated that several authors had used the concept of Bonapartism to explain events in Venezuela. It is likely that Laureano Vallenilla Lanz *padre* (the author of *Cesarismo democrático*), who received a European education, was influenced by the outlook that Marx criticized. Communist leader and historian Juan Bautista Fuenmayor, who turned this analogy into a law, was directly influenced by Marx (and perhaps by Gramsci). In the case of Karl, her use of this concept is related to the work of Schmitter and perhaps Poulantzas.

23 January, the pacts that bound labor, capital, and political parties to each other after 1958 expressed this common interest in the nation's basic source of wealth.

As the petrostate took shape, the right to rule and the right to make money became intimately intertwined. The political compromise orchestrated in Venezuela involved social classes and groupings whose relationship to each other was conditioned by their fundamental dependence on the state; it was therefore a different type of compromise. Paraphrasing Sismondi, one could suggest that in a Bonapartist compromise the state lives at the expense of society, while in a "rentist compromise," society lives at the expense of the state.

If Bonapartism à la Poulantzas were seen as a "constitutive theoretical characteristic of the very type of capitalist state," including the states of peripheral nations typically excluded in discussions of the capitalist state, one should posit the existence of "subtypes" of capitalist states and position them within a spectrum the extreme poles of which are constituted by what we may call "classical Bonapartism" and "rentier Bonapartism." The former would express the relations of a capitalist society structured around the extraction and distribution of local surplus value, the latter those of one organized around the appropriation and distribution of ground-rent.[13]

FROM THE EIGHTEENTH BRUMAIRE TO THE TWENTY-THIRD OF JANUARY

In light of these considerations, the coup against Pérez Jiménez and the transition to democracy may be better understood. The economic measures that

---

13. As in any typology, this distinction calls attention to distinguishing differences and blurs similarities that obtain in any concrete historical situation. Perhaps a careful study of what is considered the "classic" compromise would reveal the significance of ground rent in its formation. In this respect, it is important to recall that according to Marx's account, in 1851 the classes linked to various fractions of capital, land, and labor were at a stalemate in France and that Louis Napoleon came to power with the support of the peasantry. In this classic compromise the bourgeoisie exchanges the right to rule for the right to make money. Yet the bourgeoisie is not the only class concerned with making money, and profits are not the only form of revenue. In the French case, the right to make money included not only the distribution of surplus value among various fractions of capital and labor but also of rents among the peasantry and other landowning classes. Thus, ground rent also played a role in France and therefore in the formation of the classic Bonapartist compromise. What distinguishes the Venezuelan case was the central role of the state as the single national landowner and the main channel through which ground rent is distributed. In France, capitalists rather than landowners had become the major contenders for political power, and the total volume of ground rent was not centralized but distributed among multiple and atomized peasants dispersed throughout the countryside. Ultimately, however, they became Louis Napoleon's source of power.

Pérez Jiménez's regime took served to transform the economy in unplanned ways and to alter the political demands of various social groups. Despite its mercantilist orientation, the regime's actions stimulated the growth of industry and capitalist agriculture and drew foreign industrial capital, once limited to the oil enclave, directly to the center of the domestic economy. These rapid changes occurred in large part because the latifundist landholding class and the oligarchic ideology associated with it had already been dismantled, allowing the emergent modernizing political-business elite and the reformist development ideology of the triennium to delimit the terrain within which the military regime could define and legitimize itself.

The Pérez Jiménez regime, while working within the framework of oil rent–financed economic growth, sought to depoliticize the ascendant reformist model of development; it attempted to construct the physical edifice of modernity upon a quiescent social landscape. The government at once favored the expansion of propertied interests but curtailed their growing power. This process inevitably brought out increased tension within the rent-based dynamic of growth, for which the state was the central agent and focus of economic activity. The tendency for oil rent distribution to concentrate power in the state was increasingly countered by the diversification of the economy and of social classes. In a related development, the once extreme predominance of import-based commercial and financial activities in the economy, under the stimulus of the oil enclave and state revenue distribution, was now challenged by the conflicting demands of domestic capitalist production directed to the local market and by the attempt by private capitalists to influence decisions concerning the development of basic industries. These conflicts were barely addressed in the movement to bring down the Pérez Jiménez regime. They were subsumed within cross-class appeals for freedom, democracy, and constitutional rights. But they helped bring about the shift in political forces and rapid rise of a collective sentiment against the military regime which coalesced at the end of that regime. These conflicts were implicit referents in terms of which new definitions of political and economic goals were formulated by the elites who played a leading role in the opposition to Pérez Jiménez.

After the 1 January military uprising, the breakdown of the dogma of the unity of the armed forces ignited an escalating opposition, but this lack of unity of the armed forces did not lead to Pérez Jiménez's downfall. He had undermined his regime not only by closing down the channels of political communication throughout his rule and trying to silence in 1957 the voice of the market but also by weakening the military, his fundamental source of support. He transformed the autonomous and secret Seguridad Nacional into both the watchdog of the military and the agency effectively in control of the use of force. In so doing, he turned his back on the increasingly pro-fessionalized military—for which he had stood—and embraced instead a caudillo-type personal force headed by a civilian, Pedro Estrada. When in January 1958 the military demanded that Pérez Jiménez restore the military's power, he had no recourse but to behead the Seguridad Nacional, the agency that had usurped it. By relying on a privatized police institution for the use of force, Pérez Jiménez lost the support of the military, the legitimate insti-tutional representative of public force.

Pérez Jiménez was left alone only when signs of his weakness became visible, which led to a spiraling devaluation of his political currency. In panic many of his followers shifted loyalties or left the country during the first three weeks of January. Suddenly old backers of the regime in the military and the private sector turned into advocates of democracy. His quick downfall, with-out resistance from any group or sector, revealed the volatility of political actors whose powers were largely borrowed, who inhabited not a world of their own making but one largely constructed through the extraordinary powers of the state.

Starting with the first cabinet established on 24 January, private-sector leaders directly occupied key commanding positions in the new govern-ment. Arturo Sosa, closely connected with the Vollmers, was named finance minister; Oscar Machado Zuluoaga became the minister of communications. Lieutenant Colonel Rafael Alfonzo Ravard was named president of the Ven-ezuelan Development Corporation. With the replacement of the two perez-jimenista officers by two wealthy business leaders, Eugenio Mendoza and Blas Lamberti, representatives of an expanding bourgeoisie, the junta was the expression of the marriage of the right to rule and the right to make money which Pérez Jiménez had dissolved by concentrating both functions in himself.[14]

The alliance between the military, business, and the dominant political parties was based on the agreement that the winner of the elections would not monopolize state power. AD, as the most popular party, was a major promoter of the idea that the ruling political party should share political power with the other centrist parties and grant the bourgeoisie a significant voice in policy decisions and participation in the state apparatus. It was im-

---

14. Mendoza and Lamberti resigned on 18 May 1958. Without the need for their high-profile pres-ence in the junta, the defense of their interests was secured through the influence of private sector leaders in key ministries.

plicitly understood that public wealth and state power would be widely distributed, rather than concentrated in one individual or group.

The pacts signed by the political parties should be situated as ideological formulations within the wider cultural and social world from which they derived their significance and efficacy. As the development of the oil industry helped refashion a web of social relations sustained by oil money, the state became the focus of political struggles as the caretaker of this wealth. The practical centrality of the state and the foundational significance of the conceptions upon which it was premised—concerning the nature of Venezuela as an oil nation, the collective character of oil wealth, the rights of citizens to benefit from oil revenues—were increasingly taken for granted. Adam Przeworski has argued that pacts appear on the political agenda only when the conditions for a spontaneous democratic class compromise are absent or threatened (1987). What all democratic advanced capitalist nations have in common, he seems to be arguing, is not pacts but advanced capitalism itself, plus electoral and institutional conditions which generate "a spontaneous compromise that supports the coexistence of capitalism and democracy" (1987:3). Short of these conditions, democracy cannot emerge spontaneously. But what seems "spontaneous" in a particular society—what people experience as "second nature," what Bourdieu calls "habitus"—is really sedimented historical experience. Przeworski's argument assumes a model of capitalist society wherein wealth is generated by, and distributed between, capitalists and workers within a national domain. The Venezuelan case shows the historical development not of classic market "spontaneity" but of a different second nature—the "spontaneous" recognition of the need to control state intervention as a result of the formation of a capitalist society whose major source of monetary wealth rests not on the local production of surplus value but on the international capture of ground-rent. Rather than view this as an anomaly, what needs to be accounted for in each case is the historical nature of apparently spontaneous political behavior.

While conflicts centered on the role and form of specific institutions—of the state apparatus, of political parties, of interest associations and labor unions—fundamental understandings concerning their character as elements of an oil nation became second nature. This assumed a web of understandings and orientations that was the conditioning context within which Venezuelan democracy acquired definite form. The Spirit of 23 January was an expression of these implicit understandings. While this spirit took concrete form in the pacts, they helped give an institutional form to Venezuelan democracy and consolidate as natural givens the assumptions that supported it.

Accordingly, what these pacts took for granted—the assumed cultural givens that Durkheim addressed as the noncontractual foundation of contracts—were as significant as what they explicitly regulated. Their fundamental premise was that the promotion of individual and collective welfare would best occur through the expansion of the oil economy and the distribution of oil revenues by a democratic state. Thus, they were built around an agreement to respect the basic political and economic relations that sustained the oil enclave and that, in turn, were sustained by it. The explicit orchestration of alliances and the formulation of a common political and economic project presupposed an implicit accord to maintain Venezuela's international role as a major oil producer economically and politically tied to the geopolitical strategy of the United States in the hemisphere. This orchestration also assumed a commitment to contain the lower and working classes within a centralized system of limited reforms and benefits. The new political institutions would be built upon existing power relations, not against them. In these arrangements the United States was a crucial, although invisible participant. The exclusion of the Communist Party from the pacts was emblematic of this fundamental understanding. It meant the exclusion not just of a particular political group that had played a key role in the resistance against Pérez Jiménez but of a leftist tendency that had wide currency within the ranks of the reformist parties themselves, especially AD and URD. This leftist tendency was soon radicalized by the Cuban revolution, particularly after its 1961 endorsement of socialism, and by Betancourt's ever more visible middle-of-the-road orientation toward domestic and international politics.

In a context polarized by the radicalization of the Cuban revolution, which became an alluring model for large sectors of the youth of the major parties (except COPEI), the pacts could no longer contain the opposing forces. URD was the first to leave the coalition government in protest against Betancourt's attempt to impose hemispheric sanctions against Cuba at the Organization of American States meeting in Costa Rica. Then AD underwent its first division, when on 8 April 1960 most of the younger leaders and youth of AD (who in 1958 had sought to designate a nonpartisan candidate of "national unity" and who later became critical of Betancourt's social policies), founded MIR (Movimiento de Izquierda Revolucionaria) and joined a sector of the PC in armed struggle for socialism. From their perspective, Betancourt had transformed the party "of the people" into the party of the bourgeoisie.[15]

---

15. For a revealing testimony of their efforts to avert Betancourt's candidacy in 1958 and of their reasons for leaving the party and joining the armed struggle, see the interviews with Lino Martínez, Moises Moleriro, and Américo Martín in Blanco (1982).

The fundamental pact was thus the agreement to make pacts. This underlying accord entailed a commitment to avoid political conflict as well as structural change. The pacts therefore served to control the transformation of political identities during a transitional period; they sought to reform, but also to preserve, the existing structure of economic and social relations. The pacts were not just about what to do, but who to be.[16] As it turned out, post-1958 Venezuela was a time of moderate reformers, not revolutionaries.

NEOCOLONIAL DRAMAS

It is somehow fitting that what Vallenilla called the "sunny showroom" several times became the stage for a representation of the classic Bonapartist seizure of power in 1851, either as a dramatic masquerade (Vallenilla 1967) or as a scientific construct (Fuenmayor 1982; Karl 1982). While the ill-fitting costumes of the farce illuminate the illusions of historical actors, the procrustean costumes of science, by making believe that these costumes properly fit the actors, fix the actors' identities ever more firmly as impersonators of a foreign drama on the stage of the sunny showroom.

Lest this spectacle be taken at face value, we must look beyond the imperial imagination which casts domestic politics in terms of the alluring images of civilized others. In this the aim is not to reveal the true faces behind fantastic masks but to explore the constitution of political identities on the historical terrain of neocolonialism, where the colonial struggle between barbarism and civilization continues in new forms. In Latin America the aspiration to overcome underdevelopment has often turned into an insidiously tragic means of continuing the conquest and colonization by its own hand, of recognizing itself in other histories, and therefore of misrecognizing the history that unfolds in its own land.

In Venezuela, the contest between democracy and dictatorship has been cast as part of this nightmarish colonial struggle between civilization and barbarism. Ghosts of the colonial past and images of the modern future (incorporated in a cornucopia of objects and images of societies where the future has already happened) mingle in the daily battles of political actors, animating their interests and ideals. In their public battles as much as in their private fantasies, the state became a powerful site for the performance of illusions and the illusion of performance, a magical theater where the symbols of civilized life—metropolitan history, commodities, institutions, steel mills, freeways,

---

16. As Lechner suggests, the transition to democracy involves the reformulation of collective and individual identities (1985).

constitutions—were transformed into potent tokens that could be purchased or copied. As a magical theater, the state became a place possessed with the alchemic power to transmute liquid wealth into civilized life.

In this magical state, the leading performers were readily seduced by the spell of their own performance and came to incarnate the state's powers as their own. Possessed by its powers, Marcos Pérez Jiménez, like Juan Vicente Gómez before him, thought he could rule alone. As long as his performance as the state's personification was compelling, the public at large surrendered to its magic. But once the spell was broken, Pérez Jiménez appeared as an impersonator. Pressured by the armed forces, he was forced to leave the country. Occupying the space he left vacant as the single but solitary embodiment of the nation, the people now appeared at center stage as a united body with a single will to demand once again, for a brief but inaugural historical moment, democracy.

Figure 2
Relationship between nonpetroleum exports and petroleum exports
(nonrentistic), 1945–58

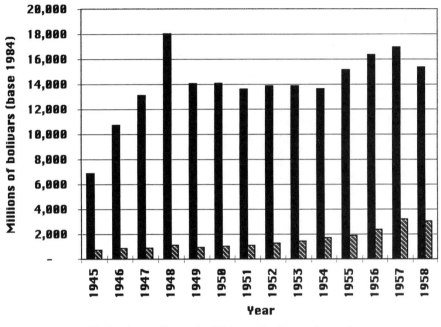

SOURCE: Baptista 1991: 118

Table 6
Evaluation of Petroleum Income, 1945–58
(in millions of bolivars, base 1968)

Year	Rentistic petroleum revenue	Value of petroleum production	Value of nonrentistic petroleum production	State share in oil revenues	Reported profits (1)	Nonrentistic profits (2)
1945	406	1,060	654	458	275	211
1946	403	1,462	1,059	552	440	388
1947	863	2,394	1,531	871	745	611
1948	1,328	3,534	2,206	1,400	1,060	992
1949	1,144	3,124	1,980	1,150	704	747
1950	1,821	3,748	1,927	1,124	970	804
1951	2,414	4,405	1,991	1,469	1,201	753
1952	2,576	4,677	2,101	1,516	1,263	720
1953	2,712	4,892	2,180	1,568	1,261	710
1954	3,102	5,337	2,235	1,699	1,412	667
1955	3,369	5,875	2,506	1,973	1,710	821
1956	4,072	6,829	2,757	3,197	2,215	914
1957	5,346	8,463	3,117	3,879	2,774	948
1958	4,753	7,662	2,909	2,825	1,616	718

SOURCE: Baptista 1991: 144. Headings of each column have been modified by the author in consultation with Baptista.
(1) Profits as reported by the oil companies
(2) Profitability of oil capital stock in Venezuela after taxes
    (Based on U.S. rate of return in the oil sector.)

Figure 3
Agricultural and industrial production, 1944–58

Figure 3
Agricultural and Industrial Production, 1944-58

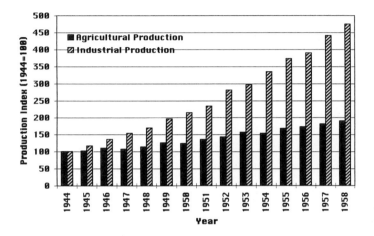

SOURCE: Baptista 1991: 124, 126

Table 7
Share of petroleum in total exports, 1945–58
(in millions of bolivars, base 1984)

Year	Total exports	Petroleum exports (nonrentistic)	Non-petroleum exports	% of petro-leum in total exports
1945	7594.5	6882.0	712.5	91
1946	11564.1	10704.9	859.2	93
1947	13960.2	13097.0	863.2	94
1948	19139.0	18031.0	1108.0	94
1949	14971.1	14052.0	919.1	94
1950	15062.2	14060.5	1001.7	93
1951	14694.0	13620.5	1073.5	93
1952	15123.6	13863.5	1260.1	92
1953	15294.5	13872.0	1422.5	91
1954	15327.1	13625.8	1701.3	89
1955	17051.6	15158.0	1893.6	89
1956	18711.2	16340.7	2370.5	87
1957	20155.6	16952.8	3202.8	84
1958	18385.4	15348.9	3036.5	83

SOURCE: Baptista 1991: 118–119.

❧ III ❧
Revival

THE PETROSTATE AND
THE SOWING OF OIL

Carlos Andrés Pérez and his mistress Cecilia Matos. (Archivo El Nacional.)

Previous page: Carlos Andrés Pérez and his cabinet in the Presidential Palace after winning the 1973 election. (Instituto Autónomo Biblioteca Nacional.)

6

THE MOTORS WARS: THE
ENGINES OF PROGRESS

¡Este hombre sí camina! (This man really walks!)

Carlos Andrés Pérez's electoral slogan

Nada camina tanto en este continente como un mito. (Nothing walks so much in this continent as a myth.)

Alejo Carpentier

In late 1973 the quadrupling of the price of crude petroleum shook the world, violently sucking up money as by a frenzied tornado from the center nations of the first world to the oil-exporting countries of the periphery. In the center nations, what came to be known as the oil shock led to visions of political and financial disaster for the industrial West which were made more real by World Bank's forecasts that predicted the continued transference of world wealth to the OPEC nations in the future. One analyst stated, "All the major symbols of Western Industrial success seemed to be on the auction block. One unified group of Arab investors tried to buy a small town in the northwestern United States—George Washington. The Arabs would buy General Motors, the Bank of America, and the Bank of England" (Aliber 1983 : 119).

While at the center the increase in oil prices led to visions of economic and political collapse, in Venezuela, as in other OPEC nations, it created the illusion that instantaneous modernization lay at hand, that the flow of history could be redirected, that oil money could launch the country into the future and grant it control over its own destiny. In December 1973, just as oil prices escalated, Carlos Andrés Pérez was elected president of Venezuela by a large margin. Suddenly, the man who had campaigned as *el hombre con energía* (the man with energy) was endowed with the energy that seemed embodied in the oil money originating in the world's energy crisis. Upon taking office he dramatically presented this conjuncture as being Venezuela's historic opportunity to overcome underdevelopment, to achieve its second independence and construct the Great Venezuela.

Carlos Andrés Pérez during the 1973 presidential campaign (Instituto Autónomo Biblioteca Nacional.)

Venezuela's first independence, achieved in 1821 after a long war against Spain led by Simón Bolívar, had not brought the state either political or economic control over society. As in other Latin American nations, civil strife decimated the economy and fragmented civil authority during the nineteenth century. Venezuela was under siege by creditors, vulnerable to international fluctuations in agricultural prices, with a social elite looking outwards toward Europe for models of civilized life. The country seemed to live in the shadow of external powers. The second independence, then, referred to the project of transcending the legacy of this stagnation by linking the one glorious moment of the nation's historic past to a dynamic, luminous future, of completing the task that Bolívar had initiated. The second independence had been repeatedly proclaimed as a goal before. What was new was the unprecedented sense of possibility, the belief that this time national progress, which had been a receding mirage, could finally become reality. This sudden rush of power created a collective state known locally as "petroleum euphoria." The nation seemed finally to be in the process of controlling its destiny.

Now the stage was set for a major performance of what may be called the theater of modernization: the ensemble of laws, practices, and rituals of rule through which the political and economic elite reproduced its power by defining the terms of national development. If the Venezuelan state had typically exercised its power dramaturgically, securing compliance through the spectacular display of its imperious presence, its sudden extraordinary financial abundance enabled it to project its presence even more fantastically than ever before. Through dazzling modernizing projects that engendered collective fantasies of progress, the state, personified in Carlos Andrés Pérez as its most effective enchanter, induced a magical state of being that was the condition of the state's appearance as the majestic agent of Venezuela's transformation. This chapter examines how the state sought to transform Venezuela through the development of the automobile industry during this period of heightened state power and collective expectations.[1]

THE AUTOMOTIVE INDUSTRY POLICY

The alliance forged among the mass-based reformist parties, the local business elite, and major U.S. corporate interests with the overthrow of Pérez Jiménez's dictatorship in 1958 established national sovereignty as its goal. This sovereignty was to be based on the establishment of democratic controls over the appropriation of oil resources and the productive investment of oil revenues. As politicians and economists debated the uses to which the new financial plenty should be put, the problem seemed to be not a lack of resources but an excess of them. This excess created an extraordinary sense of confidence. At that time it became possible in Venezuela to believe that the project of transforming ephemeral natural wealth into permanent social well-being—sowing the oil—would finally become a tangible reality.

The automotive industry policy formulated in 1962 was an important expression of this project, which was premised on the notion that Venezuela should replicate the evolution of the developed capitalist nations (Blank 1969). The industry's expansion offered the expectation of national progress

---

1. The discussion of automobile industrial policy in chapters 6 (engine production) and 7 (the production of tractors) is based on a larger study and draws on interviews with most of the state and private-sector leaders directly involved in the formulation and implementaiton of the policy. Research focused on informal interviews with managers and owners of over fifty auto parts enterprises, structured interviews with workers and managers, and archival work in the Registro de Comercio, Corporación Venezolana de Fomento, Corporación Venezolana de Guayana, Ministerio de Fomento, FEDECAMARAS, Consejo Venezolano de Industria, and FAVENPA, and attendance at other events sponsored by business associations during the 1974–79 period. Research on the ownership structure of the automobile sector led to a mapping of the major economic groups in Venezuela and their links to each other and to the state. Chapter 6 draws ideas from Coronil and Skurski (1982).

because it was thought to unite, in its advanced productive organization and in the social value of the commodity produced, the promise of collective development and of individual autonomy. At the same time, the vehicle industry was intended to benefit the new democratic regime by providing investment opportunities and industrial jobs, thus reducing the nation's technological dependence and decreasing the weight of imports in the balance of payments. Although the implementation of this program was chronically delayed, the successive administrations of AD's Raul Leoni (1964–69) and COPEI's Rafael Caldera (1969–74) subscribed to its principles. This assured an unusual degree of continuity in the program's technical staff and reinforced the ideological definition of the vehicle industry as a leading force on the road toward development and as the chrysalis of modernizing social classes.

When AD returned to power in 1974, politicians and técnicos alike felt that the new administration would finally be able to achieve the overdue goals of the automobile policy. Venezuela's entry into the Andean Pact in 1973 created an immediate obligation to formulate a new policy, for it committed the government to a program of vehicle industry "rationalization" (that is, making the irrational national industry rational) in order to coordinate the production of vehicles with the other members of this pact (Colombia, Peru, Ecuador, and Bolivia). The collective euphoria stemming from the newfound wealth which prevailed in 1974 and 1975 led government officials to view previous failures of these efforts as now easily surmountable, things of the past.

The policy on the auto industry was then made law with binding regulations to demonstrate unequivocal proof of the state's commitment to its ends. The objective of this law was to develop a fully integrated national vehicle industry. The law was drafted by functionaries from the Ministerio de Fomento (Ministry of Development), the Foreign Commerce Institute (ICE), and the Planning Ministry (CORDIPLAN). Their draft drew on the proposals that three AD economic specialists connected with powerful corporate interests had made in a study of the vehicle industry commissioned by the government in 1969.[2] Thus, the law reflected both AD's policies and the business interests of its allies. Not surprisingly, the government's internal guidelines for the policy's formulation established de facto obstacles to realizing the policy's goals and set the agenda from the start in a way that poten-

2. Both José Ignacio Casals and Constantino Quero Morales became ministers of development under Pérez; Aura Celina Casanova headed the state's Industrial Bank. Their "Estudio sobre la industria automotriz venezolana y sus perspectivas de desarrollo" (Caracas: ECODESA, 1969) was commissioned by the Venezuelan Development Corporation (CVF) from their private consulting firm.

tially limited the outcome. The guidelines directed that the "rationalization" of the industry, which implied a drastic reduction in the number of vehicle companies and models, should cause the least possible "social and economic upset" to existing firms. Second, the existing "structure of the market," based on the relative weight of each producing company, should be a determining factor in planning the reorganization of the sector. Finally, and of great importance for the future, the "historical preferences" of the Venezuelan consumer—understood as meaning a fondness for large American cars—should be respected. The boldness of the policy's goals contrasted sharply with the conservative character of its guidelines.[3]

The draft did not meet serious objections from the private sector. During 1974 the drafting commission met with the vehicle-manufacturing companies and achieved an apparent consensus that the policy was acceptable. The law was passed on 16 May 1975 (Decreto Ley 929 and 921) under the "special powers" granted the president to speed up development plans, a product of the period when major decisions were made law outside the normal framework of legislative and party controls.[4] The central goal was to have 90 percent of the vehicle's value, including the drivetrain, produced locally by 1985. Major components would be produced by enterprises having at least 51 percent of their capital from local private sources. Existing foreign companies would have to become mixed or national firms in accord with Andean Pact regulations if they intended to benefit from the common market. The manufacture of basic components (such as the drivetrain) could be undertaken by the transnational companies (TNCs) manufacturing vehicles if they formed partnerships with local capitalists under the terms of Andean Pact Decision 24. This altered the basis for antagonism between the assembly sector and the parts sector, between the vehicle TNCs and the national industrialists, as defined by the 1962 policy.

The first of the steps designed to achieve these goals was the reduction in the number of vehicle models from fifty-nine to eleven by 1985 so that manufacturers could benefit from economies of scale and the standardization of parts.[5] The next step was to increase the local content of vehicles by

3. Untitled confidential memorandum (Ministry of Development 1974). Also, interviews with members of the draft commission.

4. For a discussion of industrial policy making at this time in the context of the Venezuelan experience since 1958, see Blank (1974).

5. A passenger vehicle model was defined by the drivetrain, not by body design. A drivetrain includes the motor, the transmission, and related elements. The full production of these auto parts requires as well the establishment of a forge and foundry.

3 percent a year and to measure this content by an index system of production costs (*perfiles industriales*). Third, vehicle manufacturers were to compensate for the value of their imports of disassembled vehicle material by exporting locally made auto parts by 1979. Fourth, the firms could no longer apply their auto parts exports toward fulfilling their quota of local content for Venezuelan vehicles. Fifth, by 1980 the manufacturers were to produce the drivetrain domestically and use locally produced cast iron, steel, and aluminum. Finally, vehicle manufacturers would be permitted to manufacture only the classes of vehicles (such as those designed primarily for carrying passengers or cargo) that they produced at the time of the law's decree (a provision that hurt European and Japanese manufacturers, who were less diversified than their U.S. competitors).[6]

The Andean Pact's sectoral program assigned Venezuela the following vehicle models: one medium passenger car (A3 category, 1500–2000 cubic centimeter, or cc), the exclusive production of two large passenger cars (A4, over 2000 cc), one utility vehicle (C, maximum weight 25,000 kilos—Venezuela opted to use an auto engine in this vehicle), one medium truck (B3, between 9.3 and 17 metric tons), and one large truck (B4, over 17 metric tons). In addition, the government established bilateral agreements for two light-truck models: a "coproduction" accord with Ecuador (B1.2, between 3 and 6 metric tons) and a "coassembly" accord with Bolivia (B1.1, up to 3 metric tons).

The policy sought to achieve manufacture of the drivetrain first and production of the vehicle body as the final stage. The latter would allow domestic vehicle production to be independent of design changes in the home country. Based on the notion that drivetrain production would ensure the transfer of the essential technology, this two-phase strategy coincided both with the Andean Pact's auto program and with the conventional wisdom of the U.S. vehicle manufacturers. Moreover, local planners, swayed by the example and reasoning of the U.S. auto industry, delayed vehicle body metal stamping on the grounds that the expensive investment in machinery could not be justified for a market of Venezuela's size and should wait for the growth of the Andean market. Since this reasoning was based on the U.S. system of high-volume production and annual model changes, it is likely that the method chosen to reduce models reflected nontechnical criteria that gave the vehicle companies, as the source of the drivetrain technology, a built-in bargaining advantage and created a technical obstacle to the fulfillment of the

---

6. "Normas para el desarrollo de la industria automotriz. Resolución no. 5457, 1975," *Gaceta Oficial*, no. 1772, 16 September 1975.

policy's goal. According to a former técnico from the Ministerio de Fomento, it would be feasible to use body stamping to achieve model reduction in the intermediate stage of the industry's growth. The freezing in the growth of the number of models would strike directly at the local industry's commercial dependence on the foreign companies and at the local market's replication of U.S. consumption patterns (confidential interview 1978).[7]

The policy's premise that the existing structure of the industry be respected virtually assured that the state would select the "Big Three" U.S. companies to produce the three coveted large gasoline engines (two eight-cylinder, one six-cylinder) for use in the two A4 passenger models, in the utility vehicle, and in the B3 truck. Given the official restrictions, Renault, VW, and Fiat could bid only in the medium, four-cylinder engine category, and Toyota and Nissan could offer the engines of their utility vehicles only in the A4 category. The bargaining agenda for the large-engine bids had excluded the Japanese and European companies.

A major source of conflict was the decision to allow the manufacture of one engine per vehicle model. This obliged assemblers to use the locally made motor, even if it were not their own (the "hybrid vehicle" concept). For public planners, it was not only important technically to have the TNCs acquiesce to this program; it was also a test of the state's capacity to promote the interests of local capital as a whole. The planners shared the assumption that the state's new financial resources could be transformed directly into political power. Much in the way that OPEC nations could define new terms of association with the oil companies while maintaining their partnership with them, so, it was thought, the Venezuelan state could impose new conditions on the auto TNCs while solidifying its alliance with them.

As it turned out, the negotiations between the state and competing transnational corporations over the rights to manufacture vehicle engines in Venezuela were conditioned by the underlying conflict between two related processes triggered by the 1973 jump in international oil prices and the ensuing world recession. First was the reorganization of the world automobile industry by the transnationals. Second was the reorganization of the dominant alliance in Venezuela and the reorientation of its development program. Investments in the new projects were affected by these related transformations in the international and local contexts provoked by the oil boom.

---

7. This discussion is based on highly confidential interviews. No public information was ever made available on the bidding process, which was regarded as a top state secret. For a discussion of economies of scale, see Baranson (1978), Jenkins (1977), and White (1971).

THE INTERNATIONAL CONTEXT

As a result of the world recession of the early 1970s, international capital underwent a major restructuring in which an important element was the reorganization of the automobile industry. When center nations sought to recycle the enormous quantity of petrodollars that the OPEC nations suddenly held, the automobile transnational corporations of the United States, Europe, and Japan competed intensely for foreign markets. Yet, since they were all caught in a world recession which forced them to redefine their global strategies, the major TNCs were reluctant to invest in Venezuela. In 1973 the major world producers had hit high levels of vehicle production: the United States, over 10 million; Japan, 4.5 million; Germany and France over 3.5 million units each. Brazil for the first time produced 1 million vehicles in 1974. The combined production of these countries was over 25 million vehicles. But between 1973 and 1975 production was down everywhere: 30 percent in the United States, 36 percent in Japan, 22 percent in Germany. In 1975 the European auto industry's total production dropped 15 percent; five of the nine major producers had large losses; and several firms required government intervention.

The energy trauma affected especially the U.S. auto industry, long reliant on inexpensive gasoline to propel its large, profit-making cars. Facing a shrinking market, the U.S. automakers also had to confront the U.S. government, which enacted in 1975 new fuel-efficiency standards. To meet this dual challenge, U.S. corporations would have to invest an estimated $80 billion by 1985 in the design and production of more efficient motors and lighter cars. In the United States, this was the time of the "small car blues" (*Business Week,* 16 March 1974), when all automakers, suffering serious loses, were forced to shift production toward small cars that were less profitable but more fuel efficient. The situation at General Motors was symptomatic. Between October 1973 and March 1974, GM slid into its worst sales slump since the 1958 recession. Sales during 1974 were down 37.5 percent. Just between February and March, its share of the auto market, including imports, dropped from 44.4 percent to 37.5 percent. Unemployment in the auto sector was growing. By March 1974, GM had closed as many as fifteen of its twenty-two automobile assembly plants and three of its four body plants in order to reduce the glut of unsold big cars and convert to its now more popular smaller cars.[8] Revealingly, during this period GM was "toppled from

8. A Cadillac Coupe de Ville cost $300 more to build than a Chevrolet Caprice but sold for $2,700 more. A typical intermediate car, the Chevelle, had a return of $600 per car, the compact Nova $450, and the subcompact Vega only $125 (*Atlantic,* December 1974).

its pedestal as America's most profitable industrial corporation and replaced, ironically, by Exxon Corporation" (*New York Times,* 24 March 1974).

The other automakers also suffered serious loses. While GM moved from first to second place, Ford was displaced from third to fourth position, and Chrysler from sixth to eleventh. Altogether, the automakers' earnings fell 65 percent during 1974. Ford, Chrysler, and American Motors were all in the red for the first two quarters of 1975. In January 1975, when automakers assembled only 370 thousand cars, unemployment hit a record peak; 314 thousand workers (about 40 percent of the industry's hourly labor force) were laid off. The shift in production toward smaller cars forced these companies to compete with imported cars. During the first six months of 1975, imports captured 37 percent of the small-car market and 20 percent of the total market (*Business Week,* 28 July 1975).

Thus, at the outset of the Pérez administration, the automobile transnationals, weakened by the economic downturn, were undergoing major organizational changes. To counter their decline, these corporations sought to penetrate foreign markets, integrate their international productive operations, expand the production of certain products in third-world nations, increase their control over raw materials, develop partnerships with each other, and strengthen their ties with their home governments and national currencies.

As issues of fuel economy, raw material costs, and automobile design acquired new importance, the automobile companies needed a worldwide strategy to secure cheap raw materials, an efficient international division of productive operations, and expanding markets. They began to seek world sourcing for the production of "world cars," the internationally coordinated manufacture of standardized auto models assembled from components produced in different countries. Thus, vehicle manufacturers eventually became willing to participate in national auto industry development programs, as long as these programs could be adapted to their rapidly evolving global strategies.

Each country in which the automobile transnational corporations operated had a distinct role in their overall scheme, and this role was in turn of decisive importance in shaping the industry. As a General Motors executive in Venezuela remarked, "For GM there is no small market" (confidential interview 1978). *Business Latin America* commented on the experience of GM and Ford with the Andean Pact negotiations. "Corporate strategy should be mapped out for the area as a whole, so that bids in one country are prepared with regional priorities in mind . . . Concessions that would make the home office wince could look quite different to management if they gain firm access to a related project" (25 October 1978). In Venezuela, each concession granted meant a price exacted. The new transnational flexibility was to couple the national automobile policy more tightly to the international policy of the ever more global corporations.

THE NATIONAL CONTEXT

Local capitalists were hesitant to invest in the new projects, but for reasons different from those of the TNCs. During this period a reorganization of the dominant class alliance and a reordering of the pattern of profitability of the domestic economy occurred. As a result of the nationalizations of the iron and oil industries in 1975 and 1976, the state's principal role changed from collecting taxes on primary export products to being a direct producer of primary and industrial goods. The new integration that resulted between the state's financial and productive roles took two directions: the state's financial apparatus was expanded and centralized and became interconnected with the state's producing corporations. The government's development strategy combined the traditional goal of import substituting industrialization to establish a diversified and vertically integrated domestic industrial system, plus the new objective of creating an industrial export structure through state investment. The state's promotion of capital accumulation, which had previously rested on its protectionist role, was now complemented by the state's direct participation as the major productive agent in the economy.[9]

Pérez linked the pursuit of an economic policy directed toward "deepening" capitalist relations with the struggle to make his political faction more powerful within AD. This combination was to solidify an existing alliance between AD and certain sectors of the bourgeoisie and to forge a marriage of complicity between Pérez's political clique and his economic clique, between "bourgeois politicians" and "political capitalists." The internal struggle for leadership within AD made the traditional use of state power by the party in office to further its interests take on new forms. The party had long been dominated by ex-President Rómulo Betancourt and the old-guard leaders who were associated with the original industrial development project and the economic groups that it promoted. Betancourt sought in the early 1970s to resolve the problem of succession within the party by supporting

---

9. The government's strategy and investment program are described in the "V Plan de la Nación" (*Gaceta Oficial*, no. 1860, extraordinario. Caracas: Tipografía Nacional, 1976). Bigler analyzes the state's institutional expansion (1980). For the V Plan, the reform of state enterprises, and the oil nationalization, see Equipo Proceso Politico (1977). For administrative reform, see Karl (1982).

Pérez's presidential candidacy, seeing in him a leader of AD's younger generation who respected his authority and allegiances. However, the Pérez administration's unprecedented financial and political power permitted the
president to use his office relatively free of established political constraints.
Thus, Pérez was able at the outset of his term to capitalize on the nation's
acceptance of his power. He set out both to reorganize the state apparatus
and to secure the leadership position within AD for his faction of the party.

There were two components to Pérez's political strategy. First, he sought
to concentrate power in the office of the president while reducing the president's political accountability to his party, the legislature, and state agencies.
He obtained special powers from Congress that enabled him to bypass both
Congress and his own party. Second, he sought to achieve more autonomy
from established ties to strong economic interests in government policy making. Accordingly, he promoted a set of entrepreneurs who had backed his
candidacy, the men called the Twelve Apostles, because they had a close relationship with the president.

These entrepreneurs, especially Pedro Tinoco and Carmelo Lauría, influenced Pérez's policy (such as the nationalization of oil and iron, the V Plan,
and the administrative reform plan) and helped construct and participate in
major economic projects linking state, foreign, and local capital. While they
continued to benefit from state projects and spending under Pérez, the established economic groups and corporations were displaced from their once
uniquely privileged position of influence on state policy by the new groups.

Consequently, intense interbourgeois conflict developed during this period. Despite appearances, it did not simply reflect the opposing interests of
distinct sectoral fractions of capital. In Venezuela, petroleum income had
helped link sectors of the economy. The rise of major economic groups
with diversified and overlapping investments had served to diminish clashes
among these economic sectors at the policy level. Rather, this conflict reflected the heightened competition among capitalists for access to state projects and funds and, ultimately, for position within the entrepreneurial state.

Rival economic groups differed from each other in the composition
of their investments. While both the established and ascendant economic
groups were based primarily in finance, commerce, and real estate, the established groups had significant industrial investments in both durable and non-
durable consumer goods for the mass market. On the basis of their political
ties the ascendant groups sought to expand in all areas, including manufacturing sectors, where dominance by the established groups had been un-
questioned (for example, cement and petrochemicals). With respect to the

vehicle industry, the established groups were dominant in the auto parts sector and in the related steel and metalworking sector and had investments in the smaller vehicle assembly firms. The ascendant groups, devoid of investments in these sectors, were to become partners with the TNCs producing vehicles in some of the new vehicle projects.[10]

The automobile policy took for granted that local capitalists would invest in the automobile projects. Yet while they were willing to expand their enterprises and even to produce new auto parts, local capitalists were cautious about the larger investments planned by the policy. The policy had ambiguously stated that the fulfillment (*realización*) of the projects should be undertaken by mixed capital enterprises. The government had intended to have local investors join foreign firms at the initial state of project design. However, only one company was formed according to this plan, PLAMOANCA, a joint venture between GM and the powerful SIVENSA group (controlled by the Machado Zuloaga family). Other industrialists, weaker and less committed to the auto sector than the SIVENSA group, were unwilling to undertake investments of this magnitude, slow maturation, and risk.

During this period, the explosive expansion of circulating money created opportunities for profit which did not depend on productive investments or on efforts to increase the productivity of labor. High profits could be reaped through a variety of speculative ventures, in real estate, commerce, and construction. Local capital was particularly attracted to those areas in which it could quickly capture a portion of the *circulante*—the money in circulation. Between 1974 and 1976 the rate of private investment in industry actually declined and reached the 1972 level until 1976. The expansion of production that did occur during this period (11 percent in the manufacturing sector) resulted from the increased utilization of installed capacity. Commerce, on the other hand, expanded at a rate of 36.9 percent, reflecting a significant increase in imports. The boom, far from stimulating private investment in industry, created conditions which reinforced the traditional orientation of local capital toward investments in areas leading to large and immediate returns. In order to understand more fully this context, it is necessary to present a brief description of the structure of the domestic automobile industry.

10. The rise of the "new groups" within the bourgeoisie was a significant but poorly understood process. Their political connections are analyzed by Duno (1975) and Martín (1976). Equipo Proceso Político (1978) mistakenly argues that the new groups constitute an internationalized fraction of capital. No thorough analysis of their economic basis has been made. The only study of the "old groups" is in the works of Rangel, especially (1972).

THE ORGANIZATION OF THE VENEZUELAN
AUTOMOBILE INDUSTRY

In contrast to the first Latin American nations to industrialize, where assembly operations preceded parts production, Venezuela experienced simultaneous growth both in the terminal (assembly) and parts (supplier) sectors. The original 1962 automobile policy divided the two sectors, for it prohibited "vertical integration"—investment by assembly firms in the parts sector. Thus, the nascent parts sector could not be directly controlled by the TNC vehicle manufacturers, and local entrepreneurs were provided with a relatively protected field for industrial investment in conjunction with foreign auto parts manufacturing firms. Moreover, these state-promoted local capitalists, who were heralded as the emergent national industrial bourgeoisie, helped counter the weight of the vehicle TNCs in negotiations with state agencies.

The terminal sector. In this sector the fifteen firms employed 10,456 people in 1975, or 3.2 percent of the industrial workforce. They had gross fixed capital investments of $83 million, and production represented 6 percent of the nonpetroleum gross domestic product. The average local content of the vehicles (the percentage of a vehicle's parts which were officially counted as being of local manufacture) was approximately 35 percent of their value. This represented the purchase of $264 million in locally made parts. The assembly firms in 1975 varied considerably in size and product diversification. Seven firms assembled both autos and commercial vehicles; three, only commercial vehicles (trucks and buses); one, commercial and utility (four-wheel drive) vehicles; and one, only autos. By 1975 the U.S. Big Three automakers produced 81 percent of the nation's passenger cars and 90.2 percent of the commercial vehicles out of a total of 143,900 units.

The firms relevant for this study fall into three categories. First, the Big Three U.S. automakers (GM, Chrysler, and Ford) had wholly owned subsidiaries established in 1948, 1950, and 1962. Second, the European auto firms—Renault, Fiat, Volkswagen, and Daimler-Benz—either had joint ventures or had granted assembly licenses to locally owned companies. Third, the utility and commercial vehicle assembly companies from the United States, Europe, and Japan also operated under license or as joint ventures (except for American Motors). The latter firms, as well as the European auto firms, were all established as a result of the 1962 auto policy.

The auto parts sector. In 1975, this sector had a core of approximately seventy-five firms which produced primarily for the vehicle industry and accounted for approximately 80 percent of local parts production. A periphery, whose members produced secondarily for the vehicle industry, brought the number of firms in the parts sector to an estimated three hundred. The value of parts produced in 1975 for new autos was $264 million, with a gross fixed investment of $130 million. The sector employed fourteen thousand workers, or about 4.3 percent of the industrial workforce. Because of the diversity of the sector, it is difficult to determine its economic composition with precision.[11]

Few of the core firms were foreign subsidiaries (except for the subsector manufacturing tires), although major U.S. parts producers were partners and licensers in the principal local parts firms. While there were many small and medium local industrialists in the parts sector, the largest firms were dominated by investors from the major economic groups. The rapidly growing SIVENSA corporation, an industrial holding company formed by members of the elite of the established groups (the Machado Zuloaga and Vollmer families), was the majority owner in over twenty of the sector's leading firms.

Automobile industry interest associations. Of these associations, the two industrial chambers were created at the government's behest in 1963 to represent their sectors' corporations in the democratic planning process.[12] The Chamber of Venezuelan Auto Parts Manufacturers (FAVENPA) numbered 66 members in 1975 and 120 in 1978. Composed of the principal auto parts firms, it produced about 80 percent of local parts at that time. The representatives of SIVENSA corporation played a major role in its leadership. FAVENPA used its growing public voice to promote the interests and political role of local industrialists as a whole.

The Chamber of the Venezuelan Automobile Industry (CIVA) was publicly less active than FAVENPA. It tended to criticize government regulations as being obstructive and to attack the local parts sectors as being a low-quality, high-cost producer. CIVA's unity was frequently undermined by the dominant role played within it by the U.S.'s Big Three and by the occasional privileged treatment obtained by certain locally owned assembly firms. The Association of Distributors of Automobiles and Machines (ADAM) was founded in 1952 by major vehicle dealers to control the expansion of dealerships. The proprietors included several of Venezuela's wealthiest families,

11. Data for this section come from reports of FAVENPA, CIVA, and the Ministry of Development.

12. For automobile policy in democratic planning, see Blank (1969a and 1969b).

many of whose fortunes stem from auto sales.[13] This network provided foreign enterprises with knowledge of and access to the local political scene, although ADAM itself had little influence on policy.

THE IMPLEMENTATION OF THE POLICY

Wait and See: The Initial Opposition

The boom, as shown above, made both the automobile TNCs and local capitalists reluctant to invest in the programmed automobile projects. While the TNCs were trying to adjust their Venezuelan investments to their world-wide plans, local capitalists were seeking to develop profitable ventures in commerce, real estate, and banking. The automobile transnationals were particularly cautious with respect to prospective investments in Venezuela. Each new investment had to be evaluated even more carefully than before, since local operations should correspond to their emerging global strategies. For example, at this time, the inside position at GM in Detroit concerning its investment policies in Venezuela was simple: "GM won't invest a penny there now" (confidential interview, Chicago 1980). By weakening the auto transnationals, the oil boom impelled them to challenge more directly the Venezuelan government's automobile policy.

This challenge, of course, could not be frontal. Venezuela was an exceptionally lucrative market. While auto sales were plunging worldwide from oil price increases, in Venezuela they were growing at a rate of 20 percent, with local production expanding at a rate of 12.8 percent. The difference between domestic production in Venezuela and local demand was taken up by a large increase in imports. The pressure grew for the TNCs to secure their position within Venezuela's market. They both fought the policy and sought to increase their local profits by opposing price controls. They argued that profits were falling as a result of price controls on 40 percent of their auto production—the no-frills, "regulated" cars—and so they drastically raised the price of their nonregulated, luxury vehicles. In turn the government, responding also to the increased local demand for regulated cars, required most manufacturers to raise the local quota of regulated production to 50 percent. Demand exceeded supply for all vehicle categories in the fast-expanding Venezuelan market.

This battle over prices served to create a more fundamental challenge.

13. These include the Phelps, Degwitz, Planchart, Di Massi, Cisneros, Duarte, Zingg, Vallenilla, and Mendoza families. For a journalistic account of the early auto dealerships, see Schael (1969).

The vehicle transnationals argued that without adequate profits they would not be able to expand vehicle production to meet demand or to plan investments in the drivetrain projects. To underline their words with action, the TNCs stopped promoting the production of new vehicle parts by the auto parts firms. Since vehicle part production could expand only with the guidance of the TNCs, this was a clear indicator of their noncompliance with the local-content goals of the policy. At the same time the assembly companies successfully applied pressure where it counted. To the surprise of many of the government officials directly involved in the implementation of the policy, these companies obtained significant reductions in the local-content requirements for trucks and buses from Development Minister José Ignacio Casals. This unchallenged change—which was implemented through several statements (*oficios*) of weak juridical status—was understood by the attentive corporations as a significant message: there was going to be "flexibility" in the implementation of the law.[14]

Bidding for the Future—or for the Present?

The bidding process for the major automobile projects was seriously affected by these converging responses of local and foreign capital to the oil boom. The Venezuelan government had given private investors almost five months to present their bids (15 October 1975 to 1 March 1976). By December 1975, when it was clear that few projects would be forthcoming, the government was forced to revise the spirit, if not the letter, of its guidelines. Minister of Development Casals agreed that after the government had selected them, the TNCs could seek local partners to implement (*realizar*) the projects. Thus, because local competition for participation in the joint ventures was absent, the TNCs consolidated their control of the industry and were then free to design the projects as they wished, without having to accommodate to the pressures of local capital.

The TNCs did have to meet, however, the demands of the government. The basic requirement—that Venezuela produce engines and incorporate 90 percent of the value of the car by 1985—placed most of these corporations in a position that conflicted with their emerging worldwide strategies. The TNCs approached top government officials to enlist support for a change of policy. Their request found more than simple support from Minister Carmelo Lauría, President Pérez's closest economic advisor and the ex-

---

14. This interpretation is based on numerous interviews with executives of FAVENPA, GM, CIVA, and the Ministry of Development.

president of a major local bank. Reportedly, in a meeting with representatives of the Big Three U.S. companies, he replied to their claim that it was insane to manufacture engines locally by advising them to sabotage the policy: "In the face of something crazy, propose something equally crazy" (Ante una locura, propongan otra locura). In a separate meeting, a Renault representative received the same message.[15]

The Bids

The automakers followed Lauría's advice. They presented extraordinarily inadequate bids to the government to force it to face the consequences of its previous decision. When the government limited the bids for the major engines to established companies, it increased their leverage and reduced competition to a minimum. In this context, the strong companies presented the worst bids; and the weak ones, the best. Toyota, which had knowledge-able advisors and influential local partners (the Behrens family), decided to take a gamble and presented a bid. By law, however, its bid had to be restricted to the same category of vehicle that it produced locally (four-wheel drive utility vehicles), so its bid was not acceptable. Renault and Fiat were the competitors for the four-cylinder engine. VW did not present a bid. Its home office decided against bidding because it already had large investments in Brazil and Mexico. As a result, the government invited Hillman to present a bid, but this company also declined to do so. Renault's well-designed proposal offered a technically advanced but expensive motor (with a lightweight, aluminum block). Fiat proposed a conventional but proven engine but did so with an incomplete plan. For the diesel engine bids, only three out of the seven participants offered sufficient informa-tion: Fiat, Daimler-Benz, and Pegaso. Mack, Cummins, Ferrostaal, and Steward and Stevenson did not even meet the minimum requirements for bidding.

All of these bids presupposed the establishment of a gear box factory, a foundry, and a forge to manufacture the engine block of the various engines and other drivetrain components. However, in a major setback, no accept-able proposals for these projects were received. Without the foundry and the forge, the foreign and transmission manufacturers could simply machine their own imported components in their Venezuelan plants. A foreign con-sultant, who had helped formulate the Venezuelan automobile policy from the outset in 1962, confided that the minister of development had not given

15. Confidential interviews with several government officers and private sector leaders.

these projects enough importance and had not taken the necessary steps to elicit adequate bids.[16]

The Initial Selections, the Continual Delays

Facing this situation, the government extended the bidding period until June 1976 and urged the companies to improve their proposals. This time the government made it clear that it would not accept from the bidders criticism of the policy and that their proposals had to be complete. On the basis of the revised proposals the government made preliminary selections. The major winner was Fiat. The Italian company was awarded both the four-cylinder auto engine and the medium B3 truck engine (to be used in trucks between 9.3 and 17 tons gross vehicular weight). It was widely rumored that this selection reflected the influence within the government of the Di Mase family, Fiat's local partner in its Venezuelan assembly plant and traditionally a strong supporter of AD. In addition, President Pérez had taken the unusual step of making personal contact with Fiat's president Agnelli during his recent visit to Italy. The large engine for the B4 trucks (over seventeen tons) was awarded to Mack Truck Company, whose local partner was the prominent Duarte family. This award was legally recognized in an official agreement (acta convenio) signed in May 1977.

In relation to the larger auto engines, government técnicos, supported by a U.S. consulting firm, recommended the selection of Chrysler for the eight-cylinder engine and American Motors for the six-cylinder engine. However, government leaders objected to this recommendation. They argued that at this time these companies could not be trusted to carry out major local investments, given Chrysler's financial problems at home and AMC's secondary role as an international producer.

New Guidelines

Consequently, these basic engine decisions were delayed. Then the government ruled that in order to economize on gasoline consumption, all commercial trucks must have diesel engines. This change in the specifications for the eight-cylinder engines opened up a new round of competition. One of the eight-cylinder engines had originally been designed primarily (70 percent) for medium trucks. Now there was no need to produce two eight-cylinder engines. As local businessmen observed at the time, there was then no possibility for the Big Three to "share the spoils" (repartirse la torta).

At the highest level of government the implicit understanding had been

16. Confidential interview (1978).

that the Big Three would share the Venezuelan market. Ford would receive the eight-cylinder gasoline engine for commercial vehicles; and Chrysler and GM, the eight- and six-cylinder engines for automobiles.[17] With only one eight-cylinder gasoline engine, the market could not be divided up as originally intended. Now the plan called for only two engines for two different markets: one eight-cylinder engine for 100,000 vehicles and one six-cylinder engine for 40,000 vehicles.

The government now could no longer easily accommodate the three companies that together controlled 75 percent of the local market. Chrysler had presented the best bid for the eight-cylinder engine but was a company in serious financial trouble. American Motors had presented the best bid for the six-cylinder engine but was not a strong company internationally or locally. GM, the world automobile leader, had presented the worst bid and had shown no desire to cooperate with the government. Ford, whose bid for the eight-cylinder engine was second to Chrysler's, had no acceptable six-cylinder engine. The government found itself at an impasse. The government then proposed that Chrysler and Ford produce jointly one eight-cylinder and one six-cylinder engine in a single plant. The two companies would share the market equally. In retaliation for its recalcitrant attitude, GM would be excluded. Ford and Chrysler, however, found the proposal unacceptable. Neither company wanted to operate jointly with the other, and Ford still hoped to obtain exclusive rights to manufacture the more lucrative eight-cylinder engine.

The impasse continued. However, by objecting to any concrete decision, the three companies were in fact colluding. By blocking the implementation of the automobile policy, they were in fact pursuing their preferred path of action of avoiding an investment in Venezuela at this time, even as they preserved their right to remain in Venezuela as assemblers and importers during the profitable boom period.

The Battle to Get Good Bids

Throughout this process the government's public image as a powerful and impartial actor began to crumble. It had tried to create the impression that it was not prey to traditional considerations of political interest by taking pains to demonstrate that it could judge the engine bids on the basis of their technical merits alone. The commission to evaluate the bids had its offices in a building separate from the Ministerio de Fomento and kept its location secret to avoid corporate lobbying. This commission seems

17. Confidential interviews.

indeed to have selected the best bids, but it chose the projects of the weakest companies.

Decisions were made at the highest level of the government on other than simply technical grounds. The Fiat selection made this point clear. And the refusal to grant the bids to American Motors and Chrysler, although perhaps reasonably justified in terms of the need to choose strong companies, also reflected the significant political weight of the excluded companies. It became evident that the issue was to select not simply the best engines, but also the strongest companies. For the government, the challenge became to make the most powerful companies present if not the best, at least serious, bids.

For almost a year the government did little to change this situation. Then on 26 June 1977, the new minister of development (the third in a year), Luís Alvarez Domínguez, announced that in an effort to promote fuel economy the government had decided Venezuela would not produce the eight-cylinder gasoline engine. This decision redefined the bids for the two six-cylinder gasoline engines, expanding their potential market and therefore their appeal. These engines were intended to power, in addition to passenger cars, the four-ton truck to be produced jointly with Ecuador. Benefiting from the year's delay, the government also added several new technical requirements for these engines: low fuel consumption, pollution control meeting California standards, advanced technology, and the use of aluminum in the components. This change weakened Ford and strengthened GM. While Ford did not have a suitable six-cylinder engine, GM had a proven motor that could fulfill the policy's requirements. Some técnicos privately confided that this decision was politically motivated. Instead of specifying the number of cylinders, they argued, the government should have presented a set of performance criteria, including that of fuel efficiency. Yet while it is true that the definition of performance criteria would have enabled competition among different types of engines, regardless of the number of cylinders, the worldwide tendency was to shift production toward smaller and lighter engines. The government took an additional step to increase competition by inviting Renault to joint the Big Three in a new round of closed bidding for the six-cylinder engine. American Motors was excluded from the bidding. By inviting Renault, the government intended not only to give it a chance to remain in the Venezuelan market (it had lost to Fiat in the four-cylinder competition) but also to force the U.S. corporations to offer better bids.

Inseguridad Jurídica

At first the inclusion of Renault appeared to be simply a maneuver to increase competition. The U.S. companies seemed assured that the selection would ultimately be theirs. Yet, another set of decisions taken by the government at this time made matters less clear. These decisions, however, also revealed the extent to which the government was pursuing the policy in an ad hoc fashion. The first of these decisions came early in September 1977. At this time the president unilaterally revoked the government's selection of Mack Truck Company to produce the large diesel engine and awarded both the motor and the assembly rights for a truck and a bus to Pegaso, a company belonging to the Spanish state-owned enterprise, ENASA, which was in serious financial difficulties. This decision was taken during the visit to Venezuela of Spain's King Juan Carlos, along with other measures to grant Spain key investment possibilities in Venezuela.

These decisions, taken at the spur of the moment, reflected AD's commitment to cement ties with the Spain's young democratic regime. A few months later, Development Minister Alvarez Domínguez acknowledged that the selection of Pegaso had been a political decision. In a memorandum he prepared for his successor, he explained that the choice of Pegaso "was determined in part by the political necessity of strengthening relations with the new Spanish democracy" (*Latin American Economic Report*, 13 April 1979). The fact that Mack had been content with the commercial boom in imported trucks and had not taken any steps to produce the engine that it had been awarded in 1975 made it easier for the government to bypass its previous selection and more difficult for Mack to fight it.

The award to Pegaso not only violated the acta convenio signed on 9 May, which granted Mack the right to produce the large diesel engine, but also the national Automotive Policy Law. According to this law, no new vehicle models or assemblers could be established in Venezuela. While in the case of automobiles a model is defined by the engine and drivetrain, in the case of trucks and buses it is defined by the body type. By granting Pegaso the right to produce buses and trucks, therefore, the government was in fact permitting a new assembler to become established and to introduce new models. Local industrialists were stunned. Mack, Fiat, and Pegaso had already signed an agreement on 9 May to produce diesel engines in the Guayana region. However, the Pegaso diesel plant was designed to be built in the Andean state of Táchira, a decision that also meant the dissolution of the Guayana diesel complex.

A few days later, on 13 September, after months of arduous negotiations, the five Andean Pact nations signed in Quito a common program for vehicle production known as Decision 120. This complex program indicated that these nations had agreed not to allow the introduction of new vehicle models. Thus, the Pegaso selection also violated the spirit of a program that had been amply discussed and was about to be signed. Just prior to signing Decision 120, FAVENPA had voiced a public protest against the government for accepting the common external tariff included in this program. Local industrialists had been complaining that the proposed tariff, set at around 40 percent, was too low to protect Venezuelan industry. While in the other four countries, scarce foreign exchange and foreign-exchange controls served effectively to protect local industry against imports, in Venezuela the very abundance of foreign exchange and the existence of free convertibility made it necessary to establish high tariffs. Although local industrialists had expressed these concerns through their associations to key government officials (on 22 July FAVENPA, CIVA, the Association of Metallurgical Industrialists, and the Association of Part Importers, CANIDRA, sent a document to ICE's president Reinaldo Figueredo), the government had paid no attention to their demands. The agreement was about to be signed, and no change had been made. Thus FAVENPA contacted the journalists responsible for the economic sections of the major newspapers and asked them to give prominent attention to this issue.[18]

President Pérez was angered at finding this outburst of public criticism in the newspapers of 11 September (a Sunday). He urgently summoned the presidents of CIVA and FAVENPA, "wherever they were," to his office. President Pérez directed his attack against FAVENPA's César Rodríguez and accused the association of being an instrument of the transnational corporations and of their plans to undermine the Andean Pact. César Rodríguez challenged this accusation. He argued that FAVENPA represented national industrialists and that it was interested not in undermining the Andean Pact but in defending local industry. Reportedly, the president then significantly changed his position. He assured his critic that he would attempt to modify the tariff, although he could not promise to change unilaterally the level of the common tariff. In the meantime, he stated, local industry would be protected by all available means, including import licenses.[19]

Reportedly, sensing receptivity in the president, Cesar Rodríguez took the offensive. He said that the government itself was undermining the vehicle program by violating its principles. He explained to the president that the Pegaso decision violated not only the spirit of the program that was about to be signed in Quito but also the letter of the Venezuelan policy law. The president, surprised, turned to his minister of development, who acknowl-

18. Interviews and newspapers of 10 September.

19. Confidential interviews.

edged that Rodríguez was right. As a result of this exchange, the vehicle industry law was deliberately manipulated by the president, who issued a modification of the law in which the executive was given discretionary power to permit new vehicle models. The decree was published the next day (12 September) but it was backdated to 9 September to make it coincide with the announcement of the Pegaso decision.[20]

While this modification entitled the government to introduce new vehicle models, its subsequent signing of Decision 120 legally prohibited it from doing so. The modification of the national law could thus apply only to the Pegaso selection made on 9 September, four days before the government signed Decision 120. Yet on 16 September the Ministerio de Fomento issued an oficio which permitted the local production of the Renault R-30. FAVENPA sent a letter informing Minister Alvarez Domínguez that this move represented a violation of policy. The minister did not reply.

This set of events highlighted what the private sector called the growing "juridical insecurity" (*inseguridad jurídica*) characterizing this period. The government's disregard of the rules of the game underlined the private sector's collective weakness and divided it by confirming the benefits of seeking privileged individual access to the executive. Despite the ideological commitment to "concerted planning," relations between the private sector and the state centered around the practice of negotiating individual exceptions and securing particularistic privileges.

The Técnicos of the Ministerio de Fomento: *Politics vs. Expertise*
The transnational automobile corporations contributed to this situation by using their influence to gain state favor. They slowly moved from simply opposing the policy to explicitly proposing alternatives to it. Ford sought to negotiate directly with the president. At this time, Henry Ford II came to Venezuela and offered both to expand local investments and to establish an aluminum wheel-ring factory that would produce parts for export (*El Universal,* 18 September 1977). According to informed sources, both Ford and GM offered, if they won the bids to manufacture auto engines, to lobby the U.S. Congress to include Venezuela and Ecuador in the preferential trade system of the U.S. Foreign Trade Law. Venezuela's exclusion from this law affected a few key sectors, such as the petrochemicals industry.

While the private sector was concerned about the growing inseguridad

---

20. Confidential interviews. See "Resolución no. 4970, 9 de septiembre de 1977," *Gaceta Oficial,* 12 September 1977.

jurídica, the government's técnicos were increasingly upset by their own lack of influence in the decision-making process. In an informal exchange with a minister, one of them complained that their opinions were not taken into account. The minister quickly retorted: "Look my friend, you are here to give us your technical reports, not to make decisions." He then explained, "If decisions were made on the basis of technical criteria alone, there would be no need for ministers" (confidential interview 1978). This position, of course, was in itself reasonable. But reasons of state could hardly conceal the ties of complicity that joined politicians and businessmen in a network woven in order to advance private interests.

With great frequency this web of complicity also embraced the government técnicos. "In all of Latin America," said Max Nolff, an experienced international planning consultant, "only ministers who have técnicos whom they completely trust can make decisions on the basis of technical recommendations" (interview 1978). A top official from the automobile division of the Ministerio de Fomento expressed a similar view. "Look," he said, "Carlos Andrés Pérez's erratic style is his way of protecting himself from people he cannot trust. He constantly changes plans to make himself unpredictable." Then he added: "People might call him 'Locovén,' but he must rule like a madman in order to establish his power over those who surround him." [21] Arbitrariness and unpredictability at the highest level were thus seen as defense strategies against unreliable politicians and advisors.

In this case, however, it was not clear whether the president was using his power to advance the automotive policy or to pursue objectives which were alien to it. This was a period when the transnationals were exerting intense pressure on the state. The same companies that had initially shown little interest in investing in Venezuela were now proposing grand schemes and using their power to influence the course of events. Everyone watched everyone else's moves.

These pressures were increasingly felt inside the Ministerio de Fomento. The same técnico who acknowledged that there was a logic to President Pérez's apparent arbitrariness confided that AD was trying to set up a trap to justify removing him from his own job. Not a member of AD himself, he had kept his job because of his honesty and technical competence. The slightest show of wrongdoing could justify his replacement. He explained

---

21. *Locovén* is a play on words: *loco* means crazy, and *ven* is a suffix that stands for Venezuela and was commonly used in the names of state companies (for example, Petroven). Confidential interview 1978.

that recently the wife of a prominent AD leader asked him to grant her a permit to import a car. He refused. Just after she left, his boss (an AD leader) dropped by his office and told him, "Look, denying her that car can cost you your job." But his interpretation was that the whole event had been set up to get rid of him. "If I grant her the permit to import the car," he said, "they would have an excuse to fire me and put an adeco in here who would do what they want, now that a number of key decisions involving millions and millions are going to be taken" (confidential interview 1978).

The continuity of the automotive industry technical staff of the Ministerio de Fomento, as well as its relative political insulation throughout several administrations, was exceptional for Venezuela. This tradition began in the early sixties. At that time, Hugo Pisani, a COPEI sympathizer, was in charge of the Automotive Department of the Ministerio de Fomento. When Leonardo Montiel Ortega, a URD leader, was named director of industries of this ministry, it was expected that Pisani would be fired. Instead, Montiel Ortega, against pressure from his own party, ratified the heads of departments in their jobs. According to Pisani, "Montiel Ortega started a tradition. Ever since, we all have kept our jobs because of our honesty" (interview 1977). When Pisani decided to start his own private practice, he was asked to suggest a person to succeed him. His choice, Mariano Crespo, another COPEI sympathizer, was given the job. In turn, when Mariano Crespo also decided to join the private sector, he too was asked to propose his replacement. His candidate, Roberto Madero, was a former member of the Communist Party and had obtained his engineering degree in Czechoslovakia. Madero was appointed as well.

All of these técnicos agreed that they obtained and kept their jobs because of a combination of experience, technical knowledge, and honesty. "The world of the automobile industry in Venezuela is a small world," said Pisani. "If one does anything improper, everyone would immediately know about it" (interview 1977). But it was also an intricate world. Unlike other industrial sectors, where a few enterprises control production, in the automobile sector there is a certain degree of complexity and competition. "It came to be that both the ruling parties and private companies preferred to have people like us in the ministry," explained Mariano Crespo. "At least they all knew what to expect from us" (interview 1977).

The Ministerio de Fomento, however, was understaffed and underequipped, and its staff was underpaid. During the oil boom, with the abundance of government income it brought, the same people who were responsible for the normal workings of the ministry had to manage the negotiation of the new vehicle industry bids. The government made little provision to enable the ministry staff to evaluate the projects on the basis of the profound changes that were occurring in the structure of the world automobile industry or in the domestic economy. Its staff was overburdened and had to rely largely on the interested vehicle companies themselves for information concerning the future direction of the international vehicle industry. Nor was it equipped to monitor and evaluate adequately the compliance of the parts manufacturers with the new local-content regulations, on whose success the future goals of major-component manufacture depended. At one point FAVENPA, at the suggestion of the SIVENSA interests represented within it, even offered to help the ministry set up a computer system to enable it to keep up-to-date information on the automobile sector.

Thus while they were allowed a certain stability and protection from partisan pressures on their jobs, and their decisions had an effect on the routine operations of the vehicle companies, técnicos had limited power to formulate or implement effectively vehicle industry policy. What was construed as executive respect for their technological expertise was a means for developing a technical discourse and set of administrative practices which served to buffer and legitimize the dominant political party's efforts to articulate political and economic interests.[22]

Politics in Command: New Decisions
There were also direct means of exercising political control over the technical dimension of policy making. Political parties controlled decisions through the top positions in the Ministerio de Fomento (the minister, the director of industry, and the director of commerce). These positions were held by individuals loyal to the ruling party, although they did not have to be party members. The crucial conditions were that they give priority to political considerations and support the president. In addition, all major economic decisions were discussed and taken by the *gabinete económico* (a subgroup of the cabinet composed of the ministers involved in economic affairs and the president). At this high level the ruling party, through the leaders of its various factions, and the private sector's elite, through trusted politicians or direct representatives, could have final say over policy decisions.

Yet the above-mentioned decisions concerning Pegaso and Renault were made outside these channels. Unlike the previous decisions, the Pegaso se-

---

22. Dinkelspiel comes to the same conclusion on the basis of his insightful discussion of the Venezuelan Guayana Corporation (CVG) (1967).

lection was made by the president. The inclusion of Renault in the new engine bid was also taken without consulting with the gabinete económico. There was, thus, growing concern that major decisions would be made unilaterally. Pressures on the technical staff of the Ministerio de Fomento were interpreted as a sign of growing pressure to circumvent the normal channels of decision making and to privatize the process to a significant degree. The very importance of the new projects made this prospect very disturbing. At stake were multimillion-dollar ventures involving not only the Venezuelan but the Andean market. Henry Ford's offer to President Pérez to produce in Venezuela aluminum wheels for export raised serious concern over the future of the automotive policy.

Rhetoric and Politics: Conflict within the Triple Alliance
The extent and the expression of this concern over a possible redefinition of the automotive policy is suggested by a discussion that took place during a meeting in November 1977 organized by the Consejo Venezolano de Industria (the Venezuelan Council of Industry, the top private association of industrialists) to evaluate Decision 120; it was attended by government officials, private-sector leaders, and businessmen. The day of formal discussions was followed by a cocktail party. Although high-level political figures were present, businessmen especially gathered around Roberto Madero, the head of the automotive section of the Ministerio de Fomento (Dirección General de Materiales y Equipos de Transporte). This social occasion gave them the opportunity to talk to him informally, on their own terrain, about problems relating to government regulations and decisions. While the mood was cordial, they maintained a careful distance, which contrasted with the relaxed gossip which prevailed in conversations among themselves and with many political leaders.

The atmosphere became charged when Henrique Machado Zuloaga, a powerful local industrialist and director of the SIVENSA group, approached Madero and expressed his objections to the Ford project. He argued that exporting aluminum wheels would seriously undermine local parts producers; Ford would be able to reduce its purchase of parts from domestic manufacturers equal to the value of the aluminum wheel rings it produced and exported (up to 20 percent of its automobile local content could be deducted in this way). Machado Zuloaga insisted, as bystanders listened attentively, that the export of these rings was the equivalent to the export of Venezuela's cheap electrical energy and bauxite: little labor was used in simply stamping out wheel rings. Through this project Venezuela would continue to be a raw-materials exporter with an industrial guise. Finally, to make his argument irrefutable to the government's representative, Machado Zuloaga invoked a central tenet of the doctrine of state-led industrialization: the state serves the national interest by promoting local industry.

> The reason for the automotive policy is, has been, and should continue to be, the industrialization of Venezuela. The policy is intended to develop local industry, to expand auto parts producers. But if Ford exports these wheels our local industry will be undermined. If what we want is to export value, then the best deal we can strike is to export the gasoline that is inside the gas tank of a car.

Madero listened carefully. Machado Zuloaga had framed his particular criticism within the dominant nationalist code which Madero himself promoted. They both knew as well—without needing to make it explicit—that Henrique Machado's firm RUDEVECA, which produced steel wheels, would be adversely affected by Ford's planned project. Madero's careful response addressed the technical aspects of the issue. He argued that the wheel factory would not lead to a reduction of local-content incorporation, for once a given part is recognized as part of local content, it cannot be disincorporated. Although Ford's wheel factory might inhibit further investments in local parts, Ford needed to find means to maintain its profits. Finally, if necessary, auto parts producers could sell their parts to other assemblers.

In reply, Machado Zuloaga argued that the decision to approve the aluminum wheel plant was important not only because it would reduce Ford's purchase of RUDEVECA's wheel rings but also because it would set a negative example for other assemblers. The government's acceptance of profitability to justify the plant contradicted its own policy goals. If profits were the decisive issue, he argued, then he would present to the ministry a profitable project which not develop national industrial capacity.

> I have not done this before because I know that were I to do it, you would kick me out of your office, for you would not want me to mock you. But now I will do it. I will present a project to produce and export steel sheets with a few holes and screws in them. This project will give you an argument that you can use to object to the Ford plan. You could say that just as the Machado plan was rejected, the Ford project must be rejected.

This time Madero listened without reply. His silence suggested that he agreed with Machado's argument. Instead, he agreed to discuss the issue per-

Table 8
Production of vehicles in Venezuela, 1975–78

Firm	1975				1978			
	Passenger	Utility	Commer-cial	TOTAL	Passenger	Utility	Commer-cial	TOTAL
GM	19,797		9,906	29,703	28,029		12,226	40,255
Ford	25,270		16,491	41,761	39,881		23,916	63,797
Chrysler	28,772		7,820	36,592	19,626		16,438	36,064
AMC	1,259	4,537		5,796		6,037		6,037
FIAT	2,117		315	2,432	4,200		738	4,938
Renault	5,978			5,978	6,564			6,564
VW	6,158		540	6,698	5,002			5,002
Mercedes-Benz	1,607		410	2,017	165		21	186
Toyota		5,602		5,602		9,241		9,241
Nissan		3,765		3,765		6,871		6,871
Mack			801	801			1,606	1,606
Total of above firms	90,958	13,904	36,283	141,145	103,467	22,149	54,945	180,561
All 15 firms[a]	92,079	14,422	37,414	143,915	103,467	22,802	56,409	182,678

SOURCE: Coronil and Skurski 1982: 73, based on annual reports of CIVA and statistical reports of the Ministry of Development.

[a] Includes production of the following brands: Bluebird, Reo, Land Rover, Hillman, and International Harvester.

sonally with him in the future. The conversation then moved to other problems. Henrique Machado expressed his concern about the fact although Venezuela produced axles (his own factory, DANAVEN, was the major local producer), axles were not recognized by the other Andean nations as part of the drivetrain. "Venezuela might end up competing against cheaper axles imported through these nations." Madero assured him that this would not occur.

During the oil boom there had been a great increase in imported automobiles, which greatly upset auto parts producers. Industrialist Machado referred critically to the importation of four thousand Chevrolet Caprice units in 1976. Government official Madero responded, "It does not matter if a few wealthy Venezuelans spent eighty-five thousand bolívares [about $19 thousand]) to buy an imported Caprice." In support of Machado, a top manager of SIVENSA's auto parts subgroup PROCESA, José Bisogno, argued that four thousand cars represented sixteen thousand wheels, one month of RUDEVECA's production. Madero responded, "So your production has gone down lately?" Bisogno replied, "No, but it has not gone up. This situation is serious. These imports are the same as saying that during one month five hundred workers will do nothing." Bisogno also told Madero, "You must know that people joined the Association of Agriculturalists just to be able to import fancy four-wheel drive cars, which they drove proudly around Caracas, not on farms, as intended by the government." At this point Gerald Greenwald, the president of Ford in Venezuela, joined the conversation. Suddenly in this small group representatives of the three major social forces that together were shaping at this time the automobile policy converged: the state, local capital, and transnational corporations.

Roberto Madero was a self-made government functionary with no political affiliations. He had been a member of the Communist Youth during the tumultuous sixties at his high school in Caracas, Liceo Andrés Bello high school. Through his connections with the Communist Party, he obtained a scholarship to study engineering in Czechoslovakia. Upon his return, he worked in the Ministerio de Fomento, where he had been the head of the automobile sector since his predecessor, Mariano Crespo, left in 1973. He had not become an anticommunist like some of his former comrades but had become very critical of the Communist Party's strategy and cynical about Venezuelan politics. He remained committed, however, to contributing to Venezuela's development and felt that he could do more for the country working within the state than against it. He had managed to establish a position for himself as a responsible and honest functionary but did not feel at home among entrepreneurs. He was more comfortable among others who had also struggled within the cracks of the system. His was not a world of affluence or power, as it was for many of those whom he met at work. From a middle-class family of modest means, he seemed in appearance and style to be the typical Caracas *criollo*—outgoing, quick-witted, and proud. Less typically, he was not quite willing to seek the approval or to adopt the style of the rich and powerful.

Henrique Machado Zuloaga was also an engineer. He belonged to a major economic group and to a distinguished Caracas family of the traditional social elite whose members historically occupied important positions in Venezuela's economic and cultural world. His older brother, Oscar Machado Zuloaga, had been president of FEDECAMARAS, the leading private business association, and headed the Electricidad de Caracas, the largest private company in Venezuela. Henrique Machado had become the leader of the automobile subgroup (PROCESA) of the SIVENSA group, which had experienced significant growth under his leadership. He seemed the embodiment of the ideal local capitalist who uses his privileged education, family fortune, and name to build the productive structures of the economy. He was a competent entrepreneur who had been president of FAVENPA, but

Left: Roberto Madero, director of the automotive division of the Ministry of Development. (Revista Automotriz.) *Right:* Henrique Machado Zuloaga, director of the Grupo SIVENSA. (Archivo El Nacional.)

generally preferred to remain behind the scenes. Unpretentious, almost retiring, in some respects he was typical of the traditional sector of the Caracas elite—elegant without being flashy, polite but a bit distant.

Gerald Greenwald was the president of Ford's subsidiary in Venezuela as well as the trusted representative of Lee Iacocca (the head of Ford Company) during this critical period. (When Iacocca became president of Chrysler some years later he made Greenwald his right-hand man); at this writing, Greenwald is chairman of United Airlines. After he arrived in the country, he established a reputation as an able and personable executive at a time when Ford was in trouble in Venezuela. The company's original opposition to the automobile policy, aggravated by its contemptuous treatment of functionaries and political leaders, had alienated the government. In contrast, Greenwald behaved in a respectful and friendly fashion, entertaining Venezuelan leaders frequently in his home, in an apparent effort to repair the damage. A self-confident, suave executive, he knew how to be cautious in public and to work behind the scenes.

When Greenwald joined the group, the conversation of necessity changed. He brought up the problem of the escalating cost of automobiles

Gerald Greenwald (center), president of Ford of Venezuela, at a reception
for automotive executives at his home in Caracas. (Archivo El Nacional.)

in Venezuela. He argued that the automotive policy would necessarily lead
to intolerable increases in the price of parts and automobiles. Thus, the government should take measures to avoid increasing production costs or else
allow market prices to reflect cost increases (that is, to eliminate price controls). Thus, Greenwald's proposition in effect was that Venezuela should
exploit its comparative advantage and not undertake production under un-
favorable conditions. He expressed this idea cautiously. "Venezuela is a rich
country. It should use its resources wisely so as to produce only under favorable conditions, and therefore at reasonable prices." Clearly, this line of argument favored the new aluminum plant proposed by Ford. Madero (who
had earlier appeared to defend Ford's project) now argued:

> The government takes into account not just the short-term interests of firms
> and consumers, but the long-term interests of the nation. If the state promotes
> the automotive industry, it is because it is concerned with the development
> of the country as a whole. If you know how to produce an automobile en-
> gine, then you also know how to produce a stationary engine for agriculture,
> mining, or the construction industry. We want to expand employment and
> achieve a degree of technological independence. What good is it for us to have

inexpensive cars if there is no knowledge of how to produce them and no jobs for people? For us, the automotive industry is a means, not an end.

As Madero talked and was met with approval by Machado Zuloaga, Gerald Greenwald repeatedly interrupted him, saying, "Yes, you might be right, but I would like to know what your wife will think when she buys a car." Madero chose not to respond to these interruptions, but a member of his staff told Greenwald, "You are right, the car will be expensive, but their children will have jobs." The conversation, which initially had set local capitalists against Madero as a representative of the Venezuelan state, ended by uniting all of them against Greenwald as a representative of foreign capital. Suddenly everyone present joined Machado Zuloaga, Bisogno, and Madero against Greenwald. In this intense, spontaneous exchange the appeal to nationalist development goals had momentarily submerged divisions between government and industrialists, when the critique of those goals was offered by the foreign capitalist—despite his position as intimate participant in the local economic system.

The conversation turned then into a more technical debate. Greenwald, refusing to deal with the nationalist argument, insisted on the issue of prices at the level of cost-benefit for consumers and enterprises. Madero argued that automobile prices in Venezuela depended on two factors: local-content level and production volume. By articulating these two factors, the government could encourage economic growth without burdening excessively the consumer or the auto companies.

Greenwald disagreed. He argued that the Venezuelan market was just too small to be efficient. "For example, the handles of Ford cars are all the same, and we produce four million similar handles." Madero warned, "If you cannot produce handles cheaply here, then we'll make all the car companies use the same handles." He added, "If the auto manufacturers want to stay here, you will have to make agreements among yourselves to use common parts." Santiago González, a small local entrepreneur who produced clutches, agreed with Madero. "The axles produced by DANA and other companies are the same." As if to draw to an end this discussion, Madero said:

> Look, every time I go to Detroit I hear the same story about our market being too small. You are used to different dimensions. You don't understand that your market does not have to be the universal standard. Production can be structured differently. The equipment can be different. Instead of a six-ton

press we can use a two-ton press. Instead of six transfers to make axles, we might need only one.

The conversation remained friendly. Smiling, Greenwald kept saying that Madero could be right, but that he wanted to know what Madero's wife would think when she had to buy a car made in Venezuela. As it became clear that he was making no headway, Greenwald shifted the discussion once more. He brought up the issue of technology. "Who will build the industry? You don't have trained personnel." Madero's answer came quickly. "It does not matter that we don't have trained personnel. We will import the personnel."

In response, Greenwald asked, "Why does a country develop, to benefit whom?" Madero answered, "To benefit the country, everyone who lives in the country." Greenwald then argued that "foreign employees don't belong to the country, they come and go back, and reap the benefits of their work." Madero replied that all those who come to the country and contribute to the nation's development should receive a reward for their work. "But the results of their work will remain in the country, and the collectivity will benefit." Greenwald objected. "So it will be a situation in which the foreigners will develop the country." At this point all the Venezuelans, clearly bothered by the implication of Greenwald's remark, spoke in one voice. "The U.S. did the same, it is the melting pot, Fermi, Einstein, von Braun." Then Bisogno said, "Yes, we will be like the U.S. in 1928." Facing this strong consensus, Greenwald conceded. "Yes, immigrants contributed a great deal to the development of the U.S."

Throughout this discussion, the Venezuelans agreed that industrial activity should not be evaluated exclusively in terms of the immediate benefits it would bring to the enterprise, to its workers, or to consumers. As Henrique Machado kept emphasizing, the proper yardstick to assess any policy was the contribution that it would bring to the development of the nation as a whole. Madero, sensing that Machado was implicitly reinforcing his initial argument against the Ford wheel project, broke the consensus that had been created in the discussion with Greenwald. "Yes, but it is necessary also to take into account the profits of the enterprise. Otherwise we won't get enough investments, and the nation will be harmed as well." As Madero left, a staff coworker and old friend told him, "Look Roberto, you are too old to be playing the role of the devil's advocate. What use is there for you to argue things that you don't believe in?"

This informal exchange, occurring in November 1977, revealed more than the terms and the form of informal public discussion concerning development policy and economic activity between representatives of state and capital. It also showed a basic contradiction undermining the automotive policy and it prefigured the direction of its eventual modification.

THE MOTORS OF POWER

Minister Alvarez Domínguez informed a surprised public on 28 June 1978 that Renault and GM had been selected to make the six-cylinder engines. Ford had been excluded, he explained, because its aluminum engine was an unproved prototype that would not be ready for manufacture until 1981. While Renault's engine lacked the power to be used in the light truck as required, its merits had been proven during two years of commercial use in Europe. Furthermore, Chrysler had withdrawn from the bidding (due to the home company's financial cutbacks) but had stated in writing its willingness to mount Renault's engines in its cars if Renault won the bid. Should this occur, Venezuela might gain access to Chrysler's international markets for its engine exports.

There were also political considerations involved in this major policy upset. The semiofficial explanation emphasized the president's desire to "diversify the national origins of Venezuela's technology suppliers, to increase the country's bargaining power with the TNCs, and to counter its dependence on U.S. corporations" (Luis Alvarez Domínguez, quoted in the *Daily Journal,* 19 October 1978). The government had learned that its bargaining power was limited in relation to strong foreign companies whose local presence rooted them socially and connected them politically.

By selecting Renault, the government sought to increase its bargaining power. From the outset Ford and GM had used their power to disrupt and stall the negotiations. Since Ford, the most powerful and recalcitrant company, was unwilling to negotiate on the government's terms, the administration took steps to exclude it, creating competition instead by supporting a European company with little power within the country. Diversification of technology sources would mean diversification of the government's local allies and the potential expansion of the executive's autonomy. France reportedly offered the government military technology along with the Renault engine. The unexpected presence of the defense minister at a gabinete económico meeting at that time supports this suggestion. By contrast, Ford's representative reportedly gave an ultimatum to Minister Alvarez Domínguez: either accept Ford's engine bid or Ford will leave the country. But

A General Motors V-6 engine installed in a Ford truck to demonstrate the feasibility of "hybrid" vehicles for national production and export, at an exhibit in a Caracas hotel, August/September 1978. (Revista Automotriz.)

declining support for the administration and growing financial difficulties had reduced the executive's power to act decisively. Ford organized a campaign to halt the engine decision and to escalate the policy conflict into a motors war. Few foreign companies in other sectors could have attempted to mount such a public attack. However, the vehicle industry lends itself to the integration of foreign manufacturers into the local business community, and vehicle marketing creates consumer loyalty to the producing companies.

Ford had many resources: its weight in the economy, its political connections, its public image as a good corporate citizen, and its international power and prestige. Yet Ford's power alone could not assure success. There occurred a convergence between the opposition to the engine decision led by Ford in the private sector and the opposition to the Pérez administration led by members of AD's old guard. Tensions between AD and the president were heightened by the Renault selection procedure. Pérez had acted independently, with the minister of development as his main ally, and had failed to consult the gabinete económico. The AD leadership moved to challenge the Pérez administration in the presidential election of 1978. As the electoral consequences of poor administration and widespread corruption were recognized, AD chose a Betancourt-supported candidate, Luis Piñerúa, who promised to bring honesty to the public administration (*el hombre correcto,* or the honorable man, became his campaign slogan). A magazine article recognized that the conflict was not "over the power of the motors, but over the motors of power" (*Zeta,* 15 August 1978). Ford bluntly denied in the press that the government had made an engine "selection," claiming it was a "preselection." Minister Alvarez Domínguez replied publicly that the engine selection was definitive (*El Universal,* 11 July 1978).

Ford mobilized domestic support and simultaneously organized pressure on the Andean Pact negotiations. It had already been selected to produce Ecuador's light truck, which was to use a six-cylinder engine from Venezuela. It now notified Ecuador's government that it refused to use the GM engine because it was not powerful enough and because Ford's protection of its international name precluded such an arrangement. Ford's circle of pressure was complete. President Pérez, on seeing the Andean Pact agreement in jeopardy, suspended the engine decision without public notice on 12 July and sent técnicos from the Ministerio de Fomento and the Foreign Commerce Institute to Quito. In meetings held at the end of July, Venezuela and Ecuador established revised conditions for the bids and asked Ford and GM to improve their offers in a new round. They added the following requirements: transmissions were to be manufactured for export outside the Andean Pact (one hundred thousand automatic transmissions per year from Venezuela, seventy-five thousand manual transmissions per year from Ecuador); royalty payments for engine plant technology were to be eliminated; and an automobile training center for workers was to be established (*El Universal,* 22 August 1978). This was an important innovation in Andean Pact negotiations: two countries had agreed on common terms for a bid and negotiated jointly with the TNCs.

As local criticism mounted, the president unexpectedly removed his ally, Minister of Development Alvarez Domínguez, from the position of chief negotiator in the auto program and replaced him with the president of the Foreign Commerce Institute, Reinaldo Figueredo Planchart. Figueredo Planchart, who had become a close friend of the president, was of upper-class origins and from a family that had been involved in automobile dealerships. Alvarez Domínguez had risen to high positions because of his technical competence and political skills. As a university student he had been a leader of the Communist Party, but upon graduating as an engineer he changed political affiliations and joined the private sector. President Pérez also named Figueredo director of a new interministerial commission created to examine the auto policy. This surprise move occurred while Alvarez Domínguez was in Europe (31 July to 6 August).

The abrupt shift of authority to the Foreign Commerce Institute (ICE) triggered a brief state agency battle within the "motors wars." Development Minister Alvarez Domínguez, stunned at being undercut by the president, attempted to reassert his authority. The psychological intensity of this battle had taken its toll. After a public presentation, Alvarez Domínguez collapsed and was taken to a hospital. The development minister had generally been more accessible to private-sector influence than ICE, but during the Pérez administration ICE's Figueredo Planchart acted as a direct representative of President Pérez, and Ford found more support from ICE's president. There was no disagreement on technical grounds between the técnicos of the two agencies, who shared the auto policy's assumptions and goals. However, Domínguez would not allow his ministerial representatives to sign the new bid terms presented to the companies in Quito on 16 August under the direction of ICE's Figueredo, and he made public accusations that the TNCs were using "abusive pressures" to subvert the state's programs (*El Universal,* 19 August 1978). Insisting that he was Venezuela's sole legal nego-tiator, Alvarez Domínguez privately submitted his resignation to the president. Instead of accepting it, the president restored him to his former position in time to receive the new bids on 30 August. Figueredo of ICE now submitted his resignation, which was not accepted, and the conflict came to an end.

During this period the motors war resembled a popularity contest. The corporations sought to broaden their base of support through articles and full-page advertisements in the press. Ford's enormous publicity campaign, sponsored by its local dealers association, stressed Ford's importance in the domestic market and the advanced design of its engine. A group of local journalists was invited to tour Ford's North American facilities during the company's August celebrations of its fiftieth anniversary, and they recipro-cated with laudatory articles in the local press.

Ford's central role in the local ruling alliance and its strong links with domestic financial and banking institutions were stressed to a more select audience. Nelson Rockefeller, long influential in Venezuelan politics, voiced emphatic support for Ford at a luncheon attended by national leaders (in-cluding Rómulo Betancourt) offered him by Eugenio Mendoza, on the occasion of Rockefeller's seventieth birthday (confidential interviews).[23] GM's campaign stressed the long history of GM's operations in the country, its aid to parts manufacturers, and the proven quality and versatility of its engine. The company tried to communicate that as a good corporate citizen it respected the Venezuelan government. A common theme during this campaign was that these engines would contribute to modernizing Venezuela and propelling it toward "the future." The engines depicted in the ads emphasized the transformative capacity of technology. Venezuela's future was construed as depending on which engine was chosen.

The Final Selection: Winners without Losers
In October 1978 the government announced that GM was the victor over Ford. GM had agreed to manufacture an additional 1.2 million brake drums for export per year in Venezuela and 150 thousand axles for export per year in Ecuador. By improving its offer, GM had not only won the engine bid but also the right to manufacture the truck that Ecuador had previously assigned to Ford. Minister Alvarez Domínguez was pleased. He triumphantly announced that henceforth the Andean Pact nations would improve their bargaining power by "setting the multinational concerns against each other. . . . While they fight for the spoils, we will sit back and reap the benefits" (*Daily Journal,* 19 October 1978). Given this position, the government announced a surprising new decision. For the second six-cylinder engine selection, Ford and Renault would compete ("fight for the spoils") in another round of bilateral bidding with Venezuela and Bolivia, the co-producer of the B1.1 truck.

Although Ford had again lost, it was given yet another chance. Ford's aggressive stance had been effective. Now Ford expanded its plant in the city of Valencia to a capacity of four hundred units per day, which made it the largest U.S. auto plant in South America. By making this move, the company made obvious its intention to stay. Ford's recovery in the bidding was related to new shifts within the international automotive industry. In the summer of 1978 Chrysler withdrew from Europe, selling the controlling interest in its subsidiaries to Renault's main competitor, Peugeot-Citroen, and prepared to sell all but its Mexican installation in Latin America. Once GM won the six-cylinder engine bid, it purchased Chrysler's Venezuelan and Colombian

23. Eugenio Mendoza had been development minister under General Medina in 1942, president of the Iron Syndicate during General Pérez Jiménez's rule, and member of the ruling junta that overthrew Pérez Jiménez in 1958. As the leader of the Mendoza Group, Mendoza was a high-profile and public-minded industrialist.

operations. This gave it a strong base within the Andean Pact and compensated for the sale of its unprofitable Argentinean subsidiary. Consequently Renault could no longer rely on an accord with Chrysler to improve its position in the Venezuelan bid, changing the alignment of corporate interests that supported the Renault selection in June. Renault's regional position was weakened, GM's was strengthened, and Ford's prospects were greatly improved.

The new round of bidding marked the decline of the motors war. It became clear that the government was not going to make a final decision at this time. Although negotiations were based on the premise of national sovereignty, the internationally based vehicle manufacturers decision-making power continually subjected the negotiations to changes over which the locally based state had no control. Caught up in an intense campaign for the December election and involved in a serious political scandal (the "Carmona case," analyzed in a later chapter), the administration was to make no further politically costly decisions. The vehicle companies also preferred to delay the decision until after the election, both because their relations with the Pérez administration had been conflictual, and because they hoped the new government would change the selections of the policy itself. As a journalist noted:

> The prime actor in this scenario is still the Venezuelan government, and due to its past unpredictability in matters relating to the Andean automotive development program, no one is willing to commit himself to a definite forecast on the final outcome . . . Local and international businessmen still remember the Pegaso affair with a bad taste, and are all too aware that the government will ignore its own game rules if the "national interest" makes such violations advisable (*Daily Journal,* 19 October 1978).

The COPEI Presidency: The Engines of Progress Break Down

The election of the Christian Democratic candidate, Luis Herrera Campíns in December 1978 (with 46.6 percent of the vote to AD's 43.3 percent) brought a reevaluation of Pérez's programs, a policy of economic slowdown, and the timid promotion of a free-market economic doctrine. The transition to a new government headed by a leader of an opposition party made it easier to accept that the past—the boom period—was over. As Luis Herrera Campíns announced in his inaugural speech, he inherited a "mortgaged country." This change in economic and political conditions helped to crystallize a redefinition of the automotive policy. Reflecting the downturn of the economy, local vehicle production dropped 13.6 percent in 1979 and 1.8 percent in 1980. In this context, the government began to modify the auto policy along the lines that the TNCs had long proposed. It first freed itself from the legal and political commitments created by the previous government, suspending in April 1980 the engine selections made under Pérez and promising to make new ones by the end of the year. This suspension did not apply to the awards covered by international coproduction agreements, that is, those made with GM.

For reasons of fuel economy, the production of eight-cylinder automobiles was eliminated entirely. This gave Ford and GM the chance to produce four-cylinder autos and therefore the right to bid for the small engine which had been awarded to Fiat. However, Fiat was in violation of its two signed contracts, for it had not begun construction on either within the required period. Moreover, given the change of administration it had lost its privileged influence over the executive. Thus, the government invited new companies, GM and Cummins, to bid for the diesel engines. Mack had challenged the legal claim of Pegaso to the diesel engine and had constructed an assembly plant for diesel engines to export outside the Andean region, hoping eventually to produce for the Andean market if it won its legal claim.

As a result of these delays, local investment in the production of drivetrain parts had necessarily halted. A significant challenge to the automotive program occurred in this context. The terminal firms (notably GM) now attacked the program's traditional prohibition on vertical integration by seeking equity participation in existing firms to expand their production for export. As part of its new global productive strategy, GM wanted to make Venezuela the site for the production of certain products (such as air conditioners and automatic starters). In August 1980, significant policy changes were made. Price raises for regulated cars were granted, and price controls were to be removed by October 1981, when a two-tiered tariff system would instead regulate prices. As an interim measure intended to reduce consumer opposition to higher prices, the government allowed the assemblers to import fifteen thousand small, low-priced "popular cars" until October 1981. Since these cars were different from the models produced in Venezuela, this measure violated the Andean Pact's Sectoral Program. The mandatory production of regulated cars was removed. The 3 percent annual increase in local content was suspended for 1981 and lowered to 1 percent annually until 1985.

These measures, which affected consumers directly, received considerable press coverage. The most significant policy change, however, went basically unnoticed. The automobile policy's maximum local content for vehicles was reduced from 90 percent to 75 percent. This measure officially recognized the withdrawal of support by all sectors from the goal of national industry autonomy. The traditional goal of manufacturing a "Venezuelan car," so dramatically revitalized during the boom years, thus came to a quiet end. A year later, in August 1981, these changes were extended. The terminal sector could now fulfill 30 percent of its local content goals with parts exports until 1983 (according to the 1975 Automotive Law this allowance was to be eliminated by 1980), and the terminal sector's obligatory compensation of imports with exports of equal value was postponed indefinitely. As a result of these measures, the export of parts would occur at the expense of local parts corporations and, thus, of the diversification of auto parts production.

These changes coincided with the TNCs' efforts to make the Andean Pact nations adapt their policies to their own corporate global strategies. Ford even suggested in its new engine bid that the Andean countries only assemble vehicles and engines until their market volume justified actual production. In the interim, Ford argued, they could compensate by exporting auto parts from the region, such as aluminum wheels from Venezuela (*Número,* 15 February 1981).

The private sector did not oppose these changes, which meant a shift in investment strategies—not the end of profitable ventures but a change in profit opportunities. Clearly, commercial interests were now favored. But with this change industrial investments could now take place along less complicated lines: auto parts could be produced for export, often in association with transnational corporations. It is revealing of the difference of interests that lay behind the parts manufacturers' public policy that Gastón Texier, the new president of FAVENPA, regarded this reorientation favorably. The interests of his own factory lay in the new direction taken by the automobile policy, since it opened up the possibility that his factory could also export its products through the TNCs. Finally, the minister of development recommended the postponement of the gasoline engine decision until 1984. The justification for this delay was given in the same terms put forth before by the transnational corporations. Additional time would allow the government to evaluate the technological changes in the international auto industry. In the end, Venezuela would be the winner. But in fact, the government and the private sector had come to accept, at least for the time being, Venezuela's continued role as an importer of engines. With the "engines of progress" vanishing into a distant future, belief in progress itself receded. Concealing the chasm opened by this failure, a transparently ideological rhetoric of development replaced the illusions of development of more affluent days.

CONCLUSIONS

Export Promotion versus Import Substitution

Corporate resistance to the implementation of Venezuela's auto industry policy resulted from the increasingly global strategies of the automakers. The difficult goal of world sourcing and marketing for world cars required that national protectionist barriers be minimized, production facilities be integrated internationally, and natural resources be accessible—hence the TNCs' heightened concern with the specifics of national auto policies.

In the course of the engine negotiations, the TNCs argued for an alternative policy that would build on Venezuela's comparative advantages and on the local industry's potential participation in the global production of vehicles. In their view, the country's political stability and economic strength within the Andean Pact and the Caribbean made it an attractive base for foreign capital. Venezuela's wealth in natural resources and its development of steel, aluminum, and the hydroelectric and petrochemical industries made possible the production of energy-intensive inputs that incorporate a high coefficient of inexpensive energy for the production of lighter auto parts for export. Against the auto policy's goal of economic self-reliance and local integration, the TNCs posed the benefits of modern technology and international integration.

Venezuela's local-content rules and the goal of 90 percent local integration became the focus of corporate pressure and the locus of the conflict between import substitution and export promotion policies. According to *Business Week,* "local content requirements that hinder outside sourcing are one of the greatest obstacles facing manufacturers seeking to rationalize their productive facilities." A GM official stated, "Worldwide sourcing is a very, very complicated logistic problem and it's going to get worse . . . as protection-minded countries steadily raise their local percentage (20 November 1978). A GM official highlighted the corporate political response to indigenization. "At General Motors the trend is away from studying macropolitical stability to studying a country's regulatory process and its likely choices. In our business we can face major problems from changes in such things as 'local content' laws. And they can make all the difference between profit and loss" (*Business Week,* 1 December 1980).

Local parts makers, however, were more concerned with the ambiguous and contradictory application of the policy, which made production planning and investment uncertain, than with the analysis of policy strategies. While FAVENPA had supported the new policy, its main demand now was that the government stimulate growth in the parts sector with clear guidelines and respect for the rules of the game. As its executive director stated, "A change of local content to 75 percent would worry the theoreticians of the auto policy, but not the parts producers" (interview with Rodrigo Arcaya; interviews with local industrialists confirmed this view). The association of auto parts producers primarily criticized the government's indecision:

> Three years after the decree of the Auto Policy, its rules and the goals of local parts content have not been complied with, and this is not because the authorities responsible for the policy's implementation are ignorant of the facts. The national executive itself, author of the policy, has altered its spirit by permitting, by means of "resoluciones," the assembly of new models and brands of vehicles in the country . . . To what end was the set of regulations contained in *resoluciones* and decrees created? What is the point of a legal text whose word is not respected? (*NOTIFAVENPA*, June 1978).

In this conflict the terminal firms held that Mexico's growing auto industry exemplified the merits of export promotion, while Argentina's fully integrated, stagnant industry demonstrated the pitfalls of import substitution. The striking similarities, as well as the significant differences, between auto policy development in Mexico and Venezuela reveal why the Mexican example was favored. In both countries the automakers opposed local integration and industry rationalization measures (such as limits on the number of terminal firms and vehicle models) at the outset of policy formation in 1962. This made the industry's fragmentation and external dependence inevitable. Original goals became more difficult to implement as successive negotiations were conditioned by the existing industry structure and the class alliance that sustained it. In Mexico, in response to corporate pressure and balance of payments difficulties, the government agreed to relax both restrictions on vertical integration and the already weak requirements on local content well before the 1977 shift toward export promotion encouraged such measures. In Venezuela, a positive balance of trade facilitated the formulation of stricter local-content rules and restrictions on vertical integration but also permitted chronic delays in the policy's implementation. In each country, the evolution of regulations concerning vertical integration and local-content incorporation allowed for continuity between import substitution as it was implemented and the export promotion strategy offered as a solution to its ills.

Since an export program increases the external control and fragmentation of the local industry (through the dependence it creates on foreign clients' product specifications and demand fluctuations), an outward-oriented growth strategy is easier to pursue if the stage of inward growth has retained the basis for external integration. In Mexico the vehicle industry export program had built on the growing interpenetration of the Mexican and U.S. economies resulting from Mexico's proximity to the United States, supply of cheap labor, diversified industrial structure, and expanding oil industry. In Venezuela, export promotion at this stage was more a means to undermine a protectionist policy and to reduce the separation between the terminal and the parts sectors than a development strategy in itself, since petrodollar recycling continued to define the local industry's internal dynamic and its role in the international industry. In each case, export strategies furthered the international integration of the vehicle industry.

The Venezuelan government's position concerning the revision of the auto policy was largely reactive. Responding to industry changes and corporate pressure, it allowed de facto noncompliance to create conditions for the policy's modification. Minister of Development Alvarez Domínguez had suggested the possibility on 31 January 1978 to the English-language newspaper, the *Daily Journal,* commenting that the policy's goal of 90 percent local integration by 1985 "was not a rigid one, and was subject to the flexibility imposed by the existing conditions affecting the industry and the evaluation of numerous contingent factors."

Alvarez Domínguez subsequently called the 1975 Auto Policy Law an expression of the "optimism" of the boom years of 1974 and 1975. "The objectives of the law, which should have been stipulated as a body of modifiable regulations, became rigid law because at that time we thought we could do everything." He recognized that the legalization of the objectives expressed the government's commitment to the auto policy but felt that "if the automotive industry could no longer be the heart of Venezuela's development, then the government could transplant another heart" (interview 1980). Hector Hurtado, the strongest promoter of the 1962 auto policy and both minister of hacienda and president of the Venezuelan Investment Fund under Pérez, shared this skepticism concerning the policy's aims. "The goal of 90 percent was included in the law because of the enthusiasm of the técnicos: it was not worth arguing about it with them" (interview 1980).

Electoral considerations also contributed to the decline of government support for the auto policy. Alvarez Domínguez later admitted, "Certain economic decisions were not taken because they would have an electoral cost" (interview 1980). A key apostle confided, "Carlos Andrés Pérez is a smart politician. He chose the engines when it was too late to go ahead with the decisions. He was not going to take on the political problem of making expensive cars or of alienating his allies" (confidential interview 1980).

State Power: Capital Accumulation and Social Reproduction
These post hoc justifications highlight two points. First, the Venezuelan state's industrial policies were highly sensitive to the evolving goals of its allies in the dominant alliance. Despite its economic resources, the state's power as policy maker is contingent on actions taken by leading members of the alliance. The tension between the state's monetary abundance and its structural limits creates a tendency for policy goals to be inflated, for policy implementation to be reactive, and for state planners to favor strategies that minimize their risks and preserve existing arrangements. Policy makers cultivated the ability to reproduce the present while claiming the future.

Second, the emerging reorientation of the auto policy reflected an adaptation not only to the reorganization of the international auto industry but also to the new focus of the national development project. Under Pérez, the state publicly maintained its traditional commitment to autonomous development. The promotion of industrial exports was presented as a logical extension of import substitution. However, international support for export promotion as an alternative had found local acceptance and had begun to be assimilated into the rhetoric of nationalism. "The world economic powers have been alluring and deceiving us with import substitution in an attempt to keep us forever as parasites of their system," stated ex-President Pérez privately (interview, September 1980). In fact, the state's promotion of intermediate industries with export potential, along with the rapid expansion of projects resting on external financing, technology, and supplies, consolidated an unstated withdrawal of support from import substitution. As the domiciliated foreign bourgeoisie,[24] the local bourgeoisie, and the state converged to support the goal of national development through export promotion, the auto industry was treated less as a leading sector of the economy than as a processing sector for basic industry outputs. The goal sought was no longer to integrate the vehicle industry and the local bourgeoisie within the nation but to link local and transnational capital within global productive structures.

The evolution of the conflict over alternative development models was constrained by the reinforcement of rent-based growth. The spending spree triggered by the sudden abundance of petrodollars stimulated not only

---

24. By domiciliated foreign bourgeoisie, I mean the sector of foreign capital that becomes rooted socially and politically in the host nation. For the "doctrine of domicile," see Sklar (1975:186).

productive investments but also a tendency toward "retrogression":[25] the strengthening of state-centered commercial and financial nonproductive practices, which consolidated the rentier character of the Venezuelan economy. Oil-financed imports supplied productive units with their means of production, supplemented or replaced locally produced consumer goods, and created profit opportunities that lessened the need to develop labor's productivity. These conditions made for an incoherent pursuit of industrial policy. The government undertook overambitious projects in all areas of the economy, projects that were poorly coordinated and lacked provisions to resolve the conflicting demands they made on resources and manpower. The private sector criticized only the government's increasing control of the economy and its mismanagement of public enterprises, for the latter created demand for private services and products.

The result was a heightened tendency for the private sector to privatize the state and for the state to extend public control over the economy. Given the state's expanded role as a financial and productive agent, private investment became inextricably bound up with political access to executive and state agencies. Local economic groups and foreign corporations intensified their struggle to form alliances with state capital. Consequently the fusion between the economic and political domains, typical of Venezuelan rentier capitalism, became more marked. Competition among capitals was not carried out in a separate economic system, nor was it strictly a struggle over accumulation. Rather, accumulation, the continual transformation of money capital into productive capital, became another element in the intensified struggle over the appropriation of oil rents.

Despite its limitations, the Automotive Policy Law had threatened to alter a basic rule of the game: the implicit accord that the Venezuelan auto industry would remain an assembly-based, limited operation and a commercial outlet for TNC exports. Full vehicle manufacture in Venezuela would disrupt the industry's established commercial and productive structure and commit the corporations to a major investment under terms that would reduce the links between their local and international operations and restrict their behavior concerning ownership, model changes, and standardization. Thus, while they competed to avoid exclusion from the lucrative Venezuelan market, their common interest in preserving the import and assembly character of the local industry allied them in the attempt to subvert the policy. Their collusion underlined the limitations of state power to policy makers.

25. On this concept, see Brenner (1977:41-53).

"The auto transnationals appear to struggle," Carlos Andrés Pérez told me in private, "but in reality there are underlying accords. When we attempted to implement the automotive policy we noticed how the transnationals divided up markets and fields of action and influence in order to obstruct our plan" (interview, September 1980).

Policies by States, Policies of States

In subaltern nations, import substitution and export promotion policies are formulated *by* states but are not policies *of* states. The dominant analytical approach to policy making in third-world nations assumes both that host states and transnational corporations are independent actors and that they pursue distinct interests. Bargaining models of the policy process build on these assumptions and thus reproduce common illusions: the belief that states defend national interests, that the pursuit of profit maximization brings local and transnational capital into opposition, and that policy outcomes depend on these actors' differential bargaining power. A structural focus on the dynamic of productive relations, class alliances, and political coalitions leads to a different view not only of who bargains over what but also of what bargaining is. If policy making appears to be a drama enacted by discrete social actors, this focus reveals the relationships that constitute the actors and the structures that underlie the drama. By highlighting the Durkheimian, noncontractual dimensions of policy making, it renders visible the extent to which this process reflects and reproduces the values and relationships in which it is embedded.

This analysis shows how the automotive policy conflict became a locus of constraints on the development of capitalism in Venezuela. The struggle over the engines reflected not only a tension between import substitution and export promotion development strategies but also an intensification of the disjuncture between the logics of worldwide capital accumulation and of domestic social reproduction. Whereas this disjuncture has allowed for a degree of expanded capital accumulation (at the cost of heightened social repression) in Brazil, and during some periods in Mexico and Argentina, in Venezuela it undermined the pursuit of *either* development strategy and consolidated the rentier character of the economy. "National development" in Venezuela has been premised on the local expansion of industrial capitalism, but industrialization has expanded only within the limits of a national social structure whose internal organization and links to the world market have been built on the extraction and circulation of oil rents.

The motors war expressed and consolidated significant changes not only in the aims of industrial policy in Venezuela but also in the identities of major social actors and in the conditions that structured their field of action. What began in 1974, however illusorily, as a moment of empowerment—of belief in the domestic capacity to modernize the nation—ended in a heightened simulacrum of power—the pretense of sovereign control in the face of uncontrollable domestic and international events and forces. The modification of the automotive policy, in fact the abandonment of its original goals, took place slowly and undramatically and was presented as an improvement. During a period when an overflowing stream of oil wealth seemed to bless Venezuela and dazzling state development projects conjured up collective fantasies of progress, the intertwining of powerlessness and the illusion of power worked to dissolve the distinction between pragmatic flexibility and obligatory submission. Actors accommodated swiftly to new conditions without subjecting the past to critical evaluation. The ground for differentiating between versatility and inconstancy cracked. Between the cracks one could fleetingly see that the magic of oil money could no longer sustain the magical state, as national oil money dissolved into the global financial torrents of international capital.

7

MIRAGES OF EL DORADO: THE DEATH OF A TRACTOR FACTORY

In many market-economies, government restrictions upon economic activity are pervasive facts of life. These restrictions give rise to rents of a variety of forms, and people often compete for the rents. Sometimes, such competition is perfectly legal. In other instances, rent seeking takes other forms, such as bribery, corruption, smuggling, and black markets.

Ann Krueger[1]

In Venezuela, in order to be called dishonest, you have to be a gangster.

a Venezuelan industrialist

THE SYSTEM OF CIRCULATION

If money talks, we must understand what it said during the oil boom in Venezuela. In the course of the administration of Carlos Andrés Pérez, after the 1974 fourfold increase in oil prices, money circulated in Venezuela in larger quantities and through more channels than ever before. In only five years government expenditure was larger than all previous government spending combined since the beginning of this century. This abundance of money expanded or created networks for building personal fortune and fed the illusion, as money passed from hand to hand, that it could be made to fall into what Keynes once called men's "greedy palms" (1963 : 183). Clearly, the impact of this sudden plenty, interpreted through notions of money as an external substance or force—"a shower of petrodollars," "a gift from God," "rivers of money"—was conditioned by the preexisting context. At the same time, this change in the form and extent of the flow of money effected a corresponding change in social relations and values. It is the nature of these related changes that I propose to explore now.

A visible result of this sudden inflow of petrodollars was that the local production of value became more subordinated than ever to the appropriation of circulating money. A no less real but more elusive outcome was the

---

1. It should be noted that the concept of rents used by neoclassical economics differs from the Marxist notion. In Krueger's work, rents result from social impediments to free competition (1974 : 291-92).

fact that the character of circulation itself changed. The petrodollar torrent drowned production; in contrast, this torrent bloated circulation. As the links between circulation and production were eroded by petrodollars, so too were the constraints which had previously inhibited the expansion of circulation as a distinct system of social relations and values. As these constraints were eroded, circulation expanded beyond customary limits, stretching or violating normative boundaries. The breach of normality created a new sociality.

An ethnographic account of the short life of FANATRACTO, a tractor and engine factory, reveals the inner logic of the system of circulation as it was freed from the constraints of productive practice and ideology. In the previous chapter, I showed how the negotiations to choose the companies to produce automobile engines in Venezuela were indefinitely stalled. The justification for the delays, cast by a technical discourse as being a conflict between export promotion and import substitution industrialization strategies, was shown to conceal a more fundamental opposition between production and rent appropriation. In turn, this fundamental opposition reflected the tension between the actual social dominance of circulation over production and the political need to eclipse it and to present the state and the bourgeoisie as champions of production. Here I will show how the logic of circulation worked even in the case of a project that had reached the stage of production.

MIRAGES OF EL DORADO

On 22 September 1978, President Pérez started up a tractor assembled in southeast Venezuela by FANATRACTO (National Factory of Venezuelan Tractors and Motors). This event had special significance. The production of agricultural machinery had been a long-standing goal in Venezuela's import substitution industrial strategy. In addition, FANATRACTO was the first major factory built in Ciudad Bolívar, the capital of Bolívar state, in the Guayana region. This region, the site of the mythical El Dorado during the Spanish Conquest, had become during this century the hope of Venezuela's economic diversification and independence. As we saw with the case of the Iron Syndicate, its rich natural resources—hydroelectric power, iron, and bauxite—fueled dreams of a future of abundance even without oil. Five years earlier, just before retiring in 1973 as CVG president and as an early leader, since he headed the hydroelectric project under Pérez Jiménez, of the state's efforts to industrialize this region, General Rafael Alfonzo Ravard declared that "the progress of Guayana in the last twenty years has been El Dorado

President Carlos Andrés Pérez and FANATRACTO's president, Anton von Enzbeg, at the inauguration of FANATRACTO. (Private collection.)

marching toward man" (*El Universal,* 30 November 1973). FANATRACTO appeared to embody the new El Dorado, the future marching toward Venezuela. In his speech at the inauguration of the factory, President Pérez proclaimed, "We have nothing to fear tomorrow, when the sources of our oil become exhausted, because Venezuelan industry and agriculture will be the solid and firm basis on which will rest the well being of Venezuelans" (*El Universal,* 23 September 1978).

Two years later FANATRACTO was dead. The assembly of tractors had begun in July 1978 in a pilot plant. The construction of the full-scale plant had started in June 1978 and was completed at the end of 1980. The final plant, a smaller version of a John Deere tractor factory located in Spain, came to occupy 27 thousand square meters of enclosed, dust-free space (a requirement for the production of diesel engines) built on a total area of 127 thousand square meters. The factory, with an initial investment of over Bs. 70 million ($18 million) was ready to function at the beginning of 1981. But no tractor was ever manufactured there. Instead, the factory was abandoned. The promise of production became the reality of decay. The factory's corpse awaited the combined onslaught of undomesticated natural forces— encroaching vegetation—and "unsocialized" human beings—the *margina-*

Table 9
The death of FANATRACTO: main actors

Institutions

ACO S.A.: A conglomerate owned by ALCOA Aluminum Co. and by diverse Venezuelan investors. Distributor of Deere products.

ACO Inversora: Subsidiary of ACO, holder of 15 percent of FANATRACTO's shares.

CAVENDES: An investment bank owned by major local economic groups, underwriter of 20 percent of FANATRACTO's shares.

CVG: Corporación Venezolana de Guayana, the state holding company for the industrial development of the Guayana region. Owner of 45 percent of FANATRACTO's shares.

John Deere Co.: A U.S. transnational, the world's largest manufacturer of agricultural machinery, and 20 percent shareholder in FANATRACTO.

Ministry of Development: Ministerio de Fomento, the agency responsible for the state's industrial policy and promotion activities.

FANATRACTO: The company, of mixed capital, created to manufacture tractors in Venezuela.

"Gabinete económico": Economic Cabinet, a subgroup of the Cabinet.

Individuals

Carlos Guillermo Cordido Valery: President of FANATRACTO, from the Caldera faction of COPEI.

Luis Herrera Campins: President of Venezuela (1979–84), COPEI party.

Harry Mannil: President of ACO.

José Porras Omaña: Minister of Development, succeeded Quijada.

Concepción Quijada: Agriculturalist and tractor importer, brother of Manuel Quijada.

Manuel Quijada: Minister of Development, friend of President Herrera.

Carlos Andrés Pérez: President of Venezuela (1974–79), AD party.

Andrés Sucre: President of the CVG.

---

dos, or slum-dwellers, who were believed to be ready to tear it down to take its bathroom fixtures and other usable parts. "The government does not even want to protect the factory," lamented one of its private promoters, "and so I have had to stretch our budget to pay some guards with our own money. But soon it will be all over. The factory will be torn apart by the marginados and swallowed up by the jungle" (confidential interview, August 1981).[2]

FANATRACTO died in relative silence. From the outset the media paid little attention to its troubles. Its promoters did not use the newspapers to arouse the political support that it needed to survive. When in October 1980 they were forced to halt operations and dissolve the company, there was no significant public expression of protest. In a country where newspapers are

2. FANATRACTO's president, Anton Von Enzberg, presented a less gloomy view. He told me that the factory was protected by a maintenance budget designed to last until 1985. Taking literally the comment about FANATRACTO "being swallowed up by the jungle," he noted that the jungle was two hundred kilometers away (personal interview, 13 July 1983).

commonly used by the bourgeoisie as a means to exert public pressure, to build a sense of collective identity, and even to communicate private messages among restricted elite groups, the limited use of the media seems puzzling. From the perspective offered by the media, it appeared as if only a few people were attached to FANATRACTO, as if it, like the marginados, had no major *dolientes,* or mourners (literally, people in pain or sufferers— a term commonly used to refer to people affected by a loss). I have taken FANATRACTO's apparent lack of dolientes as a clue that has guided my investigation of its early death. Since in Venezuela the social importance or power of individuals is marked at their death by their dolientes, as reflected in the number and size of the published notes of condolence (whose proper dimensions and institutional provenance are determined by a tacit code), I have taken a leap and assumed that this company's quiet death reflected its lack of social importance. I have also assumed that FANATRACTO's quiet end, given the status of its promoters, was a loud message. Deciphering this message, then, would be a key to understanding its death.

THE ORIGIN OF FANATRACTO

The goal of establishing a tractor factory was set during the administration of Rómulo Betancourt (1959–64), discussed during that of Christian Democrat Rafael Caldera (1969–74), and finally concretized during the presidency of Carlos Andrés Pérez. The oil boom helped this plan take on ambitious dimensions. Under Pérez, the state decided to combine the construction of a tractor factory with the establishment of a diesel complex which would produce three different types of diesel engines: 60 to 120 horsepower for tractors and small trucks; 120 to 170 horsepower, for medium trucks; over 170 horsepower, for large trucks and buses. These engines were part of the Andean Pact assignments to Venezuela. By combining in one site the production of three different types of engines, the state hoped to maximize economies of scale.

On 9 October 1975 the government invited interested firms to bid for the production of the engines. The corporations which won the original bids (Deere the small engine, Fiat the medium, and Mack Truck the large) opposed the government's plan. They presented technical objections to the joint production of common engine elements and argued for setting up separate factories for each engine. The boom, however, had created within the government the sense that money conferred boundless political power. As in other areas of state policy, in this case government planners believed they could impose their nationalist demands on transnational companies. A Ministry of Development officer in a private interview proudly said:

> We invited their representatives to a meeting, put all of them together in one room, and told them what we wanted to do. We will have a common forge, and will produce certain common elements for all the engines. The whole thing will be managed by one administration. They presented objections, but could not refute our arguments. We established the conditions and forced the transnationals to accept them (interview, Jorge García Duque 1978).

The state, through the Ministry of Development, managed to establish these conditions. Through the president, however, it violated them. Upon the visit of King Juan Carlos of Spain to Venezuela, President Pérez revoked on 9 September 1977 the selection of Mack to produce the large diesel engine and awarded both the motor and the assembly rights for truck and bus to Pegaso, part of the Spanish state-owned company ENASA. The details of this decision were discussed in the previous chapter. Suffice it to recall here that the government justified its decision in terms of the political need to strengthen Venezuela's relationship with Spain's new democratic regime and that by doing so it violated legally sanctioned contracts. Its actions in this case had two important consequences: first, the dismemberment of the Guayana diesel complex for political reasons as the result of the president's selection of the city of Cumaná as the site of the Pegaso plant; and, second, increased concern within the private sector that the state would redefine at will the rules by which it operated. One of the country's leading auto entrepreneurs stated off-the-record: "After the Pegaso affair, I cannot convince any transnational to do serious business with Venezuela. How can I persuade them to invest a large sum in Venezuela, if I cannot assure them that the government will not whimsically change the rules of the game?" (confidential interview, Caracas, September 1980).

Within the private sector, the Pegaso incident served to inhibit productive investments, whether promoted by capitalists or by the state. Yet it also made capitalists aware of the dangers of not investing at the right time. The Pegaso selection was only partly the result of state arbitrariness; the private sector's resistance to investing in industry at all was also responsible. Although Mack had been awarded the diesel engine as early as 1976, it had not begun to build the factory and instead had used delaying tactics. Once again the dominance of commercial activities curbed industrial expansion. Had Mack begun construction, it would have been more difficult for President Pérez to revoke its original selection. As a result, Mack found itself without government support in its industrial venture and facing a formidable new competitor in the commercial sector. On the basis of this experience, a Mack consultant (and an ex-functionary of the Ministry of Development) told Mack executives, "Even if we do not manage to kick Pegaso out, you must move into production, even if it is only for export and without much protection. If Pegaso folds or is unable to meet the competition of Peru's Volvo, Mack will be here" (interview, September 1980). From this perspective, production did not stand in opposition to circulation; rather, industrial investment was seen as a means to preserve commercial dominance.

THE CREATION OF FANATRACTO

FANATRACTO was the offspring of this survival imperative to industrialize or perish which was imposed on commercial ventures by import substitution policies. Foreign tractor producers had been obliged to submit bids for the production of tractors. For some of them, the local market was not large enough to justify industrial investment but was sufficiently lucrative to entice them to invest in productive facilities in order to preserve their commercial presence. The state presented them with a stark alternative: the loser would be excluded, and the winner would have a captive market. In addition, the state guaranteed the winner adequate financial support and sufficient tariff protection against cheaper imports.

Feasibility studies had shown that with an annual market of four thousand tractors, Venezuela could support only one tractor plant, and even then only if it received generous state protection. The plan to build this plant was justified on the basis that it could be a means of promoting agricultural production by reducing the costs of its inputs. Tractors, unlike trucks or buses, need to be serviced on site. As a result of Venezuela's small and multibrand market, tractors were poorly serviced and had a limited average life. Agricultural fields were sown with dead tractors.

The state wanted to counteract the negative impact of this situation on agricultural production and prices by developing an adequate national service network. This could only be established, however, in a single-brand market. A commercial monopoly was not feasible politically. The government could not justify it in principle, and if it did, it would meet the opposition of existing dealers. The establishment of an industrial monopoly, on the other hand, could be justified on both political and technical grounds. The firm would have to meet certain conditions: state equity participation, to keep the company from favoring some private interests over others and from charging excessive prices; investment by a local dealership to ensure mainte nance and political support; and investment by a foreign tractor manufacturer to supply modern technology.

Thus was FANATRACTO born. Total investment was estimated at Bs. 168 million ($39.1 million). Of the initial Bs. 50 million investment, John Deere Company (winner of the bid) held 20 percent, ACO Inversora (a subsidiary of ACO S.A., a local conglomerate that distributed Deere and other vehicle products) had 15 percent; CAVENDES (an investment bank acting as an underwriter), 20 percent intended for sale to other distributors; and CVG (a state corporation), 45 percent. FANATRACTO was, thus, a special instance of a joint venture. It united state capital with local and foreign private capital through an alliance of four types of social actors: a transnational corporation, a private local conglomerate, a private local bank, and a state corporation. Of these, two deserve special mention: the CVG, the state enterprise, and ACO S.A., the local private investor.

CVG AND ACO

Of the numerous public enterprises in Venezuela, CVG had a good reputation for the relative efficiency of its firms (although it was known as well for disregarding the social impact of its giant enterprises on the Guayana region). Since its establishment in 1960, General Alfonzo Ravard, an MIT engineering graduate, had insulated it from party politics by managing it according to "technical" criteria—what Dinkelspiel has analyzed as a "technological administrative style"—which attempted to divorce it from the larger implications and demands of the policies it pursued (1967). General Ravard's successor, Argenis Gamboa, a University of Pittsburgh engineering graduate, continued his professional managerial tradition. As a result, an unusual degree of administrative continuity and technical expertise supported CVG's enterprises. The boom had reduced CVG's relative isolation from national party politics, but Andrés Sucre, its president under COPEI, promised to maintain its priorities.

ACO Inversora (FANATRACTO's principal local private investor, and a subsidiary of ACO S.A., hereafter ACO) seemed to be a highly promising partner as well. Several features made ACO appear to be a strong ally. It was a large holding company that brought together transnational capital (ALCOA owned 41.9 percent of its common stock) and a diversified group of local investors (two thousand shareholders, according to ACO's annual reports), including prominent local families.[3] It was also a diversified conglomerate

3. Tamayo Rivero, Degwitz, Mendoza Fleury, Mendoza Goiticoa, Villasmil, and Brillembourg.

specializing in the distribution of automobile and agricultural machinery whose forty-two companies linked commercial, financial, service, and industrial sectors. Further, it was the largest single independent dealer of Deere agricultural and industrial products in the world outside the United States, had been professionally managed since its founding in 1954, had a well-trained staff, and had experienced phenomenal growth in recent years.[4] More than 75 percent of ACO's earnings came from its commercial activities. The government allowed a mark-up on the sale of tractors of 30 percent over their CIF price. Between 1974 and 1977, ACO's share of the tractor market jumped from 19.7 percent to 36 percent (ACO S.A. 1974–79).

ACO Inversora (hereafter Inversora) was a subsidiary holding company of which 40.9 percent was owned by ACO and 59.1 percent by ACO's directors and shareholders. Through its operating subsidiaries (many of them former ACO subsidiaries), Inversora was involved in the distribution of cargo vehicles and heavy machinery, the leasing of equipment, manufacturing, and coffee exporting. Inversora was established in 1976 to make possible ACO's diversification and growth. Venezuela's decision to join the Andean Pact in January 1974 and its acceptance of Decision 24, which regulated foreign investment in the region, restricted ACO's expansion because ALCOA had a large share in the company. According to Decision 24, new foreign investment in specified areas, including purchasing, marketing, or distributing goods, was restricted to national companies—those in which foreign participation was less than 20 percent. "Mixed" companies, in which foreign capital had under 50 percent of the capital, were allowed to continue to conduct existing operations but were not permitted to expand activities in these areas. By shifting its stock, then, ALCOA's indirect ownership of 17 percent in Inversora (through its 41.9 percent ownership of ACO) became less than the 20 percent minimum. Thus, Inversora was classified as a national company by the Superintendency of Foreign Investment (SIEX), and was entitled to expand into new industrial and commercial areas. Needless to say, FANATRACTO was the type of industrial project restricted to national companies.

The project's main promoters, however, were not in a hurry to get the project under way. CVG was involved in a number of larger projects: the

---

4. In 1973–77, net sales went from $71.1 million to $212 million, an annual average compound growth rate of 31 percent. Net income rose from $4.3 million to $15.9 million, at a 39 percent rate, and sales of Deere products rose at a rate of 51 percent. In 1977 agricultural equipment was 19.6 percent of ACO's sales and grew at a rate of 33.6 percent in 1973–77.

Table 10

Ownership structure of ACO S.A.

Shareholders	Percentage
Aluminum Company of America ("Alcoa")	41.9
Albur, C.A.[a]	21.9
Inversiones Diversas C.A.[b]	8.4
Sindicato Tamayo, S.A.[c]	8.9
Juan Simón Mendoza F.	2.4
Harry Mannil[d]	1.6
Empresa Mil S.A.[e]	1.5
Sindicato Santa Clara S.A.[f]	0.9
Arnold Orav[g]	0.8
Urbanización Central C.A.[h]	0.7
Officers, employees, and other shareholders	11.0
	100.00

[a] Juan Simón Mendoza owns over 90%
[b] Owned by Ricardo Degwitz
[c] Owned by the Tamayo family
[d] President and Chairman of the Board of the Company
[e] Owned by the Villasmil family
[f] Owned by Arturo Brillembourg
[g] Vice President of Operations and a Director of the Company
[h] Owned by Juan Simón Mendoza
SOURCE: CVG files.

Plan IV of SIDOR, the state steel mill, intended to quadruple steel production within five years; the effort to double aluminum production by expanding ALCASA and creating VENALUM; and the increase of hydroelectric power through the expansion of the Guri dam. ACO, for its part, wanted to continue to reap commercial benefits from the oil boom for as long as possible. While a pilot plant had been built to assemble tractors and train local personnel, ACO's president Harry Mannil slowed down the assembly of tractors, apparently to avoid antagonizing other tractor importers, as well as his suppliers of imported tractors (confidential interview, September 1980).

Electoral considerations, on the other hand, played a crucial role in speeding the construction of the factory. President Pérez had wanted to initiate tractor production in Venezuela, but his term was about to end without the factory operating. Thus, he had to be content with the prospect of turning on the ignition of a tractor assembled in the pilot plant, which he did just ten weeks before the 1978 presidential election.

Table 11

Ownership structure of ACO inversora S.A.

Shareholders	Percentage
ACO S.A.	40.9
Albur, C.A. [a]	22.5
Inversiones Diversas C.A. [b]	8.3
Sindicato Tamayo, S.A. [c]	7.8
Officers, employees, and other shareholders	20.5
	100.00

[a] Juan Simón Mendoza owns over 90%
[b] Owned by Ricardo Degwitz
[c] Owned by the Tamayo family

SOURCE: CVG files.

Table 12

Ownership structure of FANATRACTO

Shareholders	Percentage
Corporación Venezolana de Guayana (CVG)	45
John Deere Co.	20
CAVENDES	20
ACO Inversora S.A.	15
	100.00

SOURCE: CVG files.

THE DEATH OF FANATRACTO

The surprising defeat of AD in the December election brought to power a Christian Democratic administration headed by Luis Herrera Campíns. One of the first acts of his gabinete económico was to name a committee to evaluate the national automotive policy. It formed a subcommittee to assess FANATRACTO which was composed of representatives of the Ministry of Development, the Planning Office (CORDIPLAN), and the Ministry of Agriculture. After a four-month study, the subcommittee issued a report approving the FANATRACTO project and recommending that the government give it full support. It made two important suggestions: FANATRACTO should be granted a 50 percent tariff protection; and while the tariff went into effect, a system of import licenses should be established which would only allow the entry of tractors of different horsepower than those produced by the company.

Table 13
ACO's annual growth (percentage)

	1974	1975	1976	1977	1973–1977
Automotive vehicles	67.9	24.8	21.3	35.9	36.3
Agricultural equipment	17.4	83.6	20.7	13.6	31.1
Industrial and construction machinery	26.2	100.5	20.5	29.9	41.1
Replacement parts	21.9	49.0	22.6	30.8	30.6
Service and other	49.1	(13.6)	(5.4)	(18.4)	—
TOTAL	32.3	44.4	22.6	27.3	31.4

SOURCE: CVG files; ACO S.A. annual reports.

The report evaluated the major objections that had been made to the project (primarily by farmers and importers of agricultural equipment): first, domestically produced tractors would be high priced;[5] second, expensive tractors would raise agricultural costs;[6] third, a monopoly in this key sector would have negative consequences.[7] The report emphasized FANATRAC-TO's contribution to the nation's overall development goals: the creation of skilled jobs, the establishment of backward linkages, foreign-exchange saving, technology transfer, and the promotion of national autonomy.

Yet the minister of development, Manuel Quijada, inexplicably did not convey the results of this report to the gabinete económico. Instead, he took a series of steps which delayed any decision. He requested new information about all aspects of FANATRACTO while allowing tractors to be imported by granting numerous import licenses. On 20 June 1980 he decided to demand from the firm a revision of its local-content program. In a letter addressed to its president, Quijada expressed concern over FANATRACTO's impact on agricultural costs and explained that "any decision about this industry has to take into account its effect on agricultural activity" (CVG

5. The report argued that the surcharge would only be 33.4 percent, assuming full production, with 60 percent local content, and a 33 percent increase in the cost of locally made parts over imported ones.

6. Two alternatives were presented in the report. Given an average tractor life of five years, a 35 percent increase in tractor costs would lead to a Bs. 0.037 per kilogram increase in average agricultural production. Alternatively, given an average tractor life of seven years (resulting from standardization and improvements in service and maintenance), agricultural costs would be reduced by Bs. 0.05 per kilogram.

7. It argued that the state's controlling investment would prevent the firm from favoring any particular private interests or from raising prices speculatively. The state, if necessary, could increase its control by becoming the majority shareholder. It did recommend that the cost structure of tractor production be studied to determine the price distributors should charge.

Table 14
ACO's net sales (in millions of dollars)

	1977	%	1976	%	1975	%	1974	%	1973	%
Automotive, trucks, and buses	383.124	42.0	281.923	39.4	232.490	39.8	186.345	46.1	111.006	36.4
Agricultural machinery	170.553	18.7	150.076	21.0	124.338	21.3	67.725	16.7	57.688	18.9
Jeep CJ's and wagoneer vehicles	141.015	15.5	110.329	15.4	79.696	13.6	55.993	13.8	64.284	21.0
Industrial and construction machinery	132.133	14.5	101.69	14.2	84.364	14.4	42.072	10.4	33.348	10.9
Replacement parts	68.906	7.6	52.699	7.4	42.971	7.4	28.843	7.1	23.669	7.7
Service and other	15.765	1.7	19.311	2.6	20.405	3.5	23.621	5.9	15.847	5.1
TOTAL	911.496	100.0	716.028	100.0	584.264	100.0	404.599	100.0	305.842	100.0

SOURCE: CVG files; ACO S.A. annual reports.

Table 15

ACO's net profits (percentage of net sales)

	1977	1976	1975	1974	1973
Automotive, trucks, and buses	18.9	17.7	16.8	16.4	16.0
Agricultural machinery	20.9	22.9	24.9	25.3	19.4
Jeep CJ's and wagoneer vehicles	14.9	13.5	11.9	12.2	12.1
Industrial and construction machinery	26.1	24.1	19.4	16.0	17.6
Replacement parts	25.2	26.4	32.1	31.1	20.9
Service and other	2.6	33.1	13.8	22.0	11.9

SOURCE: CVG files; ACO S.A. annual reports.

Table 16

ACO's sales of tractors

Year	ACO S.A.		Total imports		ACO's share %
	Units	%	Units	%	
1974	538	—	2728	—	19.7
1975	957	77.9	3033	11.2	31.6
1976	1259	31.6	3300	8.8	38.2
1977	1336	6.1	3700	12.1	36.1

SOURCE: CVG files; ACO S.A. annual reports.

1980). Quijada also insisted that the contract with Deere specify that FAN-ATRACTO be given exclusive rights to manufacture Deere tractors in the Andean region and that Deere agree to buy tractor parts and motors every year (having a value equivalent to twenty-five hundred tractors) for export outside the Andean region. If these conditions were met, the government would agree to suspend all tractor import licenses and grant FANATRACTO a 25 percent tariff protection.

Minister Quijada's position was part of an overall shift in government policy which also reflected a change in the international climate of economic opinion. Liberalization had become the preferred formula for the treatment of stagnant economies in development and financial agencies. While elsewhere in Latin America it was pursued relatively systematically, in Venezuela it was used in a rather ad hoc manner. There was no need, as in countries with authoritarian regimes such as Chile, to use economic doctrines as a means of political legitimation. Rather, liberalization was used inconsistently in response to conjunctural economic problems. For example, when the private sector was reluctant to invest because of diminishing margins of profit in certain sectors, the government invoked liberalization in order to eliminate price controls on products which had long been frozen to protect consumers.

Liberalization also served to justify the granting of licenses to import tractors, with the result that during this period the market became saturated. Under these conditions the assembly of tractors in FANATRACTO's pilot plant became unprofitable. Between 1978 and 1979, the assembly of 992 tractors (149 in 1978 and 843 in 1979) brought a loss of Bs. 8,128,000. The 1980 projected production was 995 tractors at an estimated loss of Bs. 9,400,000.[8] The conditions established by Quijada were clearly unreasonable. An ACO leader confided, "We really needed only 30 percent protection. We asked for more because we wanted to have more margin to play with."[9] More margin meant, of course, higher profits. Now FANATRACTO's breathing space had shrunk. Even if it met all of Quijada's conditions, it would receive only a 25 percent tariff. In a country where cars received a minimum tariff protection of 60 percent, it indeed seemed unreasonable to expect that tractors, despite their lower level of local content, could be profitably produced under these conditions. Unable to change Quijada's position, and facing a growing financial crunch, FANATRACTO did what most enterprises linked to the state do when in trouble: it asked the state for financial aid.

Used as a last resort, the request for financial assistance was a means to buy time for FANATRACTO. At that moment the expectation was that, given more time, something could suddenly happen *(de repente algo puede pasar)*: Minister Quijada could change his mind; the president might be persuaded to support FANATRACTO; or a new minister might be appointed. The continued experience of incoherence fed the expectation of further inconsistency and fluctuation. It made sense for the company's promoters to act in terms of the structural inconsistency of the system. Thus, if the government appeared to contradict itself by simultaneously promoting and undermining its company, it was reasonable for its promoters to appeal to a state bank for financial aid just to shore it up at a time when the Ministry of Development had conditioned its survival on its capacity to be cost-effective. The company's request seemed absurd only from a perspective that assumed

8. Total production came to 1,400 tractors.
9. Confidential interview (15 September 1980). However, according to Von Enzberg, FANTRACTO's president, this level of protection was needed to compensate for higher cost resulting from increased local content in a later phase of the project (interview, 13 July 1983).

consistency in state policies; in the Venezuelan context, FANATRACTO acted as expected.

Its promoters decided to appeal to the person closest to President Herrera, Gonzalo García Bustillos, his minister secretary. In a letter dated 2 July 1980, Carlos Guillermo Cordido Valery, FANATRACTO's president, asked García Bustillos to support his request for a Bs. 10 million loan from the Industrial Bank (owned by the state). The carefully worded letter avoided any hint of confrontation with the minister of development. Instead it focused on the company's urgent need for money to meet its pressing obligations. The tone and message of the letter were set in its opening paragraph. "Although the Ministry of Development declared itself to be disposed to support . . . FANATRACTO, . . . this support has arrived late" (CVG 1980). Quijada's disposition to support the firm, of course, was a public appearance, one conditioned by the company's compliance with his stringent requirements. Since FANATRACTO's management had tactically decided to accept them—because everything was "absurd"—it felt entitled to cite Quijada's professed support.

Cordido Valery explained his strategy in a letter he wrote the next day to Andrés Sucre, the CVG president. "We have focused exclusively on the problem with the Industrial Bank because raising the issue of general support for the project could create delays which could adversely affect the urgent needs of the company" (CVG 1980). He went on to explain that he had signed the request, as the president of the company, but that if Sucre felt that he (Sucre) should sign it, as the president of the firm's major shareholder, to feel free to do so. He made arrangements, as well, for a meeting with García Bustillos, who they wished to impress with the urgency of their request. The care Cordido gave to each detail in the letter reveals the precarious position that he felt the company was in. Because it was clear that Minister Quijada had President Herrera's support, Cordido felt he had to measure every step. His strategy paid off. On 14 July, Luis Ugueto, the minister of finance, sent a letter to Minister Secretary García Bustillos informing him that the "gabinete económico had decided to grant FANACTRACTO its loan request."[10]

This financial support did not reflect a change of policy toward the company. Rather, it was an instance of a characteristic response in Venezuelan politics: the attempt to cushion conflict on a mattress of petrodollars. Money was used, if not to keep those who counted happy, at least to lessen the

10. Despite this decision, according to Von Enzberg, FANATRACTO's president, the Industrial Bank gave FANATRACTO only Bs. 3 million (personal interview, 1983).

political cost of state decisions. This oil-supported subsidization of consensus promoted ambiguity in social practices and values by prolonging artificially the life of conflicting social actors. The use of money as social glue was both the expression and the foundation of a political culture of ambiguous rules and of a political life of continuous intrigue. In this instance the loan was clearly not meant to solve FANATRACTO's problems. This was not a case of keeping an enterprise going by throwing money at it *(a realazos)* but of avoiding its immediate death. During the company's extended life, its promoters would try both to press for a change of policy and to comply with Quijada's requirements. While construction of the modern factory advanced rapidly to ready it for operations in early 1981, Deere evaluated new programs for exports, technological assistance, and local content incorporation.

In October 1980, however, Minister Quijada privately told CVG's Andrés Sucre that the government would simply never give FANATRACTO protection. As a result of this information and of continuing financial troubles, the company's board decided to suspend its operations. The kiss of death came on 5 November. The *Gaceta Oficial* published a resolution of the Ministry of Development which eliminated the requirement of import licenses for tractors and established a tariff of only 1 percent. This decision contradicted previous agreements and signaled the end of any possibility of compromise. As a result, FANATRACTO's board decided to end the company's operations and to sell all its assets.

The press was virtually silent. Only the newspapers of Ciudad Bolívar in Guayana mourned the closing of FANATRACTO. An advertisement in a national newspaper actually celebrated the company's demise. The Agricultural Association reprinted an earlier paid article in which it criticized the project. No tractor plant should be created, it stated, which could not produce tractors at the same price as their imported counterpart. Of course this position contradicted basic tents of Venezuela's industrialization ideology. Yet it was boldly and simply asserted.

The silent acceptance contrasted sharply with the fireworks of the motors war. The struggle for the company had been reduced to private negotiations with the minister of development. The limited press attention was meaningful only for those with inside knowledge. When the company closed, the lone voice of an industrial association leader (Mr. Godayol, of the Association of Mechanical and Metallurgical Engineers, AIMM) accused the businessman Concepción Quijada of "pressuring successfully for FANATRACTO's shutdown." Minister Quijada responded vehemently, "The only Venezuelan aspect of FANATRACTO's tractors was the air in the tires." He insisted that the company had been unwilling to produce with a tariff of 25 percent and reiterated that the government would not grant it more protection. For him, the issue was not just economic but moral:

> If AIMM wants to keep the factory in operation, let them create a special fund to do so. Some people in Venezuela still cannot get accustomed to the fact that a government can make decisions purely in the national interest . . . but with time, they will become accustomed to an environment of morality, which is what we want to implant in Venezuela (*The Monthly Report,* October 1980).

A few months later, Minister Quijada, in a significant postscript for FANA-TRACTO, was fired from his post. Facing growing opposition from the private sector and public discontent with the state of the economy, on 4 January 1981 President Herrera invited Quijada for breakfast and informed his friend that the government needed a change of image. He offered him the post of ambassador in Spain. Quijada refused it.

The new minister, Porras Omaña, was a very different figure. He did not match the president's preference for a minister free from ties with the private sector. On the contrary, he was known for using his ties with the state to further the interests of a major economic group. During the Betancourt period he had worked as director of industry for the ministry; he had then been a strong supporter of protectionism. He left the government to work for the powerful, AD-linked Di Mase economic group, a family heavily involved in banking and the owner of the Fiat assembly plant. At the time of his appointment, he was executive vice president of the Di Mases' Banco de la Construcción de Oriente. Like Quijada, however, Porras Omaña was also the president's personal friend, had studied in the same high school in Barquisimeto, and could also offer the president the personal loyalty and trustworthiness he apparently sought.

POSTMORTEM: THE FORCES AGAINST FANATRACTO

It was to be expected that FANATRACTO would be opposed by an alliance of farmers and importers of agricultural machinery. Farmers have traditionally been free to import their inputs; some of them, in fact, have become major importers in their own right. One of the most outspoken leaders of the farming sector voiced his opposition to the project when it was inaugurated in September 1978. On that occasion Concepción Quijada, ex-president of FEDECAMARAS (the top business association) and current president of the Association of Cotton Growers, told a journalist, "I have never supported the assembly of tractors in Venezuela under the pretext of developing a national industry because agricultural production is already having difficulties and cannot be taxed with new costs that would be impossible to overcome" (*El Universal,* 20 September 1978). He warned that it could survive only if protected by high tariffs and cautioned farmers and cattlemen to watch its development with concern.

Manuel Quijada

What was not expected in September 1978 was that AD would lose the presidential election and certainly not that Concepción Quijada's brother, Manuel, would be named minister of development. If Herrera's victory was a surprise, his choice of Quijada was, for most, unimaginable. Manuel Quijada was not a member of COPEI, had no background in industrial affairs, and had, moreover, been involved in an armed leftist uprising in 1962 against President Betancourt. Even a sympathetic journalist felt obliged to deal with this theme. In a seven-hour interview with Quijada, a reporter elicited a strong reaction from him by commenting that many were surprised by his appointment, given his lack of credentials and his suspect political background. "People say that your curriculum vitae had to be searched for in the DISIP" (the secret police agency). Quijada replied, unperturbed, "Yes, but only one part of it." The other part, he asserted, had to do with the personal qualities that the president recognized in him. Herrera Campíns had chosen him, he claimed, because he wanted a person with clear ideas, independent of the economic groups, whom he could trust. For Quijada, economics was not a matter of knowledge but of common sense. "I am not an economist; I don't even know how to handle economic terms. I believe that economics is more a problem of logic than of profound theoretical knowledge" (*Número,* 21 December 1980).

Quijada then, in response to another comment by the journalist, presented his vision of Venezuela. His interviewer observed, "People have said that Quijada was an appropriate Minister for the 'Republic of the East,' but not for the Ministry of Development." (The "Republic of the East" is the name given to a loose association of intellectuals—poets, professors, artists—who talk about life and politics in the bars of Sabana Grande, a commercial center in the eastern part of Caracas. They have organized themselves as a Republic, appoint Ministers and, half in jest, from time to time make public pronouncements.) Quijada replied:

> It may well be so, because in the Republic of the East you find only those who are capable, who are intelligent, who have been frustrated by mediocrity.

Without any doubt, the "Republic of the East" is the only place where people do not talk about business deals. People there talk about the important things in the life of a country, of Culture, or of Man. What happens is that people criticize the "Republic of the East" because it seems—it only seems, but it is not true—that people there drink a lot. It is strange that in an orgiastic country like this *(en un país de orgía)* people regard only the members of the "Republic of the East" as sinners of alcoholism. (*Número,* 21 December 1980.)

His vision of Venezuela affected his choice of policies. Before the eleventh convention of the Association of Venezuelan Industrialists, Minister Quijada expressed his strong opposition to protectionism and criticized the use of import licenses as an instrument of industrial policy:

Traditionally in Venezuela all local industry has been protected and overprotected. This protection has been granted without establishing whether it can be justified economically, both in terms of the effective use of local productive factors and of the social use of the goods produced. The criteria used by the state for establishing tariff protection had been guided more by the desire to industrialize at any cost than by the need to establish factories which could, because of their economic efficiency, have a positive social impact. Also, the granting of tariffs, in some cases, reveals the degree of influence that an industrial promoter may have on any given government . . . The elimination of the mechanism of import licenses is a moral and economic necessity. From an economic point of view, import licenses become a means of absolutely restricting access to external markets, which consolidates monopolistic situations that cancel policies directed at stimulating competition. In its moral aspects, it is no secret that licenses constitute an inexhaustible source of corrupt cliques and of unwarranted privileges. (*Producción,* 10 August 1980.)

Although Milton Friedman could have subscribed to these statements, it would be a mistake to see Minister Quijada as a follower of Chicago school economics. In Quijada's world, these words expressed a different meaning: they were less an endorsement of liberalism than a rudimentary critique of capitalism. Just as Proudhon, the staunch critic of the institution of private property, regarded property as a counterweight to the power of the state (Hirschman 1977 : 128), Quijada was critical of capitalist privilege in Venezuela, viewing liberalization as a means to counteract its institutionalization.

Like many people of his generation and background, Quijada was critical of the course that capitalism had taken in Venezuela. This sense of dissatisfaction was at the root of the 1962 armed leftist uprising in which he played an important role. Almost two decades later, as minister, he saw capitalism as a necessary stage in the development of mankind; he intended not to fight it but to humanize it. Capitalism had to be humanized because it was unjust, indifferent to poverty and inequality. This indifference reflected its fundamental flaw: a narrowness of spirit resulting from the relentless pursuit of profit that it fostered. To the crude materiality of the capitalist ethos, Quijada opposed a transcendental spirituality. This spirituality was rooted in Spanish medieval theology and in mercantile notions which regarded capitalist investment as demeaning and money as meant to circulate, not to be saved. Thus, Quijada's spiritualism could not provide a guideline for practical action in a capitalist setting. In this respect Quijada criticized capitalism from a precapitalist standpoint. He fit within a current of Latin American intellectuals who see themselves as standing above the mundane concerns of material existence.

At the heart of Quijada's vision of Venezuela was his interpretation of the natural origin of its wealth and the social misuse of it. In his long and often rambling interview, Quijada suggested that because Venezuela consumed natural, not social wealth, it was unable to sustain the development of civilized life.

> How is it possible that in a country like ours, its wealth is being consumed by just one generation? This wealth does not belong to us as a generation because natural wealth belongs to all the generations of Venezuela, the present one and the ones to come. We have been consuming it for the enrichment of one social class of our generation, and, by the way, this social class has used these riches very badly. I say that it has used this wealth very badly because in Venezuela there is no quality of life, not only at the level of the popular classes, but also at the level of the well-to-do classes, because for us art, for instance, is cheap. It is much more pleasurable for us to get drunk in Miami than to live in Venezuela under other circumstances, or than to go to Europe to see the European cultural world . . . There is, of course, an intellectual class, a very important one, but that does not mean that there is quality of life. There is not quality of life in the most developed cities, and even less in those of the interior. The problem that we have in the interior is that there is not quality of life there. That's why there is a sort of wall, a sort of horde, of poverty, surrounding this country, and creating a sense of threat, of fear. Because they cannot find a comfortable life in the interior they come here. The cities of Venezuela, the big cities, are besieged cities (*Número*, 21 December 1980).

Quijada represented a cultural tradition that stood in ambivalent tension before the advance of capitalism—that accepted its dynamism but rejected its spirit. As a noted Venezuelan historian, Germán Carrera Damas, has observed:

From the end of the eighteenth century until World War II what crushed
concerned Venezuelans most was the sense of suspended time, of stagnation,
of a society that moved nowhere, which exhausted itself in itself, in its wretch-
edness, its hunger, its poverty, its smallness. There is no worse fate for a people
than this. It is a hundred times better to live in the midst of problems. For this
reason, that crazy but enlightened man Antonio Guzmán Blanco distinguished
himself from his contemporaries by his horror of stagnation and by being able
to sell his soul to the devil in order to break away from stagnation.[11] Thus, he
was able to do this to sell his soul to the devil, to expanding capitalism. (*El
Nacional,* 30 November 1980.)

On the ideological map of Venezuela, Quijada presented himself as a
fighter for the nation's lost soul. Corresponding to his vision of a split between culture and business, between spirituality and materiality, was a notion of the two Venezuelas: a corrupt nation ruled by money and the "Republic of the East . . . the only place where people do not talk about business
deals." Within this opposition, foreigners were the preferred embodiment of
capitalism as evil. As outsiders, they represented capital as an alien force, un-
mediated by the crosscutting network of relations that linked the domestic
business and intellectual communities and mitigated the negative association
attached to the pursuit of money. It was from the standpoint of the Republic
of the East that Quijada attacked FANATRACTO.

In Quijada's opposition to FANATRACTO there were other factors at
play as well. His older brother Concepción had helped him while he was
jailed and then exiled in 1962, during which time he studied art in Florence
(confidential interview, September 1980). Now it was Manuel's turn to re-
ciprocate. His brother felt no need to conceal the benefits he gained from
having ties to the minister. In a meeting with ACO leaders he boasted,
"FANATRACTO will never work. I am getting a license to import several
hundred tractors. You will not be able to compete against me."

Politics and Money
This ostentatious display of power was becoming normal. If before the boom
a certain discretion marked the private use of public power, now arrogance
stamped its mark on its use, as if flaunting power confirmed having power.
The frantic pursuit of money erased further the line separating the public and
private realms. In many circles, to refrain from using public power for private

11. Guzmán Blanco, who ruled Venezuela intermittently during the latter third of the nineteenth
century, actively promoted the development of the coffee export sector and the incorporation of
Venezuela into the world market.

ends became tantamount to being stupid. While in Venezuela being clever *(vivo)* has always been associated with being quick—with having the ability to grasp immediately a situation—now to be clever meant to find ways to get rich quickly. Wherever it was, money tended to define the situation. From a perspective that privileged the pursuit of money, the state, as the main distributor of oil money, was perceived as a source of wealth, as a tool for private enrichment.

At the highest level of state power, the president needed a relative degree of independence from the influence of money and of party politics. At this level, honesty was a practical matter; it consisted less in not being dishonest than in knowing how to deal with dishonesty. The rupture of an implicit rule of Venezuelan politics—broken by Carlos Andrés Pérez and high officers of his administration—that top leaders let others steal but did not steal themselves, had led to administrative chaos. The growing monetization of politics and politicization of money now reduced the president's capacity to act. President Herrera's choice of Quijada was a paradoxical response to this situation. By choosing a personal friend, a non–party member, and a person unrelated to any economic group, President Herrera hoped to gain independence from party control and private sector influence. He hoped to gain as well the support of a minister who had no independent basis of power and whose ideas he respected—including Quijada's distrust of the business community and his preference for the "important things in the life of a country, of Culture, or of Man." But the unintended consequence of this escape into the personal realm was to intensify not only the politicization of personal relations but also the personification of political life.

Cordido Valery

President Herrera's choice of development minister also reflected intraparty political rivalries. By selecting Quijada, the president made clear his intent to block the person widely regarded as COPEI's choice for development minister: none other than Carlos Guillermo Cordido Valery. Cordido Valery had occupied high positions in the Ministry of Development during Caldera's presidency, had dedicated his career to industrial matters, and was regarded in both private and public sectors as an able economist. During the Pérez administration he worked as a private consultant for several economic groups involved in the vehicle industry and was an adviser of FAVENPA (the interest association of auto parts producers). One factor offset his credentials: he was associated with the Caldera faction within COPEI. The infighting between *calderistas* and *herreristas* precluded the choice of Cordido Valery as minister of development.

According to an implicit political code, Cordido Valery could not be excluded from the government; for the sake of party harmony, he had to be given an important position in the new administration. However, he clearly regarded the presidency of FANATRACTO as a stepping stone toward the post of minister. As the business community became increasingly alienated by Quijada, Cordido Valery's constant and not always tactful criticisms of him made his own ambitions too transparent. Minister Quijada needed little prompting to undercut Cordido's ambition. He knew that the end of FAN-ATRACTO would end Cordido's threat to him as well.

Monopoly: For or Against?

If the establishment of an industrial monopoly would have raised significant opposition under any conditions, in this context it is understandable that Minister Quijada was particularly receptive to his brother's objections. There were objective grounds for concern. Since ACO Inversora and Deere were partners in FANATRACTO (together they held 35 percent of its shares), it was difficult for the government to ensure that they would not collude. Even if the state was FANATRACTO's largest shareholder, and if CAVENDES were to sell its 20 percent as planned, it was clear that ACO and Deere would be in a privileged position to control the production, distribution, and pricing of tractors in Venezuela. The viability of the plan depended on the state's capacity to control and police the enterprise. Minister Quijada, however, did not want to give Cordido Valery the power to pursue this option.

Quijada's opposition to FANATRACTO thus cannot be seen as resulting simply from his interest in his brother's commercial success as a tractor importer or farmer, or in preserving his cabinet post against competition from Cordido, or from his ambivalence toward capitalism. These economic and political interests were not decisive in themselves, for they did not express the standpoint of organized social constituencies. Rather, Quijada's position was effective because it articulated different social and moral universes, poorly organized in themselves. In this context, economic liberalization did not correspond to the doctrine of any influential social group. As presented by Quijada, it was a means both of revitalizing capitalism and of resisting its pernicious advance in Venezuela. But here paradox built upon a paradox: in opposing FANATRACTO, Quijada in practice supported its private-sector promoters, ACO and Deere, which were industrial investors in the firm but also defenders, as commercial interests, of liberalization.

In this conflict, the struggle over strategies and principles was intertwined with a battle over positions. The rivalry between Manuel Quijada and Cordido Valery became so open that FANATRACTO's directors privately asked CVG's Sucre to remove Cordido from the presidency of the firm. They argued that he was a liability, since Quijada would obstruct FANATRACTO or anything else that could possibly enhance Cordido's image. Sucre, however, was not interested in rocking the boat to defend the company. He preferred to let the conflict work itself out. When the firm closed, two influential CVG managers (Ricardo Martínez and Roberto Alamo) told Sucre, "The general would not have allowed this to happen" (referring to General Ravard, CVG's former president) (interview, September 1981). Thus, Cordido had to fight in the name of the state against its representatives.

Deere, ACO, and Harry Mannil

Cordido Valery's remaining allies in FANATRACTO were its private shareholders, Deere and ACO. It must be remembered, however, that originally Deere had misgivings about investing in Venezuela. It decided to do so only because it was forced to do so by the state and was assured financial assistance and tariff protection. As the largest producer of agricultural equipment in the world, Deere was in a strong position. Unlike Deere's main rivals, Massey-Ferguson and International Harvester, whose sales depended on the external market, Deere controlled the U.S. market: only 23 percent of its sales were outside North America, in contrast to Massey-Ferguson's 70 percent and International Harvester's 32 percent. Yet ACO, as the largest independent dealer of Deere products outside the United States, made Deere interested in preserving Venezuela's lucrative market. Although for Deere, the possibility of an industrial monopoly was potentially attractive, it raised important doubts. A productive monopoly was politically sensitive and economically risky. On the other hand, as ACO's commercial partner, Deere had seen its tractor market share rise from 19 percent to 33 percent in three years. Profits had jumped accordingly, without complex investments and labor problems. In short, Deere would accept being forced into a monopoly situation if the state granted it full support, but would not promote it if the project raised political waves and came under attack.

FANATRACTO's main private sector promoter, ACO, was run by Harry Mannil. Born in Estonia, he arrived penniless in Maracaibo in 1946. His first success was his ascent as an employee of BECO, a department store owned by the Blohm family, of German descent. This company, founded in

1942, was a political product of World War II. For many years the Blohm family's company, Blohm and Company, was involved in the import-export business: commercial agents since the nineteenth century, Blohm was strictly a family company. Its main shareholders were Jorge and Ernesto Blohm, the sons of its founder, Otto Blohm, and their cousins, Enrique Heinz and Carlos Alfredo, sons of Alfredo Blohm. As World War II advanced, the United States pressured to gain control of German investments in Latin America. Although the Blohms were Venezuelan citizens of German ancestry, they were forced to reorganize their company. Unwilling to submit to the government's demands, Enrique Heinz and Carlos Alfredo sold their shares to their cousins, who then negotiated the organization of the new company with a tripartite commission involving the Venezuelan state, the United States, and Great Britain. The new company was named BECO. The Blohms had only one vote per hundred shares. Foreign and local private capital was invited to participate in the new company. The major local capitalists were Eduardo Tamayo, Miguel Alfonzo Rivas, and Guillermo Villasmil. The most powerful shareholder, however, was a U.S. company: Aluminum Company of Pittsburgh (ALCOA), with 25 percent of the shares.

ALCOA was represented by Mr. Tata, a U.S. citizen born in Estonia who "played a decisive role on the board of directors" (Gerstl 1977:276). As a result of a conflict in 1954 between the Blohms and Mr. Tata, ALCOA decided to leave BECO and establish another company, ACO, on 8 September 1954. Following BECO's example, ALCOA invited local capitalists to participate in the new company. Of the initial Bs. 1 million investment, ALCOA subscribed 45 percent of the shares; Juan Simón Mendoza, 25 percent; and Eduardo Tamayo, Eugenio Mendoza, and Ricardo Degwitz, 10 percent each. A month later, Bs. 14 million were added, with each partner investing more or less a proportionate amount, except for Mendoza, who waited until 1961 to begin increasing his share in the company. Two new small investors were Guillermo Villasmil and Arturo Brillembourg. Harry Mannil moved to ACO with Mr. Tata and replaced him in 1972 as its president. Since then, he had managed the company according to U.S. standards.

Mannil's economic success gave him access to the upper social circles of Maracaibo. He married Masula D'Empaire, the granddaughter of Samuel Belloso, a commercial tycoon and banker. Yet the Mannils remained largely aloof from the upper social circles of Caracas. They related to Venezuela through the world of business and through its indigenous margins or mysterious past, as if it were an exotic object of consumption. The Mannils promoted the commercial production and marketing of the textile work of the

Guajiro Indians and, together, gathered the largest private collection in Venezuela of pre-Columbian art. These activities placed them at odds with local anthropologists, who criticized their relation with the Guajiro people as well as the means they used to build their archeological collection. Rejected by these intellectuals, the Mannils were also kept at a distance by the Caracas upper class. A report on Venezuelan elites written for the U.S. embassy stated, "Mannil is not yet fully accepted within the Venezuelan social elite. Possibly because of this he sent his wife to the United States for the birth of their children, so that they would carry dual U.S./Venezuelan citizenship, in case they should ever decide to leave Venezuela" (mimeo:n.d.). Yet in characteristic Venezuelan fashion, they were indirectly accepted through their offspring. In 1977, after this report, the Mannils' daughter, Helmi, married Martín Tovar Larraín, son of Martín Tovar Zuloaga and Yolanda Larraín Basalo, of two elite families. The marriage did not invalidate the report's observation, for it illustrated the flexibility of Caracas's higher social circles and their permeability to successful outsiders. The bride's links to the Belloso and D'Empaire families facilitated this marriage and made it fit the accepted pattern of intraelite marriage.

ACO, more than Deere, was divided. To some extent, it was also satisfied with its extraordinary commercial success and was concerned with the political risks of monopolization. On the other hand, it was more receptive than Deere to the idea of FANATRACTO. ACO's broad local capital base and the expectation that it would bring immense profits and political legitimacy weakened its resistance to the establishment of an industrial monopoly. Harry Mannil, ACO's president, could thus say that it promoted FANATRACTO only for "patriotic reasons" and confide that in Venezuela the "great advantage of moving into industrial production is that in commerce there is competition and fair prices, in production there is monopoly and speculative profits" (personal interview, September 1978). FANATRACTO's potential for extraordinary profits was the lure which both worried and attracted ACO.

ACO's support for the project, however, did not stop its organizers from acting with restraint. ALCOA's strong presence in ACO most certainly encouraged caution. It may be recalled that Mannil decided as early as 1978 to slow down FANATRACTO's production program in order to avoid alienating the existing tractor importers and that as a result President Pérez had to grant tractor import licenses in 1978. Once this crack had been opened, the protectionist wall could easily crumble, as it did when Minister Quijada passed out import licenses in 1979, drowning FANATRACTO in a sea of cheaper tractors. A financial evaluation of ACO, written by a U.S. firm, candidly observed that the company used industrial investment as an instrument of commercial domination:

> Inversora is participating along with several other Venezuelan and foreign companies in several projects to manufacture transportation and agricultural equipment. While some of these projects are expected to contribute significant earnings to Inversora in the future, management feels such projects are also important to insure an adequate future supply of imported products and thus protect and potentially enlarge the ACO group's market share for such products (CVG 1980).

FANATRACTO's potential for industrial success thus conflicted with the commercial social basis of its own promoters. If the company were successful it would eliminate from the market a large number of tractor brands then imported by influential companies which were involved with ACO.[12] All the major tractor importers stood to lose with FANATRACTO's success and were thus set against it. Since they were ACO's natural political and economic allies, ACO was concerned not to alienate them. ACO was thus divided. It promoted FANATRACTO as long as it was the protected offspring of state policies but dropped it when the state withdrew support from it. Most important of all, it sought to preserve the conditions which had made possible its own commercial success.

POLICY MAKING AND THE STATE

As shown here, Minister Quijada did not stop FANATRACTO by himself. Since he did not represent a coherent social group or political current, his opposition to this company was effective because it coincided with that of other constituencies, themselves divided and inconstant. Agricultural producers and tractor importers, who have always depended on the state, changed from a position of cautious criticism during the Pérez administration to one of active resistance when President Herrera experimented with liberalization. ACO, which combined industrial and commercial interests, shifted its support as conditions changed, refashioning its identity from that of a promoter

---

12. Ford Company, which had 37 percent of the auto market, was ACO's main supplier of vehicles (ACO accounted for 23.8 percent of Ford's sales in 1977). Ford tractors were also sold by a company belonging to J. J. González Gorrondona, a close associate of President Pérez. One of ACO's founders and a powerful business leader, Eugenio Mendoza was a major importer and distributor of tractors through his firm, Maquinarias Mendoza.

of industrialization for "patriotic reasons" to that of a seeker of comparative advantage. Harry Mannil, in a special report of *Chief Executive* (a U.S. quarterly business journal, "written primarily by and for chief officers in American industry") wrote in strong support of free-trade policies. "While government regulation may have short range effects, in the long run market forces will dominate our world economy" (autumn 1981). Throughout this policy conflict, actors took a wait-and-see attitude and were ready to adapt quickly to changing conditions.

More than any other local social actor, the state had the means to adapt to new situations. Unable to control the changing conditions in which it operated, it adapted to them by constantly manipulating and redefining laws and rules. Authorized as it was to make rules, the state felt empowered to break them as well. The line separating law making from law breaking was vanishing. Observed a prominent lawyer (interview, 1981), "In Venezuela, the lawmaker makes the tricks to cheat on the law" *(el que hace la ley hace la trampa)*. For the private sector, the state's visible changeability was seen as the source of economic instability. Thus, businessmen constantly demanded a climate of "juridical security" and well-defined rules of the game.

In this case, the state acted without meeting strong opposition from the private sector. The strongest criticism was voiced by *The Monthly Report,* a private newsletter published in English and sold mostly to foreign companies. Its detailed criticism expressed the need of transnational as well as local capital to have clear guidelines for their industrial investment in Venezuela. Against the contingent logic of circulating money—as reflected in the state's changing policies—*The Monthly Report* presented the structural logic of industrial capital. I quote the report at length:

> Indeed, it is difficult to imagine why the Government continues cutting off its nose to spite its face. Besides the fact that Venezuela will remain dependent on foreign supply sources for an integral part of its food production system, the key point is that the Government once again has broken its word. FANA-TRACTO was established in Venezuela at the insistence of the Government (*not* Acción Democrática). No tractor producer wanted to establish a domestic manufacturing operation under the terms set by the Government. Food producers are correct in asserting that the market is too small to achieve proper economies of scale. Venezuelan-made tractors by necessity always will cost more than their imported counterparts. However, the idea behind FANA-TRACTO was to establish a local operation which also would provide an efficient national service and maintenance network to care for a market of *standardized* tractors. This was the prime consideration behind the Government's

efforts to induce foreign producers to invest here. John Deere did not want to set up a local factory, but reluctantly agreed to bid when the Government (*not* AD) promised that the winner would receive 50-percent tariff protection from imports, and that the winner would be the *sole* provider of tractors to Venezuela. Now the Government (*not* COPEI) has blithely decided that FANATRACTO cannot produce economically enough to justify its existence, and that the maximum protection it should receive in any case is just 25 percent. This view is absurd. Why should tractors be subject to 25 percent at a time when the Government has agreed that most motor vehicles require 60-100 percent tariff protection? Whatever the merits of the Government's present view, the fact remains that the plant was created on the basis of a firm Government commitment to 50-percent protection. When the Government abruptly changed its mind, it should have offered FANATRACTO some kind of compensation for the losses they were about to absorb . . . Venezuela's credibility as a serious, law-abiding nation has been further eroded. In effect, potential investors increasingly are questioning the advisability of investing in Venezuela. Without trust in Government, and without real assurances that investments will be permitted reasonable protection and rates of return, new investment will simply not materialize. Imported tractors will continue to flood Venezuela. Most lack parts and service networks, and the farm sector's already sizable tractor graveyard will continue to grow, dotting the nation's farm lands with rusting hulks of steel. And the nation will continue suffering an agricultural sector that loses up to 50 percent of all crops in any given year, mainly due to a lack of standardized, well-maintained harvest infrastructure. (26 October 1980:15.)

DOING BUSINESS WITH MONKEYS

One of the main promoters of FANATRACTO, a técnico who had worked for the government in the early 1960s and now worked for the private sector, was shocked by what happened to it: "Andrés Sucre laughed when FANATRACTO closed down. As far as I am concerned, he is as responsible for the millions the state lost on it as if he had stolen the money." According to him, importers benefited from the demise of the tractor factory, but the state's policies could not be seen as designed to favor the commercial sector. "The degree of incoherence is such that there was no intent to favor the commercial sector. Things just happened that way." He saw himself as having different concerns from those of politicians and businessmen and identified with the civilizing character of the industry which industrialization discourse had long asserted:

No one cares. The trauma is mine. And I have a trauma because of the lessons I learned from great economists and engineers—from people like Jean Tinberger—for whom the development of a country is measured by its capacity to develop a foundry, a forge, and a steel industry. (Interview, September 1980)

As a técnico, he defined himself by his unbending commitment to the form and prescriptions of development planning. A technocratic conception of planning as science, often wielded as a shield to protect plans from the play of politics, consolidated the prevailing understanding of development as a neutral process, a sequential succession of stages linked by the logic of industrial growth. A steel mill, a foundry, and a tractor factory were links in a natural chain, objective entities without which there could be no development. From this perspective, the end of FANATRACTO was a signpost indicating that the country had fallen out of the development track, that it was going nowhere:

Just as apes must acquire new skills to develop into humans, human beings must learn to develop iron and steel if they want to get out from underdevelopment. When GM was negotiating with the state the establishment of a motor factory in Venezuela, I had to explain to its vice president, Mr. Estes, what

FANATRACTO: the empty factory. (Private collection.)

had happened to FANATRACTO. As I told him the story, I could see what he was thinking. I told myself, "They would sign anything, and they will. But they will establish an escape clause. They are signing a contract with monkeys. Nothing matters. The issue for us is not imperialism, it is that we let ourselves be imperialized. (Interview, September 1980.)

THE SCAR OF POWERLESSNESS

For its critics, the end of FANATRACTO meant that business would continue as usual, the status quo would be preserved. For its supporters it was another sign that Venezuela resisted change, that "the future" remained an unattainable illusion. For winners and losers alike, the death of FANATRACTO left the imprint of the daily violence of a normality built upon the slippery foundations of circulating petrodollars. This was not just the visible normality of apparently unrestrained power—of grandiose plans, loose commitments, illegal actions. It was also the underlying normality of underdevelopment, of the lack of control over the forces of historical change. Powerlessness in the midst of riches fostered a sense of inconsequence, of unaccountability, of society as spectacle. If changes were ultimately ineffective, what remained—short of a radical transformation—was the spectacle of change, the show.

Policy makers and capitalists proclaimed the goal of transforming Venezuela but seemed intent on preserving established relations and able only to spend Venezuela's vanishing petrodollars, not to reproduce the conditions that elsewhere had made "history" possible. The frantic agitations of everyday struggle, in their apparent lack of historical significance, seemed inconsequential, the senseless movement of an aimless nation, the distraction of a society at a standstill: "Wearying with the constant repetitions of the same tensions and relaxations; antagonisms that periodically seem to work themselves up to a climax only to lose their sharpness and fall away without being able to resolve themselves" (Marx 1972:35).

As in Marx's description of the France of Louis Bonaparte during the political crisis of 1848–51, when historical progress seemed to have come to a halt, in the Venezuela of the 1980s, when money seemed unable to buy progress, a sense of drama in history gave way to a sense of history as drama. Monetary abundance had managed only to conceal what people understood as Venezuela's backwardness. As resources shrank, the prospect of stagnation reasserted itself all the more starkly behind the mask of change.

As in other third-world nations, in Venezuela the experience of conquest, colonization, and underdevelopment had left as a scar the sense of existing in the shadow of history. Around this scar Venezuelans wove their personal and collective lives. The wound remained at the center, structuring social experience as a necessary, if often concealed, confrontation with the reality of historical subjection. Few would experience the death of FANA-TRACTO as a personal trauma. But only because this trauma was part of a common experience of collective subordination could it be expressed from within in terms of a colonial discourse that defined Venezuela as a primitive society, as a nation of monkeys.

THE CONTINGENT LOGIC OF CIRCULATION

Dominant interpretations of industrializing third-world nations tend to forget that these societies are market dominated but not market organized. They therefore assume that economic and political interests are organized in terms of an idealized model of capitalist rationality and deduce from this model the constitution of social agents as well as that of state policy. In order to develop an alternative view, I have used the story of FANATRACTO as a thread to illuminate a social fabric. By linking together structure, agent, and action, this thread has allowed me to analyze the formation of state policy in relation to the reproduction of society—to show how social agents constituted themselves as they expressed and shaped their social world, a world whose apparent incoherence expressed the underlying logic of rent-propelled circulation.

It would thus be a mistake to assume that FANATRACTO was the locus of a conflict between local industrial and commercial capital or between the state and private capital or between imperialism and Venezuela. As I have tried to show, ACO and Deere, FANATRACTO's major private capital shareholders, could hardly be said to represent the interests of industrial capital: their commercial interests were fundamental even as they invested in the factory. Similarly, the conflict between private commercial interests and the state's industrial policy was overshadowed by the opposition within the state between two political factions and two personalities, one representing protectionism and industrial promotion, the other liberalization and free trade. But even in this case the defense of principles was tied up with the defense of positions. If circumstances changed, it was clear that principles would change accordingly.

It would also be a mistake to analyze this case using a closed-system model of capitalist society in which the nation is abstracted from the international system. Against the ideal of the capitalist nation as an internally integrated system, this analysis highlights the need to contextualize and particularize capitalist relations in time and space dimensions that preserve the links between global and local developments. In this case, therefore, I have tried to show how FANATRACTO's ill-fated evolution becomes intelligible in the light of Venezuela's distinctive relation to value formation—as an exporter of strategic raw materials and the recipient, through the state, of a large flow of internationally generated value in the form of mineral rents.

FANATRACTO became the locus of the sharp disjuncture between the vast flow of domestically circulating value and the limited scope of local productive capacity. More than ever before, during this period production was valued in terms of its relationship to circulation. Industrial profits were seen as an extension of commercial earnings; industry, as a means of commercial domination. Without eliminating the local production of value, circulation subordinated it to the appropriation of oil rents.

As the massive inflow of petrodollars made profits increasingly unrelated to production, money making as a goal became an independent activity, an end that defined its own means. This fact had momentous significance. It involved a shift away from the ensemble of values associated with capitalist production toward those related to commercial and financial speculation. While the ideology of production became more transparently ideological, the practice of speculation generated its own legitimating ideology. The ideal model of the conquering bourgeois, the builder of society, receded before that of the businessman, or rather, the wheeler and dealer *(el negociante),* a clever seeker of personal fortune. Quickness, adaptability, and improvisation were valued over constancy, continuity, and discipline.

Yet the limitless pursuit of individual gain was a goal rent with ambiguity, for the personal appropriation of oil money entailed the privatization of national wealth. Thus the model of the clever wheeler and dealer reflected only one side of the oil coin. The other side, viewed from a perspective that privileged the collective dimension of oil wealth, reflected the image of the profit seeker as a corrupt person or as a pirate *(pirata).* A popular slang term, pirata condensed two referents: the adventurer in search of plunder and the impostor whose false appearance fails to conceal his or her ineptitude. Use of the word came to refer to thieves of social riches and of social trust, adventurers in pursuit of instant wealth, for whom society was an expanding frontier whose rules were to be broken, for whom the nation was loot. *Piratería* (piracy) came to designate the ensemble of practices characterized by incompetence, corruption, and deceit.

FANATRACTO was an offspring of the euphoria and sense of power fueled by the oil boom. The project was part of the multimillion-dollar plan to turn Venezuela from an underdeveloped nation into an industrial power: La Gran Venezuela. By the time the factory was completed in 1980, the context had changed dramatically. Venezuela was paying the costs of excessive and careless borrowing and spending, unrealistic development plans, and widespread piratería. Declining oil revenues, growing external debt and slow industrial growth were among the factors which led to President Herrera's sporadic moves toward liberalization of the economy. As abundance evaporated, euphoric optimism was replaced by the ideology of realism. But both perspectives reflected the same underlying process. Realism and liberalization at this stage, just as optimism and protectionism earlier, were the social forms through which money talked.

Underlying the disparate elements that combined to undo FANATRACTO, then, was a common foundation: the consolidation of a contingent logic rooted in the dominance of rent money and motivated by the value attached to capturing it. It was in terms of this fluid logic that the state could break commitments, violate agreements, and waste investments and that its decisions could find social acceptance. Words and actions had no fixity; a capricious fluidity dissolved their constancy. In the pursuit of money, people adapted to its changing forms. Thus, it came to be possible to accept turning FANATRACTO, as it was ready to start production, into a potential corpse in the heart of Guayana, just another mirage of El Dorado.

8

THE DEVIL'S EXCREMENT:
CRIMINALITY AND SOCIALITY

We are sinking in the Devil's excrement.

Juan Pablo Pérez Alfonzo

Money, more than any other form of value, makes possible the secrecy, invisibility and silence of exchange. By compressing money into a piece of paper, by letting it glide into a person's hand, one can make him a wealthy person.

George Simmel

The extent of the power of money is the extent of my power. Money's properties are my properties and essential powers, the properties and powers of its possessor. Thus, what I am and am capable of is by no means determined by my individuality . . . Do not I, who thanks to money am capable of all that the human heart longs for, possess all human capacities? Does not money, therefore, transform all my incapacities into their contrary?

Karl Marx

MONEY AND SOCIALITY

When the first tractors ever assembled in Venezuela were coming out of FANATRACTO's pilot plant in Ciudad Bolívar, on 28 July 1978 at 2:30 in the afternoon, Ramón Carmona, a thirty-six-year-old Venezuelan lawyer, was murdered on the busy Andrés Bello Avenue of Caracas. Three armed men stepped out of a car and in public view gunned him down. It all happened very fast. Carmona resisted being forced into the car but could not run away or get help before being shot. One indignant witness could only shout, "That's no way to kill a man!" but quickly quieted when a gun was pointed at him. The three men got back into the car and disappeared. On the street remained Ramón Carmona, his body "stitched" vertically in professional gunman style, from neck to right thigh by eleven machine gun bullets.

On the face of it, the deaths of FANATRACTO and of Ramón Carmona were unrelated; in all likelihood Carmona did not even know that FANATRACTO existed. Yet I argue that both Carmona and FANATRACTO were

Table 17
The Carmona case: main actors

Raymond Aguiar: Gladys de Carmona's lawyer.

Virgilio Avila Vivas: governor of Margarita, involved in the Playa Moreno project.

David Morales Bello: AD leader, prominent lawyer, and an "apostle" of President Pérez.

Renato Campetti: Italian businessman, developer of Playa Moreno, owner of the briefcase.

Ramón Carmona: Campetti's lawyer, murdered by gunmen

Gladys de Carmona: a lawyer, wife of Ramón Carmona.

Piero de la Corte: Italian businessman involved in the sale of frigates, friend of Campetti and Metimano.

Antonino D'Antona: Campetti's chauffeur, retained his briefcase, brought labor charges against him.

Juan Martín Echevarría: minister of justice, former director of the PTJ (federal police).

Cecilia Matos: President Pérez's secretary and mistress—the "Second Lady."

Giulio Metimano: Former manager of the Boca de la Verità restaurant, protection broker.

Alberto Martínez Moncada: judge in the Carmona case, forced to resign by PTJ pressure.

Manuel Molina Gásperi: director of the PTJ (Federal Police).

Mayra de Molina: D'Antona's lawyer, wife of Manuel Molina.

Carlos Andrés Pérez: president of Venezuela (1974–79), AD leader.

Gladys de Carmona displays her husband's briefcases to demonstrate that political ends rather than robbery had motivated his murder. (Archivo El Nacional.)

the victims of the same forces. Through the analysis of FANATRACTO I showed how, during the oil boom, the expansion of the circulation of rent money undermined production and turned the pursuit of money into an end that defined its own means. Now, through the investigation of another death—the murder of Carmona—I explore the dynamics of the system of circulation outside the formal sphere of the economy. Through both cases, by analyzing the outer boundaries of the system of circulation, I examine its inner structure.[1]

Sowing Carmona

Carmona had known that his life was in danger. He also knew of the dangers of being kidnapped; he used to tell his friends that it was always best to resist kidnappers. According to his wife, "Ramón always used to say it and to proclaim it: when one is kidnapped—be it by the police, the guerrillas, or thieves—one must let oneself be killed on the spot, and one should never get into the kidnapper's car" (Castellanos 1979:171). True to his word, on 28 July Ramón Carmona resisted. When his assailants failed to make him enter the car, they shot him. Still alive, Ramón Carmona was taken to a nearby hospital, where he died on arrival. His last words were, "They screwed me" *(Me jodieron)*.

The next day the police reported that Carmona had been killed by thieves. At his burial, however, a friend of his gave an emotional speech in which he blamed the police:

> We are living in an ill-fated hour because we lack juridical security, because criminals, swindlers, and thieves are protected by genuflecting police and judges, because we are being asphyxiated by corruption . . . Your death, Ramón Carmona, had already been tried and sentenced. It must be stated with your own frankness that your death was conceived in the very hovels of the police; of a debased police, of a police that took the twisted path of blackmail

---

1. This chapter is based on published accounts. Carmona's Murder involved very powerful individuals who were entangled in a complex web of illegal transactions. Many people linked in one way or another to this case have died, either murdered or in accidents, including Manuel Molina Gásperi and Raimund Aguiar. Although I interviewed some of the participants in the events analyzed here, including President Pérez and Gladys de Carmona, I decided to base my account on publicly circulating printed information and media reports. My interest in this instance is to examine the claims that were made at the time, not to determine their veracity. The usual caveats about the fragmentary character of any interpretation apply in particular to this chapter.

and political repression; of a police that, rather than uncovering the crime, covered it up, and that instead of preventing the crime, supported it and executed it. (Castellanos 1979:101.)

At this time, Carmona's widow, Gladys de Carmona (herself a combative lawyer, nicknamed *la Turca*—the Turk), told the press that her husband had not been killed by common criminals and that he had not been robbed. To prove her point, she showed the journalists his four briefcases and said that both his jewelry and the money he was carrying when killed had been left on him. She did not mention that twenty hours after the murder she had received a call from a friend who assured her that her husband was killed by the Policía Técnica Judicial (the Judicial Technical Police, the federal police force for the investigation of criminal cases, hereafter the PTJ). Her informer gave her the names of the murderers and told her that the plan had been not to kill her husband on the street but to "sow" him—to kidnap and kill him and then to bury him elsewhere. She kept this information to her herself but publicly declared that she would not rest until finding who had killed him. "I want them alive" *(Los quiero vivos)* became her battle cry.

Throughout the heated public investigation that followed the murder, Gladys de Carmona emphasized that what had to be done was to discover the "intellectual," not the "material," author of the murder. For her, the important question was not who had pulled the trigger but who had given the order to kill. Extending this reasoning, I will ask not who gave the order but why was it given. I will seek the answer not in the psychological makeup of the actors but in the intersection of individual interests with contradictory social principles. By laying out "the structural conditions for various forms of conscious actions" (Bhaskar 1979:124), I intend to render the murder intelligible.

I see the murder as a thread in a net which was woven to catch money. How did it come to be that, during the oil boom, the relentless pursuit of money became a normative practice in ever-wider social circles? The progressive blurring of normal boundaries was evident throughout Venezuelan society. This change was so pervasive that it seemed not only irreversible but also natural. Those who denounced the "erosion of public morality" recognized that illegal behavior had established its own legitimacy. Gonzalo Barrios, AD's president and its most astute analyst (a man with a reputation for honesty), publicly commented on the new mood with resigned laconicism: "In Venezuela, public officials steal simply because they have no reason not to steal" (*El Nacional,* 28 September 1978). "Stealing" in this context was a euphemism that named only the tip of the iceberg of illegality.

Ramón Carmona and Gladys de Carmona. (Archivo Ultimas Noticias.)

The demise of both FANATRACTO and Carmona resulted from this blurring of norms. Yet these events came to occupy a different place in Venezuelan public opinion. The protracted death of FANATRACTO went largely unnoticed. Only those directly linked to it knew about its problems, and not even they brought the matter to public attention. In contrast, the events surrounding the murder of Carmona were a focus of public interest from the outset. The murder could have been dismissed as one of the many common crimes occurring in a large city. But the political battle waged around it turned into a national drama. Its setting, the normally hidden domain of state-centered illegal transactions, was suddenly brought into public view.

DEATH AS SPECTACLE

For several months after the murder, the Carmona case was national news. The facts came to light in a piecemeal and confusing fashion; each revelation raised new questions. First it was learned that at the time of his death Carmona was defending Renato Campetti in a case brought against him by his employee, Antonino D'Antona. The latter's lawyer was Mayra Vernet de Molina, the wife of the PTJ's director Manuel Molina Gásperi. The day after the murder, while the PTJ announced that the murderers had been common thieves, Gladys de Carmona initiated her quest to find out who had killed her husband. When she declared to the press that she wanted her husband's murderers alive, she communicated to an attentive public that she believed this was no common murder. She took it upon herself to investigate this case and proclaimed that she would not rest until establishing who had been "the murder's mastermind" *(el autor intelectual del asesinato).*

The next move was taken by the PTJ. After failing to demonstrate that Carmona had been killed by common criminals, the PTJ suggested that the murder had been a crime of vengeance. A week later, on 8 August, the PTJ declared it had evidence that the murder had been a crime of passion. That same day a radio station (Radio Continente) aired a taped telephone conversation in which Gladys de Carmona said that she was going to put a bullet through her husband's head. At first this evidence seemed to confirm the PTJ's version. At this time it had come to light that Ramón Carmona had been a notorious womanizer and that just before his murder he had been with one of his lovers in a Caracas hotel. It also became known that his wife was extremely upset with him over his behavior.

Gladys de Carmona, however, succeeded in turning the apparently incriminating tape of her phone conversation into evidence against the PTJ. First she showed that the taped conversation in fact had occurred two hours after the murder was committed. She explained that her husband had agreed to have lunch with her that day and that she was furious because she could not find him anywhere. At 4:30 P.M. (the murder had occurred at 2:30) she called one of his friends (José Novoa) and told him, "If Ramón is with a woman, I am going to put a bullet between his two eyes" (Castellanos 1979: 83). While her quick explanation weakened the PTJ's version, the very existence of the tape revealed that for untold reasons the police had been keeping close track of Carmona's steps and that now, in complicity with a radio station, it was trying to discredit his widow. These events increased her credibility. Her husband had been widely known in legal circles. He had defended several powerful figures accused of fraudulent business deals and violent crimes. Because of his daring, he had devoted friends and fierce enemies. Backed by a group of lawyers and well-connected friends, Gladys de Carmona mounted a campaign to press for resolution of the case.

A sector of the media played a crucial role in exposing this case. The daily newspaper *El Nacional,* the television station, Radio Caracas, and especially the magazine *Resúmen* followed the story in detail. According to one of the judges in charge of the Carmona case, Rafael Rodríguez Corro, the media acted as the true special prosecutor (the judge in charge of investigating the case). In his opinion, while the press brought out information that both aided and changed the course of the legal process, the government "tried to undermine the legitimate right of the press to inform freely." He added that if it had not been for the attitude of the media, "this case would not have been exposed to public opinion, at least when it was, because there was an effort to keep it hidden, at least until the end of the electoral period" (*Resúmen,* 17 December 1978). Because it became an element in political struggles, the crime broke "all records of media coverage through the written press, the radio and TV" (*Resúmen,* 28 December 1978).

Critics of corruption from different political camps held up the Carmona case as a mirror for Venezuelan society to look at itself. Jorge Olavarría, the director of *Resúmen,* a magazine supported by the traditional economic groups (Mendoza, Vollmer), stated:

> The blood of Carmona has fallen over all of us. This blood came out of the poor people killed with righteous "energy."[2] This blood was nurtured by the shameless demagoguery which denounces corruption but which ostentatiously practices it. This blood was let when we accepted, without complaining, the first abuse, the first murder, the first corrupt person. This blood pours forth because of cowardice, indifference, comfort-loving selfishness. And the case itself, rotten in its origins, in its roots, and in its consequences, is no accident. It is a symptom of the purulence of a delinquent society, one which attacks those who have the courage to speak up and which protects those who have shamelessly become its accomplices and concealers. (*Resúmen,* 19 November 1978.)

Leftist critics pointed to this scandal as an example of the utter corruption that had come to characterize the whole society. Two well-known political leaders and university professors, Domingo Alberto Rangel and Pedro

2. "Energy" is a clear reference to President Pérez, one of whose electoral slogan was "Democracy with Energy." He also campaigned as "the man with energy."

Duno, wrote the preface and commentary of a book titled *Los quiero vivos* (I want them alive), based on interviews with Gladys de Carmona. The book was written as an immediate response to the murder. Immersed in the moment, it assumed that the prevailing understanding of what had happened is known and true and does not offer an account of the facts of the case. Rhetorical statements take the place of analysis. Potential insights are left undeveloped and presented as satisfactory explanations. It is as if the critique of reality were part of the spectacle.

The major force behind the media's exposure of this case was the interest of political and economic groups in discrediting the Pérez administration. COPEI, among the opposition parties, had the most to gain from the electoral damage it could inflict on AD through disclosure of a political scandal. It used its influence in the judicial system to pursue this case and mobilized public opinion through the media. On 19 October, two weeks before the December presidential election, a prominent leader of COPEI, Rodolfo José Cárdenas, blamed the government for the murder. He turned suspicion regarding the PTJ into certainty. Given this premise, his argument was straightforward: since the murder had been committed by the government's police with the consent of its director, Molina Gásperi, the government was responsible for the crime. According to Cárdenas:

> The PTJ is an organ of the Government. The PTJ forms part of the Government, a very important part. It is impossible that the Government talk about the PTJ as if it were an alien body, as if it were a private security agency, as if it were a body like the Boy Scouts. (*Resúmen*, 19 November 1978.)

As was common in this period, he concluded his article by making a call to cleanse the nation, one resonant with Catholic notions of evil and atonement:

> This is a propitious time for purification. Could the nation triumph over the vested interests that are entwined around a murder? There are cats, there are murderers. There are rats, and large ones. The hair on the dogs of crime bristles as they bark at peaceful citizens. (*Resúmen*, 19 November 1978.)[3]

More contradictory, but equally significant, was the role played by AD. The nomination of Luis Piñerúa Ordaz (who was backed by Rómulo Betancourt) as AD's presidential candidate had heightened the tension existing be-

---

3. *GATO* (Cat), the *Grupo Armado Táctico Operacional* (Armed Tactical Operational Group), was the name of the PTJ's elite brigade suspected of being involved in this crime.

tween the Betancourt and Pérez factions of the party. Piñerúa's electoral identity as "the honorable man" (*el hombre correcto*) was an implicit criticism of the dishonorable man, Carlos Andrés Pérez. On the one hand, it was widely reported that the Pérez faction used its influence in the judicial system, largely through AD leader David Morales Bello's patronage connections with judges, to keep the Carmona case from developing further. The Betancourt faction, on the other hand, was torn by the conflicting goals of undermining Pérez's internal power within AD and protecting Piñerúa's electoral chances. Party discipline and electoral considerations dissuaded the Betancourt faction from taking a public stand against Pérez. But despite its possible electoral cost, Betancourt felt it necessary to back the judicial investigation of the Carmona case. In so doing, he hoped not only to erode Pérez's power but also to give proof of AD's claim to represent a moral force in Venezuelan society. The major traditional economic groups supported this effort. Concerned with the worsening of the economy and with the explosive growth of the "apostle groups" under Pérez, they threw their weight behind the investigation of this case.

As the story unfolded, the case generated its own source of support: the public. As each new element brought more exciting events and influential actors onto the center stage, an avid public intensified the pressure to reveal the plot. As the plot was revealed, a complex structure of illegal transactions involving the use of the state for private enrichment by a covert social network centering on the president himself was exposed. The public's curiosity about these illicit deals was presented by the media as being a cleansing force. As *Resúmen* argued, for the health of Venezuela it was necessary "to uncover completely the garbage that contains the Carmona case in its entirety" (*Resúmen*, 19 November 1978).

THE PURSUIT OF EL DORADO

The Italians

The search for fortune brought together the characters of this chronicle. As often occurs with complex stories, this one had a simple beginning. After World War II, when Europe was in ruins, Venezuela underwent an oil boom as a result of the postwar reactivation of world trade. Between 1944 and 1950 local oil production doubled—from 700,000 to 1,500,000 barrels per day. European residents in Venezuela—mostly Italians and Spaniards—spread the rumor among their relatives and friends in Europe that "money could be found rolling in the streets of Venezuela." Among the many Italians who then immigrated to Venezuela in pursuit of their El Dorado were Renato Campetti, born in Giulianova, Abruzzo, in 1922, and Antonino D'Antona, born in Trapani, in 1924. They met in the Venezuelan port of Puerto la Cruz in 1948. Both were young and penniless. Their encounter was brief, and from that moment their lives took different paths. Thirty years later their paths were to cross again. Out of that second encounter the Carmona case sprang.

By the time of their second meeting, D'Antona's search for fortune had been unsuccessful. He had lived a life of adventure: he had been the captain of a fishing ship (hence his nickname "the Captain"), mined for gold and diamonds in the rivers of Guayana, played pool for money, and been a friend of the famous novelist Papillón—but had made no money. When a second generation of Italians came flocking to Venezuela to make their fortune after the 1974 oil boom, D'Antona worked at a Caracas restaurant, La Boca de la Verità (The mouth of truth) as a parking attendant. It was at this restaurant that he once again met Renato Campetti, who remembered him from the 1948 days of Puerto la Cruz and hired him not only to serve as his personal valet and chauffeur but also as the chauffeur for Campetti's company, Playa Moreno, when Campetti was away.

Campetti, by contrast, had been very successful in business. From Puerto La Cruz he had gone to the remote plains city of San Fernando de Apure where his first venture, a laundromat, ended in failure. Burdened by debts and attracted by the boom of the Caracas construction industry, which was fueled by public spending during the dictatorship of Pérez Jiménez (1948-58), Campetti left the interior to try his luck in the capital. There, through Italian friends, he obtained profitable contracts to build military garrisons. Campetti soon realized the benefits of the links between business and politics and became an active organizer of the Italian community's political support for the dictator. When Pérez Jiménez was ousted in 1958, Campetti, frightened by the popular reaction against those who had conspicuously profited from their connections with his regime, felt he had to leave the country. He left behind in Venezuela a network of friendships and contacts and took the lesson of his American experience to Italy: money and politics go together; to get money, one must get close to those who are in power.

In Italy Campetti became the sales representative for Latin America of a large Italian tractor company (SAME) and sold tractors to several nations. His most spectacular transaction was a deal that he struck with Fidel Castro in which he managed to break the economic blockade and sell Cuba fifteen hundred tractors. His fortune grew quickly. In Paraguay he bought a large hacienda, became close to the dictator General Stroessner (who nominated him consul ad honorem in Milan) and expanded his business activities. His major interest, however, remained in Venezuela. He came back to Caracas, paid off his old debts, and reestablished his contacts. His biggest deal came when he sold the Caldera government two Italian oil ships: the *Independencia I* and *Independencia II*. This transaction reestablished Campetti's position in certain circles. It is a significant fact—although one not publicly known in Venezuela—that these ships had first been offered to the Caldera administration by a Venezuelan businessman at a much lower price. This businessman was not only a COPEI supporter but also a personal friend of President Caldera. Unlike Campetti, however, he had offered no bribes to the state officials who handled the purchase (confidential interview, November 1978). Campetti had learned to use the informal mechanisms that increasingly linked business and politics in Venezuela.

Playa Moreno

From his previous stay in Caracas, Campetti also learned that land was a key to wealth in Venezuela. He set his eyes on Margarita, an island off the northeastern coast of Venezuela which had been recently declared a tax-free zone and was experiencing a commercial and tourist boom. Campetti was interested in purchasing Playa Moreno, a large plot of land that was being sold in Margarita. He needed partners. Rising oil prices had strained the Italian economy; wealthy Italians were escaping taxes by smuggling liras out of Italy, buying dollars in Switzerland, and seeking lucrative investments in other countries. In Italy Campetti had established a network of powerful connections. Through his Italian wife he became the uncle-in-law of Sebastiano Cameli, an offspring of a famous Genovese ship-building family. The Cameli family in turn linked him to other influential people: the Deninos, also involved in ship building; the Martinellis, active in the beer business; Ignacio Barbuscia, representative of Ford in Italy; and Bambo Kessouglu, another shipbuilder and owner of the Sun Line Company. These individuals, among others, became Italian shareholders of Playa Moreno (Invernizzi, *Resúmen,* 8 April 1979).

Playa Moreno included a plot of public land measuring 1.2 million square meters which had been sold, through the influence of Margarita's Governor Avila Vivas and Ecology Minister *(Ministro del Ambiente)* Gabaldón, to a local group of investors. They had originally paid only Bs. 0.125 (about three cents) per square meter, immediately selling part of the land after its purchase to the developers of Playa Moreno for 240 times as much—Bs. 30

(about seven dollars) per square meter. Both groups of investors remained partners in Playa Moreno. For the Italian investors the history of the land and the jump in its price was unimportant. They wanted to make profits, and at Bs. 30 per square meter Playa Moreno was a good buy. Moreover, their association with influential Venezuelans seemed to guarantee success. President Pérez wanted to turn Margarita into a major international and national tourist site, and he used the resources of the state to promote its development. Governor Avila Vivas built local roads and services for Playa Moreno. Needless to say, because of its high-placed supporters, the red tape *(permisología)* that in Venezuela can stall a project indefinitely did not plague Playa Moreno: all permits were granted quickly. Everything was working smoothly. Unexpectedly, a violation of a traditional code of honor, involving Campetti and D'Antona, clouded these dreams of fortune.

The Briefcase

In exchange for D'Antona's services as chauffeur and valet, Campetti had offered him a good monthly salary and a large payment upon conclusion of the Playa Moreno transaction (reportedly $100 thousand). D'Antona needed the money; Campetti needed a man in whom he could trust. However, he was careless in his treatment of D'Antona. When Campetti was about to leave Venezuela on a trip in May 1978 without having paid his salary for three months, D'Antona angrily quit his job and demanded his salary and severance pay (Bs. 30,000, about $7,000). In a hurry to board his plane for New York, Campetti attempted to pacify D'Antona by stuffing in his hands a few thousand bolívares. However, D'Antona was not satisfied. A journalist recounts, "The Captain, who is a man of honor, was offended by this, and he returned the money. Campetti responded, 'Then get screwed' *(E allora vaffanculo),* and he left for the airplane" (Castellanos 1979:100). He had left in D'Antona's care, as was his custom, his personal belongings; in this case these were a suitcase with clothing and a briefcase. A few days later, when Campetti returned from New York, D'Antona was not waiting for him at the airport.

Campetti took a taxi and went to the Tamanaco Hotel where he usually stayed when he was in Caracas. As early as 1957 this hotel was described, in a brief essay on Caracas written by Mariano Picón Salas (Venezuela's foremost essayist) as a "vestibule" into Venezuela's economic life:

> For the ambitious foreigner who comes to Venezuela and is able to meet the expenses of the first week's stay, the Tamanaco Hotel is an obligatory social battlefield. There he can begin to establish a network of relationships, and for

those who have good planning and strategy it can become the wide vestibule of fortune. For those who know the magic words, Aladdin sometimes walks through the streets of Caracas with his miraculous lamp that offers mining concessions, land to be developed, enterprises to be created (1976:233-34).

Thirty years later, during the oil boom, an Italian journalist offered the following description of the Tamanaco Hotel:

A river of thousands of millions of dollars flows toward the state's coffers, inspiring both inside and outside Venezuela dreams of greatness and of easy earnings. In Caracas, the Tamanaco Hotel has become a center of international transactions. By its swimming pool fantastic deals are discussed, made, lost, and dreamt up (*Resúmen,* 15 April 1979).

From the Tamanaco Hotel Campetti sent a messenger to ask D'Antona to return his belongings. D'Antona, however, gave back only the suitcase and said he would return the briefcase only when paid what he was owed. Campetti, refusing to act under pressure, decided to attend to other business, presumably hoping that in the meantime the Captain would come to his senses and realize that it would be in his interest to return the briefcase.

While Campetti was in Margarita handling matters related to Playa Moreno, D'Antona, not knowing what to do, got together with his Italian friends in one of the cafes of the Republic of the East, a cosmopolitan area of Caracas with many cafes and restaurants where intellectuals, politicians, and foreigners gather to gossip and exchange ideas about life and politics. He complained that he had not been paid, that he was old, that Campetti was rich. His friends examined the briefcase. One of them, Giulio Metimano, suggested that with the briefcase he could get what he wanted. Metimano had been the manager of La Boca de la Veritá, where D'Antona had worked parking cars. He has been described as a man of many acquaintances, as a police agent and a "protection broker" (Carmona 1979:97). According to his friends, his name fit him well; Metimano literally means "stick your hand in." Among his acquaintances was Manuel Molina Gásperi, the head of the PTJ. Following Metimano's suggestion, D'Antona presented his case, and the briefcase, to Mayra de Molina, a lawyer and the wife of the PTJ's director.

The Extortion
Reportedly, Mayra de Molina paid little attention to the dispute between boss and employee, a matter that would normally be handled by a department of the Labor Ministry. What caught her attention was the contents of the briefcase. On Friday, 22 June 1978, the telephone operator of the

Margarita Concorde Hotel recorded a message to Renato Campetti that asked him to call Mayra de Molina.

Campetti knew he had to respond to a call from the wife of the head of the PTJ. On Monday, 25 June, Campetti sent two lawyers (Leopoldo Robles and Coromoto Texier de Armas) to talk to Mayra de Molina in her law firm (Coromoto Texier was the wife of Hernán de Armas, one of Campetti's partners in Playa Moreno). Mayra de Molina presented the case as a simple labor dispute. She asked D'Antona to formulate himself his own demand. The recompense he demanded had jumped from Bs. 30 thousand to 1 million (from almost $7 thousand to $230 thousand). Surprised by this change, Campetti's lawyers left the office. The same day D'Antona filed in the PTJ a labor complaint and left Campetti's briefcase in its custody. He later explained that he did not want to be seen as a thief; that he was only using the briefcase as a means to get what was rightfully his. Yet Leopoldo Robles, who had attended another meeting with D'Antona and Mayra de Molina declared in court that in that meeting, "the Captain said that, besides his severance pay, he demanded Bs. 1 million, because he was no longer the stupid man he had always been" (Castellanos 1979:50). Robles added that D'Antona considered that Campetti owed him a present, and that since he now had many expenses and Campetti was wealthy, he should be given "Bs. 1 million to have a secure old age" *(Para pasar su vejez tranquilo)* (Castellanos 1979:50).

The PTJ threw its weight against Campetti. It raided both his Tamanaco Hotel room and the Caracas office of Playa Moreno, had his bank account blocked (in 1977 Campetti had withdrawn Bs. 8 million, $1.8 million), asked INTERPOL to arrest him if found anywhere in the world, and had him followed everywhere in Caracas. At this point it all seemed to amount to a simple case of extortion: the powerful wife of the head of the PTJ was pitted against a rich but powerless foreigner whose very wealth made him at once suspect of wrongdoing and an attractive target for extortion. But one crucial detail was missing: Campetti was no "orphan" (a term used to refer to people without connections to the higher spheres of power).

The Rings of Power: Cecilia Matos

In America, Campetti had learned that money and politics go together, that to get money, one must get close to the powerful. At the center of President Carlos Andrés Pérez's personal clique was a woman, Cecilia Matos. Affectionately called *la negra* (the dark one) because of her olive skin, Cecilia Matos was one of fourteen children from a humble family raised in Cabimas, a once booming, but now decaying, oil town in Zulia. She was Pérez's mistress and secretary when he was president of AD's congressional force during the Christian Democrat administration of Rafael Caldera (1969-74). In that position, Pérez had played a crucial role in obtaining congressional approval for Caldera's policies, since COPEI was in the minority in congress. He also developed a network of relations outside AD's traditional political and business circles. This network was the basis for the formation of the infamous inner clique of apostles during Pérez's presidency. As his secretary and mistress, Cecilia Matos became Pérez's confidant and intermediary for distributing favors and negotiating deals. When he became president, she too ascended. Known by intimates as the Second Lady, she helped coordinate the network of social relations and political transactions which made up the informal side of Pérez's presidency.

In Venezuela, as in most Latin American nations (and unlike the United States) the private lives of politicians are regarded as being their own affair as long as they maintain the appearance of respectability. Yet for heads of state, privacy is often difficult to obtain. The strict but highly visible security measures imposed by the agency charged with security for the president necessarily transformed his every outing into a public event. Pérez made a virtue out of necessity. He had established his political image as that of an energetic man. By cultivating his image as a womanizer, he reinforced his prestige as a man of action. This image came to have a special dimension as a result of his many passing affairs with upper-class women. He made it clear, however, that he respected certain standards. He visited Cecilia Matos regularly but spent the night in his own home when he was in Caracas. And he underlined the seriousness of his relationship with Cecilia Matos, with whom he had a child, by insisting that those close to him accept her as one of them. He is reported as having frequently said that those who did not accept her did not accept him (*Resúmen,* 17 February 1980).

Because of her role as intermediary, the figure of Cecilia Matos became highly charged, the locus of contending views of Pérez. For his critics, she came to symbolize the unbridled personalism of Pérez's presidency. Oscar Machado Zuloaga, the president of the nation's largest private company and a leader of the Vollmer-Zuloaga economic group, saw her as a dissolver of established boundaries. In discussing the increase of corruption during the oil boom, he was concerned to clarify that there are two kinds of businessmen: the corrupt and the moral. Those who are moral take care to keep their business affairs separate from their political friendships. He spontaneously offered as evidence of his own morality the fact that he had never even seen Cecilia Matos:

There are entrepreneurs who try to see her, and who even go to her parties. That's what I mean when I say that there are differences between two different types of entrepreneurs. I never used my relationship with Rómulo Betancourt to solve an economic problem (interview, August 1980).[4]

The 1974 oil boom brought good fortune to Cecilia Matos. She moved to a large mansion in La Lagunita, one of the most prestigious and wealthy suburbs of Caracas. This home of the Second Lady became known as the Second Casona (Casona is the name of the president's residence) because there, in the informal atmosphere of luxurious parties and meals, policy decisions were taken, public officials were appointed or fired, and business deals were discussed and closed. The very abundance and quality of liquor and food was an index of power. Mr. Vásquez, the ex-chef of Caracas's best restaurant (Henry IV) and of the Presidential Palace, became the chef of the Second Casona. In this setting, away from the limiting conventions and protocol of public life, the power of political office and the power of money combined to generate a new etiquette, a code of conduct congruent with the nature of the decisions taken. Informality was in part an expression of power. More fundamental, it was its necessary social form, one congruent with the nature of the power that was expressed through it. To have power meant to have the capacity to break and redefine rules. A cynical interpretation of the Golden Rule gained currency: "Those who have the gold make the rules." Since in Venezuela the state had the gold, this rule took yet another form: "those who make the rules get the gold."

Cecilia Matos had gained access to the world of the wealthy. Perhaps in grateful recognition of the source of her good fortune, she wore a gold replica of an oil tower on a chain around her neck. She said she never took it off; it was a gift from "Papi," as she affectionately called President Pérez (confidential interview, August 1978). As she became more powerful, she also felt entitled to redefine rules. One well-established political norm in Venezuela was that the media could not report on the president's private affairs; Cecilia Matos's anonymity was not to be violated by the media. In November 1977 her close friend and President Pérez's subsecretary at the Presidential Palace, Gladys López de Vázquez, gave a spectacular party in the

4. In restricted circles it was known that Machado Zuloaga had previously objected openly to what he regarded as Pérez's unprincipled conduct, as well as his attempt to intervene in private management decisions. He had resigned from the presidency of VIASA (an airline company of mixed state and private ownership) when President Pérez requested that the same stewardesses who had attended his 1977 flight to the Middle East, when parties reputedly took place, be assigned to his upcoming trip to Mexico in 1977.

ballroom of the Caracas Hilton Hotel to celebrate her daughter's fifteenth birthday. However, in fact, a magazine wrote, "the center of the spectacle was Cecilia, and all the Ministers paraded before her table" (*Resúmen,* 17 December 1980). The November issue of the magazine *Páginas* carried a full report of the party, describing the expensive decorations and luxurious liquors and food and showing a picture of Cecilia Matos being greeted by Carmelo Lauría, President Pérez's most powerful minister.

The article created a commotion. It suddenly brought into the open a submerged reality; now everybody could see the woman who before could not even be named in print. The context was an extravagant party that only the very wealthy could afford. It was widely believed that the article had been published by Pérez's enemies to tarnish his image. Luis Esteban Rey, of AD's Betancourt fraction, used this occasion to write an article condemning the emphasis on luxury consumption and the corruption of morals that were corroding Venezuelan society. There were rumors that the police would confiscate *Páginas* and jail the journalist who reported on the party. But it was later found out that Cecilia Matos had asked her friend, Osmel Soussa, a society columnist, to report on it. "It was an explicit order of Cecilia to go public, because she was tired of the anonymity she had been forced to undergo for so long" (*Resúmen,* 17 February 1980). At a time when Cecilia Matos felt powerful, she tested her power and claimed her right to exist in the public eye. It was by apparently trivial moves like this that rules were changed, that new ways of acting and defining reality were formed and imposed.

Campetti had become part of Cecilia Matos's circle. It was a circle of people drawn together by wealth in a spiraling ascent toward the alluring symbols of status in the Western world. In 1977, during one of her frequent trips to Europe, Cecilia Matos stayed at Campetti's newly acquired mansion in Portofino, Italy, which he had bought from Fiat's Umberto Agnelli for around $1 million. Out of such encounters with the riches of the Old World were constructed the dreams of the newly rich in Venezuela. From their outsider's view, this world seemed to be made up of discrete, purchasable things. They surrounded themselves with its glittering tokens of superiority—in the words of a Venezuelan observer, "clothing, automobiles, jewelry, mansions, trips, yachts, more and better clothing, automobiles, jewelry, mansions, trips, yachts" (Duno 1975:58). In this manner, through an obsessive, escalating pursuit of luxury, they made for themselves a new social identity, a sense of belonging to a superior world, a higher position in their own world. This marriage of power and luxury generated, according to the same observer, "a dialectic which impels you to escalate, to give up your scruples" (1975 : 58). The dreams brought forth the means.

Ramón Carmona

Campetti sought the help of Cecilia Matos. Not wanting to bother the president with this matter, Cecilia Matos asked for her sister's advice. Nancy Matos was also an influential woman. As President Pérez's private secretary in the Presidential Palace, she had developed important contacts. Her advice was that Campetti seek the legal protection of Ramón Carmona, a lawyer known for his legal skill and combative spirit. Omar Salaverría, a friend of both Campetti and Carmona, introduced them. In a meeting which included Campetti's own lawyers, Hernán de Armas and Coromoto de Armas, Carmona insisted that Campetti should only pay D'Antona's wages and severance pay. While Carmona worked on the case, Campetti, worried by the PTJ's involvement, lived in the home of his friend, Salaverría. There he felt protected. Salaverría's neighbor was Erasto Fernández, who had been the director of the federal political police (DIGEPOL) under Betancourt and later became the head of the security forces of one of the leading economic groups in Venezuela.

At the time, Piero de la Corte, an Italian friend of Campetti's, came to Venezuela to help him. Little has been publicly disclosed about him. The media have stated only that he was Campetti's partner but noted that he was not involved in Playa Moreno. *Resúmen* suggested the nature of their association by explaining that the military, for reasons of national security, had prohibited the media from reporting on the recent purchase by the navy of six Italian military vessels. *Resúmen* knew how to make its silence speak.

During his brief stay in Caracas, de la Corte met with the PTJ's Molina Gásperi, his wife Mayra de Molina, Campetti, and Metimano. These meetings, despite being confidential, took place in restaurants, within public view: power not only made privacy unnecessary but made the public space its own. De la Corte was able to tell Campetti details of what was going to happen to him, which of his bank accounts would be blocked, which steps the police would take next. His informant was Metimano, the ex-manager of La Boca de la Verità. Metimano, in turn, confided that his own source of information was "el Capo" (the boss). Campetti felt reassured by this proximity to power.

Campetti, however, was surprised by de la Corte's advice to pay not only the Bs. 1 million ($230 thousand) D'Antona had demanded but Bs. 400 thousand ($192 thousand) more for Mayra Vernet de Molina. Carmona persuaded

Gladys de Carmona (white blouse), widow of Ramón Carmona, and Mayra Vernet de Molina (checkered dress), wife of Molina Gásperi, the director of the Policia Técnica Judicial (PTJ) at a court hearing. (Archivo El Nacional.)

Campetti to refuse. De la Corte, upset by what he felt was his friend's stubbornness, left for Italy. There he complained to Campetti's wife about Carmona. He told her that Carmona was the major obstacle to a quick solution to her husband's legal problems. In phone conversations with his wife, Campetti learned that she viewed Carmona as an untrustworthy lawyer, one with an extensive police record and known links to the Mafia.

While from Italy Campetti's wife pressured him to drop Carmona as his lawyer, in Caracas Mayra Vernet de Molina threw the weight of the PTJ against Campetti, and Carmona manipulated the levers of the judicial system against Campetti's ex-chauffeur, D'Antona. At this stage Carmona had the upper hand. Through his friendship with Judge Alberto Martínez Moncada, Carmona was able to accuse D'Antona of extortion and to obtain on 7 July a court order for his arrest. This decision, however, left much to be desired. The court order affected only D'Antona and was obtained without a thorough investigation. Judge Martínez Moncada did not summon any of the individuals supposedly involved in the extortion: Mayra de Molina, Manuel Molina and his subordinates at the PTJ, and D'Antona himself. Moreover, despite the court order, the PTJ did not detain D'Antona. Clearly, at this

Gladys de Carmona heads a demonstration demanding justice place in front of the National Congress three days after the murder of her husband. (Archivo El Nacional.)

point Carmona's concern was not to attack D'Antona but to extricate Campetti from the PTJ. Having persuaded the court that Campetti was being extorted, he managed to obtain another court order that cleared the restrictions that the PTJ had imposed on him. His bank accounts were unblocked, and the INTERPOL arrest order was rescinded. Campetti was free to leave for Italy.

Campetti was vindicated. His lawyer had come through with a victory. It remained for him to recover his briefcase, but Carmona could be trusted to do that. Before leaving for Italy, Campetti celebrated his triumph with Carmona. In his euphoria, he promised Carmona he would have his friend, Piero de la Corte, sign a document in a Venezuelan consulate in Italy certifying that the Molinas had tried to extort him. This promise made Carmona especially happy. For a long time he had wanted to discredit Mayra de Molina. He felt she used her position as wife of the PTJ director to gain unfair advantage in her private practice. He had opposed her in many legal battles, but one had special significance because it involved his own relatives. In 1976 Gladys de Carmona's sister, Gina de Jaimes, and her husband, Marcelo Jaimes, founding members of the PTJ and leaders of AD's branch within the PTJ, were fired by Molina Gásperi. Reportedly Molina, resenting Gina de

Jaimes's higher position within the PTJ's branch of AD, fired them both, inventing false charges and using the media to discredit them. When Rámon Carmona tried to defend them legally, Mayra de Molina used her influence to have one of her friends assigned as the judge of this case. Thus, Carmona was forced to abandon this legal battle.

It was reasonable then to expect that Carmona, as Campetti's lawyer and as Molina's old adversary, would welcome the opportunity to combat his long-standing rival. But it is also reasonable to suppose that there was something else at work in this case. Carmona must have assessed the significance of Campetti's briefcase. If it contained documents which could establish that top leaders were involved in illegal transactions, the possession of these records would give him enormous power. He first tried to obtain them legally. As part of Campetti's defense he used his influence over Judge Martínez Moncada to order the PTJ to hand over the briefcase to the court. He must have known, however, that the PTJ would probably keep the most crucial materials. But by putting direct pressure on the Molinas he could force them to return the documents or to make a deal.

On 10 July, two days before leaving for Italy, Campetti gave Carmona two powers of attorney: one to continue the legal proceedings against D'Antona, the other to initiate a procedure against "PTJ officials who could be guilty of the crime of extortion" (*Resúmen,* 19 November 1978). On 25 July, Carmona obtained a tax solvency certificate for Playa Moreno; the PTJ, usurping the Treasury's functions, had tried to accuse Campetti of tax evasion. This resolved, Carmona now felt free to move against the Molinas. But he still needed the document from Piero de la Corte. After many phone calls to Campetti in Italy, on 28 July Carmona got the reply he wanted: de la Corte had signed the letter accusing Molina of extortion. Those who witnessed this conversation at the Playa Moreno office in Caracas heard him tell Campetti: "Perfect, brother . . . Molina is screwed." Reportedly, he then made a local call and told a friend, "Brother, I already have the document; I also have the tax solvency from the Treasury, and D'Antona has an order of arrest. Manuel Molina is through. On Monday I will give a press conference and will expose them all" (Carmona 1979:60). But other people had also heard this conversation. Immediately after these phone calls, Carmona left the offices of Playa Moreno. A friend drove him to the Hotel Cuatricentenario, where Carmona spent some time with his lover. He left the hotel at ten minutes past two in the afternoon, when she gave him a ride to Andrés Bello Avenue. It was then, as he walked from the car toward a friend's office, that three men intercepted and killed him.

LEGALITY/CRIMINALITY

The web of social relations that trapped Carmona also shaped the legal net used to catch the murderers. The net was designed to select who would be caught while keeping the appearance of legality. Throughout this case the legal process showed a disturbing isomorphism with the murder itself. A complete reconstruction of this inconclusive process would require a separate analysis. This brief account of the legal process will serve both to illustrate the similarity between the legal and the criminal realms and to deepen the analysis of the murder itself.

Tribus

It is important to note that, although the Venezuelan judicial system is formally autonomous, in practice it is closely articulated with the party system and is extremely responsive to political pressures and private influence. While Venezuelan law forbids most public officials from practicing their profession independently, they often use public office as a means to enhance their private careers. The judicial system was particularly afflicted by this privatization of public functions. Its most common mechanism was the establishment of informal links between public tribunals and private law firms *(bufetes)*. This association is popularly called *tribubufete* or simply *tribu,* a play on the words *tribunal, bufete,* and *tribu* (tribe). Tribu connotes in this context a form of subsociality, or at best, a backward form of sociality—the sociality of primitive groups, not of civilized society. The heads of these tribes, who are often called *caciques* (chiefs), derive their power from their ability to mediate between the tribe and society.

None other than Rómulo Betancourt commented on the widespread influence of tribes during this period. At the rally to proclaim Luis Piñerúa AD's presidential candidate for the 1978 elections, Betancourt gave a fiery speech in which he called for a battle against the corruption of Venezuela's legal system. "It is necessary to put an end to the calamity that the Judicial system is an archipelago in which each party has its own plot . . . An end must be put to the fact that a good number of tribunals are grocery stores *(pulperías)* where verdicts are bought and sold" *(Resúmen,* 5 August 1979). Manuel Molina Gásperi and his wife Mayra de Molina, by informally linking his PTJ to her private legal office, had established a powerful and feared tribu in Venezuela's legal archipelago.

Perhaps the most powerful person in Venezuela's tribunals was David Morales Bello, an AD leader who was a skillful lawyer and a trusted Apostle.

Morales Bello was also influential in the PTJ, as indicated by his selection by a graduating class of the PTJ's elite forces, GATO (the *Grupo Armado Táctico Operacional,* or Armed Tactical Operational Group), to be its *Padrino* or godfather. (It is a common practice in Venezuela for a graduating class to name itself after an admired public figure, who becomes its godfather or godmother.) To complete this circle of influence, Morales Bello's son was the PTJ's legal counsel.

On this occasion, the politicization—or rather, the privatization—of the legal process was inevitable. Given the structure of Venezuela's legal system and the multiplicity of interests at play, it was to be expected that every actor would try to bend the law. All struggled both to defend their immediate interests and yet to preserve the underlying structure of alliances that bound them together. The result was a stalemate—it became impossible either to cover this case up completely or to resolve it conclusively.

There was ample evidence that profound irregularities marred the legal process. Judges were extorted, threatened, and discouraged from pursuing their work. Violence was present everywhere, making it difficult for judges to act, for witnesses to speak, for journalists to report. The judge assigned to investigate the case, Dr. Alberto Martínez Moncada, resigned after receiving threats against his family and being publicly exposed as a participant in a case of extortion. The judge who succeeded him, Dr. Guevara Sifontes, also received several death threats. And Gladys de Carmona, the main force behind the investigation, was followed everywhere and constantly threatened. Her home was machine-gunned twice. The public suspected the presence of hidden motives or pressures behind the public actions of the people involved in this case.

Even attempts to create the pretense of legality backfired. While trying to present himself as an advocate of justice, President Pérez unwittingly acknowledged that he had influenced key witnesses. He had sent his personal representative to let them know that he felt that they "were being pressured" and to reassure them that they could speak freely. As a consequence of the government's action, the witnesses changed their testimony. As he candidly put it, "As a result of the government's pressure, they recognized the officials supposedly involved in the crime" (Peña 1979:13).

Fabricating Criminals

On 29 July, the day after Carmona was killed, Molina Gásperi piloted the PTJ's plane to Miami to pick up Minister of Justice J. M. Echevarría and the Apostle David Morales Bello. They had secretly gone to Washington to obtain information about the U.S. congressional investigation of Boeing's bribes to foreign governments. A $2 million bribe by Boeing to the Venezuelan officials who had purchased the presidential plane had been revealed. Reportedly, Echevarría and Morales Bello were to try to keep this explosive subject quiet.

Inexplicably, Minister of Justice Echevarría had not requested the permit to leave the country required of high public officials before traveling, which made his trip illegal. Moreover, no good explanation was offered for Molina himself having flown to meet Echevarría and Bello in Miami. Apparently, they could not find seats on a commercial flight and had requested the PTJ's plane. When pressed to explain why Molina had to go himself, President Pérez justified Molina's trip as simply a question of personal choice. He flew himself, Pérez said, "because he just felt like it. No one asked him to do it" (Peña 1979:26). Upon their return, Minister Echevarría and Molina presented a united front as regards the Carmona murder, declaring that it was the work of common criminals who would soon be caught. The trip and its aftermath suggest that the minister of justice and the PTJ's director had colluded to cover up the murder from the outset.

While the PTJ was using the media to convince the public that it was about to find the murderers, Molina was privately attempting to control Campetti and de la Corte. He reportedly forced them to come to Venezuela by threatening to use the INTERPOL against them if they refused to do so. Once they arrived in Caracas, Molina closely controlled their movements. They were restricted to the Caracas Hilton Hotel and to outings with Molina to luxury restaurants and to his house. Gladys de Carmona was blocked in her repeated attempts to arrange a meeting with Campetti. Then, on 4 September, Campetti confirmed under questioning by the PTJ his recent public declaration that there actually existed no document accusing Molina of extortion. Gladys de Carmona was outraged by this statement and could only hope to challenge it by interrogating Campetti in court.

After the PTJ failed to show that Gladys de Carmona had killed her husband, it attempted, by fabricating witnesses and motives, to bolster its initial argument that Carmona had been the victim of common criminals. Yet this attempt was undermined by the media's denunciations of the torture and bribery of witnesses. The discovery of the corpse of Oswaldo Farrera (also known as Watusi), a common criminal, had particular impact. Under strange circumstances he had been released from jail the day before Carmona was killed and was found dead on 17 August. It was widely rumored among his jailmates that a deal had been struck with him: he would be released from jail if he killed Carmona. On 30 July the PTJ received a phone call from an anonymous source who declared having heard Farrera say in jail that a lawyer was trying to get him out of jail "for the purpose of killing Dr. Carmona Vásquez" (Castellanos 1979: 152).

Farrera's corpse was found near a house presumably used to torture prisoners. Reports that other bodies had been discovered in the vicinity of this "house of torture," as the press called it, supported the argument that Farrera's death had not been a common crime. As the PTJ's efforts to accuse common criminals also backfired, it became the major target of suspicion. Members of its elite GATO brigade were suspected of having committed murder. This intensified suspicions about Molina Gásperi. The view that he had ordered the murder was gaining ground. Molina's motive, according to this view, was his old professional rivalry with Carmona and his fear of being publicly accused of extortion. The public was aware, however, that it would not be easy to accuse Molina, who besides being the head of the largest national police force, was an AD party faithful trusted by the president and the minister of justice. People joked that just as the United States had its president resign because of Watergate, Venezuela could have its head of police ousted because of the "Watergatos."

The Rules of the Legal Game

Yet at this time a sudden violation of the rules of the game undermined Molina's position. This fact, together with AD's continuing loss of electoral support, made it possible for Molina to come under attack. Although from the outset the PTJ was suspected of being involved in the crime, the judge in charge of this case, Dr. Alberto Martínez Moncada, let the PTJ carry out its investigation. Witnesses were questioned at the PTJ by the PTJ; Molina Gásperi was never summoned to give declarations. The investigation moved slowly and ineffectively. According to Raimund Aguiar, the main lawyer working with Gladys de Carmona and a friend of Judge Alberto Martínez, there had been an agreement between the judge and the head of the PTJ not to implicate the PTJ in this case.[5] Reportedly, the PTJ had possessed information for over a year that Judge Martínez had tried to extort the directors of the Banco Latino (an important local bank, whose president was Pedro Tinoco, one of President Pérez's most influential Apostles). Molina had kept this information within the PTJ and had threatened Judge Martínez with

---

5. Aguiar became an important figure in denouncing the irregularities of this case. He himself was gunned down and killed (following many death threats) in Caracas in 1982.

Piero de la Corte (with dark glasses) and Renato Campetti (with clear glasses) in front of the Policía Técnica Judicial. (Archivo El Nacional.)

exposing him if he pursued the investigation of the case. According to Aguiar, Molina had let Judge Martínez know that if "he kept screwing around and being a nuisance, and kept directing the investigation against him, he would expose what happened with the Banco Latino" (Castellanos 1979:273).

Thus, Molina had kept Judge Martínez in check through extortion and blackmail. In addition to the threat of exposing him publicly, Molina also threatened him and his family. The PTJ mounted psychological warfare against the judge, constantly sending him death threats and following him everywhere. As a result of this:

> Alberto was really scared: Alberto had left this investigation in the hands of the PTJ and of two low-level officials of the Public Ministry. As we know, it is impossible for the investigation to have been in worse hands. Alberto did not cooperate actively to deviate the course of the investigation. He simply acted like an ostrich: he hid his head in a hole and forgot about the world. And he let the PTJ and the two public officials do what they wanted. (Castellanos 1979:274.)

The Breach of Rules

At one point, however, when Campetti and Piero de la Corte were giving declarations in the PTJ, Judge Martínez secretly disappeared for a few days,

A journalist who was a friend of Molina's wrote an article revealing that the judge was in Aruba and suggesting that he had "escaped" from Venezuela. He was upset by this. He was already sensitive to public criticism, for Judge Rodríguez Corro had accused him of unjustifiably separating the Playa Moreno and Carmona cases. He felt that only Molina could have known that he had gone to Aruba and that the article was an attempt to humiliate him. According to Aguiar, the judge interpreted the newspaper information as a "breach of the rules of the game." The agreement had been that "Manuel Molina does not say anything about Alberto Martínez Moncada, and Alberto does not say anything about Manuel Molina Gásperi" (Castellanos 1979:274).

The breach of the rules of the game led to an open war. Judge Martínez also "decided to break the rules of the game" (Castellanos 1979:274). He took three steps: he summoned Molina, Campetti, and Piero de la Corte to give dispositions in court; gave a court order forbidding the Italians from leaving the country; and most important, ordered the PTJ to hand over the investigation of the case to him. Manuel Molina, fearing loss of control over the case, disclosed to the media the information about the judge's involvement in the extortion of Banco Latino officials. At the same time, he

Major figures involved in the Carmona case: David Morales Bello, an associate of Carlos Andrés Pérez and prominent lawyer (left); Minister of Justice Juan Martín Echevarría; and the director of the Police, Manuel Molina Gásperi (center). (Archivo El Nacional.)

intensified the "psychological warfare" against the judge. A few days later Martínez resigned. He later explained that what worried him was not the reports about his involvement in the Banco Latino extortion but the threats against his wife and children. He had discovered across from his house a hidden PTJ surveillance post from which his moves were observed and photographed. When he tried to take command of this case, the threats against his family became unbearable (Castellanos 1979:42).

Although Judge Martínez's efforts to pursue an independent course of action lasted only a few days, his actions forced Molina to violate the law at a moment when public attention was centered on him. Despite the court order forbidding the Italians from leaving Venezuela, on 10 September Molina personally escorted them to the airport and helped them board an airplane to Italy. As a result of this action, on 12 September Molina was fired as head of the PTJ. In de la Corte's opinion, Molina took them to the airport because he had given them his word previously that "we would be able to leave the country if we appeared to give declarations" (El Universal, 14 October 1978). For Gladys de Carmona, as for those who believed that Molina had masterminded the murder alone, his actions were proof of his guilt. For Resúmen, on the other hand, Molina's erratic behavior toward the Italians— his change from their "pursuer" to their "protector"—suggested that Molina might have been obeying orders from "above" (3 December 1978). At this point it is not possible to assess the validity of either position. But it can be asserted that Molina's destitution—for violating a court order, not for being implicated in the murder—benefited President Pérez. With Pérez worried about the erosion of his popularity only weeks before the December presidential election, this measure removed Molina from the center stage and thus reduced the government's public exposure in this scandal.

The Rings of Power: Security Forces

When Molina was fired, he was immediately offered a job as the security forces director and legal consultant of the Cisneros Group, a major economic group whose leader was one of the "Apostles" of President Pérez, at a monthly salary reported to be Bs. 30 thousand (almost $7 thousand). Given the links between President Pérez and the Cisneros family, this offer probably reflected either a compromise between Pérez and Molina or an attempt by Pérez to appease him. In either case, the offer shows that behaving like a gangster—using the PTJ as a private instrument of force to pursue individual gain through violent and illegal means—was both institutionally permitted and politically rewarded.

Clearly, Molina's services were considered both highly valued and socially acceptable. As the top police official in the country, Molina had acquired an intimate knowledge of the upper circles of business and politics. This knowledge could be very useful for an economic group (Molina's extortion of Judge Martínez is just one example of the possible uses of this form of knowledge). This offer also provides a glimpse into the complex network of connections which brought together the state and economic groups and included the informal association between private and public security forces. The inner rings of power were forged through this type of association. These rings linked the upper levels of state and bourgeoisie, sealed their solidarity in a web of complicities, consolidated their might, and created the conditions for the fusion of legality and criminality.

Electoral Pressures

As electoral polls showed a decline in support for AD, the president decided to ride the tide of popular opinion concerning the PTJ's involvement in the murder. On 11 October, Minister of Justice Juan Martín Echevarría declared to the press that a detective of the elite GATO brigade, Anoel Pacheco, had been the murderer and that the PTJ's inspector of the brigade of disappeared persons, Gilberto Castillo, had acted as a cover. The big question—who had masterminded the murder—remained officially unanswered, but on this occasion Echevarría declared that the crime's instigators "would be detained and taken to court as soon as it is found who they are" (*Resúmen*, 14 December 1978).

Gladys de Carmona and her lawyers stepped up their work. In order to capture maximum public attention, they made the dramatic announcement that PTJ's Molina Gásperi had masterminded Carmona's murder on 4 November, when much of the country was watching a Venezuelan fight in a world championship boxing match. They emphasized publicly that no one higher than Molina was involved in the murder. According to them, "the criminal responsibility did not go beyond the leadership of the PTJ . . . the rest of the criminal participation in this case should be sought from that position down" (*Resúmen*, 24 December 1978).

The care taken to blame no one higher than Molina seems strange, particularly since the case against him was not altogether persuasive. His apparent motive—his need to defend himself against the accusation of extortion—had barely been investigated. Mayra de Molina was not even accused for her role in the extortion. It was also not clear why a man with Molina's power would have wanted to resort to murder to defend himself against charges of extortion, supposedly backed by a document signed by Piero de la Corte, a foreigner without recognized influence in Venezuela. It is reasonable to assume that as head of the PTJ Molina did not have to resort to murder to block the charges against him. On the other hand, it could still be argued that Carmona was known for being a shrewd and daring lawyer and that it was reasonable for the Molinas to try to avoid by any means being made the center of a politically sensitive trial.

The accusation against Molina alone, however, was a logical outgrowth of the suspect manner of handling the Carmona case. The separation of the investigation of the murder from the Playa Moreno case had meant that additional suspects and motives had also been excluded from consideration. In this light, the effort to blame only Molina appears to have been politically motivated. Then, on 25 November, just a week before the presidential election, President Pérez declared that he believed that the media had already indicated who had murdered Carmona. This declaration was taken to mean that Pérez had ceased to support Molina.

Molina Speaks Up: Bottomless Corruption

Molina was eventually forced to serve a jail sentence for violating the court order forbidding Campetti and de la Corte to leave the country. Arrested on 25 October 1978, he kept a guarded silence during his months in jail. His silence was not broken even by a reported plan to kill him in jail and make the murder appear a suicide. In February 1979, Molina was freed on parole. But just when it seemed that he was being brought back to a position of power, President Pérez declared that he still believed that the media had already indicated who had masterminded the murder. Then, a few days before the end of Pérez's presidential term in March, a court order was issued for the arrest of Molina as "a material coauthor" of the murder. But Molina had already gone into hiding. In a clandestine radio press conference on 7 March he declared that the court order against him was the result of presidential pressure and that he was "the president's prisoner." He then managed to escape the country. At this point he felt free to talk and gave a foreign journalist new information which redefined the situation and placed responsibility for the murder on the president himself.

Molina's accusation was straightforward. Carmona had not been killed by the PTJ's GATO but by agents of the DISIP, the government's political police. The DISIP planned the murder and used a common criminal, Oswaldo Farrera (Watusi), to execute it. Extortion was not an issue. The crime was decided in "the Presidential Palace because Carmona knew too much."

Carmona had learned not only about the deals between Campetti and Cecilia Matos in Playa Moreno but also about a larger scandal: "the military frigates, the six war ships sold by Cantieri Navali Riuniti, of Riva Trigoso." This transaction involved "a deal of more than $600 million, including a bribe of $60 million, $40 of which would have ended up in the pockets of Cecilia Matos" (*Resúmen,* 8 April 1979).

Later investigations revealed that the purchase of the warships had indeed been marred by great irregularities. Suffice it to say here that Campetti, making use of his connections in Italy, was reportedly the link with the Italian shipmakers and that the local intermediaries in this transaction were close to President Pérez (the Di Mase brothers and Alberto Aoun). The comptroller general's annual report shows that the government had paid $100 million above the market price for these ships. The comptroller general, Dr. Muci Abraham, later declared that he had resisted bribes and traps by the businessmen involved in this transaction (they set up a situation to make it appear that he was accepting bribes). After a short term in office he was replaced by a man who was closer to President Pérez (*Resúmen,* 24 June 1979).

The 25 March issue of the Italian magazine, *L'Expresso,* which had first published the interview with Molina, did not circulate in Venezuela. *Resúmen* reported that a Venezuelan diplomat in Rome had tried to bribe the journalist not to publish this article. The implication of these two events, according to *Resúmen,* was that the new COPEI administration (in office since March 1979) may have decided "to cover up for the sins of the previous administration" (*Resúmen,* 15 April 1979). This interpretation is plausible, given the structure of solidarity binding AD and COPEI, based on ties of complicity and mutual protection. For others, however, Molina's implication of the president was a smokescreen to direct attention away from himself.[6] Gladys de Carmona and her lawyers still maintained that Molina alone had masterminded the murder.

A Delinquent Society? A Society of Accomplices?
When the complicity of the PTJ in the murder seemed evident, one of the judges in charge of this case declared that the murder of Carmona had also been the murder of the PTJ as an institution (*Resúmen,* 17 December 1978). But a deeper loss was involved. The Carmona case became a crucible for the social definition of political categories. Occurring in the midst of a heated electoral campaign, it served to focus public debate on the nature of

6. Molina was killed in 1985 in an unexplained private airplane crash.

Venezuelan society. Discussion centered on the quality of political life and the character of the people. The case was presented as a mirror of Venezuela.

The same outspoken social sector that actively constructs the nation's public image—politicians, intellectuals, private sector leaders, journalists concurred in seeing a change in this identity. The commonly held view of Venezuela as a normal, decent society was now presented as mere appearance, a façade that concealed a vast underworld of corruption. This underworld was not restricted to a small circle. Rather, the Carmona case was defined as a microcosm of the whole nation. By revealing the underworld of the powerful and of the legal system itself, the case served to crystallize a changed collective conception of Venezuelan society. The definition of the state as the locus of corruption led to a projection onto all of society of the qualities attributed to it.

In the waning days of the oil boom, the state became the locus not only of the struggle for resources but also of the frustration over the lack of progress. This focus on the state created the sense that Venezuela was a nation of thieves and "pirates," a delinquent society. For this reason, the murder of Carmona, involving the state so intimately, was taken as the symbol of other deaths, of the death of the PTJ as an institution, of legality, of decency, of the very sources of morality and sociality in Venezuela. On its editorial page just before the 1978 presidential election, *Resúmen* asked:

> What is our society like? Do we live in a delinquent society? The case of the Carmona murder prompts us to reflect on this. Is this an accident, or is it perhaps symptomatic of a society that has reached the heights of purulence and is beginning to experience the end typical of all delinquent societies that fall apart by themselves? . . . The government wants us to believe that the Carmona case is only a human accident, which occurred within the best institutional setting. It is difficult for us to believe this illusion because Molina is not the first one, not the only one. And we all know this. His crime was to have allowed his greed and his intoxication to reach a level that could not be accepted even by a delinquent society. But this extreme level does not minimize or excuse the horde of speculators, of extorters, of abusers of power, who constitute the marrow of the bones of the delinquent society in which we live (19 November 1978).

Leftist critics held a similar view. For Domingo Alberto Rangel and Pedro Duno, the Carmona case was a "sort of mirror . . . in which a society had to look at its true face." They asserted that "in that crime all the ills of our public life paraded on the stage of the investigation of the causes of the crime which ended the existence of Ramón Carmona. Ours is a deformed and weak society, one that conceals its defects in order not to disturb the digestion of petroleum" (Carmona 1979:8).

CORRUPTION AS PETROLEUM INDIGESTION

The perception of petroleum as the cause of Venezuela's corruption had become widespread during this period. Petroleum was seen as a toxic substance, the excessive consumption of which was threatening the health of the nation, its institutions, and its populace. The absorption of massive quantities of petrodollars into Venezuela—seemingly the most important transformation undergone by petroleum once extracted and the main form in which it appeared in society—constituted a threat to a body politic, whose digestive system was under assault and failing. The entire society was seen as breaking down under the corroding force of accumulated toxins, waste, and excrement. During this period, the digestive metaphor became the central image to express the impact of petrodollars on the social body. In its repeated use and elaboration, it expressed the dominance of relations of consumption in society and the lack of controls on them. By 1978 there was a growing sense that the oil boom had only apparently expanded social powers by increasing the capacity to consume, that in reality it had reduced social control by undermining social nexuses, replacing sociality with criminality.

Petroleum came to be seen primarily as a form of money. Paradoxically, at a time when petroleum as material substance was thus being further socialized—divested of its natural materiality and transformed into just another word for money—as money, it was renaturalized, endowed with natural powers and treated as an external force. This understanding of petroleum conflated powers that were attributed to money, to political office, and to nature. As conditions deteriorated, petroleum came to symbolize uncontrollable powers. It condensed common associations that connected oil seen as the dark inside of nature and as the viscous lubricant of all transactions in Venezuelan society, to notions of money as a corrupting force—what Simmel once called "the complete heartlessness of money." As a negative power, petroleum came to be seen as an evil force, as "the Devil's excrement." In 1975, OPEC's founder, Pérez Alfonzo, wrote a visionary book titled *Hundiéndonos en el excremento del diablo* (We are sinking in the Devil's excrement). By 1978, this phrase for oil had become a common expression. It was often used to support the view, most forcefully expressed by Pérez Alfonzo, that oil had undermined Venezuelan society by making it, as Uslar Pietri had feared in 1936, into a parasite of nature. While Venezuelans had treated this dark effusion of nature as God's gift, it had turned out to be the Devil's excrement.

The digestive metaphor thus came to express the relationship between society and nature as one between society and moral powers. The nation was feeding itself with an alien discharge; it had taken for good food what was actually harmful waste. Indigestion was thus a symptom of the moral disease of a society that had inverted the relationship between production and consumption, that could no longer distinguish food from waste, good from evil. Venezuela had lost control over itself: intoxicated by oil as waste, it had become transformed into waste. The identification of both the nation and individuals with excrement became an ever more common shorthand explanation for everyday problems. Conversations were casually interspersed with comments such as *"somos una mierda," "es que este es un país de mierda"* (we are a piece of shit; it's that this country is made of shit).

Heartless Money

This notion of petroleum as an independent force, as the dissolvent of morality in Venezuela, runs through a fictionalized account of the Carmona case which was written during this period. *Relajo con energía* (Disorder with energy), a hastily written short novel, provides a glimpse into the way the murder of Carmona was experienced and represented. The novel is built around a group of characters who are involved in the murder. Through extensive use of monologues and dialogues, the reader is presented with both the imagined subjectivity and the private speech of characters known only through the media. That which is widely speculated regarding the intimate working of power is presented here as fact and is represented and interpreted in terms of commonly held perceptions. Clearly, much of the source for the novel was political gossip. The best journalistic account of the Carmona case makes the point that the Republic of the East was the place to go to find out about the Carmona case (Castellanos 1979:23). The author of the novel, Argenis Rodríguez, was a permanent citizen of the Republic of the East.

In this fictional account, President Pérez presents oil as the defining force in a society whose population and leaders are too backward or corrupt to control it: "Venezuela is a country without morality, or mystique, or religion. Venezuela is not Iran. Venezuela is a poor country of a million square meters and populated by illiterate peasants. Venezuela lives off of petroleum and all of it is going to come into my hands" (Rodríguez 1980:62).

The book's minister of development presents this version of the president's "development ideology":

It has been said that our system works by giving people a free hand. We cannot stop the development of a country. The development of a country like ours is based upon speculation, and our role is to promote speculation in every area. Our country will be made strong by the process of stealing from the government. Our state is wealthy, and the best way to distribute money well is by letting people do what they want (Rodríguez 1980: 53-54).

An ambitious young congressman extols the independent power of money: "Money makes an ass move. Money makes a woman move. Money makes the Party move. And one becomes someone out of nothing with the money one can get. A good party member is not the one who knows history, but the one who knows how to get some dough, wherever it is" (Rodríguez 1980:77).

A conception of money as an independent power and of power as manipulation structures a chapter titled "From the Private Diary of the Minister of the Interior," in which the minister expresses his thoughts about the Carmona case and provides a cynical interpretation of what happened. In this monologue, Cardona represents Carmona and Sierpe is Molina:

During these five years of Carlos Andrés Pérez we have been brought to an abyss by this thing that we call democracy. It is sheer luck that the military did not do anything. Why? Nobody can explain it. In the party we have no explanation for this fact. The Social Christians cannot explain it either. Even the Americans cannot explain it. Something strange is happening in Venezuela. The explanation may be very simple: there is money, and everyone has a gun. A twelve-year-old youngster can find a gun and assault any passerby. And in fact he knows this, and things like that happen a thousand times a day. There is no one who has not been held up. And our society, in its total emptiness, tolerates more than three thousand death threats by telephone. Per day, yes sir, per day. We had Cardona's phone tapped. Yes, we knew he was no little angel. We knew that he was screwing with a Mendoza. We knew that he was getting divorced from his wife behind her back. Yes, we had him under watch. But at the same time we had our friend Sierpe, our top policeman, under observation. And we knew that our chief police officer, together with his wife, who is a lawyer, wanted to get Bs. 1 million from one of Cardona's clients. And what did we do? Fold our arms and let Sierpe order the kidnapping of Cardona. What did Cardona do? Nothing. Just boring, petty things. He would threaten Sierpe with a press conference and declare that the Chief of the Police was also the chief of the bandits. Didn't we know this ourselves? And we did not do anything because we did not want to do anything. We enjoyed the show and wanted to know how far they would go in pursuit of the loot.

Because Cardona asked for an interview with the President, and the President, who knew about this mess, did not even answer him. Until the fatal hour came. A very bad hour, by the way. It was 2:30 in the afternoon. The donkey's hour. The hour when one sleeps because one has drunk too much scotch. Or from the feast that we gulped down at Gorrondona's (or gonorrhea's) house, who was taking a whole state bank to the United States. We rewarded him for that. Because our system has been characterized for rewarding those who steal a lot. We screw the petty thief, for being an asshole (Rodríguez 1980: 85-86).

Argenis Rodríguez, the author of this novel, has said that he wrote it with a critical intention. He dedicated it to his young son so that he "will never think of imitating or following the example of the characters that appear in the book" (*Resúmen* 5 February 1980). The title of his work, *Relajo con energía,* directly refers to one of Pérez's 1973 electoral slogans, "Democracy with Energy." Rodríguez said that he chose this title because:

This is the language that the Venezuelan people understand. Here everyone knows what *relajo* means: "laxity," "disorder," "corruption." And we also know what "energy" means. Energy is something we know about through other forces that are not social, but rather, technical. But the man who wanted one day to offer democracy with energy delivered neither one nor the other. We did not get to have either democracy or energy. What we did get was a mess, an uncontrollable, energetic mess. (*Resúmen,* 3 February 1980.)

The book's subtitle is also revealing: "A Brief Account of the Destruction of a Country" *(Breve relación de la destrucción de un país)* alludes to Bartolomé de las Casas's account of the Spanish Conquest. It suggests a similarity between the destructive character of both forms of conquest. Just as for the Spanish conquistadores America was a territory to be plundered, for contemporary Venezuelans their country had become a place to be looted. How representative are Rodríguez's views? A review of this work concludes:

Is this a pessimistic, defeatist book? Each reader will determine this, but for us, before we resolve this little problem, it is interesting to point out that the harsh realism which is portrayed in this book corresponds, unfortunately, to reality. The history of contemporary Venezuela has a supreme protagonist, one that stands above all others. It is not development or underdevelopment. It is not wealth or poverty. It is not justice or social injustice. It is, unmitigatedly, corruption. Large and small. From above and from below. (*Resúmen,* 3 February 1980.)

As in his previous work, Rodríguez reduces Venezuela to a sordid spectacle. He leaves no space free from corruption, points to no areas of resistance. Its overall impact is to take an image of the state as a gang of criminals and accomplices and project it to the whole nation.

EXPLOSIVE SCANDALS, BUSINESS AS USUAL

By 1978 it was becoming clear to the public that the nation's petrodollars had been wasted. The most effective slogan in the electoral campaign was COPEI's "Where is the money?" *(Donde están los reales?).* The Carmona case gave part of the answer: corruption, in its myriad forms, had grown to match the dimensions of the state's expanded income. The awareness that the bonanza might not last forever only heightened the speed at which public money was thrown into circulation and was privately appropriated. Because of its ramifications, the Carmona case was one of the immediate causes of AD's electoral defeat in the 1978 elections (Blank 1980:215).

The fact that the case was important did not mean that it was likely to be solved. By December 1978, *Resúmen* argued that the Carmona case in fact would never be solved. It concluded this from the way it had been handled and presented to the public:

As a legal case, the Carmona case is deader than Carmona. Some lawyers, who care about the flashes of the media but who possess only meager research resources, do not measure the distance between their optimism and the weakness of their case. While this is the real situation, and not the imaginary one of the public which believes that Molina has been condemned and that justice has been met, Secretary Lauría and Minister Mantilla visit the widower. They make serious, strong pronouncements, they state that "No matter what, at any cost, justice will be attained," and they gain the only thing they care about: time. Time not only to make it to the elections, so that the case will not hurt more than necessary a candidate who later could make them pay. Time also to get closer to these hallucinatory days in which the whole nation enters into the imaginary world of Christmas trees, Spanish nougat, Chilean wines, Italian bread, and multiflavored *hallacas.* After that . . . then one hands the whole package to the new government: *"chi vediamo dopo, caro amico"* (See you later, dear friend) (3 December 1978).

The political circumstances which led to the exceptional public disclosure in the Carmona case disappeared later. Other scandals came up and in varying degrees captured the public's interest. Despite their differences, each scandal went through a similar cycle of initial public involvement, subsequent decline of concern, and final oblivion. Ever since the establishment of the democratic regime in 1958, public scandals—the experience of each scandal and of its succession as one in a seemingly unending series—created a sense of agitation and change. Despite the scandals, cases of corruption remained unsolved. Thus this sense remained superficial, disproportionate to the deeper and enveloping presence of a familiar reality that seemed not only unchanging but unchangeable.

Even when their guilt was exposed in a scandal, the powerful seldom ended up in jail. They remained rich and powerful and became more admired for managing to preserve their position in the face of attack. A journalist commenting on the Carmona case expressed a common view. "In Venezuela only people who are fools *(pendejos),* or broke, go to jail. Clever people *(vivos)* never do" (Castellanos 1979:42). This immunity of the powerful cannot be explained without understanding the role that oil rents have played in establishing a particular pattern of solidarity within the dominant class. This class defined itself as the custodian and manager of the nation's major resource. Clearly, there had been intense competition within this class for supremacy; the cleavage between politicians and businessmen was significant. But this common role helped reduce differences among its members. Their competition presupposed a fundamental alliance to preserve the conditions that made competition possible.

The form of this competition could vary. The oil boom heightened the significance of illegal transactions in the struggle for state funds. By 1978 the public outcry against the explosive expansion of corruption, while also manipulated as an element in this competition, reflected the need to redefine the rules of the game. But according to an implicit rule, internal differences within this class ought to be resolved informally, if not as among friends, then as among partners. This partnership was premised on the class's having privileged access to public resources. The chronic blurring of boundaries separating the proper from the improper use of this privilege was both a condition for the existence of this class and an expression of its power.

In molding the form of competition among its members, oil money acted not just as the glue of existing power relations but also as a dissolvent of any effort to undermine them. Ties of complicity everywhere may complement the structural solidarity of a social class. But in Venezuela, in the absence of more fundamental forms of social interdependence, rent money made it possible for ties of complicity to constitute a structural form of class solidarity.

In this light, it is understandable why the Carmona case, like most scandals, would not be satisfactorily solved. The point of a scandal was not to achieve justice or determine what actually happened. Scandals were the expression of a power struggle whose object was to redress a particular breach or imbalance by informal means. Public opinion was mobilized to realign forces within the dominant class, not to reach a conclusive legal outcome. Existing ties of reciprocity built around a complex web of complicity served as a deterrent against the formalization of conflict resolution through the legal system. A scandal transformed a case into a spectacle. The spectacle delivered not the binding consequences of legal decisions but the show, the illusion of consequences.

But of course there were consequences. Existing power relations were not transformed but were constantly reproduced and realigned. These changes were often presented as fundamental transformations, and yet their real significance remained hidden. Political life was lived from moment to moment. Exceptions to the rule were the rule. The exercise of power, based on this fluid manner of constructing social reality, made the contingent structural.

CONCLUSION: THE FORM OF INFORMALITY

Unlike fictional murders, real ones do not always leave behind the clue that could allow one to unravel their mystery and uncover their perpetrators. In this case, whether Carmona was killed by Molina or by President Pérez, through the PTJ or the DISIP, or even by Pérez through Molina, we may never know. But what is significant is that these various alternatives were believed to be plausible. My intent has been to establish their intelligibility, not their truth—to understand not just the social conditions that made the murder possible but also the particular form that the murder took and the way in which it was socially represented. If I have then analyzed the murder as part of a system of social relations, it must be recognized that it was only through that murder that this system surfaced to public view. By bringing into the open a normally hidden reality, the murder became the condition for its own analysis. I see the murder of Carmona as a breach of a code and as the expression of an alternative code. During the oil boom, criminality established its claim as a normal form of sociality. Its ideals were brought out into the open. Its heroes left the clandestine world and proudly paraded in public places, making deals in restaurants, broadcasting their accomplishments in private clubs, flaunting their loot everywhere, seeking the company of society's notables.

At the close of the oil boom, the shift in the definition of ideal behavior in the economic realm was matched by a shift in the normative definition of political behavior. Just as the ideal of the *bourgeois conquerant* receded before that of the clever merchant or speculator, the notion of the responsible citizen paled before that of the independent individual, a person free from social constraints. To be someone, one had to be clever, daring, and rich; and to be rich, one had to have the power to stand outside the law and above social constraints.

Although they were more a matter of emphasis than of sharp differentiation, these shifts in normative standards became significant in the conduct and representation of social life. By projecting these standards onto the public arena, the political struggle centering on the Carmona case magnified their differences and exaggerated their opposition. Yet the contrast that was expressed through images that opposed citizens and gangsters, entrepreneurs and pirates, work and plunder, health and intoxication, corresponded to the fundamental tension giving distinctive character to Venezuelan society: the conflict between the public character of oil money and the private nature of its appropriation. Underlying the struggles for social ascent was a conception of petroleum as ready-made collective wealth whose private appropriation could be justified only if it promoted the collective welfare. Yet as black gold, petroleum gave power to those individuals who possessed it, transforming, by virtue of its power to confer power, the nature of power in society and the human capacity to define collectively the possible and the desirable.

Figure 4
Agricultural and industrial production, 1973–80

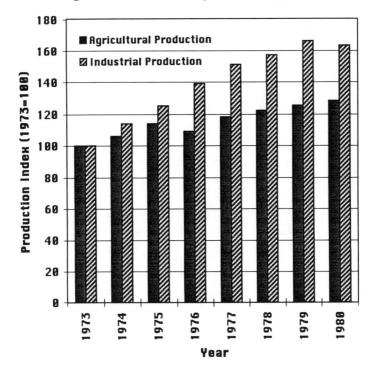

SOURCE: Baptista 1991: 126

Table 18
Employment, 1973–80

Year	Total population	Economically active	Employed	Unemployed	Unem-ployment rate (%)
1973	11,748,395	3,673,778	3,468,418	205,360	5.59
1974	12,117,759	3,813,613	3,540,611	273,001	7.16
1975	12,522,721	3,966,121	3,709,534	256,587	6.47
1976	12,934,310	4,118,658	3,871,689	246,969	6.00
1977	13,341,371	4,275,765	4,072,699	203,066	4.75
1978	13,779,195	4,440,179	4,235,242	204,937	4.62
1979	14,237,753	4,605,261	4,357,919	247,342	5.37
1980	14,703,316	4,818,012	4,534,098	283,914	5.89

SOURCE: Baptista 1991: 263

Table 19
Share of petroleum in total exports, 1973–80
(in millions of bolivars, base 1984)

Year	Total exports	Petroleum exports (nonrentistic)	Nonpetroleum exports	% of petroleum in total exports
1973	26,857.1	20,109.9	6,747.2	75
1974	34,535.2	23,893.4	10,641.8	69
1975	29,582.7	21,887.4	7,695.3	74
1976	31,531.4	23,687.9	7,843.5	75
1977	29,611.3	23,116.8	6,494.5	78
1978	29,828.6	23,031.7	6,796.9	77
1979	38,605.2	28,521.8	10,083.4	74
1980	41,116.8	28,964.5	12,152.3	70

SOURCE: Baptista 1991: 119.

Table 20

Evaluation of petroleum income, 1973–80

(in millions of bolivars, base 1968)

Year	Rentistic petroleum income	Value of petroleum production	Value of nonrentistic petroleum production	State share in oil revenues	Reported profits(1)	Nonrentistic profits(2)
1973	13,459	19,980	6,521	13,037	2,665	2,055
1974	37,422	46,563	9,141	39,720	2,286	3,435
1975	27,806	37,966	10,160	29,858	1,815	3,479
1976	28,038	39,257	11,219	29,328	3,761	4,395
1977	30,188	41,724	11,536	26,991	7,805	4,622
1978	26,408	40,028	13,620	25,731	6,221	5,139
1979	43,789	62,435	18,646	39,618	12,480	8,117
1980	59,651	83,664	24,013	56,026	14,813	9,709

SOURCE: Baptista 1991: 145. Headings of each column have been modified by the author in consultation with Baptista.

(1) Profits as reported by the oil companies

(2) Profitability of oil capital stock in Venezuela after taxes

    (Based on U.S. rate of return in the oil sector).

❧ IV ❧
Sequel

BLACK GOLD:
MONEY FETISHISM AND MODERNITY

27 February 1989, Caracas. (Archivo El Universal. Photo: José Cohen.)

Previous page: Carlos Andrés Pérez, "the man who really walks" ("el hombre que camina"), during the 1988 presidential campaign. (Archivo Ultimas Noticias.)

9

Harvesting the Oil: The Storm of Progress

In my life I have demonstrated that material wealth does not appeal to me.
What really appeals to me is History.[1]

Carlos Andrés Pérez

Interviewer: How do you want to be remembered by History?
Carlos Andrés Pérez: As I was, as a man who dedicated his life—and I have
spent more than fifty years in politics—to the struggle for democracy and
freedom in Venezuela and Latin America, and who managed to promote
the modernization of Venezuela.[2]

Interview, 21 October 1994

THE MYTH OF PROGRESS

The pursuit of modernity in Venezuela, cast by official discourse as the
nation's quest to resemble metropolitan centers, was the legitimating
aim of policy and politics throughout most of this century. Despite limited
achievements and persistent setbacks, it was a widely held belief that Venezuela had steadily progressed toward this objective since the reestablishment
of democracy in 1958. For this reason Venezuela has been largely absent from
the international scholarship on Latin America, which has focused on nations
with more dramatic histories—histories marked by revolutions, economic
swings, and harsh dictatorships and, more recently, by the "transition" from

1. *En mi vida he demostrado que la riqueza material no me atrae. A mí lo que sí me atrae es la historia.* I have
taken this quote from a compact disk titled "No me perdonan" (They don't forgive me) produced
by Alonso Toro, a young Venezuelan musician, whose imaginative musical compositions incorporate
fragments of political speeches in rhythmic structure in order to mimic the role of repetition in
political life. The title comes from a speech by Pérez in which he repeats that his political enemies
don't forgive him—*no me perdonan*—because he is the only politician who has been twice elected
president of Venezuela; he turns criticism of his rule into an expression of envy.

2. *Entrevistador: ¿Cómo quiere ser recordado por la Historia?*
*Carlos Andrés Pérez: Como lo que fuí, como un hombre que dedicó su vida—y yo tengo mas de 50 años en la
vida política—a la lucha por la democracia y la libertad en Venezuela y en la América, y que logró impulsar la
modernización de Venezuela.*

  I interviewed Pérez in his home, where he was under house arrest afer having been impeached
for corruption.

authoritarianism to democracy. Treated as an exception, Venezuela was cited as a model of a successful transition to democracy or as having a "consolidated" democracy. In one of the books addressing Venezuela's changed status the editors remark, "So exceptional was Venezuela, such a model of socially conscious democracy, that the nation was paid scant attention. To foreign journalists, social scientists, and politicians, Venezuela seemed predictable, and hence of little interest" (Goodman et al. 1995:4).

The myth of Venezuela as a wealthy democratic nation steadily advancing toward modernity continued to hold into the 1990s despite problems that had become evident by 1978. It took not just the currency devaluations, a prolonged decline in the standard of living, massive popular riots resulting in the massacre of four hundred people in 1989, but two abortive military coups in 1992 to shatter what Cabrujas had called the state's "myth of progress." The political elite sought to silence the critique of its economic and ideological shift, and to define the riots as an expression of anarchic currents within a population unaccustomed to a rational economy and to making sacrifices for the nation (Coronil and Skurski 1991; Coronil 1994). The attempted coups of 1992, in contrast, brought a sense of instability at the very top, undermining the elite's self-confidence, and challenging prevailing international and political opinion about Venezuela.

The breakdown of dominant perceptions about Venezuela opened a space for views that had previously been kept marginal but that now appeared as revelations. From this space, it became possible to say that the coups "revealed for all to see that the country suffered many serious problems and its 'model' political system was miserably dysfunctional." The recognition that Venezuela "suffered from the political, economic, and social problems common to most Latin American countries" led to the "collapse of Venezuelan exceptionalism" (Goodman et al. 1995:5-6; see also Levine 1994). From this changed perspective, what before had been celebrated as a model democratic state, a dynamic party system, and a growing economy, is now described as a bloated state dominated by closed elites (a "cogollocracia"),[3] a clientelistic party system ("partidocracia"),[4] and a protected market

---

3. "Cogollo" is the top of the sugar cane or the heart of garden plants; it is used metaphorically to refer to the elite.

4. Many Venezuelan scholars had long analyzed the elitist and demobilizing aspects of the political system (for example, Malavé Mata 1987). Some U.S. scholars have also noted the limited character of Venezuela's democracy. For a lucid synthesis of Venezuela's contemporary history that underlines this aspect, see Hellinger (1991); for a carefully researched interpretation of Venezuela's elitist party structure, see Coppedge (1994).

Carlos Andrés Pérez in his residence "La Ahumada," under
house arrest, August 1994.
(Fundación Andrés Mata.
Photo: Luis R. Bisbal.)

that nurtured parasitical oligopolies (see Goodman et al. 1995; McCoy
et al 1995).

These polar views underline the need to attend to the continuities between Venezuela's alleged exceptional past and its purportedly typical Latin
American present. The recognition of these continuities will make it easier
to see how Venezuela's exceptional financial wealth made it possible for
the state to implement dazzling development plans which obscured structures typical of other Latin American nations. As in a fun-house mirror, Venezuela's image as a wealthy modernizing nation reflected not only an extraordinary physiognomy but also a rather typically malformed anatomy.

Given that Venezuela's development project was premised on the projection of this exceptionalist myth about itself, what has collapsed is the myth.

I began my argument in this book by citing playwright José Ignacio Cabrujas's insight that "oil wealth had the power of a myth." For him, oil wealth transfigured politicians into magicians who embodied the myth of progress and gave it specific form. Presiding over the 1974 oil boom, Carlos Andrés Pérez incarnated this myth like no other president in Venezuelan history, turning it, in Cabrujas's words, into a "hallucination." Ironically, a decade later, during his second presidency (1989-93), Pérez helped shatter the myth of progress by disowning the oil-protected past as an irrational fantasy and turning to the free market as the rational means of achieving progress.

THE PERSISTENT MYTH

Pérez's successors, COPEI's Luis Herrera Campíns (1979-84) and AD's Jaime Lusinchi (1984-89), continued to act as the incarnations of the myth of progress under conditions in which it was increasingly difficult to do so. Using financial resources obtained from a sharp increase in oil prices in 1979 as well as from continued foreign borrowing, they sought to perpetuate the existing political system while making some adjustments in order to obtain more foreign exchange. Courting both popular sectors and foreign creditors, they preserved the political and economic centrality of the state, channeling public resources to favored private interests, demobilizing the population through patronage, publicity, and repression, further concentrating wealth at the top, and placing the burden of the debt on the working population for generations to come.

Nevertheless, the escalating foreign debt and declining economy weakened the state's role during the 1980s. The foreign borrowing begun under Pérez spiraled. During Herrera Campíns's administration Venezuela's official foreign debt increased from close to $9 billion to nearly $24 billion. His failure to obtain financing to consolidate the debts contracted during the oil boom by the state's decentralized institutions signaled Venezuela's loss of international credit. Efforts to activate the economy, such as his 1983 devaluation of the currency, failed to induce a rise in productivity, for they were accompanied by subsidies for "essential" imports for protected industries. As a result of the state's inability to promote the expansion of the domestic economy, local businessmen lost confidence in the local market. In this context, benefits obtained through protectionism came to be redirected from the domestic economy into an ever-expanding current of capital flight.

Under Lusinchi's administration the myth of progress met its limits. He courted local sectors by maintaining a modified version of the protectionist and distributionist system he inherited, but he also responded to international pressures by implementing some IMF stabilization measures. These measures, in Venezuela just as much as in countries ruled by military regimes, led to a drop in real wages and consumption levels (McCoy 1989). Yet the Venezuelan elite could benefit from a system designed to supply dollars at preferential rates for certain imports (the National Preferential Exchange Office, RECADI). As a channel for the massive illicit appropriation of state funds, this system became, "monetarily, probably the largest in the country's history" (Perdomo 1995:331). Lusinchi, heir to a tradition which regarded indebtedness as a sign of Venezuela's backward past (recall that General Gómez paid Venezuela's foreign debt in 1930 even though this did not make economic sense), was committed to paying the debt "to the last cent," as he promised in his inaugural speech. During his administration, the debt service reached $30 billion, consuming almost 50 percent of the nation's foreign exchange, yet the debt principal was reduced only from $35 to $32 billion. The real debt, although it remained largely invisible until the next administration, was higher yet, for the "floating debt" (short-term loans obtained by state agencies which were not officially approved or registered) raised the debt to nearly $43 billion (Karl 1995). Lusinchi continued to spend in a final burst of state munificence until, as Pérez was to discover, the international reserves were practically depleted ($200 million). With the state having no international credit to meet its rising external and internal obligations, when Pérez took office he would have to use more than half of the state's annual foreign exchange income (over $5 billion) to pay its creditors. The possibility of financing the myth of progress had come to an end.

PÉREZ'S NEW MYTH: THE GREAT TURNAROUND

As if following a script by Cabrujas, who had said that it would be suicidal for a presidential candidate in Venezuela "not to promise us paradise" because the "state has nothing to do with our reality" (1984:17), the 1988 presidential campaign proceeded as if nothing had changed in the last decade. Pérez campaigned across the country in 1988 without suggesting, as I saw while traveling with his campaign, that a different reality would have to be faced. In each town, in each public gathering, he presented himself as a savior who offered, as Cabrujas said, "paradise." As in the previous election, he made his speed and energy his trademark. He passed through towns as an apparition, either in a large motorcade led by a team of skilled motorcycle riders who resembled Hollywood stuntmen or walking so fast that no one could interact with him. His campaign's signature slogan was "Estas manos que ves son las de Carlos Andrés" ("These hands that you see are those of Carlos Andrés"), but he continued to be known as "the man with energy" and "the man who really walks"; these slogans from 1973 and the new campaign were repeated together in the meetings orchestrated throughout the nation, linking the past to the present. His appearance in each town, waving his upraised hands and promising prosperity, was directed at impressing everyone with his exceptional power; each spectacle unfolded as if its aim were not so much to convince people as to leave them dumbfounded.

With the November 1988 polls indicating that Pérez would win, it was difficult to remember that ten years earlier he had been publicly accused of corruption and that his own party had sought to distance itself from him when his term ended. Then it had been common for people to refer to him derisively as *Locovén* (the suffix *ven*, short for Venezuela, was used to designate the state-owned companies Pérez created during his administration; *Locovén* combines this suffix with *loco,* which means crazy). By attributing the failure of the national development project to Pérez's impulsiveness and personalization of power, *Locovén* expressed the general sentiment that Pérez had lost touch with reality, that he, in effect, incarnated the mad state project of the Great Venezuela.

Yet if in Venezuela political reality was constructed, as Cabrujas put it, through tricks of prestidigitation, Pérez turned out to be the country's most compelling magician. As part of AD's effort to reestablish its public image after its candidate lost the 1978 election, AD's ethics committee sanctioned Pérez for corruption and unsuccessfully sought to expel him from the party.[5] Pérez managed to overcome his party's opposition and to rebuild his leadership within the party, cultivating alliances with financial backers at the top and reviving his support from below, particularly among labor. As a critic of Jaime Lusinchi's administration he regained the allegiance of the party's base and was elected AD's presidential candidate in its primary.[6]

By 1988 a wide array of groups embraced Pérez as their candidate. The

5. For an account of this episode, which centered on the overprice of the frigate Sierra Nevada, see Malavé Mata (1993). For a version of this incident by Gumersindo Rodríguez, a close Pérez associate, see Blanco Muñoz (1989:497–500).

6. Pérez had supported Lusinchi against Piñerua when they competed to be chosen as AD's presidential candidate in 1978, but became his rival for supremacy within AD once Lusinchi was president.

excesses of his presidency were recast as the inevitable expression of structural problems that affect oil-producing nations during boom periods; earlier accusations of Pérez's corruption were now dismissed as the product of Machiavellian publicity campaigns directed at tarnishing his public image.[7] While the economic groups linked to Pérez expected him to support their interests, within the Left Pérez appeared as the only viable candidate who could promote fundamental reforms. Rumors circulated of secret conversations between Pérez and leaders of the leftist parties, of agreements with Latin American presidents, of daring social reforms.

Pérez's aggressive emphasis on foreign policy in his first term, which cast Venezuela as a leader in promoting the establishment of democracy and of autonomous development throughout Latin America, established his image as a defender of Latin American independence. "We know he is a *pillo* (a scoundrel)," a friend told me almost with resignation, "but he is the only political leader in Venezuela, and perhaps in Latin America, who can mastermind a continental political alliance against the IMF and redefine the debt problem." This opinion by a noted economist who had held a top planning position under President Caldera (1969-74) echoed a widely repeated statement during the campaign: "*Carlos Andrés es tan loco que de repente puede echar una vaina*" (Carlos Andrés is so crazy that just maybe he could shake things up).[8]

People reflected humorously on their own shift of perspectives. Another widespread observation during the 1988 electoral campaign captured this reversal: "In 1978 we called Carlos Andrés *Locovén*. Now we are calling him *venloco* (come here, crazy one)." By turning *Locovén* into *venloco*, the expression shifts from a name to a sentence in which *loco* becomes a positive term that refers to a daring person. Instead of dismissing Pérez as the em-

7. For instance, I was told that *Resumen,* whose investigative reports during the 1978 campaign played a key role in linking Pérez to the Carmona case, had published disinformation about Pérez from circles close to Rómulo Betancourt. I was also told that this "information" itself was planted by Pérez. Yet, eighteen years later, Resúmen's director, Jorge Olavarría, still endorsed the account his magazine had given of the Carmona case (interview, August 1996).

8. This colloquial statement is difficult to translate, but captures how Venezuelans express their belief that the unexpected might happen. *De repente* means "suddenly." *Vaina* is an expression used so frequently by Venezuelans that other Latin Americans identify us by our use of this word or by the exclamative *coño* (female genitals), which is used almost as frequently, despite the fact that it is considered even more vulgar. Vaina literally means sheath, but it is generally used to mean problem, nuisance, bother, or thing. In this context it conveys the sense of a change, a problem for others. I am grateful to Jean Paul Dumont, who made me aware that vaina also connotes vagina (yet another case of native blindness).

bodiment of a mad state, *venloco* asks him to come back as a visionary leader who could turn history around.[9]

"Making History" became a familiar slogan during the 1988 electoral campaign. Pérez often asserted that he was seeking the presidency for the second time because he was interested in "History," not in money. Many echoed his phrase. Others, perhaps more cynical, or perhaps wishing to back up his claim with a fool-proof argument, said: "Carlos Andrés already has *todos los reales* (tons of money). If he now wants to bother with the presidency instead of enjoying his *reales*, it is because he really wants to make History." [10] The second time around, however, not oil money but the international financial system defined from the outset the terms under which he would make History.

Pérez won the 4 December 1988 elections by a wide margin (53 percent of the votes). His inauguration ceremony—popularly called *la coronación*—was an impressive ritual of rule that sought to revive the state's splendor and to promote the expectation that Pérez could turn history around. Drawing representatives of 108 nations to the event (including twenty-two heads of state), Pérez projected his image as an international leader. Among those present were Cuba's Fidel Castro on his first visit to Venezuela since 1959, Nicaragua's Sandinista leader Daniel Ortega, and Dan Quayle, on his first foreign visit as U.S. vice president. The presence of Castro and Ortega fueled collective expectations that Pérez would make a radical announcement.

The myth of progress could be countered only in equally mythical terms. As an incarnation of this myth, Pérez constructed his image as a powerful leader by relying on the unexpected, on impulsive decisions often made outside formal political institutions and regular control that produced the illusion that he could make anything happen. This style of politics sustained the expectation that he was in tune with History's pulse, that through him the nation was already on the path to progress. Because it made for frequent

---

9. Using this positive sense of crazy, José Martí (1853–95), the Cuban writer and independence leader, once stated: "the impossible is possible. We, the crazy ones (*los locos*), are the ones who are rational"; Cintio Vitier, a Cuban writer, relates Fidel Castro's invasion to Cuba in the *Granma* to Martí's notion that only crazy people can make history (1975: xlii). In Argentina, "las madres de la Plaza de Mayo," who defied the military dictatorship's repression to protect silently the disappearance of their children, were dismissed by the military junta as "las locas de la Plaza de Mayo." The mothers, who played a key role in overthrowing the dictatorship, resignified the meaning of *locas* by imparting to it positive meanings related to courage and vision in the face of oppression.

10. The *real*, a coin from colonial times, denotes both money in general and a particular coin, half a bolívar.

blunders in the conception and execution of state projects, this style could be sustained only by speed—but then no politician was faster than Pérez, the "man who really walks," "the man with energy." Speed made it possible for Pérez to deny mistakes by leaving them behind, frenetically advancing from one spectacular undertaking to another and keeping the expectant collectivity open to the marvels of his power.

Speed, however, required not just Pérez's magic, but the magic of money; as a myth-making machine the state was fueled by an ongoing stream of petrodollars. By 1989, as diminishing petrodollars had to be used to service the debt, Pérez transformed the task of facing reality and opening the economy into yet another myth. But to the extent that the state had been "a state of dissimulation" ("un estado de disimulo"; Cabrujas 1987:7), without torrents of oil money it could only simulate its dissimulation. The new myth could only self-destruct.

THIS STORM WE CALL PROGRESS

> Where we perceive a chain of events, [the angel of history] sees one single catastrophe which keeps piling wreckage upon wreckage and hurls it in front of his feet . . . This storm irresistibly propels him into the future to which his back is turned, while the pile of debris before him grows skyward. This storm is what we call progress.
>
> *Walter Benjamin*

Still feeding the hope that he would restore the prosperity that people associated with the 1973 oil boom, Pérez referred during the presidential campaign to the International Monetary Fund (IMF) as *la bomba solo-mata-gente* (the bomb that only kills people). At his inauguration he issued a call to debtor nations to lobby against the oppressive policies of international banks. But at the same time that Pérez publicly denounced international capital, he privately sent a message to the IMF that he would comply with its stringent conditions.

Soon after his inauguration he shifted his public position. Presenting it as a historical turning point, he announced *El Gran Viraje*, the Great Turnaround: the shift toward an open economy in compliance with the IMF's austerity program. In theory, this meant turning away from the parochial oil-protected national market toward the competitive global market. In practice, it meant dismantling the complex network of protections—state employment, loans, subsidies, tariffs, price controls, and wage regulations—that had constituted the populist model of development for more than half a century. Neither the business sector nor the working population was prepared for this change.

At a time when much of the population expected Pérez to restore prosperity, businesses hoarded basic consumer goods in the expectation that he would lift price controls. The resulting shortage of goods, which extended to coins themselves, the openly defiant stance of commercial firms, and the indifference of the government created a widely shared sense of deception and impotence in the face of uncontrollable powers.

In this context, Pérez raised the price of domestic gasoline, the cheapest in the world, to begin to bring it to world market levels. Assuming that this measure would be accepted as a reasonable economic step, the government did not prepare the population for its application. Yet, in Venezuela's petro-democracy, this measure shattered the bond that united the body politic as the collective owner of the nation's natural body; by violating what people considered their birthright, it ruptured a moral bond of protection between state and people. In response to this measure, on 27 February private owners of buses and vans doubled their fares, defying government regulations. Abused by government and business, workers and students who relied on these means of transportation began spontaneous protests which soon expanded into massive rioting and looting, escalating from neighborhood grocery stores to commercial centers in Caracas and other cities. For two days, several hundred thousand people in the capital and many other cities participated in this collective upheaval; over a thousand stores were burned and looted in Caracas alone.

Government leaders were shocked. After thirty years of stability supported by oil income and the parties' control over popular sectors, these leaders believed that el pueblo was incapable of independent action. The stunned government responded to this social explosion with massive repression. In Caracas thousands of troops occupied the streets, fired indiscriminately at residences in working-class barrios and people on the streets, killing at least four hundred. The government gained control of the streets only after suspending constitutional guarantees, arresting several thousand people, and imposing a state of siege. Lasting five days, this was the largest and most violently repressed revolt against austerity measures in Latin American history (Coronil and Skurski 1991).

The government resisted efforts by human rights organizations to investigate what had happened, took no legal action against those responsible for the indiscriminate and excessive violence, and assumed no responsibility to-

La Nueva Peste, Cementerio del Sur, Caracas. Bodies of victims of the 27 February 1989 massacre buried in garbage bags. (COFAVIC.)

ward the relatives of the victims or the wounded.[11] While the official figure remains at 277 dead, a human rights organization created to defend the victims of this massacre, COFAVIC (Committee of Relatives of the Innocent Victims), identified 400 bodies; it is possible that many more people were killed. The most shocking discovery was a mass grave in Caracas's public cemetery whose existence was widely rumored. In a section called la Nueva Peste (the New Plague), the successor to a mass grave for victims of a past epidemic, the government had secretly buried sixty-eight people in plastic garbage bags during the riots. These findings fueled widely held beliefs among the poor that a far higher number of people had been killed and secretly disposed of. The government, however, continued to discourage efforts to investigate these violent events and did not alter the official figure it had given before la Nueva Peste was discovered.

Years later Pérez still insisted that "there were less than three hundred

11. COFAVIC asserted that three years after the February massacre, "impunity continues to be the main enemy." The military tribunal before which they have presented all their carefully researched cases, "has not produced even one arrest order, while the same tribunal in charge of the proceedings related to the military coup of 4 February 1992 [an attempted coup against Pérez] has produced in less than one month over 150 arrest orders. This calls into question once again the credibility of military justice" ("Tres años de impunidad," *Referencias*, año 4, No. 41, 1, March 1992, p. 4).

people killed." He dismissed my question about COFAVIC's list by discrediting the source: "This is a lie. If this list exists, the identifications are invented. The *Petejota* (the Technical Judicial Police) are very honest in relation to this, nothing was covered up. There was a mass grave, it is true; but people buried there had already been identified." Pérez concluded: "It would have been regrettable if one, two, or three people had been killed. The historical truth is that not even three hundred people were killed" (interview, October 1994). Pérez's unwillingness to modify the original official figure was not just the usual assertion of the government's unaccountability, but also a political attempt to control the terms of public discourse and to deny alternative claims.[12]

These events marked a crisis of the populist project that had defined the relationship between state and pueblo since 1936. With the shift to free-market policies and the dismantling of populist developmentalism, dominant discourse began to present the people not so much as the virtuous foundation of democracy, but as an unruly and parasitical mass to be disciplined by the state and made productive by the market. From the perspective of the popular sectors, on the other hand, the elite was increasingly defined as a corrupt "cogollo" that had privatized the state, looted the nation's oil wealth, and abused the people.

For months after the 27 February riots, as living conditions continued to deteriorate, scattered protests involving state employees and professionals, as well as students and workers, escalated throughout the nation. They made increasingly public the view that the people had been betrayed by their leaders and that democracy had become a facade behind which an elite had used the state for its own advantage. This view found unexpected support within the military, which had been a loyal supporter of the democratic regime. Its mid-level officers and lower-level members also faced a drastic decline in real wages and prospects for mobility. Paralleling the stratification in the political parties, mid-level officers saw the upper-level officers as politicized and complicit in a corrupt state that had obliged the military to suppress civilian protest.

Just as the government had assumed the passivity of the popular sectors,

12. In 1992 Pérez had stated that the people discovered in la Nueva Peste "were registered in the morgue"("La exhumación avanza con lentitud," *Referencias*, año 3, No. 27, p. 3). He now asserted to me that they had been buried in la Nueva Peste because their relatives had not taken the bodies from the morgue. Yet COFAVIC had demonstrated that the bodies were buried in secret, and the three bodies that were identified by the forensic commission, aided by international experts, had not been registered in the original government list.

it had taken the military's loyalty for granted, since it had been successfully incorporated into the patronage system controlled by the democratic parties. On 4 February 1992 a group of mid-level army officers from the clandestine Movimiento Bolivariano Revolucionario-200 (Revolutionary Bolivarian Movement-200) almost toppled and killed Pérez. Invoking Bolivarian principles of justice and sovereignty, the movement's statements blamed a corrupt elite for appropriating the nation's wealth, undermining its financial sovereignty, neglecting to protect its frontiers, widening the gap between wealthy and poor, and using the military to repress social protests. The coup's leader, Lieutenant Colonel Hugo Chávez, became a popular hero overnight. A man of humble social origins and darker-skinned than most high-ranking military officers, Chávez was seen as a man of the people, the embodiment of the patriotic leader committed to fulfilling the populist promise of national sovereignty and social equity. Ten months later, on 27 November, a second, less popular, bloodier military coup was mounted by high-level officers, including some from the air force who bombed the presidential palace. While in both cases the bulk of the military remained loyal to the government, these coups made clear that deep institutional fissures within the military had undermined the regime.[13] As during the turbulent middle years of this century (discussed in part 2), the coups' leaders claimed to defend democracy by restoring its concern for substantive achievements rather than formal procedures.

In response to the coups, the political parties intensified the effort to decentralize and revitalize the political system along lines proposed by COPRE (the Commission for State Reform). Since Congress approved a reform of the electoral system, replacing presidentially appointed regional officials with directly elected mayors and governors, the December 1992 gubernatorial and mayoral election was seen as an opportunity to strengthen Venezuela's battered democracy. In a clear repudiation of AD, the opposition parties COPEI, Causa R, and Movimiento al Socialism (MAS) won most governorships and many mayorships. But while this vote expressed the capacity of the opposition parties to organize around local concerns and leaders, an abstention rate of nearly 50 percent revealed a widespread rejection of political parties and deep skepticism concerning Venezuela's democratic institutions.

The failed coups and the electoral results showed the extent to which Pérez had lost popular support as well as control over the military. In a sudden and complex turnaround, a growing collective sentiment that political

13. For discussions of the coups, see Ochoa 1992, Aguero 1995, and Burggraaff and Millett 1995.

stability and the national welfare depended on removing Pérez from power was expressed through mounting protests and public debate. Congress impeached Pérez on charges of corruption in May 1993—he was accused of illegally using $17 million from the secret fund of the Ministry of the Interior in order to support Violeta Chamorro's fledgling democracy in Nicaragua and to finance his lavish inauguration.[14] While observers disagree about the legality of Pérez's impeachment, they agree that this measure was taken by the political elite to salvage a threatened system.[15] Just as Pérez had incarnated the myth of progress, he now had to enact the myth that he was responsible for its failure.

Senator Ramón Velásquez, who was also a historian, was selected as the interim president, whose major task was to restore confidence in the democratic system and to oversee elections for president and Congress.[16] Rafael Caldera, a politician known for his rigorous personal honesty, broke from his party, COPEI, to run on a platform critical of neoliberal reforms, with the support of MAS and Convergencia Nacional, a coalition of sixteen parties. Caldera was elected president with 31 percent of the vote; AD and COPEI, the parties which had historically dominated the democratic regime, saw their vote decline to 47 percent from 93 percent in the 1988 election. Abstention reached a record 44 percent level, compared to 22 percent in 1988. This sudden high level of withdrawal from electoral politics marked a deepening collective sense of political exclusion.

Facing a collective repudiation of the party system, Caldera also inherited a troubled economy whose problems were magnified by an unprecedented banking crisis that surfaced three weeks before he took office. The banking system had become an arena for financial speculation and oligopolistic competition as a result of the lack of effective banking laws and regulatory agencies and of Pérez's deregulation of the economy. Banks attracted the public's money by offering unrealistically high interest rates, and loaned it freely to their own directors and associates, who carried out highly speculative projects. On 10 January 1994, the government of Ramón Velásquez

14. For a comprehensive account of this incident, see Chitty La Roche (1993).

15. Editorial Centauro collected a wide-ranging collection of articles by friends and critics of Pérez who agree that the legal procedure against Pérez was marred by irregularities and that his impeachment was in response to political considerations (1994).

16. Velásquez was widely respected as a historian as well as a principled and independent politician, even though he was identified as an AD sympathizer. After he took office the level of social tension declined notably. In conversation people frequently contrasted Velásquez's "common sense" to Pérez's "megalomania" and "disconnection from reality."

bailed out the Banco Latino at a cost of almost $1.8 billion. Not only the public's savings (1.2 million depositors), but state funds were deposited in this bank, including the resources from the banking regulatory agency. During the four years that its long-time chairman, the apostle Pedro Tinoco, served as the head of Central Bank under Pérez, the Banco Latino had become the second largest in the country and a symbol of the Pérez administration's ostentatiousness and corruption. "Probably no other bank in the world had more members of its board with private jets. Banco Latino's Chairman, Gustavo Gómez, had three" (*Wall Street Journal,* 4 February 1994).

The Banco Latino bailout marked the beginning of an unprecedented banking crisis. As people tried in vain to withdraw their savings from other private banks, the Caldera government took over almost the entire private banking system at an estimated cost of over $8.5 billion or 75 percent of the 1994 national budget. A substantial portion of this money, which was given directly to the banks to back up deposits, was taken by the bankers, who fled to Europe and the U.S. before arrest warrants were issued. This was one of Latin America's worst banking crises; proportionately, it was more than ten times as severe for the Venezuelan economy as the failure of savings and loan institutions was to the United States in the early 1990s (*New York Times,* 16 May 1994). Amidst rumors of coups and popular uprising, Caldera suspended constitutional guarantees and established exchange controls.

In the past, the elite had appropriated the public's oil wealth through the mediation of the state, which exerted some control over its distribution and use. Now, the banking elite directly took the public's personal savings, as well as large sums of government money, through the unregulated market. If the coups showed deep schisms within the military parallel to those in the polity, the banking crisis revealed the deterritorializing pull of the global market on the business elite. The pursuit of money in the speculative internationalized market eroded the elite's attachment to the domestic economy and undermined customary business standards.

As we saw, at the end of the first Pérez administration there was a widely held belief that the business sector was divided between reputable businessmen, whose investments were linked to the nation's development, and unprincipled speculators, who sought profits by any means in pursuit of their own private advantage. Since the traditional elite was implicated in the financial crisis, this distinction became untenable. As a depositor in the Metropolitan Bank who lost his savings stated bitterly about the trust he had placed in the bank's board of directors: "They were members of the country's business aristocracy. They were the best names. Honest people,

people with blue blood." But now he regarded them as people who "don't have a country." As he put it, "Their country is money" (*Washington Post*, 27 June 1994).

As a result of the liberalization that began in the 1980s, the business sector shifted its focus from the state to the market. But this shift had taken place through the state; some of the most powerful economic groups had used their political connections to diversify and invest abroad. Since the 1974 oil boom, capital flight has been estimated as between $60 and 90 billion— between two and three times the amount of the foreign debt. Conglomerates that expanded internationally have been in a better position to adapt to the new context by using their financial power to reorganize their local operations. "We have reinvented ourselves," said Gustavo Cisneros, one of the leaders of the Cisneros Group. "Any group in Latin America who doesn't do what we are doing will be lost, gone, retired," he added, referring to the group's new ability to compete in international markets (*Wall Street Journal*, 16 November 1994).[17]

Ironically, the absence of state controls and privileges has intensified oligopolistic practices and competition, leading to a concentration of power in the private sector. As the banking crisis revealed, the lack of state regulations in the financial sector stimulated unconstrained profit-making practices. In what two analysts have called "an oligopolistic frenzy" (Naím and Frances 1995 : 189), the liberalization of the economy encouraged major economic groups to control the market by any means. No longer able to rely on state support, major economic groups have pursued profit-making by controlling key aspects of the market—from the monopolization of inputs to the construction of public opinion through the media. While some of the economic groups which grew under protectionism have now declined, others, particularly those with diversified national and international investments, have become new centers of economic and political power. Under neoliberalism, centralized power has not been dispersed, it has changed form. The com-

17. The Cisneros Group, which had become one of Venezuela's major conglomerates during Pérez's first term, was deeply implicated in the Banco Latino, in part through its links to its founder and chairman, Pedro Tinoco, who had been a chairman of the Cisneros-owned Cada supermarket chain. Gustavo Cisneros, the group's chairman, is a member of Chase Manhattan Bank's international advisory board and a close associate of Carlos Andrés Pérez. About half of the group's $4 billion of revenue in 1993 came from subsidiaries abroad, including investments in such companies as Univision, the Spanish-language TV network in the United States, Xtra International, a supermarket chain with fifty-six stores in Puerto Rico, the Virgin Islands and Florida, and the Spalding and Evenflo companies, makers of sports equipment and baby products (*Wall Street Journal*, 16 November 1994).

manding heights have shifted from the state to these more diffuse and invisible private centers of public power.[18]

In the automobile sector studied in this book, the auto parts enterprises linked to major conglomerates have been in a better position to adapt to the open market and to withstand the decline in automobile production. Vehicle production declined from 182,678 in 1978 to a low of 27,637 in 1989, but has steadily increased to 96,401 vehicles in 1995. The value of automobile parts production in 1995 was $765 million ($265 for the domestic market and $500 million for exports). The Sivensa Group, controlled by the Machado Zuloaga family and encompassing the most important firms in the automobile parts sector, has preserved a dominant position by directing its production to exports, which now make up more than half of its earnings. On the other hand, without any protection, FANATRACTO, despite some attempts to revive it as a tractor factory or to use it for other activities (such as storing grain or repairing freight-cars), remains a useless shell in the midst of the Guayana region.

The crisis of the protectionist state and the opening up of the economy have split the nation into two: an internationally connected upper class and its local associates (about many of whom it could be said that "money is their country"), and an impoverished majority that includes a shrinking middle class. A *New York Times* article entitled "Whatever Happened to Venezuela's Middle Class?" underlines the drastic drop in the standard of living in Venezuela (in the last twenty-five years the share of household income spent on food has increased from 28 to 72 percent) and describes what it calls the "death" of the middle class: "The country is entering its fourth year of recession, and the inflation at 54 percent last year is the highest in South America. Venezuela's middle class, once accustomed to shopping sprees in Miami, has been reduced to near-poverty" (9 February 1996). For the vast majority of the population, the situation is of course worse: facing the highest inflation in Latin America in 1996 (70 percent), around 70 percent of Venezuelans live in poverty, and 30 percent of these in critical poverty.

Caldera came to power promising to limit neoliberal measures and to

18. The changing structure and practices of the business sector need to be studied. Although the Grupo Cisneros has suffered a significant loss of prestige and power in Venezuela, it is likely that it will continue to play a dominant role in the domestic economic and public life. While in the transition to the free market some of the major conglomerates have declined (for example, the Grupos Mendoza and Corimón), others have continued to expand, and in some cases not just by diversifying internationally, but by deepening their already significant investments in domestic productive structures (the Grupo Polar).

improve the population's standard of living. But lacking financial resources to support his plans, Caldera could only delay responding to the demands of foreign creditors. On 14 March 1996, Caldera, visibly upset, announced his new economic plan: the "Agenda Venezuela," an IMF austerity program which would further the plan begun by Pérez. In exchange for new international loans, he agreed to impose the standard set of "internal adjustments," including an immediate 600 percent increase in the price of gasoline. In a historical irony, Teodoro Petkoff, a well-known former guerrilla leader and founder of the Movimiento al Socialismo (MAS), as head of the state's planning agency CORDIPLAN, was the person responsible for implementing this program. In a sign of the convergence, in some respects, of criticisms of protectionism made by the right and the left, Petkoff, a socialist politician and longtime critic both of local and international capital, became the program's most effective promoter.

President Caldera commented on the irony that he had been elected with the mandate to reverse the turn to neoliberalism: "I had to take these measures because there is nothing else that can be done" ("porque no hay más remedio," literally "because there is no other cure"). He noted, however, that he also had taken these steps because of commitments to participate in regional markets in Latin America which are organized according to liberal principles. And he noted that "while international capital and the IMF pressured Venezuela to accept these measures, the government managed to complement them with important social welfare programs." As he stood up from the interview, he told me informally: "Teodoro believes in these measures more than I do" (interview, August 1996).[19]

As in other Latin American countries, the free market has been promoted not only by its adamant proponents, but by its previous critics. Yet this endorsement raises complex questions about political agency in neocolonial contexts. How are we to understand policies implemented by subaltern states within severe internal and external constraints? How are we to interpret the ideology and practice of state sovereignty in global conditions that undermine it? What does "believing" in neoliberal measures mean for Caldera or for Petkoff?

For Carlos Andrés Pérez or for Rafael Caldera, new modalities of globalization transformed the context in which the national state had to pursue

---

19. As a result of the continuing decline of the economy and of the effects of these liberal measures on the working population, Caldera's popularity was reduced by half in two years, from 66 percent in May 1994 to 33 percent in September 1996.

its perduring goal, "the modernization of Venezuela"—the goal for whose fulfillment Pérez hopes to be remembered. Yet the failure of most development projects in Venezuela and elsewhere has led to the recognition that the pursuit of modernization has produced not progress but greater inequalities. With the shift from the state to the market as the central source of advancement, progress is still presented as the product of modernizing plans, but it increasingly appears as an individual rather than as a national objective. The neoliberal privatization of the market has entailed the individualization of the pursuit of progress.

Thus, instead of dissolving the myth of progress, the demythification of national progress has led to the mythification of individual progress. If the pursuit of progress had previously been presented as the common goal of a united collectivity, blurring its internal divisions, it now appears as an individual aim, intensifying the nation's growing polarization. In Venezuela, this division has split the nation into two. While the internationalized elite moves easily between ever more insecure domestic enclaves of privilege and the metropolitan centers, the majority is restricted to an increasingly impoverished social environment palpably marked by abandonment and neglect. As the storm of progress keeps piling wreckage upon wreckage, it is no longer possible to deny the catastrophe it has left behind by looking toward the future. The tragedy of modernity is that its promise of universal progress cannot be fulfilled in the terms in which it has been cast.

Oil painting on bolívar bills by José Rafael Castillo Arnal: Simón Bolívar on a one-hundred-bolívar bill (center); a masked urban protester, figures known as *encapuchados* (hooded ones), on a ten-bolívar bill (left); and an indigenous woman painted on a five bolívar bill (right). J. R. Castillo, a painter from Caracas, critically depicts the ruling elite's political project in paintings on canvas and bills. (Collection of the artist.)

10

BEYOND OCCIDENTALISM: A SUBALTERN MODERNITY

World history travels from east to west; for Europe is the absolute end of
history, just as Asia is the beginning . . . It is in the West that the inner sun
of self-consciousness, which emits a higher radiance, makes its further
ascent.

[Humanity] is the miracle worker, in so far as, in the course of human history, it masters nature, both within human beings and outside them, ever
more completely, and subordinates nature as the impotent material of its
own activity.

Georg W. F. Hegel

WITHIN THE LABYRINTH

Like history, writing is a contest of positions. I have written this account
by creating a space from which to reflect on Venezuela's labyrinthine
history without making the customary separations between the inner and
the outer, the local and the global, geography and history. From this space I
have sought to develop a position from which to apprehend societies defined
as marginal to the modern world and, in the same movement, to deflect the
"radiant" imperial light that consigns them to the margins. If through a contrapuntal reading of Jorge Luis Borges and Jacques Derrida we can imagine
history as a labyrinth whose exits are entrances into an expanding labyrinth,
my position claims no special privilege. "For every poet," Derek Walcott
said, "it is always morning in the world, and History a forgotten insomniac
night" (1992:26). Guided by a stance that looks backward at the destruction
that has taken place and remembers it as an "insomniac night," this position
claims the present as the morning in a world that refuses this past. At the risk
of fixing its provisionality in a labyrinth that presents no exits, I would like
to underline some of the principles that orient this perspective and the view
of Venezuela it brought forth.

While Hegel's Eurocentrism has been a central target of the critique of
historicism for unobjectionable reasons, I have joined this critique to two of
Hegel's insights in order to counter both his provincial universalism and his

critics' abandonment of a totalizing vision. First, the West was formed not independently of other cultures but by subsuming them within its history. The West's self-fashioning as the self-made center of world history should therefore be seen as the mystifying effect of power relations. Second, the universalization of the West has been achieved through its domination of nature (which I take as a description of the value attached to mastery and exploitation, not as a normative proposition). Given the territorial division of the world into politically independent nations, the domination of nature, therefore, has entailed as well the subjection of some nations by others.[1]

Building on a long tradition of critical reflection on colonialism and imperialism and taking the postmodern emphasis on the fragmentary as a useful moment in a holistic and relational analysis, I have argued for the need to recast Occidentalist histories which assume a sharp separation between the West and its periphery. In light of my analysis of Venezuelan state formation, I have proposed that the theoretical recognition of the centrality of nature in the historical formation of capitalism contributes to integrate the histories of (post)colonial and metropolitan regions; to conceptualize capitalism as a global process that involves multiple social agents in complex worldwide interactions; to view modernity as a relational process involving the contrapuntal constitution of subaltern and Occidentalist modernities; to conceive the state, in its role as a sovereign landlord over a national territory, as an economic agent with its own base of economic power; and to develop a dialectical approach that frees our understanding of history from teleological narratives locked in binary oppositions, opening a space for exploring the actions and potential solidarities of heterogeneous actors formed within increasingly interrelated material and cultural conditions.

BLACK GOLD'S MAGIC

My analysis of the historical formation of the Venezuelan state is premised on the elaboration of these propositions. If we accept that the West has defined its position vis-à-vis nature as "the miracle worker" that "subordinates nature as the impotent material of its own activity," I have approached the making of this "miracle" on Venezuelan terrain by exploring how the al-

---

1. I discuss elsewhere Hegel's conception of Europe as the center of history by linking his philosophy of history, as outlined in his *Lectures on the Philosophy of History,* to his analysis of the master/slave dialectic developed in *The Phenomenology of Mind* (Coronil 1996). For an argument that what is required is to "think with Hegel against Hegel," which usefully engages the modern/postmodern divide, see Bernstein (1991 : 293-319).

chemic change of black gold into money entailed the transfiguration of the social agents involved in this history-making process. The Venezuelan state has presented itself as the miracle worker that could turn its dominion over nature into a source of historical progress. But largely because much of its power is borrowed from the powers of oil money rather than being produced through its mastery over nature, the state has been limited to magic performances, not miracles. By analyzing the enactments that have constituted it as a magical state, I have examined its historical transformation during this century, tracing its role in the frenetic rise of Venezuela as a financially wealthy oil nation and its no less violent fall as an indebted third-world country.

When the foreign oil industry was established on Venezuelan soil, Venezuela rapidly changed from a stagnant agricultural society, torn by civil strife and indebted to foreign powers, into the world's major oil exporter. From the outset, the vast inflow of oil money led to the expansion of domestic economic activities, particularly in the areas of commerce, services, and real estate rather than in the productive sectors. The infusion of oil money into the domestic economy helped naturalize wealth, disconnecting it from the productivity of local labor by basing it on the valorization of a mineral resource which required little labor for its extraction. In so doing, it promoted the notion that riches reside directly in nature. It also politicized national wealth, making its monetary magnitude dependent on the bargaining relation between the state and oil companies and its local acquisition reliant on access to its state-mediated channels of domestic distribution. Ironically, these developments, triggered by the activities of the most advanced transnational corporations on Venezuelan soil, reinforced certain strands of social experience rooted in a history of conquest and colonization. The mirage of El Dorado had haunted the early conquerors who were drawn ever deeper into the Amazonian jungle in their obsessive quest for the riches that indigenous people assured them lay just behind the next mountain. This mirage reappeared faintly with every discovery of mineral wealth throughout succeeding centuries. With the gushing forth of oil, the submerged images of El Dorado shone again brightly, appearing as endless streams of black gold circulating throughout the vessels of the social body, nourishing it and awaiting capture.

As the oil industry came to occupy a central role in the domestic economy and as producing wealth was identified with capturing oil rents, capitalism in Venezuela developed by establishing a singular relationship among nature, the nation, and the global economy. This constitutive relationship did not preclude but rather encouraged the rapid expansion of domestic productive structures. However, it conditioned their internal organization and productive dynamics, limiting the depth of Venezuelan industrialization and promoting the development of diversified oligopolistic economic groups which integrated financial, commercial, and industrial holdings. If under capitalism the "production process . . . absorbs circulation as a mere phase of production" (Marx 1967: 328), in Venezuela—because the distribution of oil rents came to prevail over the production of value—the circulation process absorbed production as a phase of circulation. Thus, in a contradictory process, the implantation of subsidiaries of the most advanced transnational corporations on the soil of a stagnant agricultural society simultaneously promoted and undermined the development of productive relations. Paradoxically, oil money, the outcome of the activities of some of the most dynamic transnational corporations, reinforced in Venezuela economic conceptions and practices stemming from the Spanish discovery and colonization of the Americas which treated wealth less as the result of productive labor than as the reward for activities not directly connected with production, including conquest, plunder, or pure chance.

From the dictatorial rule of Juan Vicente Gómez at the opening of this century to the democratic regime of Carlos Andrés Pérez at its close, the grounding of state power in the oil economy became more abstract, generalizing the state's dominion over the nation but ultimately ceding significant control to international capital. After Gómez's death, collective pressure to participate in the political and natural bodies of the nation helped forge a singular relationship between the democratization of political life and the constitution of a protectionist state. State power, rooted during the Gómez dictatorship in the state's ownership of the nation's subsoil, came to rest on the state's ability to secure and manage increasing flows of petrodollars to finance national development projects. The liquidity, abstractness, and permutability of these monetary resources granted a different public visibility to oil. Circulating throughout the body politic as money, oil ceased to be identified as a material substance and became a synonym for money. Just as oil came to be seen abstractly as money, the state became the general representative of a political community of shared ownership of the nation's natural body.

In the hands of the Venezuelan state, money throughout this century was the universal equivalent that embodied the promise of universality. In exchange for the nation's money, the state promised to bring modernity to Venezuela—to replace its parochial system of production and mode of life with the modern structures and culture of the metropolitan centers. "To sow the oil" condensed this aspiration: the exchange of the nation's subsoil for international money was justified in terms of the nationalist project to replenish the nation's nonrenewable natural body with renewable forms of social wealth. The Faustian trade of money for modernity did not bring the capacity to produce but the illusion of production: money brought modern products or factories capable of generating only a truncated modernity. By creating an industrial structure under the protective mantle of petrodollars, the modernization programs of General Marcos Pérez Jiménez and President Carlos Andrés Pérez promoted industries that showed a persistent tendency to function more as traps to capture oil rents than as creative means to produce value.

The 1973 oil boom exploded the limits of this Faustian exchange of oil for the illusion of progress. As foreign banks recycled petrodollars into loans, the state mortgaged the national subsoil in order to obtain loans to finance its vast plan to create the Great Venezuela. Thus, oil wealth brought debt money. The combined circulation of petrodollars and debt dollars within the body politic intensified the pattern of wasteful investment and corruption that had characterized the use of oil rents from the outset. These combined resources were dissipated in inefficient enterprises, domestic consumption, and capital flight, leaving as their main domestic harvest the highest debt per capita in Latin America and a decimated economy.[2]

Even as the debt crisis is partially controlled by a variety of mechanisms (limited repayment, renegotiation of its terms, shifting bad loans from the credit to the debit column of the lending institutions' records), in Venezuela, as in other third-world countries, "the legacy of the crisis is aggravated by the inability of Latin American countries to find an adequate niche in the international trading system" (Halperín Donghi 1993 : 402). Thus, as I argue in this book, what is fundamental for understanding the dynamics of underdevelopment is not so much the direction of value flows as the place of third-world nations in the global structure of production and distribution.

In order to receive new loans to service the foreign debt, to finance development projects, and to gain the trust of international capital, Venezuela has been required to turn away from the "fantasy" world of petroleum wealth to the "real" world of the market—from protected to competitive capitalism. While Carlos Andrés Pérez's *El Gran Viraje* (The Great Turn-around) initiated this process in 1989, the demand to face "reality" continues

---

2. Venezuela was not exceptional. According to economist Jeffrey Sachs (who in his role as consultant helped implement neoliberal "shock" programs in Latin America and Eastern Europe), among developing nations, "Much of the heavy borrowing did not finance investment at all. It was used, instead, to finance current consumption spending as well as capital flights by the private sector" (1989:13).

to exert its hegemonic force, even as it is resisted not only by popular sectors and fractions of the elite, but also by Pérez's successor, Rafael Caldera. The shift from the illusion of magic to the illusion of the real corresponds to the movement from powers embodied in oil to those residing in money—from the material fetishism of land to the abstract fetishism of money.

Up to the first presidency of Carlos Andrés Pérez, oil wealth supported the fetishization of the state as the unchallenged agent of Progress. As I show in this book, as the state's incarnation, Juan Vicente Gómez, Marcos Pérez Jiménez, and Carlos Andrés Pérez came to embody—in the premiere, debut, and revival of the myth of progress—the transformative powers residing in the nation's natural body. Since the debt crisis of the 1980s, global money, parading as the neutral embodiment of economic rationality, has broken the magical spell of the indebted state, delegitimizing its parochial authority and constraining its power over the nation; the president is no longer the magically endowed agent of progress. Ironically, a state that was constituted as a national state through its control over petroleum was undone when it used the nation's subsoil to underwrite loans to finance a project of industrial development designed to end the nation's dependence on petroleum.

There is a certain perverse progression in the historical arc covered in this account. If during most of this century the circulation of the state's petrodollars throughout the domestic economy subordinated domestic productive structures to the logic of rent capture, now the circulation of international money has come to dominate the local economy, determining the conditions under which it must operate. Political control that was exercised directly through the state, incarnated in the figure of the dictator or democratic leader, is now exerted indirectly through the power of global money depersonalized in the "neutral" figure of the international market. In the name of the abstract universality of the market, international capital imposes its rationality on the national state in exchange for loans that promise it momentary relief from the burden of the past.

TOWARD A CRITICAL CARTOGRAPHY OF MODERNITY

This book has covered the rather unusual history of the transformation of Venezuela throughout this century. From a debt-ridden agricultural society threatened by the combined military might of its imperial creditors in 1902, it first became a wealthy OPEC oil exporter that during the 1973 oil boom threatened to alter center/periphery relations and then, in the 1980s, turned into an indebted nation internally torn by the polarizing pull of international capital. I would like to conclude by suggesting again that Venezuela's tempestuous history, far from having little general relevance, makes more visible similar transformations taking place elsewhere, not only in the third world but also in center nations. Thus, Robert Reich has noted how the globalization of the economy has polarized the U.S. population into an affluent sector linked to the transnational economy and a majority working in the domestic service sectors and forced to experience declining living conditions. Concerned that this polarization may lead to the "secession of the successful," he calls for a renewed commitment to the nation from those who have carved affluent transnational enclaves within an increasingly impoverished domestic landscape.[3]

The 1973 oil boom was not only a watershed in the transformation of the Venezuelan state but also a turning point that triggered the polarizing global dynamics of contemporary capitalism at the national and international levels. Ironically, the attempt by OPEC nations to reverse long-established patterns of international inequality eventually led not only to a heightened concentration of power beyond their borders but to a modification in the structure of power itself. Instead of the "uniformed imperialism" of direct political control and territorialized fixed markets of an old imperial age (Nairn 1977: 356), we are seeing the emergence of the multiform imperialism of fluid finance capital, flexible modes of accumulation, and deterritorialized markets, and the formation of a world ordered by shifting political, economic, and cultural boundaries.

The familiar map of modernity is being redrawn by global transformations in culture, politics, and production that are widely associated with the emergence of postmodernity. As a result of these transformations—linked to revolutions in technologies of production and communication as well as to massive reconfigurations of geopolitical power and populations worldwide—familiar geographical categories are uprooted from their original territorial sites and attached to new locations. These changes alter the relationship between geography and history. While deterritorialization entails reterritorialization, this dual process makes more visible both the social constructedness of space and the geographical grounding of histories. These changes modify also the spaces and targets of imperial subjection and of political contestation. Contemporary empires must now confront subaltern subjects within

---

3. The literature on recent trends in globalization and transnationalism support the notion of polarization. See, for example, Sassen (1991). For an insightful general discussion of this literature, see Rouse (1995).

reconfigured spaces at home and abroad, as the Other, once maintained on distant continents or confined to bounded locations at home, simultaneously multiplies and dissolves. At an increasing pace, collective identities are being redefined in new social places that cannot be mapped with antiquated categories. This reconfiguration of space/time makes it more difficult to sustain the old Eurocentric narratives of universal history, but also creates conditions for a decentered universality.

Yet the West's self-constitution through the domination both of other societies and of nature continues to draw legitimacy from a map of the world polarized into centers of modernity and backward areas waiting to be "enlightened"—now through the "internal adjustments" of liberal reform rather than through the civilizing mission of direct external control. At a time when globalization under neoliberal principles is making more abstract and invisible the underlying dynamics that draw this imperial map—leading some to confuse analysis with the bedazzling description of what they see as the blazing fragments of a depthless and orderless postmodern world—it is more necessary than ever to understand the disordering order that divides humanity against itself and sets it against nature.

If imperial power now unfolds within global financial circuits that link metropolitan and peripheral dominant sectors across national boundaries, subaltern subjects also proliferate within reconfigured spaces at home and abroad, enabling new understandings about their worldwide connections and common predicament. By illuminating this elusive world order, I hope this account of state transformation in Venezuela may join these emergent understandings and help counter the ongoing formation of dominant centers on the backs of subaltern others, anywhere.

REFERENCES

ARCHIVES

Archivo de El Nacional

Archivo de El Universal

Archivo de FEDECAMARAS

Archivo de la Corporación Venezolana de Fomento

Archivo de la Corporación Venezolana de Guayana

Archivo de la Fundación Boulton

Archivo de Ultimas Noticias

Archivo del Consejo Venezolano de Industrias

Archivo del Ministerio de Fomento

Archivo del Ministerio de Hacienda

Archivo del Ministerio de Minas e Hidrocarburos

Archivo Histórico de Miraflores

Archivo Fundación Andrés Mata

Instituto Autónomo Biblioteca Nacional, Archivo Audiovisual

Instituto Autónomo Biblioteca Nacional, Archivo de Hojas Sueltas

Registro Mercantil de Comercio

NEWSPAPERS

Ahora (1936–38)

The Daily Journal

El Diario de Caracas

Economía Hoy

Fantoches

El Heraldo (1954–56)

El Mundo

El Nacional

El País

Ultimas Noticias

El Universal

MAGAZINES

Auténtico

Bohemia

Business Latin America

Business Week

Número

The Monthly Report

Referencias

Resúmen

Revista de las Fuerzas Armadas

Revista Producción

VENECONOMIA

Zeta

BOOKS AND ARTICLES

Abente, Diego. 1987. "Venezuelan Democracy Revisited." *Latin American Research Review* 22(1): 225–40.

Abouhamad, Jeannette. 1970. *Los hombres de Venezuela*. Caracas: Universidad Central de Venezuela.

Abrams, Philip. 1988. "Notes on the Difficulty of Studying the State." *Journal of Historical Sociology* 1(1): 58–89.

Acedo de Sucre, María de Lourdes; and Carmen Margarita Nones Mendoza. 1967. *La generación venezolana de 1928*. Caracas: Oficina de Estudios Sociales y Económicos.

Acedo Mendoza, Carlos. 1967. *La vivienda en el area metropolitana de Caracas*. Caracas: Cuatricentenario de Caracas.

Acedo Mendoza, Manuel. 1976. *Por qué Eugenio Mendoza*. Caracas: Fundación Eugenio Mendoza.

Acosta, Irma. 1974. *¿Que carajo hago yo aquí?* Caracas: Tipografía El Sobre.

Acosta Espinosa, Nelson; and Heinrich Gorodeckas. 1985. *La adequidad*. Caracas: Ediciones Centauro.

Acosta Saignes, Miguel. 1987. *Latifundio*. Caracas: Procuraduría Agraria Naciónal.

Acosta Silva, Manuel. 1976. *Historias del 28*. Caracas: Talleres Tipográficos de la Escuela Técnica Popular.

Acuña, Guido. 1989. *Pérez Jiménez: un gendarme innecesario*. Caracas: Pomaire Venezuela, S.A.

Adelman, Morris. 1972. *The World Petroleum Market*. Baltimore: Johns Hopkins University Press.

Adolfo Ruíz, Gustavo. 1991. *La educación de Bolívar*. Caracas: Fondo Editorial Tropykos.

Agnew, Jean Christophe. 1986. *Worlds Apart: The Market and the Theater in Anglo-American Thought, 1550–1750.* Cambridge: Cambridge University Press.

Aguero, Felipe. 1995. "Crisis and Decay of Democracy in Venezuela: The Civil-Military Dimension." In *Venezuelan Democracy under Stress,* ed. Jennifer L. McCoy, Andrés Serbin, William C. Smith, and Andrés Stambouli. New Brunswick: Transactions Publishers, pp. 215–36.

Aguilera, Jesús Antonio. 1975. *La población de Venezuela: dinámica histórica, socio-económica, y geografía.* Caracas: Universidad Central de Venezuela.

Ahmad, Aijaz 1987. "Jameson's Rhetoric of Otherness and the 'National Allegory.'" *Social Text* 17 (fall): 3–25.

———. 1992. *In Theory.* London: Verso.

Alavi, Hamza. 1972. "The Postcolonial State." *New Left Review* 74: 59–81.

Albornoz, Orlando. ND. *Reforma de estado y educación.* Caracas: COPRE.

Alejandro Vargas, Francisco. 1981. *Los símbolos sagrados de la nación venezolana.* Caracas: Ediciones Centauro.

Alexander, Robert J. 1964. *The Venezuelan Democratic Revolution. A Profile of the Regime of Rómulo Betancourt.* New Brunswick: Rutgers University Press.

———. 1990. *Venezuela's Voice for Democracy.* New York: Praeger.

Aliber, Robert. 1983. *The International Money Game.* New York: Basic Books.

Allen, Henry J. 1940. *Venezuela: A Democracy.* New York: Doubleday.

Almoina de Carrera, Pilar. 1987. *El héroe en el relato oral venezolano.* Caracas: Monte Avila Latinoamericana.

Almond, Gabriel A., and Sidney Verba. 1963. *The Civic Culture: Political Attitudes and Democracy in Five Nations.* Princeton: Princeton University Press.

Alshereidah, Mazhar. 1973. *Nigeria: Petroleo y sangre.* Caracas: Universidad Central de Venezuela.

Althusser, L. 1970. *Reading "Capital."* London: New Left Books.

Alvarez, Ruben Darío. 1987. *La democracia venezolana, criatura deforme.* Caracas.

Amariglio, Jack; and Antonio Callari. 1993. "Marxian Value and the Problem of the Subject: The Role of Commodity Fetishism." In *Fetishism as Cultural Discourse,* ed. Emily Apter and William Pietz. Ithaca: Cornell Univeristy, pp. 186–216.

Amin, Samir. 1974. *Accumulation on a World Scale.* New York: Monthly Review Press.

———. 1976. *Unequal Development.* London: Monthly Review Press.

———. 1978. *The Law of Value and Historical Materialism.* New York: Monthly Review Press.

———. 1989. *Eurocentrism.* New York: Monthly Review Press

———. 1990. *Delinking.* London: Zed Books.

Amnesty International. 1987. *Political Prisoners in Venezuela.* London: Amnesty International.

———. 1988. *Memorandum al gobierno de Venezuela.* London: Amnesty International.

Amuzegar J. 1982. "Oil Wealth: A Very Mixed Blessing." *Foreign Affairs* 60: 814–35.

Anderson, Benedict. [1983] 1991. *Imagined Communities*. London: Verso.

Anderson, Perry. 1974. *Lineages of the Absolutist State*. London: Verso.

Aniyar, Lolita. 1992. *Democracia y justicia penal*. Caracas: Congreso de la República.

Antonorsi-Blanco, Marcel; and Ignacio Avalos Gutiérrez. 1980. *La planificación ilusoria*. Caracas: Editorial Ateneo de Caracas.

Appadurai, Arjun. 1986. "Introduction: Commodities and the Politics of Value." In *The Social Life of Things,* ed. Arjun Apadurai. Cambridge: Cambridge University Press, pp. 3–60.

———. 1991. "Global Ethnoscapes: Notes and Queries for a Transnational Anthropology." In *Working in the Present,* ed. Richard Fox. Sante Fe: School of American Research, pp. 191–210.

———, ed. 1988. *The Social Life of Things: Commodities in Cultural Perspective*. Cambridge: Cambridge University Press.

Apter, Emily; and William Pietz. 1993. *Fetishism as Cultural Discourse*. Ithaca: Cornell University Press.

Aranda, Sergio. 1977. *La economía venezolana*. Bogotá: Siglo XXI.

———. 1983. *Las clases sociales y el estado en Venezuela*. Caracas: Editorial Pomaire.

Araujo, Jesús. 1990. *Juan Vicente Gómez*. Caracas: Escuela Técnica Popular.

Araujo, Orlando. 1969. *Situación industrial de Venezuela*. Caracas: Ediciones de la Biblioteca, Universidad Central de Venezuela.

Arcila Farías, Eduardo. 1974. *Centenario del Ministerio de Obras Públicas*. Caracas: MOP.

Arendt, Hanna. 1958. *The Human Condition*. Chicago: University of Chicago Press.

Arguedas, José María. 1977. *Formación de una cultura naciónal indoamericana*. Mexico: Siglo Veintiuno.

Armstrong, Nancy. 1990. "Occidental Alice." *Differences: A Journal of Feminist Cultural Studies* 2(2): 3–40.

Arraíz Jiménez, Antonio. 1983. "Bs. 1.300.000 diarios de ganancia líquida se llevan los petroleros." Caracas, Julio de 1936, 193–208, in Pensamiento Político Venezolano del Siglo XX. Documentos para su Estudio. El debate político en 1936. Caracas: Congreso de la República.

Arrighi, Giovanni. 1979. "Peripheralization of Southern Africa, I: Changes in Production Processes." *Review* 3: 161–91.

Arroyo Talavera, Eduardo. 1988. *Elecciones y negociaciones: los límites de la democracia en Venezuela*. Caracas: Fondo Editorial CONICIT.

Asad, Talal. 1987. "Are There Histories of Peoples without Europe?" *Comparative Studies in Society and History* 29: 594–607.

Ascanio, Consuelo. 1985. "Consideraciones sobre la situación del café venezolano entre 1908 y 1935." *Tierra Firme* 3 (October–December): 613–28.

Asturias, Miguel Angel. 1946. *El señor presidente*. Buenos Aires: Editorial Losada S.A.

Attali, Jacques. 1977. *Bruits: essai sur l'économie politique de la musique.* Paris: Presses Universitaires de France.

Avendaño Lugo, José Ramón. 1982. *El militarismo en Venezuela: la dictadura de Pérez Jiménez.* Caracas: Ediciones Centauro.

Azócar, Gustavo. 1992. *El Amparo: crónica de una masacre.* Madrid: Editorial Planeta Venezolana, S.A.

Balandier, George. 1970. "The Colonial Situation: A Theoretical Approach." In *The Sociology of Black Africa: Social Dynamics in Central Africa,* trans. D. Garman. New York: Praeger.

Ball, Michael. 1977. "Differential Rent and the Role of Landed Property." *International Journal of Urban and Regional Research* 1(3): 380–403.

———. 1980. "On Marx's Theory of Agricultural Rent: A Reply to Ben Fine." *Economy and Society* 9 (August): 304–26.

Baloyra, Enrique A. 1974. "Oil Policies and Budgets in Venezuela, 1938–1968." *Latin American Research Review* 9(2): 28–72.

Baloyra, Enrique; and John D. Martz. 1976. *Electoral Mobilization and Public Opinion: The Venezuelan Campaign of 1973.* Chapel Hill: University of North Carolina Press.

———. 1979. *Political Attitudes in Venezuela: Societal Cleavages and Political Opinion.* Austin: University of Texas Press.

Banaji, Jairus. 1970. "The Crisis of British Anthropology." *New Left Review* 64: 71–85.

Banco Central. 1978. *La economía venezolana en los últimos treinta y cinco años.* Caracas: Banco Central.

———. 1979. *Informe económico.* Caracas: Banco Central.

———. Various years. *Memoria.* Caracas: Banco Central.

Baptista, Asdrúbal. 1991. *Bases cuantitativas de la economía venezolana 1830–1989.* Caracas: Ediciones María di Mase.

Baptista, Asdrúbal; and Bernard Mommer. 1987. *El petróleo en el pensamiento económico venezolano: un ensayo.* Caracas: Ediciones IESA.

Baran, Paul. 1957. *The Political Economy of Growth.* New York: Monthly Review Press.

Baranson, Jack. 1969. *Automotive Industries in Developing Nations.* Washington: International Bank for Reconstruction and Development.

Barber, Karin. 1982. "Popular Reactions to the Petro-Naira." *Journal of Modern African Studies* 20(3): 431–50.

Baretta, Silvio; R. Duncan; and John Markoff. 1978. "Civilization and Barbarism: Cattle Frontiers in Latin America." *Comparative Studies in Society and History* 20(4): 587–605.

Barker, Francis. 1984. *The Tremulous Private Body: Essays on Subjection.* London: Methuen.

Barreto, Daisy. 1995. The Cult of María Lionza in Venezuela: Between Legend, History, Myth, and Ideology. Unpublished manuscript. Caracas.

Barrios, Gonzalo. 1981. *La imperfecta democracia.* Caracas: Centauro.

———. 1989. "Untitled speech." In *Diario de Debates del Senado, República de Venezuela, XIX,* vol. 1. Caracas: Imprenta del Congreso de la República, pp 143–48.

Bartra, Roger. 1987. *La jaula de la melancolía.* Mexico City: Grijalbo.

Basadre, Jorge. 1980. *La multitud, la ciudad y el campo en la historia de Perú.* Lima: Ediciones Treintaitres.

Battaglini, Oscar. 1993. *Legitimación del poder y lucha política en Venezuela 1936–1941.* Caracas: Universidad Central de Venezuela.

Baudrillard, Jean. 1981. *For a Critique of the Political Economy of the Sign.* Saint Louis: Telos.

———. 1983. *Simulations.* New York: Semiotext.

Baumol, William J. 1974. "The Transformation of Values: What Marx 'Really' Meant (An Interpretation)." *Journal of Economic Literature* 12(1): 51–62.

Bautista Fuenmayor, Juan. 1979. *1928–1948: veinte años de política.* Madrid: Editorial Mediterráneo.

Bautista Urbaneja, Diego. 1992. *Pueblo y petróleo en la política venezolana del siglo.* Caracas: Ediciones CEPET.

Benjamin, Walter. 1969. *Illuminations.* New York: Schocken Books.

Bennett, Douglas C. 1984. "The World Automobile Industry and Its Implications for Developing Countries." In *Profits, Progress and Poverty: Case Studies of International Industries in Latin America,* ed. Richard F. Newfarmer. Notre Dame: University of Notre Dame Press, pp. 193–226.

———. 1985. *Transnational Corporations versus the State: The Political Economy of the Mexican Auto Industry.* Princeton: Princeton University Press.

Bennett, Douglas; and Kenneth Sharpe. 1979a. "Agenda Setting and Bargaining Power: The Mexican State vs. Transnational Corporations." *World Politics* 32(1): 57–89.

———. 1979b. "Transnational Corporations and the Political Economy of Export Promotion: The Case of the Mexican Automobile Industry." *International Organization* 33(2): 177–201.

Bentaleb, Fatima. 1984. "La rente dans la société et la culture en Algérie." *Pétrole et Société* 26 (January–March): 75–104.

Bergquist, Charles. 1986. *Labor in America: Comparative Essays on Chile, Argentina, Venezuela, and Colombia.* Stanford: Stanford University Press.

Bergsten, Fred; Thomas Horst; and Theodore H. Moran. 1978. *American Multinationals and American Interests.* Washington: Brookings Institute.

Berlant, Lauren. 1991. *The Anatomy of National Fantasy: Hawthorne, Utopia, and Everyday Life.* Chicago: University of Chicago Press.

Bernal, Martin. 1987. *Black Athena.* New Brunswick: Rutgers University Press.

Beroes, Agustín. 1990. *RECADI: la gran estafa.* Caracas: Planeta.

Bernstein, Richard J. 1991. *New Constellation: The Ethical-Political Horizons of Modernity/Postmodernity.* Cambridge: MIT Press.

Berrefjord, Ole; and Per Heum. 1984. "Offshore Petroleum Activities and the Development of the Political Economy in Norway." *Pétrole et Société* 26 (January–March): 203–9.

Berroeta, Pedro. 1987. *Rómulo Betancourt: los años del aprendizaje. 1908–1948.* Caracas: Ediciones Centauro.

Betancourt, Rómulo. 1956. *Venezuela, política y petroleo.* Mexico City: Fondo de Cultura Económico.

———. 1975. *Venezuela, dueña de su petroleo.* Caracas: Ediciones Centauro.

———. 1979. *Venezuela, Oil and Politics.* Boston: Houghton Mifflin.

———. 1983. "Discurso pronunciado en el mitin de las izquierdas." Caracus, Septiembre de 1936, 291—94, in Pensamiento Político Venezolano del Siglo XX. Documentos para su Estudio. El debate político en 1936. Caracas: Congreso de la República.

Bhabha, Homi. 1985. "Signs Taken for Wonders: Questions of Ambivalence and Authority under a Tree Outside Delhi, May 1817." *Critical Inquiry* 12(1): 144–65.

———. 1990. "DissemiNation: Time, Narrative, and the Margins of the Modern Nation." 291–322 In *Nation and Narration,* ed. Homi Bhabha. London: Routledge.

Bigler, Gene. 1980. "State Economic Control versus Market Expansion: The Third Sector in Venezuelan Politics." Ph.D diss., Johns Hopkins University, Baltimore.

Bigler, Gene; and Frankln Tugwell. 1986. "Banking on Oil in Venezuela." In *Bordering on Trouble: Resources and Politics in Latin America,* ed. Andrew Maguire and Janet Welsh. Bethesda: Adler and Adler, pp. 152–89.

Bitar, Sergio; and Eduardo Troncoso. 1983. *El desafío industrial de Venezuela.* Buenos Aires: Pomaire.

Blanco Muñoz, Agustín. 1981. *La conspiración cívico-militar.* Caracas: Universidad Central de Venezuela.

———. 1983. *Habló el General.* Caracas: Universidad Central de Venezuela.

Bland, Gary; Johanna Mendelson Forman; Louis W. Goodman; and Moisés Naím, eds. 1995. *Lessons of the Venezuelan Experience.* Baltimore: Johns Hopkins University Press.

Blank, David Eugene. 1969. "Policy Making Style and Political Development: The Introduction of a System of Democratic Planning in Venezuela, 1958–1968." Ph.D diss., Columbia University, New York.

———. 1971. "Political Conflict and Industrial Planning in Venezuela, 1958–1974." 84–106 In *Venezuela, 1969,* ed. Philip B. Taylor Jr. Baltimore: Johns Hopkins University Press.

———. 1973. *Politics in Venezuela.* Boston: Little, Brown and Company.

———. 1974. "The Politics of Industrial Planning in Venezuela, 1958–1974: Variations on the Theme of Democratic Planning." *Fifth National Meeting of the Latin American Studies Association,* San Francisco.

Bloch, Maurice; and Jonathan Parry. 1989. *Money and the Morality of Exchange.* Cambridge: Cambridge University Press.

Block, Fred. 1977. "The Ruling Class Does Not Rule: Notes on the Marxist Theory of the State." *Socialist Revolution* 7: 6–28.

Bohm-Bawerk, Eugen von. [1896] 1949. *Karl Marx and the Close of His System,* ed. Paul M. Sweezy. New York: Augustus M. Kelley.

Bond, Robert D. 1975. "Business Associations and Interest Politics in Venezuela." Ph.D diss., Vanderbilt University, Nashville.

———. 1977. *Contemporary Venezuela and Its Role in International Affairs.* New York: New

York University Press.Borges, Jorge Luis. 1978. *Doctor Brodie's Report.* New York: E. P. Dutton.

Bottome, Robert; and John Seeeney. 1987. *The Economic Outlook for Venezuela, 1987–1992.* Caracas: VeneEconomía.

Braudel, Fernand. 1967. *Capitalism and Material Life 1400–1800.* New York: Harper and Row.

Braverman, Harry. 1975. *Labor and Monopoly Capital.* New York: Monthly Review Press.

Brenner, Robert. 1977. "The Origins of Capitalist Development: A Critique of Neo-Smithian Marxism." *New Left Review* 104 (July–August): 82–87.

Brewer-Carías, Allan Randolph. 1975. *Cambio político y reforma del estado en Venezuela.* Madrid: Editorial Tecnos.

Briceño Iragorri, Mario. 1971. *Pérez Jiménez presidente: la autoelección de un déspota.* Caracas: Ediciones Centauro.

Briceño-León, Roberto. 1990. *Los efectos perversos del petroleo.* Caracas: Fondo Editorial Acta Científica Venezolana.

Bright, Charles; and Susan Harding, eds. 1984. *Statemaking and Social Movements.* Ann Arbor: University of Michigan Press.

Brito Figueroa, Federico. 1966. *Historia económica y social de Venezuela.* Caracas: Universidad Central de Venezuela.

Brito García, Luis. 1988. *La máscara del poder: del gendarme necesario al demócrata necesario.* Caracas: Alfadil.

———. 1989. *El poder sin máscara.* Caracas: Alfadil.

Broehl, Wayne G. 1968. *The International Basic Economy Corporation.* New Hampshire: National Planning Association.

Brunhoff, Suzanne de. 1973. *Marx on Money.* New York: Urizen Books.

Brunner, José J. 1993. "Notes on Modernity and Postmodernity in Latin American Culture." *Boundary 2* 20: 35–54.

Buci-Glucksmann, C. 1979. *Gramsci and the State.* London: Lawrence and Wishart.

Buck-Morss, Susan. 1995. *The Dialectics of Seeing.* Cambridge: MIT Press.

Buiter, Willem H.; and Douglas D. Purvis. 1980. *Oil, Disinflation, and Export Competitiveness: A Model of the "Dutch Disease."* Coventry: University of Warwick Press.

Burggraaff, Winfield J. 1972. *The Venezuelan Armed Forces in Politics 1935–1959.* Columbia: University of Missouri Press.

Burggraaff, Winfield J.; and Richard L. Millett. 1995. "More than Failed Coups: The Crisis in Venezuelan Civil-Military Relations." In *Lessons of the Venezuelan Experience,* ed. Louis W. Goodman, Johanna Mendelson Forman, Moisés Naím, Joseph S. Tulchin, and Gary Bland. Washington: Woodrow Wilson Center Press, pp 54–78.

Bye, Vegard. 1979. "Nationalization of Oil in Venezuela: Re-defined Dependence and Legitimization of Imperialism." *Journal of Peace Research* 16(1): 57–78.

Caballero, Manuel. 1992. *El tirano liberal.* Caracas: Monte Avila.

Cabrera, Elery. 1985. "Gómez el 'Buen elemento.' " *Tierra Firme* 3 (October–December): 685–88.

Cabrujas, José Antonio. 1987. "El estado de disimulo." In *Heterodoxia y estado: 5 respuestas* (special edition of *Estado & Reforma)*. Caracas: COPRE, pp. 7–35.

Calcaño, Luis Gómez; Thais Maingón; and Margarita López Maya. 1989. *De Punto Fijo al pacto social: desarrollo y hegemonía en Venezuela (1958–1985)*. Caracas: Fondo Editorial Acta Científica Venezolana.

Caldera, Rafael. 1989. Untitled speech. In *Diario de Debates del Senado, República de Venezuela, XIX*. Vol. 1 (January–June), Caracas: Imprenta del Congreso de la República, pp. 135–40.

Cammack, Paul. 1986. "Redemocratization: A Review of the Issues." *Bulletin of Latin American Research* 4: 39–46.

Campos, Manuel Rodríguez. 1991. *Pérez Jiménez y la dinámica del poder (1948–1958)*. Caracas: Eldorado Ediciones.

Canclini, Néstor García. 1989. *Culturas híbridas: estrategias para entrar y salir de la modernidad*. Mexico: Grijalbo.

Caporaso, James A. 1978. "Dependence and Dependency in the Global System." *International Organization*, 32(1): 1–12.

Capriles Ayala, Carlos. *Los años treinta y cuarenta*. Caracas: Consorcio Ediciones Capriles.

Cardoso, Fernando Henrique. 1973. "Associated-Dependent Development: Theoretical and Practical Implications." In *Authoritarian Brazil: Origins, Politics and Future*, vol. 1, ed. Alfred Stepan. New Haven: Yale University Press, pp. 142–76.

———. 1985. "La democracia en América Latina." *Punto de Vista* 23 (April): 1–9.

Cardoso, Fernando Henrique; and Enzo Faletto. 1979. *Dependency and Development in Latin America*. Berkeley: University of California Press.

Carmona, Gladys de. 1979. *Los quiero vivos*. Valencia: Vadell Hermanos.

Carnoy, M. 1984. *The State and Political Theory*. Princeton: Princeton University Press.

Carpentier, Alejo. 1977. *Reasons of State*. London: Readers and Writers Cooperative.

Carrera Damas, Germán. 1968. *Boves: Apectos socioeconómicos de la Guerra de Independencia*. Caracas: Ediciones de la Biblioteca de la Universidad Central.

———. 1969. *El culto a Bolívar*. Caracas: Instituto de Antropología e Historia, Universidad Central de Venezuela.

———. 1972. *Historia contemporanea de Venezuela*. Caracas: Universidad Central de Venezuela.

———. 1980. *Una nación llamada Venezuela*. Caracas: Universidad Central de Venezuela.

Carrier, James G. 1992. "Occidentalism: The World Upside Down." *American Ethnologist* 19(2): 195–212.

Casals, José Ignacio; Aura Celina Casanova; and Constantino Quero Morales. 1969. *Estudio sobre la industria automotriz venezolana y sus perspectivas de desarrollo*. Caracas: ECODESA.

José Ignacio Casals and Constantino Quero Morales became ministers of development under Pérez; Aura Celina Casanova headed the state's Industrial Bank. Their "Estudio sobre la industria automotriz venezolana y sus perspectivas de desarrollo" (, 1969) Castellaños, José Emilio. 1979. *El terrible fantasma de CARMONA*. Caracas: Editorial Ateneo de Caracas.

Castellanos, José Emilio, 1979. *El terrible fantasma de Carmona*. Caracas: Editorial Ateneo de Caracas.

Castillo D'Imperio, Ocarina. 1985. "Gómez en el saber popular." *Tierra Firme* 3 (October–December): 645–48.

———. 1990. *Los años del bulldozer: ideología y política 1948–1958*. Caracas: Fondo Editorial Tropykos.

Castro Leiva, Luis. 1985. "El debate sobre el desarrollo del país en el siglo XIX." In *Apreciación del proceso histórico venezolano*. Caracas: Universidad Metropolitana.

Catalá, José Agustín. 1989. *El estallido de febrero*. Caracas: Ediciones Centauro.

———, ed. 1994. *Otros juicios sobre el proceso al ex presidente*. Caracas: Ediciones Centauro.

Chakrabarty, Dipesh. 1992. "Postcoloniality and the Artifice of History: Who Speaks for 'Indian' Pasts?" *Representations* 37 (winter): 1–26.

Chandra, Biban. 1980. "Karl Marx: His Theories of Asian Societies and Colonial Rule." In *Sociological Theories: Race and Colonialism*. Paris: UNESCO.

Chatelus, Michel; and Yves Schemeil. 1984. "Towards a New Political Economy of State Industrialization in the Arab Middle East." *International Journal of Middle Eastern Studies* 16: 251–65.

Chatterjee, Partha. 1986. *Nationalist Thought and the Colonial World: A Derivative Discourse?* London: Zed Books.

———. 1993. *The Nation and Its Fragments: Colonial and Postcolonial Histories*. Princeton: Princeton University Press.

Chen, Xiaomei. 1992. "Occidentalism as Counterdiscourse: *He shang* in Post-Mao China." *Critical Inquiry* 18: 686–712.

Chi-Keung Ko. 1981. "Dependent Development of an Export Platform Economy: Taiwan." Ph.D. diss., University of Chicago.

Chitty La Rocha, Nelson. 1983. *250 millones: la historia secreta*. Caracas: Editorial Pomaire.

Chomsky, Noam. 1991. "The New World Order." *Agenda* 62: 13–15.

Chossudovsky, Miguel. 1977. *La miseria en Venezuela*. Valencia: Vadell Hermanos.

Clifford, James; and George E. Marcus, eds. 1986. *The Poetics and Politics of Ethnography*. Berkeley: University of California Press.

Cohen, David William. 1994. *The Combing of History*. Chicago: University of Chicago Press.

Cohn, Bernard. 1980. "History and Anthropology: The State of Play." *Comparative Studies in Society and History* 22: 198–221.

———. 1981. "Anthropology and History in the 1980s: Towards a Rapprochement." *Journal of Interdisciplinary History* 12: 227–52.

———. 1987. *An Anthropologist among the Historians and Other Essays*. New Delhi: Oxford University Press.

Collier, David, ed. 1979. *The New Authoritarianism in Latin América*. Princeton: Princeton University Press.

Comaroff, Jean. 1985. *Body of Power, Spirit of Resistance: The Culture and History of a South African People*. Chicago: University of Chicago Press.

Comaroff, Jean; and John Comaroff. 1986. "Christianity and Colonialism in South Africa." *American Ethnologist* 13: 1–19.

———. 1989. "The Colonization of Consciousness in South Africa." *Economy and Society* 18: 267–96.

———. 1990. "Goodly Beasts, Beastly Goods: Cattle and Commodities in a South African Context." *American Ethnologist* 17: 195–216.

———.1991. *Christianity, Colonialism, and Consciousness in South Africa*. Vol. 1 *of Revelation and Revolution*. Chicago: University of Chicago Press.

———. 1992. *Ethnography and the Historical Imagination*. Boulder, CO: Westview Press.

Comaroff, John L. 1982. "Dialectical Systems: History and Anthropology." *Journal of Southern African Studies*. 8: 143–72.

Conybeare, J. A. 1981. "The Rent Seeking State and Revenue Diversification." *World Politics* 35: 25–42.

Cooper, Fred; and Ann Stoler. 1989. "Tensions of Empire: Colonial Control and Visions of Rule." *American Ethnologist* 16: 609–21.

Coppedge, Michael. 1994. *Strong Parties and Lame Ducks: Presidential Partyarchy and Factionalism in Venezuela*. Stanford: Stanford University Press.

Corden, W. M.; and J. P. Neary. 1982. "Booming Sector and De-industrialization in a Small Open Economy." *Economic Journal* 92: 825–48.

Cordero Velásquez, América. 1985. "1928: las concesiones petroleras y la corrupción." *Tierra Firme* 3 (October–December): 567–78.

Córdova, Armando. 1973. *Inversiones extranjeras y subdesarrollo*. Caracas: Universidad Central de Venezuela.

Cornejo-Polar, Antonio. 1989. "Indigenist and Heterogeneous Literatures: Their Dual Sociocultural Status." *Latin American Perspectives* 16 (spring): 12–28.

Coronil, Fernando. 1988. *The Magical State: History and Illusion in the Appearance of Venezuelan Democracy*. Working Paper no. 112. Notre Dame, IN: Helen Kellogg Institute for International Studies, University of Notre Dame.

———. 1992. "Can Postcoloniality Be Decolonized? Imperial Banality and Postcolonial Power." *Public Culture* 5(1): 89–108.

———. 1994. "Listening to the Subaltern: The Poetics of Neocolonial States." *Poetics Today*. 15(4): 642–58.

———. 1995. "Transculturation and the Politics of Theory: Countering the Center, Cuban Counterpoint." Introduction to *Cuban Counterpoint: Tobacco and Sugar* by Fernando Ortiz. Durham: Duke University Press, pp. ix–lvi.

———. 1996. "Beyond Occidentalism: Towards Non-imperial Geohistorical Categories." *Cultural Anthropology*, 11(1): 51–87.

Coronil, Fernando; and Julie Skurski. 1982. "Reproducing Dependency: Auto Policy and Petrodollar Circulation in Venezuela." *International Organization* 36(1): 61–94.

———. 1991. "Dismembering and Remembering the Nation: The Semantics of Political Violence in Venezuela." *Comparative Studies in Society and History* 33(2): 288–337.

Corradi, Juan E.; Patricia Weiss Fagen; and Manuel Antonio Garretón, eds. 1992. *Fear at the Edge: State Terror and Resistance in Latin America.* Berkeley: University of California Press.

Corrigan, Philip; and Derek Sayer. 1985. *The Great Arch.* New York: Basil Blackwell.

Cox, Robert W. 1979. "Ideologies and the New International Economic Order." *International Organization* 33(2): 257–301.

Croce, Arturo. 1977. *Petróleo, mi general.* Caracas: Monte Avila Editores.

Croes, Hemmy. 1973. *El movimiento obrero venezolano (elementos para su historia).* Caracas: Ediciones Movimiento Obrero.

Crosby, Alfred W., Jr. 1972. *The Columbian Exchange: Biological and Cultural Consequences of 1492.* Westport, CT: Greenwood Press.

Crump, Thomas. 1981. *The Phenomenon of Money.* London: Routledge and Kegan Paul.

Cruz, Rafael de la; and Heinz Sonntag. 1985. "The State and Industrialization in Venezuela." *Latin American Perspectives* 12(4): 75–104.

Daalder, Hans. 1962. *The Role of the Military in the Emerging Countries.* Gravenhage: Mouton.

Dávila, Luis Ricardo. 1992. *Imaginario político venezolano.* Caracas: Alfadil Ediciones.

Davis, Natalie Z. 1981. "Anthropology and History in the 1980s." *Journal of Interdisciplinary History* 12(2): 267–75.

de Ipola, Emilio; and Juan Carlos Portantiero. 1984. "Crisis social y pacto democrático." *Punto de Vista* 21(August): 13–20.

De la Plaza, Salvador. 1970. *La formación de las clases sociales en Venezuela.* Caracas: Cuadernos Rocinante.

Derby, Lauren. 1994. "Haitians, Magic, and Money: Raza and Society in the Haitian-Dominican Borderlands, 1900 to 1937." *Comparative Studies in Society and History* 36(3): 488–526.

Derrida, Jacques. 1974. *Of Grammatology.* Baltimore: Johns Hopkins University Press.

Díaz Sánchez, Ramón. 1973. *Transición política y realidad en Venezuela.* Caracas: Monte Avila.

Dinkelspeil, John. 1967. "Administrative Style and Economic Development." Ph.D. diss., Harvard University, Cambridge.

Dirks, Nicholas B. 1987. *The Hollow Crown: Ethnohistory of an Indian Kingdom.* Cambridge: Cambridge University Press.

———, ed. 1992. *Colonialism and Culture.* Ann Arbor: University of Michigan Press.

Dobb, Maurice. 1946. *Studies in the Development of Capitalism.* London: Routledge and Kegan Paul.

———. 1973. *Theories of Value and Distribution since Adam Smith.* Cambridge: Cambridge University Press.

Dodge, Stephen Charles. 1968. "The History of the Development of the Guayana Region." Ph.D. diss., University of Minnesota, Minneapolis.

Doyle, Kenneth O., ed. 1992. "The Meanings of Money." *American Behavioral Scientist,* 35(6): 641–840.

Dumont, Jean Paul. 1976. *Under the Rainbow: Nature and Supernature among the Panare Indians.* Austin: University of Texas Press.

Dumont, Louis. 1977. *From Mandeville to Marx: The Genesis and Triumph of Economic Ideology.* Chicago: University of Chicago Press.

Duno, Pedro. 1975. *Los doce apóstoles.* Valencia: Vadell Hermanos.

Dussel, Enrique. 1993. "Eurocentrism and Modernity." *Boundary* 2: 65–76.

Eagleton, Terry; Fredric Jameson; and Edward Said. 1990. *Nationalism, Colonialism, and Literature.* Minneapolis: University of Minnesota Press.

Economic Commission for Latin America and the Caribbean. 1995. *Economic Survey of Latin America and the Caribbean 1993.* Vol. 2. Santiago, Chile: CEPAL.

Eftekhari, Nirou. 1984a. "La Norvège et le "mal hollandais.'" *Pétrole et Société* 26 (January–March): 181–202.

——. 1984b. "La rente et la dépendance en Algérie." *Pétrole et Société* 26 (January–March): 31–74.

El Nacional. 1989. *El día que bajaron los cerros.* Caracas: Editorial Ateneo de Caracas.

——. 1990. "Cuando la muerte tomó las calles." *El Naciónal* (Caracas).

Eldred, Michael. 1984. "A Reply to Gleicher." *Capital and Class* 23 (summer): 135–40.

Elias, Norbert. 1978. "The Civilizing Process." Trans. E. Jephcott. New York: Urizen Books.

Ellner, Steven. 1979. "The Venezuelan Left in the Era of the Popular Front, 1936–45." *Journal of Latin American Studies* 10 (May): 169–84.

——. 1980. *Los partidos políticos y la disputa por el control del movimiento sindical en Venezuela, 1936–1948.* Caracas: Universidad Católica Andrés Bello.

——. 1981. "Factionalism in the Venezuelan Communist Movement. 1937–1948." *Science and Society* 45(1): 52–70.

——. 1982. "Populism in Venezuela, 1935–48: Betancourt and 'Acción Democrática.'" In *Latin American Populism in Comparative Perspective,* ed. Michael Conniff. Albuquerque: University of New Mexico Press.

——. 1987. *The Venezuelan Petroleum Corporation and the Debate over Government Policy in Basic Industry, 1960–76.* Glasgow: University Press of Glasgow, Institute of Latin American Studies.

——. 1988. *Venezuela's Movimiento al Socialismo: From Guerrilla Defeat to Innovative Politics.* Durham: Duke University Press.

Elson, Diane. 1979. *The Representation of Labour in Capitalism.* London: CSE Books.

Emmanuel, Arghiri. 1972. *Unequal Exchange: A Study of the Imperialism of Trade.* New York: Monthly Review Press.

Entrikin, Nicholas. 1991. *The Betweenness of Place: Towards a Geography of Modernity.* Baltimore: Johns Hopkins University Press.

Equipo Proceso Político. 1978. *CAP: 5 años.* Caracas: Proceso Político.

Escobar, Arturo. 1994. *Encountering Development.* Princeton: Princeton University Press.

Escobar, Ticio. 1988. "Postmodernismo/precapitalismo." *Casa de las Américas* 168:13–19.

Escovar Salom, Ramón. 1985. "Venezuela: the Oil Boom and the Debt Crisis." In *Latin America and the World Recession,* ed. Esperanza Durán. Cambridge: Cambridge University Press, pp. 120–29.

España, Luis Pedro. 1989. *Democracia y renta petrolera.* Caracas: Instituto de Investigaciones Económicas y Sociales, Universidad Católica Andrés Bello.

Espinasa, Ramon V. 1989. "Petroleo, economía e historia." Introduction to *Democracia y renta petrolera,* by Luis Pedro España. Caracas: Instituto de Investigaciones Económicas y Sociales, Universidad Católica Andrés Bello.

Esser, Klaus. 1976. *Oil and Development, Venezuela.* Berlin: German Development Institute.

Esté, Raul. 1987. *La masacre de Yumare.* Caracas: Fondo Editorial "Carlos Aponte."

Evans, Peter. 1979. *Dependent Development: The Alliance of Multinational, State, and Local Capital in Brazil.* Princeton: Princeton University Press.

Evans, Peter; Dietrich Rueschemeyer; and Theda Skocpol. 1985. *Bringing the State Back In.* Cambridge: Cambridge University Press.

Evans, Peter; Dietrich Rueschemeyer; and Evelyne Huber Stephens. 1985. *States versus Markets in the World System.* Beverly Hills, CA: Sage Publications.

Evans-Prichard, Edward E. 1937. *Witchcraft, Oracles, and Magic among Azande.* Oxford: Clarendon.

Ewell, Judith. 1984. *Venezuela: A Century of Change.* London: C. Hurst and Company.

Fabar, Al. 1978. "Auto in the Eighties: Uncars and Unworkers." *Radical America* 13: 31–7.

Fabian, Johannes. 1983. *Time and the Other: How Anthropology Makes Its Object.* New York: Columbia University Press.

Fagan, Stuart I. 1977. "Unionism and Democracy." In *Venezuela: The Democratic Experience,* ed. John D. Martz and David J. Myers. New York: Praeger Publishers, pp. 174–94.

Fagen, Richard, ed. 1979. *Capitalism and the State in U.S.–Latin American Relations.* Stanford: Stanford University Press.

Falcón Urbano, M, F. *Desarrollo e industrialización en Venezuela.* Caracas: FACES.

FAVENPA. 1972. *La industria nacional de partes y piezas automotrices.* Vols. 1–3. Caracas.

Ferguson, James. 1988. "Cultural Exchange: New Developments in the Anthropology of Commodities." *Cultural Anthropology* 3(4): 488–513.

———. 1990. *The Anti-politics Machine: "Development," Depoliticization, and Bureaucratic Power in Lesotho.* Cambridge: Cambridge University Press.

Fernández de Amicarelli, Estela. 1991. "La estructura categorial del discurso político venezolana: variaciones en la oposición civilización-barbarie: Francisco de Miranda y Simón Rodríguez. 1790–1850." *Revista Interamericana de Bibliografía* 41(1): 63–81.

Fine, Ben. 1980. "On Marx's Theory of Agricultural Rent: A Rejoinder." *Economy and Society* 9(3): 327–31.

———. 1986. *The Value Dimension: Marx versus Ricardo and Sraffa.* New York: Kegan Paul.

Fishlow, Albert. 1990. "The Latin American State." *Journal of Economic Perspectives* 4 (summer): 61–74.

Fleet, Michael. 1977. "Host Country–Multinational Relations in the Colombian Automobile Industry." *Interamerican Economic Affairs* 32(1): 3–32.

Franco, Jean; Juan Flores; and George Yúdice, eds. 1992. *On Edge: The Crisis of Contemporary Latin American Culture.* Minneapolis: University of Minnesota Press.

Ford Motor de Venezuela. 1975. *Estudio de la industria automotriz en Venezuela.* Caracas.

Foster, Robert J. 1990. "Value without Equivalence: Exchange and Replacement in a Melanesian Society." *Man* 25 (March): 54–69.

Foucault, Michel. 1980. *Power/Knowledge: Selected Interviews and Other Writings, 1972–1977.* Ed. Colin Gordon. New York: Pantheon.

———. 1994. *The Order of Things.* New York: Vintage Books.

Frank, Andre Gunder. 1972. *Lumpenbourgeoisie and Lumpendevelopment: Dependence, Class and Politics.* New York: Monthly Review Press.

———. 1978. *Dependent Accumulation and Underdevelopment.* New York: Monthly Review Press.

Frankel, S. Herbert. 1977. *Two Philosophies of Money.* New York: St. Martin's Press.

Fraser, Nancy. 1989. *Unruly Practices.* Minneapolis: University of Minnesota Press.

Fuenmayor, Juan Batista. 1975. *Historia de la política contemporánea venezolana, 1899–1969.* Caracas: Universidad Central de Venezuela.

———. 1982. *Historia de la Venezuela política contemporánea.* Caracas.

Fuenzalida, Edmundo; and Osvaldo Sunkel. 1974. *Transnationalization, National Disintegration and Reintegration in Contemporary Capitalism.* Brighton, England: IDS International Working Paper no. 18.

Fundación Eugenio Mendoza. 1976. *Venezuela Moderna, 1926–1967.* Caracas: Fundación Eugenio Mendoza.

Fundación John Boulton. 1976. *Política y economía en Venezuela. 1810–1910.* Caracas: Fundación John Boulton.

Furtado, Celso. 1970. *Economic Development of Latin America.* Cambridge: Cambridge University Press.

Gadant, Monique. 1984. "Boumediène, le discours de l'Etat." *Pétrole et Société* 26 (January–March): 105–26.

Gallardo, Freddy Vivas. 1993. *Venezuela–Estados Unidos 1939–1945: la coyuntura decisiva.* Caracas: Universidad Central de Venezuela.

Gallegos, Rómulo. [1929] 1959. *Doña Bárbara.* In *Obras Completas* 1:493–799. Madrid: Aguilar, S.A.

García Araujo, Mauricio. 1971. *El gasto público consolidado en Venezuela.* Caracas: Artegráfica.

García Canclini, Néstor. 1988. "Culture and Power: The State of Research." *Media, Culture and Society* 10: 495.

———. 1990. *Culturas híbridas: estrategias para entrar y salir de la modernidad.* Mexico City: Grijalbo.

García Iturbe, Reinaldo. 1961. *La siderúrgica: su ruta hacia la Koppers.* Caracas: Pensamiento Vivo.

García Marquez, Gabriel. 1977. *El otoño del patriarca.* Barcelona: Ediciones G.P.

———. 1991. *The Autumn of the Patriarch.* Trans. Gregory Rabassa. New York: Harper Perennial.

García Ponce, Guillermo; and Francisco Camacho Barrios. 1982. *Diario de la resistencia y la dictadura 1948–1958.* Caracas: Ediciones Centauro.

Gellner, Ernest. 1983. *Nations and Nationalism.* Oxford: Basil Blackwell.

Gereffi, Gary; and Lynn Hempel. 1996. "Latin America in the Global Economy: Running Faster to Stay in Place." *NACLA Report on the Americas,* 29(4): 18–27.

Gereffi, Gary; and Miguel Korzeniewicz, eds. 1994. *Commodity Chains and Global Capitalism.* New York: Praeger.

Ghalioun, Burhan. 1984. "Rente pétrolière et transformations sociales en Norvège." *Pétrole et Société* 26 (January–March): 163–80.

Gibson, Ross. 1992. *South of the West: Postcolonialism and the Narrative Construction of Australia.* Bloomington: Indiana University Press.

Giddens, Anthony. 1987. *The Nation-State and Violence.* Vol. 2 of *A Contemporary Critique of Historical Materialism.* Berkeley: University of California Press.

Gil Fortoul, José. 1953. *Historia constitucional de Venezuela.* 4th ed. Caracas: Ministerio de Educación.

Gilmore, Robert L. 1964. *Caudillism and Militarism in Venezuela, 1810–1910.* Athens: Ohio University Press.

Gil Yepes, José Antonio. 1978. *El reto de los élites.* Madrid: Editorial Tecnos.

———. 1981. *The Challenge of Venezuelan Democracy.* New Brunswick, N.J.: Transaction Books.

Godzich, Wlad. 1994. *The Culture of Literacy.* Cambridge: Harvard University Press.

González Abreu, Manuel. 1980. *Venezuela Foránea.* Caracas: Universidad Central de Venezuela.

González Guinán, Francisco. 1954. *Historia contemporánea de Venezuela.* 15 vols. Caracas: Presidencia de la República.

González Ordosgoiti, Enrique. 1991. "En Venezuela todos somos minorías." *Nueva Sociedad* 111: 128–40.

Goodman, Louis W.; Johanna Mendelson Forman; Moisés Naím; Joseph S. Tulchin; and Gary Bland, eds. 1995. *Lessons of the Venezuelan Experience.* Washington: Woodrow Wilson Center Press.

Goux, Jean-Joseph. 1990. *Symbolic Economies: After Marx and Freud.* Ithaca: Cornell University Press.

Gramsci, Antonio. 1971. "Selections from the Prison Notebooks." Trans. Quentin Hoare and George Nowell Smith. New York: International Publishers.

Greenberg, Stanley B. 1980. *Race and State in Capitalist Development: Comparative Perspectives.* New Haven: Yale University Press.

Gregory, Christopher A. 1982. *Gifts and Commodities.* London: Academic Press.

Griffin, James M.; and David J. Teece. 1982. *OPEC Behavior and World Oil Prices.* London: George Allen and Unwin.

Grindle, Merilee S., ed. 1980. *Politics and Policy Implementation in the Third World.* Princeton: Princeton University Press.

Guha, Ranajit. 1983. *Elementary Aspects of Peasant Insurgency in Colonial India.* New Delhi: Oxford University Press.

————. 1988. "The Prose of Counter-insurgency." In *Selected Subaltern Studies,* ed. Ranajit Guha and Gayatri Spivak. New Delhi: Oxford University Press, pp. 37–44.

————. 1989. "Dominance without Hegemony and Its Historiography." In *Subaltern Studies,* vol. 6, ed. Ranajit Guha. New Delhi: Oxford University Press, pp. 210–309.

Habermas, Jürgen. 1987. "The Philosophical Discourse of Modernity." Trans. Frederick Lawrence. Cambridge: MIT Press.

Hall, Stuart. 1986. "The Problem of Ideology—Marxism without Guarantees." *Journal of Communication Inquiry* 10(2): 5–27.

Hallwood, P.; and S. Sinclair. 1981. *Oil, Debt, and Development: OPEC in the Third World.* London: Allen and Unwin.

Harris, Olivia. 1989. "The Earth and the State: The Sources and Meanings of Money in Northern Potosi, Bolivia." In *Money and the Morality of Exchange,* ed. Maurice Bloch and Jonathan Parry. Cambridge: Cambridge University Press, pp. 232–68.

Harstock, Nancy C. M. 1983. *Money, Sex, and Power.* New York: Longman.

Hart, Keith. 1989. "Heads or Tails? Two Sides of the Same Coin." *Man* 21(4): 637–56.

Harvey, David. 1989. *The Condition of Postmodernity.* Cambridge: Basil Blackwell.

Hassan, Mostafa. 1975. *Economic Growth and Employment Problems in Venezuela.* New York: Praeger.

Haug, W. F. 1986. *Critique of Commodity Aesthetics: Appearance, Sexuality and Advertising in Capitalist Society.* Minneapolis: University of Minnesota Press.

Haussman, Ricardo. 1981. "State Landed Property, Oil Rent and Accumulation in the Venezuelan Economy." Ph.D diss., Cornell University, Ithaca.

Hegel, G. W. F. 1967. *The Phenomenology of Mind.* New York: Harper Torchbooks.

————. 1975. *Lectures on the Philosophy of History.* Cambridge: Cambridge University Press.

Hebdige, Dick. 1979. *Subculture: The Meaning of Style.* London: Methuen.

Hein, Wolfgang. 1980. "Oil and the State of Venezuela." In *Oil and Class Struggle,* ed. Peter Nore and Terisa Turner. London: Zed Press, pp. 224–51.

Hein, Wolfgang; and Konrad Stenzel. 1973. "The Capitalist State and Underdevelopment in Latin America: The Case of Venezuela." *Kapitalistate* 2: 31–48.

Hellinger, Daniel. 1985. "Democracy in Venezuela." *Latin American Perspectives* 12: 75–82.

————. 1991. *Venezuela: Tarnished Democracy.* Boulder, CO: Westview Press.

Henwood, Doug. 1996. "The Free Flow of Money." *NACLA Report on the Americas* 20(4): 11–17.

Herman, Donald L. 1980. *Christian Democracy in Venezuela.* Chapel Hill: University of North Carolina Press.

Hermoso, José Manuel. 1991. *1936: Programas y poder.* Caracas: Editorial Kinesis.

Herrera Campíns, Luis. 1978. "Transición política." In *1958: Tránsito de la dictadura a la democracia en Venezuela,* ed. Salcedo Bastardo et al. Caracas: Editorial Ariel.

Hill, Christopher. 1969. *Reformation to Industrial Revolution, 1530–1780.* Harmondsworth: Penguin.

Hindess, Barry; and Paul Q. Hirst. 1975. *Pre-capitalist Modes of Production.* London: Routledge and Kegan Paul.

Hirschman, Albert O. 1958. *The Strategy of Economic Development.* New Haven: Yale University Press.

———. 1968. "The Political Economy of Import-Substituting Industrialization in Latin America." *Quarterly Journal of Economics* 42(1): 3–32.

———. 1977. *The Passions and the Interests.* Princeton: Princeton University Press.

Hobsbawm, Eric J.; and Terence O. Ranger. 1983. *The Invention of Tradition.* Cambridge: Cambridge University Press.

Holloway, John; and Sol Picciotto. 1978. *State and Capital: A Marxist Debate.* Austin: University of Texas Press.

Hotelling, H. 1931. "The Economics of Exhaustible Resources." *Journal of Political Economy* 39: 139–75.

Howard, Harrison Sabin. 1975. *Rómulo Gallegos y la revolución burguesa en Venezuela.* Caracas: Monte Avila Editores, C.D.

Hugh-Jones, Stephen. 1992. "Yesterday's Luxuries, Tomorrow's Necessities: Business and Barter in Northwest Amazonia." In *Barter, Exchange and Value,* ed. Caroline Humphrey and Stephen Hugh-Jones. Cambridge: Cambridge University Press, pp. 42–74.

Humphrey, John. 1982. *Capitalist Control and Workers' Struggle in the Brazilian Auto Industry.* Princeton: Princeton University Press.

Hyde, Lewis. 1978. *The Gift: Imagination and the Erotic Life of Property.* New York: Vintage Books.

Izard, Miguel. 1970. *Series estadísticas para la historia de Venezuela.* Mérida: Universidad de los Andes.

———. 1981. *El miedo a la revolución.* Madrid: Editorial Universal.

James, C. L. R. 1963. *The Black Jacobins. Toussaint L'Ouverture and the San Domingo Revolution.* New York: Vintage Books.

Jameson, Fredric. 1981. *The Political Unconscious.* Ithaca: Cornell University Press.

———. 1984. "Postmodernism, or the Cultural Logic of Late Capitalism." *New Left Review* 146: 53–92.

———. 1986. "Third-World Literature in the Era of Multinational Capital." *Social Text* 15 (fall): 65–88.

Jenkins, Rhys Owen. 1977. *Dependent Industrialization in Latin America: The Automobile Industry in Argentina, Chile and Mexico.* New York: Praeger.

————. 1987. *Transnational Corporations and the Latin American Automobile Industry.* London: Macmillan.

Jessop, Bob. 1982. *The Capitalist State: Marxist Theories and Methods.* New York: Columbia University Press.

————. 1983. *Theories of the State.* New York: New York University Press.

————. 1990. *State Theory: Putting the Capitalist State in Its Place.* University Park: Pennsylvania State University Press.

Kaci, Djamel; and Kendillen Leïla. 1984. "L'Algérie, proie de son quotidien." *Pétrole et Société* 26 (January–March): 127–46.

Kalmanovitz, Salomón. 1978. *Desarrollo de la agricultura en Colombia.* Bogotá: DNP/UEA.

Kantorowicz, Ernst H. 1957. *The King's Two Bodies: A Study in Medieval Political Theology.* Princeton: Princeton University Press.

Karl, Terry Lynn. 1982. "The Political Economy of Petrodollars: Oil and Democracy in Venezuela." Ph.D diss., Stanford University.

————. 1987. "Petroleum and Political Facts: The Transition to Democracy in Venezuela." *Latin American Research Review* 22(1): 63–94.

————. 1995. "The Venezuelan Petro-state and the Crisis of 'Its' Democracy." In *Venezuelan Democracy under Stress,* ed. Jennifer L. McCoy, Andrés Serbin, William C. Smith, and Andrés Stambouli. New Brunswick: Transactions Publishers, pp. 33–58.

Karlsson, Weine. 1975. *Manufacturing in Venezuela.* Stockholm: Almquist and Wiksell International.

Kaufman, Robert; and Barbara Stallings, eds. 1989. *Debt and Democracy in Latin America.* Boulder, CO: Westview Press.

Kazancigil, Ali. 1986. *The State in Global Perspective.* Paris: UNESCO.

Keenan, Thomas. 1993. "The Point Is to (Ex)Change It: Reading *Capital,* Rhetorically." In *Fetishism as Cultural Discourse,* ed. Emily Apter and William Pietz. Ithaca: Cornell Univeristy Press, pp. 152–85.

Keynes, John Maynard. 1963. *Essays in Persuasion.* New York: W. W. Norton and Co.

Kliksberg, Bernardo; and Pedro José Madrid, eds. 1975. *Aportes para una administración pública latinoamericana.* Caracas: Universidad Central de Venezuela.

Klor de Alva, Jorge. 1992. "Colonialism and Postcolonialism as (Latin) American Mirages." *Colonial Latin American Review* 1: 1–23.

Kolb, Glen L. 1974. *Democracy and Dictatorship in Venezuela, 1945–1958.* Hamden: Connecticut College Press.

Kornblith, Miriam. 1991. "The Political Constitution-Making: Constitutions and Democracy in Venezuela." *Journal of Latin American Studies* 23 (February): 61–89.

Kouznetsov, Alexander. 1988. "Materials Technology and Trade Implications." In *Materials Technology and Development* (issue 5 of *Advance Technology Alert System*). New York: United Nations, pp. 67–71.

Krause, Ulrich. 1982. *Money and Abstract Labour: On the Analytical Foundations of Political Economy.* London: Verso.

Krispin, Karl. 1994. *Golpe de Estado Venezuela 1945–1948.* Caracas: Editorial Panapo.

Kronish, Rich; and Kenneth Mericle eds. 1984. *The Political Economy of the Latin American Motor Vehicle Industry.* Cambridge: MIT Press.

Krueger, Anne O. 1974. "The Political Economy of the Rent-Seeking Society." *American Economic Review,* 64(3): 291–303.

Kurth, James. 1975. "The International Politics of Postindustrial Societies: The Role of the Multinational Corporation." In *Stress and Contradiction in Modern Capitalism,* ed. L. Linderberg, R. Alfor, C. Crouch, and C. Offe. Lexington: Lexington Books, pp. 11–44.

Kurtzman, Joel. 1993. *The Death of Money.* New York: Simon and Schuster.

Kusch, Rodolfo. 1962. *América profunda.* Buenos Aires: Hachette.

Laclau, Ernesto. 1971. "Feudalism and Capitalism in Latin America." *New Left Review* 67: 19–38.

———. 1977. *Nationalism, Populism, and Ideology.* London: Verso Books.

———. 1990. *New Reflections on the Revolution of Our Time.* London: Verso.

Lan, David. 1989. "Resistance to the Present by the Past: Mediums and Money in Zimbabwe." In *Money and the Morality of Exchange,* ed. Maurice Bloch and Jonathan Parry. Cambridge: Cambridge University Press, pp. 191–208.

Larrazábal, Radamés; and Leticia Barrios G. 1991. *El colapso del populismo y el auge de la oligarquía financiera* Caracas: Universidad Central de Venezuela, Colección Rectorado.

Latin American Subaltern Studies Group. 1993. "Founding Statement." In *The Posmodernism Debate in Latin America,* ed. John Beverley and José Oviedo. Special issue *Boundary* 2 (fall): 110–21.

Lechner, Norbert. 1977. *La crisis del estado en América Latina.* Caracas: El Cid.

———. 1987. *Cultura política y democratización.* Buenos Aires: Consejo Latinoamericano de Ciencias Sociales.

———, ed. 1981. *Estado y política en América Latina.* Mexico City: Siglo XXI.

Lefebvre, Henry. 1991. *The Production of Space.* Trans. Donald Nicholson-Smith. Originally published as *La production de l'espace.* Paris: Anthropos, 1974.

Leff, Nathanial. 1979. "Monopoly Capitalism and Public Policy in Developing Countries." *Kyklos* 32: 718–38.

Lefort, Claude. 1988. *Democracy and Political Theory.* Minneapolis: University of Minnesota Press.

LeGoff, Jacques. 1988. "The Medieval Imagination." Trans. A. Goldhammer. Chicago: University of Chicago Press.

Lenin, Vladimir Illich. 1971. "Selections from *The Development of Capitalism in Russia.*" In *Essential Works of Lenin,* ed. H. Christman. New York: Bantam Press.

Levine, Daniel H. 1973. *Conflict and Political Change in Venezuela.* Princeton: Princeton University Press.

————. 1985. "The Transition to Democracy: Are There Lessons from Venezuela?" *Bulletin of Latin American Research* 4(2): 47–61.

————. 1990. "Popular Groups, Popular Culture and Popular Religion." *Comparative Studies in Society and History* 32: 718–64.

Lewis, W. Arthur. 1949. *The Principles of Economic Planning.* London: D. Dobson.

Lezama Lima, José. 1969. *Expresión americana.* Santiago de Chile: Editorial Universitaria.

Lichtman, Richard. 1975. "Marx's Theory of Ideology." *Socialist Revolution* 5: 45–76.

Lieuwen, Edwin. 1959. *Petroleum in Venezuela: A History.* Berkeley: University of California Press.

————. 1961. *Venezuela.* London: Oxford University Press.

Lindeman, John; and Wayne C. Taylor. 1955. *The Creole Petroleum Corporation in Venezuela.* Washington: National Planning Association.

Linz, Juan; and Alfred Stepan, eds. 1978. *The Breakdown of Democratic Regimes: Latin America.* Baltimore: Johns Hopkins University Press.

Lipietz, A. 1983. "Towards Global Fordism?" *New Left Review* 132: 33–47.

Lippi, Marco. 1979. *Value and Naturalism in Marx.* London: New Left Books.

Liscano, Juan. 1950. *Folklore y cultura: ensayos.* Caracas: Editorial Avila Gráfica.

Lojkine, Jean. 1977. *Le marxisme, l'état et la question urbaine.* Paris: Presses Universitaires de France.

Lombardi, John V. 1977. *Venezuelan History: A Comprehensive Working Bibliography.* Boston: G. K. Hall.

————. 1982. *Venezuela: The Search for Order, the Dream of Progress.* New York: Oxford University Press.

Longuenesse, Elisabeth. 1984. "Rente pétrolière et structure de classe dans les pays du Golfe." *Pétrole et Société* 26 (January–March): 147–62.

López, Gilberto. 1985. "La Venezuela gomecista." *Tierra Firme* 3 (October–December): 649–62.

López Maya, Margarita. 1994. Las relaciones de los EE.UU. con Venezuela durante el trienio. Doctoral diss, Universidad Central de Venezuela, Caracas.

López Maya, Margarita; and Luis Gómez Calcaño. 1985. Desarrollo y hegemonía en la sociedad venezolana: 1958 a 1985. Mimeo. Caracas: CENDES.

López Borges, Nicanor. 1971. *El asesinato de Delgado Chalbaud.* Caracas: Ediciones Centauro.

López-Sanz, Rafael. 1993. *Parentesco, etnia y clase social en la sociedad venezolana.* Caracas: Universidad Central de Venezuela.

Love, Joseph. 1980. "Raul Prebisch and the Origins of the Doctrine of Unequal Exchange." *Latin American Research Review,* 15(3): 45–70.

Lovera, Alberto. 1977. Desarrollo urbano y renta del suelo en Valencia. B.A. thesis, Universidad Católica Andrés Bello, Caracas.

Lovera de Sola, Roberto J. 1985. "Catálogo bibliográfico sobre el tiempo y gobierno de Juan Vicente Gómez." *Tierra Firme* 3 (October–December): 663–84.

————. 1991. "Los libros de la democracia: esquema para un repertorio bibliográfico." *Boletín de la Academia Naciónal de la Historia* 74: 195–208.

Lubrano, Aldo; and Rosa Haydée Sánchez. 1987. *Del hombre completo a Jaime es como tú: Recuento de un proceso electoral venezolano.* Caracas: Vadell Hermanos.

Lucena, Hector. 1982. *El movimiento obrero petrolero: Proceso de formación y desarrollo.* Caracas: Ediciones Centauro.

Lukacs, George. 1971. *History and Class Consciousness.* Cambridge: MIT Press.

Machillanda, José. 1993. *Cinismo político y golpe de estado.* Caracas: Italgráfica.

MacPherson, C. B., ed. 1978. *Property: Mainstream and Critical Positions.* Toronto: University of Toronto Press.

Magallanes, Manuel Vicente. 1987. *Sistemas electorales, acceso al sistema político, y sistema de partidos.* Caracas: Publicaciones del Consejo Supremo Electoral.

Malavé Mata, Hector. 1987. *Los extravíos del poder: euforia y crisis del populismo en Venezuela.* Caracas: Consejo de Desarrollo Científico y Humanístico, Universidad Central de Venezuela.

Malloy, James M., ed. 1977. *Authoritarianism and Corporatism in Latin America.* Pittsburgh: University of Pittsburgh Press.

Mamalakis, Markos. 1978. "La teoría mineral del crecimiento: la experiencia latinamericana." *El Trimestre Económico* 45 (October–December): 841–78.

Mandel, Ernest. 1978. *Late Capitalism.* London: Verso.

Mandel, Ernest; and Alan Freeman, eds. 1984. *Ricardo, Marx, Sraffa.* London: Verso.

Mann, Charles C.; and Mark L. Plummer. 1994. *Noah's Choice: The Future of Endangered Species.* New York: Alfred A. Knopf.

Maravall, José Antonio. 1986. *Culture of the Baroque: Analysis of a Historical Structure.* Minneapolis: University of Minnesota Press.

Marcus, George E.; and Michael M. J. Fisher. 1986. *Anthropology as Cultural Critique.* Chicago: University of Chicago Press.

Markoff, John. 1996. *Waves of Democracy, Social Movements and Political Change.* Thousand Oaks, CA: Pine Forge.

Márquez, Joaquín Gabaldón. 1978. *Memoria y cuento de la generación del veintiocho.* Caracas: Consejo Municipal del Distrito Federal.

Márquez, Wálter. 1992. *Comandos del crimen: la masacre de el Amparo.* Caracas: Fuentes Editores.

Marshall, Alfred. 1961. *Principles of Economics.* London: Macmillan.

Marta Sosa, Joaquin. 1984. *Venezuela: elecciones y transformación social.* Caracas: Ediciones Centuaro.

Martín, Américo. 1976. *Los peces gordos.* Valencia: Vadell Hermanos.

Martínez, Aníbal. 1966. *Our Gift, Our Oil.* Vienna: the author.

————. 1973. *Historia petrolero venzolana en 20 jornadas.* Caracas: EDRECA Editoria.

————. 1980. *Gumersindo Torres: The Pioneer of Venezuelan Petroleum Policy.* Trans. Patricia Pernalete. Caracas: Petroleos de Venezuela.

Martín Frechilla, Juan José. 1994. *Planes, planos y proyectos para Venezuela: 1908–1958 (Apuntes para una historia de la construcción del país).* Caracas: Universidad Central de Venezuela.

Martz, John D. 1964. *The Venezuelan Elections of December 1, 1963.* Washington: Institute for the Comparative Study of Political Systems.

———. 1966. *Acción Democrática: Evolution of a Modern Political Party in Venezuela.* Princeton: Princeton University Press.

———. 1979. *Political Attitudes in Venezuela: Societal Cleavages and Political Opinion.* Austin: University of Texas Press.

Martz, John D.; and Enrique Baloyra. 1979. *Electoral Mobilization and Public Opinion: The Venezuelan Campaign of 1973.* Chapel Hill: University of North Carolina Press.

Martz, John D.; and David Myers. 1977. *Venezuela: The Democratic Experience.* New York: Praeger.

Marx, Karl. 1963. *The 18th Brumaire of Louis Bonaparte.* New York: International Publishers.

———. 1967. *Capital.* New York: International Publishers.

———. 1968. *Theories of Surplus-Value.* Moscow: Progress Publishers.

———. 1973. *Grundrisse: Foundations of the Critique of Political Economy (Rough Draft).* Harmondsworth: Penguin Books.

———. 1981. *Capital.* Vols. 1–3. New York: Vintage Books.

Massarrat, Mohssen. 1980. "The Energy Crisis: The Struggle for the Redistribution of Surplus Profit from Oil." In *Oil and Class Struggle,* ed. Peter Nore and Terisa Turner, Westport, CT: Hill, Lawrence, pp. 26–68

Massey, Doreen. 1992. "Politics and Space/Time." *New Left Review* 196: 65–84.

Masur, Gerhard. 1966. *Nationalism in Latin America: Diversity and Unity.* New York: Macmillan.

Matta, Roberto da. 1991. *Carnivals, Heroes and Rogues.* South Bend: University of Notre Dame Press.

Matthews, Robert D., Jr. 1977. *Violencia rural en Venezuela, 1840–1858.* Caracas: Editorial Ateneo de Caracas.

Mauss, Marcel. 1954. *The Gift: Forms and Functions of Exchange in Archaic Societies.* Trans. I. Cunnison. London: Cohen and West.

Mayobre, Eduardo. 1985. "The Renegotiation of Venezuela's Foreign Debt During 1982 and 1983." In *Politics and Economics of External Debt Crisis: The Latin American Experience,* ed. Miguel S. Wionczek. Boulder, CO: Westview Press, pp. 325–47.

Mayobre, José Antonio. 1970. *Las inversiones extranjeras en Venezuela.* Caracas: Editorial Monte Avila.

Maza Zavala, D. F. 1991. Prologue to *1936: programas vs. poder,* by José Manuel Hermoso. Caracas: Editorial Kinesis, pp. i–viii.

Mbembe, Achille. 1992. "The Banality of Power and the Aesthetics of Vulgarity in the Postcolony." *Public Culture* 4(2): 1–30.

McBeth, Brian S. 1983. *Juan Vicente Gómez and the Oil Companies in Venezuela, 1908–1935.* Cambridge: Cambridge University Press.

———. 1985. "El impacto de las compañias petroleras en el Zulia (1922–1935)." *Tierra Firme* 3 (October–December): 537–50.

McBeth, Brian S.; and William M. Sullivan. 1985. *Petroleum in Venezuela: A Bibliography.* Boston: G. K. Hall.

McCoy, Jennifer L. 1986. "The Politics of Adjustment: Labor and the Venezuelan Debt Crisis." *Journal of Inter-American Studies and World Affairs* 28(4): 103–38.

———. 1989. "Labor and the State in a Party-mediated Democracy: Institutional Change in Venezuela." *Latin American Research Review* 24(2): 35–67.

———. 1989. "Venezuela: Austerity and the working class in a Democratic Regime." In *Paying the Costs of Austerity in Latin America*, ed. Howard Handelman and Werner Baer. Boulder: Westview Press, pp. 195–223.

McCoy, Jennifer L.; Andrés Serbin; William C. Smith; and Andrés Stambouli, eds. 1995. *Venezuelan Democracy under Stress.* New Brunswick: Transactions Publishers.

Medina Febres, Mariano. 1991. *1936 MEDO 1939: Caricaturas de lucha.* Caracas: Ediciones Centauro.

Meek, Ronald L. 1956. *Studies in the Labor Theory of Value.* New York: Monthly Review Press.

Mehlman, Jeffrey. 1994. "Remy de Gourmont with Freud: Fetishism and Patriotism." In *Fetishism as Cultural Discourse,* ed. Emily Apter and William Pietz. Ithaca: Cornell University Press, pp. 84–91.

Meillassoux, Claude. 1981. *Maidens, Meal, and Money: Capitalism and the Domestic Community.* Cambridge: Cambridge University Press.

Melcher, Dorothea. 1992. *Estado y movimiento obrero en Venezuela (represión e integración hasta 1948).* Caracas: Academia Naciónal de la Historia.

Merhav, Meir. 1971. *Posibilidades de exportación de la industria venezolana.* Caracas: CORDIPLAN.

Michaels, Walter Benn. 1985. "The Gold Standard and the Logic of Naturalism." *Representations* 9 (winter): 105–32.

Mignolo, Walter. 1991. "Canons A(nd) Cross-Cultural Boundaries (Or, Whose Canon Are We Talking About?)." *Poetics Today* 12(1): 1–28.

———. 1992. "On the Colonization of Amerindian Languages and Memories: Renaissance Theories of Writing and the Discontinuity of the Classical Tradition." *Comparative Studies in Society and History* 34(2): 301–30.

———. 1995. *The Darker Side of the Renaissance.* Ann Arbor: University of Michigan Press.

Mikesell, Raymond F., ed. 1971. *Foreign Investment in the Petroleum and Mineral Industries: Case Studies of Investor–Host Country Relations.* Baltimore: Johns Hopkins University Press.

Miliband, Ralph. 1969. *The State in Capitalist Society.* London: Winfield and Nicholson.

———. 1970. "The Capitalist State—Reply to Poulantzas." *New Left Review* 59: 53–60.

———. 1973. "Poulantzas and the Capitalist State." *New Left Review* 82: 83–92.

Mills, Lady Dorothy Rachel Melissa. 1931. *The Country of the Orinoco*. London: Hutchinson and Co.

Ministerio de Fomento. 1974. Untitled confidential memorandum.

———. several years. *Memoria y cuenta*. Caracas: Ministerio de Fomento.

Mintz, Sidney. 1985. *Sweetness and Power: The Place of Sugar in Modern History*. New York: Penguin Books.

Mitchell, Christopher, ed. 1988. *Changing Perspectives in Latin American Studies: Insights from Six Disciplines*. Stanford: Stanford University Press.

Mitchell, Timothy. 1988. *Colonising Egypt*. Cambridge: Cambridge University Press.

———. 1991. "The Limits of the State: Beyond Statist Approaches and Their Critics." *American Political Science Review*. 85(1):77–96.

Mitchell, W. J. Thomas. 1986. *Iconology: Image, Text, Ideology*. Chicago: University of Chicago Press.

Miyoshi, Masao. 1993. "A Borderless World? From Colonialism and Transnationalism and the Decline of the Nation-State." *Critical Inquiry* 19 (summer): 726–51.

Moghadam, Ual. 1988. "Oil, the State, and Limits to Autonomy: The Iranian Case." *Arab Studies Quarterly* 10(2): 225–38.

Mogull, Robert G. 1972. "The Symbiotic Relationship of Creole and Venezuela." *Journal of Human Relations* 20(4): 459–67.

Moleiro, Moises. 1978. *El partido del pueblo*. Valencia: Vadell Hermanos.

———. 1988. *Las máscaras de democracia*. Caracas: Ediciones Centauro.

Moleiro, Rodolfo. 1993. *De la dictadura a la democracia. Eleazar López Contreras. Lindero y puente entre dos épocas*. Caracas: Editorial Pomaire.

Mommer, Bernard. 1983. *Petroleo, renta del suelo e historia*. Mérida: Universidad de los Andes.

———. 1986. *La cuestión petrolera*. Caracas: Fondo Editorial Tropykos.

Morales, Carlos. 1983. "La democracia y la economía nacional." Caracas, Septiembre de 1936, 343–48, in Pensamiento Político Venezolano del Siglo XX. Documentos para su Estudio. El debate político en 1936. Caracas: Congreso de la República.

Moran, Theodore. 1974. *Multinational Corporations and the Politics of Dependence*. Princeton: Princeton University Press.

———. 1978. *Oil Prices and the Future of OPEC*. Washington: Resources for the Future.

———. 1982. "Modeling OPEC Behavior: Economic and Political Alternatives." In *OPEC Behavior and World Oil Prices*, ed. James M. Griffin and Davie J. Teece. London: George Allen and Unwin, pp. 1–36.

Moreno, Arellano. 1968. *Mirador de la historia política de Venezuela*. Caracas: Ediciones Edime.

Moreno Fraginals, Manuel. 1976. *Sugarmill: The Socioeconomic Complex of Sugar in Cuba*. New York: Monthly Review Press.

Morishima, Michio; and George Catephores. 1978. *Value, Exploitation and Growth*. London: McGraw-Hill.

Morley, Morris; James F. Petras; and Steven Smith. 1977. *The Nationalization of Venezuelan Oil*. New York: Praeger.

Mörner, Magnus. 1993. *Region and State in Latin America's Past*. Baltimore: Johns Hopkins University Press.

Munk, B. 1969. "The Welfare Costs of Content Protection: The Automotive Industry in Latin America." *Journal of Political Economy* 77: 85–98.

Murray, Robin. 1977. "Value and Theory of Rent: Part One." *Capital and Class* 3 (autumn): 100–21.

———. 1978. "Value and Theory of Rent: Part Two." *Capital and Class* 4 (spring): 11–31.

Musgrove, Philip. 1981. "The Oil Price Increase and the Alleviation of Poverty: Income Distribution in Caracas, Venezuela in 1966 to 1975." *Journal of Development Economics* 9(2): 229–50.

Naím, Moisés; and Antonio Francés. 1995. "The Venezuelan Private Sector: From Courting the State to Courting the Market. In *Lessons of the Venezuelan Experience,* ed. Louis W. Goodman, Johanna Mendelson Forman, Moisés Naím, Joseph S. Tulchin, and Gary Bland. Washington: Woodrow Wilson Center Press, pp. 165–92.

Naím, Moisés; and Ramón Piñango, eds. 1985. *El caso Venezuela. Una ilusión de harmonía*. Caracas: Ediciones IESA.

Nairn, Tom. 1981. *The Break-up of Britain*. London: Verso Editions.

Nash, June. 1979. *We Eat the Mines and the Mines Eat Us: Dependency and Exploitation in Bolivian Tin Mines*. New York: Columbia University Press.

National Planning Association. 1955. *United States Business Performance Abroad: The Case Study of the Creole Petroleum Corporation in Venezuela*. Caracas: Department of Sociology and Anthropology, Caracas University.

Navarro, Desiderio. 1985. "Otras reflexiones sobre eurocentrismo y antieurocentrismo en la teoría literaria de la América Latina y Europa." *Casa de las Américas* 150 (May–June): 68–78.

Naylor, Thomas R. 1994. *Hot Money*. Montreal: Blackrose.

Neale, Walter C. 1976. *Monies in Societies*. San Francisco: Chandler and Sharpe Publishers.

Neuhouser, Kevin. 1992. "Democratic Stability in Venezuela: Elite Consensus or Class Compromise?" *American Sociological Review* 57 (February): 117–35.

Newfarmer, Richard F. 1979. *Transnational Conglomerates and the Economics of Dependent Development*. Greenwich, CT: JAI.

Nisbet, Robert. 1980. *History of the Idea of Progress*. New York: Basic Books.

Nolff, Max, ed. 1974. *Desarrollo industrial latinamericano*. Mexico City: Fondo de Cultura Económica.

Nore, Petter; and Terisa Turner, eds. 1980. *Oil and Class Struggle*. London: Zed Press.

O'Donnell, Guillermo A. 1973. *Modernization and Bureaucratic-Authoritarianism: Studies in South American Politics*. Berkeley: University of California Press.

O'Donnell, Guillermo; Philippe C. Schmitter; and Laurence Whitehead, eds. 1986. *Transitions from Authoritarian Rule: Comparative Perspectives*. Baltimore: Johns Hopkins University Press.

Offe, Claus. 1976. "Structural Problems of the Capitalist State." In *German Political Studies,* ed. Beyme von Klaus. Beverly Hills, CA: Sage, pp. 11–30.

O'Gorman, Edmundo. 1982. *The Invention of America: An Inquiry into the Historical Nature of the New World and the Meaning of Its History.* Bloomington: Indiana University Press.

O'Hanlon, Rosalind. 1988. "Recovering the Subject: *Subaltern Studies* and Histories of Resistance in Colonial South Asia." *Modern Asian Studies* 22(1): 189–224.

Olayiwola, Peter O. 1987. *Petroleum and Structural Change in a Developing Country: The Case of Nigeria.* New York: Praeger.

Ollman, Bertell. 1971. *Alienation.* Cambridge: Cambridge University Press.

———. 1982. "Theses on the Capitalist State." *Monthly Review* 34(7): 41–7.

O'Malley, Michael. 1994. "Specie and Species: Race and the Money Question in Nineteenth-Century America." *American Historical Review* 99(2): 369–95.

Ordosgoiti, Napoleón. 1984. *Gallegos, el poder y el exilio.* Caracas: Editorial Domingo Fuentes.

Ortiz, Fernando. 1995. *Cuban Counterpoint: Tobacco and Sugar.* Durham: Duke University Press.

Ortner, Sherry B. 1984. "Theory in Anthropology since the Sixties." *Comparative Studies in Society and History* 26: 126–66.

Oviedo y Baños, José. 1987. *The Conquest and Settlement of Venezuela.* Berkeley: University of California Press.

Pacheco, Emilio. 1984. *De Castro a López Contreras: proceso social de la Venezuela contemporánea.* Caracas: Editorial Domingo Fuentes.

———. 1985. "De Castro a López Contreras, proceso social de la Venezuela contemporánea, por Inés Quintero." *Tierra Firme* 3 (October–December): 693–95.

Pacheco, Luís Eduardo. 1968. *Orígenes del Presidente Gómez.* Caracas: Los Talleres de Artes Gráficas de los Lisiados Trabajadores de Venezuela.

Pagden, Anthony. 1982. *The Fall of Natural Man: The American Indian and the Origins of Comparative Ethnology.* Cambridge: Cambridge University Press.

Palloix, C. 1978. *La internacionalización de capital.* Madrid: H. Blume.

Panitch, Leo. 1994. "Globalisation and the State." In *Socialist Register,* ed. Ralph Miliband. London: Merlin, pp. 60–93.

Parboni, Ricardo. 1986. "The Dollar Weapon: From Nixon to Reagan." *New Left Review* 158 (July–August): 5–18.

Parker, Andrew. 1993. "Unthinking Sex: Marx, Engels, and the Scene of Writing." In *Fear of a Queer Planet: Queer Politics and Social Theory,* ed. Michael Warner. Minneapolis: University of Minnesota Press, pp. 19–41.

Parry, Benita. 1987. "Problems in Current Theories of Colonial Discourses." *Oxford Literary Review* 9: 27–58.

Parry, Jonathan. 1989. "On the Moral Perils of Exchange." In *Money and the Morality of Exchange,* ed. Maurice Bloch and Jonathan Parry. Cambridge: Cambridge University Press, pp. 64–93.

Pashukanis, E. V. 1978. *A General Theory of Law and Marxism*. London: Ink Links.

Pastor, Beatriz. 1988. "Polémicas en torno al canon: implicaciones filosóficas, pedagógicas y políticas." *Casa de las Américas* 171 (November–December): 78–87.

Pearsan, M. H. 1982. "The System of Dependent Capitalism in Pre- and Post-Revolutionary Iran." *International Journal of Middle Eastern Studies* 14: 501–22.

Peeler, John. 1985. *Latin American Democracies: Colombia, Costa Rica, Venezuela*. Chapel Hill: University of North Carolina Press.

Peña, Alfredo. 1979. *Conversaciones con Carlos Andrés Pérez*. Caracas: Acción Democrática.

Pérez, Carlos Andrés. 1973. *Acción de gobierno*. Caracas: Acción Democrática.

Pérez Alfonso, Juan Pablo. 1961. *Petróleo jugo de la tierra*. Caracas: Editorial Arte.

———. 1976. *Hundiéndonos en el excremento del diablo*. Caracas: Editorial Lisbona.

Pérez Alfonso, Juan Pablo; and Domingo Alberto Rangel. 1976. *El desastre*. Valencia: Vadell Hermanos.

Pérez Perdomo, Rogelio. 1995. "Corruption and Political Crisis." In *Lessons of the Venezuelan Experience,* ed. Louis W. Goodman, Johanna Mendelson Forman, Moisés Naím, Joseph S. Tulchin, and Gary Bland. Washington: Woodrow Wilson Center Press, pp. 311–33.

Pérez Sainz, Juan Pablo; and Paul Zarembka. 1979. "Accumulation and the State in Venezuelan Industrialization." *Latin American Perspectives* 22 (summer): 5–29.

Petkoff, Teodoro. 1979. *Corrupción total*. Caracas: Editorial Fuentes.

Petras, James; and M. Morley. 1983. "Petrodollars and the State: The Failure of State Capitalist Development in Venezuela." *Third World Quarterly* 5: 8–27.

Philip, George. 1982. *Oil and Politics in Latin America: Nationalist Movements and State Companies*. Cambridge: Cambridge University Press.

Picón Salas, Mariano. 1969. *De la conquista a la independencia: Tres siglos de historia cultural latinoamericana*. Mexico City: Fondo de Cultura Económica.

———. 1976. *Comprensión de Venezuela*. Caracas: Monte Avila.

———. 1984. *Formación y proceso de la literatura venezolana*. Caracas: Monte Avila.

Pietz, William. 1985. "The Problem of the Fetish, Part 1." *Res*, 9 (spring): 5–17.

———. 1987. "The Problem of the Fetish, Part 2." *Res*, 13 (spring): 23–45.

———. 1988. "The Problem of the Fetish, Part 3a." *Res*, 16 (autumn): 105–23.

———. 1993. "Fetishism and Materialism: The Limits of Theory in Marx." In *Fetishism as Cultural Discourse,* ed. Emily Apter and William Pietz. Ithaca: Cornell University Press, pp. 119–51.

Pilling, Geoffrey. 1973. "Imperialism, Trade, and 'Unequal Exchange': The Work of Aghiri Emmanuel." *Economy and Society* 2(2): 164–85.

Piñerúa, Luis. 1988. *Luis Piñerúa: enfrentamiento con el poder*. Caracas: Ediciones Centauro.

Pino Iturrieta, Elías. 1985a. "Matar a Gómez." *Tierra Firme* 3 (October–December): 533–36.

———, ed. 1985b. *Juan Vicente Gómez y su época*. Caracas: Monte Avila.

Plaza, Helena. 1984. *El 23 de enero de 1958*. Caracas: Garbizu & Todtmann Editores.

Pletch, Carl. 1981. "The Three Worlds, or the Division of Social Scientific Labor, circa 1950–1975." *Comparative Studies in Society and History* 23(4): 565–90.

Poggi, G. 1978. *The Development of the Modern State: A Sociological Introduction*. London: Hutchinson.

Polanco Alcántara, Tomás. 1990. *Juan Vicente Gómez: aproximación a una biografía*. Caracas: Grijalbo.

Poole, Deborah, ed. 1994. *Unruly Order: Violence and Cultural Identity in the High Provinces of Southern Peru*. Boulder: Westview Press.

Portantiero, Juan Carlos; and Emilio de Ipola. 1981. "Lo nacional popular y los populismos realmente existentes." *Nueva sociedad* 54:7–18.

Poulantzas, Nicos. 1973. *Political Power and Social Classes*. London: New Left Books.

———. 1975. *Classes in Contemporary Capitalism*. London: New Left Books.

———. 1976. "The Capitalist State." *New Left Review* 95: 63–83.

———. 1978. *State, Power, Socialism*. London: New Left Books.

Powell, John Duncan. 1971. *Political Mobilization of the Venezuelan Peasant*. Cambridge: Harvard University Press.

Prakash, Gyan. 1990. "Writing Post-Orientalist Histories of the Third World: Perspectives from Indian Historiography." *Comparative Studies in Society and History* 32(2): 383–408.

———. 1995. *After Colonialism: Imperial Histories and Postcolonial Displacements*. Princeton: Princeton University Press.

Proceso Político. 1978. *CAP: 5 años*. Caracas: Equipo Proceso Político.

Pro-Venezuela. 1973. *La política y los empresarios*. Caracas: Pro-Venezuela.

Purroy, Ignacio M. 1982. *Estado e industrialización en Venezuela*. Valencia: Vadell Hermanos.

Quero, Morales Constantino. 1978. *Imagen-objectivo de Venezuela: reformas fundamentales para su desarrollo*. Caracas: Banco Central de Venezuela.

Quintero, Inés. 1985. "De la alucinación a la eficiencia (Román Cárdenas en el Ministerio de Hacienda)." *Tierra Firme* 3 (October–December): 599–612.

———. 1989. "La reforma militar restauradora." *Boletín de la Academia Nacional de la Historia* 72: 141–52.

Quintero, Rodolfo. 1972. *Antropología del petroleo*. Caracas: Universidad Central de Venezuela.

———. 1975. *La cultura del petroleo*. Caracas: Universidad Central de Venezuela.

Rabasa, José. 1993. *Inventing America*. Norman: Oklahoma University Press.

Rabe, Stephen G. 1982. *The Road to OPEC: United States Relations with Venezuela, 1919–1976*. Austin: University of Texas Press.

Radice, Hugo, ed. 1975. *International Firms and Modern Imperialism*. Baltimore: Penguin Books.

Rafael, Vincent. 1993. *Contracting Colonialism: Translation and Christian Conversion in Tagalog Society under Early Spanish Rule*. Ithaca: Cornell University Press.

Rama, Angel. 1982. *Transculturación narrativa en América Latina*. Mexico: Siglo XXI.

Ramos, Joseph. 1986. *Neoconservative Economics in the Southern Cone of Latin America, 1973–1983.* Baltimore: Johns Hopkins University Press.

Randall, Laura. 1987. *The Political Economy of Venezuelan Oil.* New York: Praeger.

Rangel, Domingo Alberto. 1973. *Los mercaderes del voto.* Valencia: Vadell Hermanos.

———. 1974. *Capital y desarrollo: la Venezuela agraria.* Caracas: Universidad Central de Venezuela.

———. 1976. *La oligarquía del dinero.* Caracas: Universidad Central de Venezuela.

———. 1977. *Capital y desarrollo: el rey petroleo.* Caracas: Universidad Central de Venezuela.

———. 1978. *La revolución de las fantasias.* Caracas: Ediciones Ofidi.

———. 1982. *Fin de fiesta.* Valencia: Vadell Hermanos.

Rangel, Domingo Alberto; and Pedro Duno. 1979. *La pipa rota: las elecciones del 1978.* Caracas: Vadell Hermanos.

Reddy, William M. 1987. *Money and Liberty in Modern Europe: A Critique of Historical Understanding.* London: Cambridge University Press.

Reich, Robert. 1991. *The Work of Nations: Preparing Ourselves for 21st Century Capitalism.* New York: A. A. Knopf.

Renan, Ernest. 1990. "What Is a Nation?" In *Nation and Narration,* ed. Homi K. Bhabha. New York: Routledge, pp. 8–22.

Rey, Juan Carlos. 1989. *El futuro de la democracia en Venezuela.* Caracas: IDEA.

Reynolds, C. W. 1982. "The New Terms of Trade Problem: Economic Rents in International Exchange." In *Economics in the Long View,* vol, 1, ed. Charles P. Kindleberger and Guido di Tella. New York: MacMillan, pp. 189–209.

Ribeiro, Darcy. 1971. *The Americas and Civilization.* New York: E. P. Dutton and Company.

Ricardo, David. 1983. *On the Principles of Political Economy and Taxation.* Cambridge: Cambridge University Press.

Rieff, David. 1991. *Los Angeles: Capital of the Third World.* New York: Simon and Schuster.

Rincón, Fredy N. 1982. *El Nuevo Ideal Nacional y los planes económico-militares de Pérez Jiménez 1952–1957.* Caracas: Ediciones Centauro.

Roa Bastos, Augusto. 1974. *Yo el supremo.* Buenos Aires: Siglo XXI.

Rodríguez, Luis Cipriano. 1983. *Gómez: agricultura, petróleo y dependencia.* Caracas: Fondo Editorial Tropykos.

———. 1985. "Gómez y el anticomunismo." *Tierra Firme* 3 (October–December): 551–66.

Rodríguez Cárdenas, Manuel. 1954. *El retablo de las maravillas.* Caracas: Ediciones Alejandro Vallejo.

Rodríguez Trujillo, Manuel. 1978. "La industria de bienes de capital en Venezuela." *Venezuela Metalúrgica y Minera* 27 (June–July): 11–30.

Rodríguez-Valdés, Angel. 1993. *La otra muerte de CAP.* Caracas: Alfadil Ediciones.

Rodríquez Gallard, Irene. 1974. *El petroleo en la historiografia venezolana.* Caracas: Universidad Central de Venezuela.

Rosdolsky, Roman. 1977. *The Making of Marx's "Capital."* London: Pluto Press.

Rose, Sanford. 1977. "Why the Multinational Tide Is Ebbing." *Fortune* (August): 118.

Roseberry, William. 1983. *Coffee and Capitalism in the Venezuelan Andes.* Austin: University Press of Texas.

———. 1986. "Images of the Peasant in the Consciousness of the Venezuelan Proletariat." In *Proletarians and Protest,* ed. Michael Hanagan and Charles Stephenson. Westport, CT: Greenwood.

Rostow, W. W. 1960. *The Process of Economic Growth: A Non-Communist Manifesto.* Cambridge: Cambridge University Press.

Rothschild, Emma. 1974. *Paradise Lost: The Decline of the Auto-Industrial Age.* New York: Vintage Books.

Rourke, Thomas. [1936] 1969. *Gómez, Tyrant of the Andes.* New York: William Morrow.

Rouse, Roger. 1995. "Thinking through Transnationalism." *Public Culture* 7(2): 353–402.

Rubin, I. I. 1973. *Essays on Marx's Theory of Value.* Montreal: Black Rose Books.

Sachs, J. D., ed. 1989. *Developing Country Debt and the World Economy, NBER Project Report.* Chicago: University of Chicago Press.

Sahlins, Marshall. 1976. *Culture and Practical Reason.* Chicago: University of Chicago Press.

———. 1985. *Islands of History.* Chicago: University of Chicago Press.

Said, Edward. 1978. *Orientalism.* New York: Vintage Books.

———. 1993. *Culture and Imperialism.* New York: Alfred A. Knopf.

Salas Capriles, Roberto. 1980. *Se busca un industrial.* Caracas: Cromotip.

Salazar-Carrillo, Jorge. 1976. *Oil in the Economic Development of Venezuela.* New York: Praeger.

———. 1994. *Oil and Development in Venezuela during the Twentieth Century.* Westport, CT: Praeger.

Salgado, Rene. 1987. "Economic Pressure Groups and Policy-Making in Venezuela: The Case of FEDECAMARAS Reconsidered." *Latin American Research Review* 22(3): 91–105.

Sallnow, M. J. 1989. "Precious Metals in the Andean Moral Economy." In *Money and the Morality of Exchange,* ed. Maurice Bloch and Jonathan Parry. Cambridge: Cambrige University Press, pp. 209–31.

Salóm, Ramón Escovar. 1975. *Evolución política de Venezuela.* Caracas: Monte Avila Editores C.A.

Samuelson, Paul A. 1974. "Insight and Detour in the Theory of Exploitation: A Reply to Baumol." *Journal of Economic Literature* 12(1): 63–77.

Sangren, P. Steven. 1988. "Rhetoric and the Authority of Ethnography: 'Postmodernism' and the Social Reproduction of Texts." *Current Anthropology* 29: 405–35.

Santaella, Ramón. 1985. "La dinámica del espacio venezolana durante el gobierno de Gómez." *Tierra Firme* 3 (October–December): 629–36.

Sarlo, Beatriz. 1988. *Una modernidad periférica: Buenos Aires: 1920 y 1930.* Buenos Aires: Nueva Visión.

Sassen, Saskia. 1991. *The Global City.* Princeton: Princeton University Press.

———. 1994. *Cities in the World.* Thousands Oaks: Pine Forge Press.

Schael, Guillermo José. 1969. *El automóvil en Venezuela.* Caracas: Gráficas Edición de Arte.

Schael, María Sol Pérez. 1993. *Petróleo y poder en Venezuela.* Caracas: Monte Avila Editores Latinoamericana.

Schaposnik, Eduardo Carlos. 1985. *La democratización de las Fuerzas Armadas Venezolanas.* Caracas.

Scharer-Nussberger, Maya. 1979. *Rómulo Gallegos: el mundo inconcluso.* Caracas: Monte Avila Editores.

Scheper-Hughes, Nancy. 1992. *Death without Weeping.* Berkeley: University of California Press.

Schmidt, Alfred. 1971. *The Concept of Nature in Marx.* London: New Left Books.

Schwarz, Roberto. 1992. *Misplaced Ideas: Essays on Brazilian Culture.* New York: Verso.

Schwerin, Karl H. 1966. *Oil and Steel: Processes of Karinya Culture in Response to Industrial Development.* Los Angeles: Latin American Center, University of California Press.

Scott, James C. 1985. *Weapons of the Weak: Everyday Forms of Peasant Resistance.* New Haven: Yale University Press.

Segnini, Yolanda. 1985a. "Ateneo y Gomecismo." *Tierra Firme* 3 (October–December): 591–98.

———. 1985b. "Cartas al Benemérito." *Tierra Firme* 3 (October–December): 637–44.

———. 1987. *Las luces del gomecismo.* Caracas: Editorial Alfadil.

Shaik, Anwar. 1977. "Marx's Theory of Value and the 'Transformation Problem.'" In *The Subtle Anatomy of Capitalism,* ed. Jesse Schwartz. Santa Monica, CA: Goodyear, pp. 106–39.

———. 1979a. "Foreign Trade and the Law of Value: Part I." *Science and Society* (fall): 281–302.

———. 1979b. "Foreign Trade and the Law of Value: Part II." *Science and Society* (winter): 27–57.

———. 1980. "The Laws of International Trade." In *Growth, Profits, and Property,* ed. Edward Nell. Cambridge: Cambridge University Press, pp. 30–44.

Shell, Marc. 1982. *Money, Language, and Thought: Literacy and Philosophical Economics from the Medieval to the Modern Era.* Berkeley: University of California Press.

Shils, Edward. 1965. "Charisma, Order and Status." *American Sociological Review* 30: 199–213.

Shohat, Ella; and Robert Stam. 1994. *Unthinking Eurocentrism.* New York: Routledge.

Silva, Manuel Acosta. 1976. *Historias del 28.* Caracas: Los Talleres Tipográficos de la Escuela Técnica Popular.

Silva Michelena, José Agustín. 1971. *The Illusion of Democracy in Dependent Nations.* Cambridge: MIT Press.

Silva Michelena, José Agustín; and Heinz Rudolph Sonntag. 1979. *El proceso electoral de 1978.* Caracas: Editorial Ateneo de Caracas.

Simmel, Georg. 1978. *The Philosophy of Money.* London: Routledge and Kegan Paul.

Sklar, Richard L. 1975. *Corporate Power in an African State: The Political Impact of Multinational Mining Companies in Zambia.* Berkeley: University of California Press.

Skocpol, Theda. 1985. "Bringing the State Back In: Strategies of Analysis in Current Research." In *Bringing the State Back In,* ed. P. Evans, D. Rueschemeyer, and T. Skocpol. Cambridge: Cambridge University Press, pp. 3–37.

Skurski, Julie. 1985. "Forging the Nation". Unpublished manuscript.

———. 1993. "The Leader and the People: Representing the Nation in Postcolonial Venezuela." Ph.D. diss., University of Chicago.

———. 1994. "The Ambiguities of Authenticity in Latin America: *Doña Bárbara* and the Construction of National Identity." *Poetics Today* 15(4): 59–81.

Skurski, Julie; and Fernando Coronil. 1992. "Country and City in a Colonial Landscape: Double Discourse and the Geopolitics of Truth in Latin America." In *View from the Border: Essays in Honor of Raymond Williams,* ed. Dennis Dworkin and Leslie Roman. New York: Routledge, pp. 231–59.

Smith, Adam. 1976. *The Wealth of Nations.* Chicago: University of Chicago Press.

Smith, Neil. 1990. *Uneven Development.* Cambridge: Basil Blackwell.

Smith, Peter H., ed. 1995. *Latin America in Comparative Perspective.* Boulder, CO: Westview Press.

Soja, Edward. 1987. "The Postmodernization of Human Geography: A Review Essay." *Annals of the Association of Human Geographers* 77 : 289–96.

———. 1989. *Postmodern Geographies.* London: Verso.

Solberg, Carl E. 1979. *Oil and Nationalism in Argentina: A History.* Stanford: Stanford University Press.

Sommer, Doris. 1991. *Foundational Fictions: When History Was Romance.* Berkeley: University of California Press.

Sosa, Arturo A. 1974. *Filosofía política del gomecismo.* Barquisimeto: Centro Gumilla.

———. 1981. *Del garibaldismo estudiantil a la izquierda criolla.* Caracas: Ediciones Centauro.

———, ed. 1985. *Ensayos sobre el pensamiento político positivista venezolano.* Caracas: Edicionces Centauro.

———. 1995. *Rómulo Betancourt y el Partido del Pueblo (1937–1941).* Caracas: Editorial Fundación Rómulo Betancourt.

Sosa, F. Betancourt. 1959. *Pueblo en rebeldía.* Caracas: Ediciones Garrido.

Sosa Pietri, Andrés. 1993. *Petróleo y poder.* Caracas: Editorial Paneta Venezolana, S.A.

Spivak, Gayatri Chakravorty. 1988a. "Can the Subaltern Speak?" In *Marxism and the Interpretation of Culture,* ed. Cary Nelson and Lawrence Grossberg. Urbana: University of Illinois Press.

———. 1988b. "Subaltern Studies: Deconstructing Historiography." In *Selected Subaltern Studies,* ed. Ranajit Guha and Gayatri Chakravorty. New York: Oxford University Press, pp. 3–32.

Stallybrass, Peter; and Allon White. 1986. *The Politics and Poetics of Transgression.* Ithaca: Cornell University Press.

Stambouli, Andrés. 1980. *Crisis política: Venezuela 1948–58.* Caracas: Editorial Ateneo.

Steadman, Ian, et al. 1981. *The Value Controversy.* London: Verso.

Steedman, Carolyn Kay. 1986. *Landscape for a Good Woman: A Story of Two Lives.* New Brunswick: Rutgers University Press.

Stepan, Alfred. 1978. *The State and Society: Peru in Comparative Perspective.* Princeton: Princeton University Press.

Stobaugh, Robert; and Daniel Yergin, eds. 1979. *Energy Future: Report of the Energy Project at the Harvard Business School.* New York: Random House.

Stocking, George W., Jr. 1991. *Colonial Situations: Essays on the Ethnographic Knowledge.* Madison: University of Wisconsin Press.

Stoler, Ann Laura. 1995. *Race and the Education of Desire.* Durham: Duke University Press.

Suárez Figueroa, Naudy, ed. 1977. *Programas políticos venezolanos de la primera mitad del siglo XX. Tomo II.* Caracas: Universidad Católica Andrés Bello.

Sullivan, William M. 1976. "Situación económica durante el período de Juan Vicente Gómez, 1908–1935." In *Política y economía en Venezuela, 1810–1976.* Caracas: Ediciones de la Fundación John Boulton, pp. 247–272.

Tambiah, Stanley J. 1984. *The Buddhist Saints of the Forest and the Cult of the Amulets.* Cambridge: Cambridge University Press.

Tanzer, Michael. 1980. *The Race for Resources.* New York: Monthly Review Press.

Tanzer, Michael; and Stephen Zorn. 1985. *Energy Update: Oil in the Late Twentieth Century.* New York: Monthly Review Press.

Tarre Murzi, José. 1976. *Cuando el hombre no camina.* Valencia: Vadell Hermanos.

———. 1978. *Venezuela saudita.* Valencia: Vadell Hermanos.

———. 1979. *Los muertos de la deuda, o el final de la Venezuela saudita.* Caracas: Ediciones Centauro.

Taussig, Michael. 1980. *The Devil and Commodity Fetishism in South America.* Chapel Hill: University of North Carolina Press.

———. 1994. "Maleficium: State Fetishism." In *Fetishism as Cultural Discourse,* ed. Emily Apter and William Pietz. Ithaca: Cornell University Press, pp. 217–47.

Taylor, Philip B., Jr. 1968. *The Venezuelan Golpe de Estado of 1958: The Fall of Marcos Pérez Jiménez.* Political Studies Series, no. 4. Washington: Institute for the Comparative Study of Political Systems.

———, ed. 1971. *Venezuela, 1969. Analysis of Progress.* Baltimore: Johns Hopkins University Press, SAIS.

Tennassee, Paul Nehru. 1979. *Venezuela, los obreros petroleros y la lucha por la democracia.* Caracas: E.F.I. Publicaciones.

Therborn, Goran. 1977. "The Rule of Capital and the Rise of Democracy." *New Left Review* 103: 3–42.

———. 1979. "The Travail of Latin American Democracy." *New Left Review* 71: 114.

Thomas, Nicholas. 1991. *Entangled Objects: Exchange, Material Objects and Colonialism in the Pacific.* Cambridge: Harvard University Press.

Thomas, Paul. 1994. *Alien Politics: Marxist State Theory Retrieved.* London: Routledge.

Thompson, E. P. 1971. "The Moral Economy of the English Crowd in the Eighteenth Century." *Past and Present* 50: 76–136.

Timpanaro, Sebastiano. 1975. *On Materialism.* London: New Left Books.

Tinoco, Pedro. 1972. *El estado eficaz.* Caracas: Colleción los Desarrollistas.

Tollison, Robert D. 1982. "Rent Seeking: A Survey." *Kyklos* 35: 572–602.

Torres, Gumersindo. 1917. *Memoria.* vol. *I.* Caracas: Ministerio de Fomento.

Tribe, Keith. 1978. *Land, Labour and Economic Discourse.* London: Routledge and Kegan Paul.

Trouillot, Michel-Rolph. 1990. *Haiti, State against Nation: The Origins and Legacy of Duvalierism.* New York: Monthly Review Press.

———. 1991. "Anthropology and the Savage Lot." In *Recapturing Anthropology,* ed. Richard G. Fox. Sante Fe: School of American Research, pp. 17–44.

———. 1992. "The Caribbean Region: An Open Frontier in Anthropological Theory." *Annual Review of Anthropology* 21: 19–42.

———. 1995. *Silencing the Past: Power and the Production of History.* Boston: Beacon.

Tugwell, Franklin. 1975. *The Politics of Oil in Venezuela.* Stanford: Stanford University Press.

———. 1977. "Petroleum Policy and the Political Process." In *Venezuela: The Democratic Experience,* ed. John D. Martz and David J. Myers. New York: Praeger, pp. 237–54.

Turner, Bryan S. 1989. Review of *Democracy and Political Theory,* by Claude Lefort. *Sociology* 23: 331–32.

Turner, Terence. 1979. "Anthropology and the Politics of Indigenous Peoples' Struggles." *Cambridge Anthropology* 1(5): 1–42.

———. 1983. "Production, Value, and Exploitation in Primitive Society." Second Decennial A.S.A. Conference, Cambridge.

———. 1994. "Bodies and Anti-bodies: Flesh and Fetish in Contemporary Social Theory." In *Embodiment and Experience: the Existential Ground of Culture,* ed, J. C. Sordas. Cambridge: Cambridge University Press.

———. n.d. "Marx's Concept of Structure and the Structure of Marx's Model of Capitalist Production: An Anthropological Re-reading of Capital." Unpublished manuscript.

Turner, Victor W. 1967. *The Forest of Symbols: Aspects of Ndembu Ritual.* Ithaca: Cornell University Press.

———. 1969. *The Ritual Process: Structure and Anti-structure.* Ithaca: Cornell University Press.

Valero, Jorge. 1993. *¿Como llegó Acción Democrática al poder en 1945?* Caracas: Fondo Editorial Tropykos.

Vallenilla, Luis. 1973. *Auge, declinación y porvenir del petroleo venezolana.* Caracas: Tiempo Nuevo.

————. 1975. *Oil: The Making of a New Economic Order: Venezuelan Oil and OPEC.* New York: McGraw Hill.

Vallenilla, Nikita Harwich. 1986. *Banca y estado en Venezuela (1830–1940).* Caracas: Fondo Editorial Buria y Fondo Editorial Antonio José de Sucre.

Vallenilla Lanz, Laureano. 1952. *Cesarismo democrático.* Caracas: Tipografía Garrido.

Vallenilla Lanz, Laureano [son]. 1967. *Escrito de memoria.* Caracas: Ediciones Garrido.

Velásquez, Luis Cordero. 1971. *Gómez y las fuerzas vivas.* 3d ed. Caracas: Domingo Fuentes.

Velásquez, Ramón J. 1983. "Introducción." *El pensamiento político venezolano del siglo xx. Documentos para su estudio.* Vol. 3. *La oposición a la dictadura gomecista.* Caracas: Congreso de la Républica, pp. xi–lvi.

————. 1986. *Juan Vicente Gómez ante la historia.* San Cristobal: Biblioteca de Autores y Temas Tachirenses.

————. 1988. *Confidencias imaginarias de Juan Vicente Gómez.* Caracas: Congreso de la República.

Veliz, Claudio. 1980. *The Centralist Tradition of Latin America.* Princeton: Princeton University Press.

Vernon, Raymond. 1971. *Sovereignty at Bay: The Multinational Spread of U.S. Enterprises.* New York: Basic Books.

————. 1976. *The Oil Crisis.* New York: W. W. Norton.

————, ed. 1978. *Big Business and the State.* Cambridge: Harvard University Press.

Vetencourt, Roberto. 1994. *Tiempo de Caudillos.* Caracas: Impreso en Italgráfica S.A.

Vieille, Paul. 1984. "Le pétrole comme rapport social." *Pétrole et Société* 26 (January–March): 3–30.

Vilar, Pierre. 1976. *A History of Gold and Money, 1450–1920.* London: New Left Books.

Vincent, Joan. 1978. "Political Anthropology: Manipulating Strategies. *Annual Review of Anthropology* 7: 175–94

Vivas, Antonio Pérez. 1987. *Hegemonía andina (historia) y Pérez Jiménez.* San Cristóbal: Impreso en Tipografía Cortes.

Volosinov, V. N. 1973. *Marxism and the Philosophy of Language.* New York: Seminar.

Wallerstein, Immanuel. 1974. *The Modern World-System: Capitalist Agriculture and the Origins of the European World-Economy in the Sixteenth Century.* New York: Academic Press.

Walton, John. 1989. "Debt, Protest, and the State in Latin America." In *Power and Popular Protest,* ed. Susan Eckstein. Berkeley: University of California Press, pp. 299–328.

Warner, Michael, ed. 1993. *Queer Politics and Social Theory.* Minneapolis: University of Minnesota Press.

Watts, Michael. 1983. *Silent Violence: Food, Famine, and Peasantry in Northern Nigeria.* Berkeley: University of California Press.

————. 1987. *State, Oil, and Agriculture in Nigeria.* Berkeley: Institute of International Studies, University of California Press.

————. 1992. "The Shock of Modernity: Petroleum, Protest, and Fast Capitalism in an Industrializing Society." In *Reworking Modernity: Capitalism and Symbolic Discontent*, ed. A. Pred and M. Watts. New Brunswick: Rutgers University Press, pp. 21–63.

————. 1994. *Living Under Contract: Contract Farming and Agrarian Transformation in Sub-Saharan Africa*. Madison: University of Wisconsin Press.

Weber, Max. 1957. The Theory of Social and Economic Organization. Glencoe, Ill.: Free Press.

Weeks, John. 1983. "Unequal Exchange." In *A Dictionary of Marxist Thought,* ed. Tom Bottomore. Cambridge: Harvard University Press, pp. 500–2.

Wells, David. 1981. *Marxism and the Modern State: An Analysis of Fetishism in Capitalist Society*. Atlantic Highlands, NJ: Humanities Press.

White, Lawrence. 1971. *The Automobile Industry since 1945.* Cambridge: Harvard University Press.

Wijnbergen, S. van. 1984. "The Dutch Disease: A Disease after All?" *Economic Journal* 94: 41–55.

Williams, Raymond. 1973. *The Country and the City.* New York: Oxford University Press.

————. 1983. *Keywords: A Vocabulary of Culture and Society.* New York: Oxford University Press.

Wolf, Eric. 1982. *Europe and the People without History.* Berkeley: University of California Press.

Wolff, Robert Paul. 1981. "A Critique and Reinterpretation of Marx's Labor Theory of Value." *Philosophy and Public Affairs* 10(2): 89–120.

Worsley, Peter. 1984. *The Three Worlds: Culture and World Development.* Chicago: University of Chicago Press.

Wright, Winthrop R. 1990. *Café con Leche: Race, Class, and National Image in Venezuela.* Austin: University of Texas Press.

Yépez, Germán. 1985. "Los regímenes de Castro y Gómez y el debate ideológico de 1936." *Tierra Firme* 3 (October–December): 689–92.

Yergin, Daniel. 1991. *The Prize: The Epic Quest for Oil, Money and Power.* New York: Simon and Schuster.

Young, Robert. 1990. *White Mythologies: Writing History and the West.* New York: Routledge.

Yúdice, George. 1992. "Postmodernity and Transnational Capitalism in Latin America." In *On Edge: The Crisis of Contemporary Latin American Culture,* ed. Juan Flores, Jean Franco, and George Yúdice. Minneapolis: University of Minnesota Press.

Zapata, Juan Carlos. 1991. *El dinero, el diablo, y el buen dios.* Caracas: Alfadil Ediciones.

Ziems, Angel. 1979. *El gomecismo y la formación del ejército naciónal.* Caracas: Editorial Ateneo de Caracas.

Žižek, Slavoj. 1989. *The Sublime Object of Ideology.* London: Verso.

————. 1991. *For They Know Not What They Do: Enjoyment as a Political Factor.* London: Verso.

INDEX